JOHN, HIS GOSPE

John, His Gospel, and Jesus

In Pursuit of the Johannine Voice

Stanley E. Porter

WILLIAM B. EERDMANS PUBLISHING COMPANY
GRAND RAPIDS, MICHIGAN / CAMBRIDGE, U.K.

Published 2015 by
Wm. B. Eerdmans Publishing Co.
2140 Oak Industrial Drive N.E., Grand Rapids, Michigan 49505 /
P.O. Box 163, Cambridge CB3 9PU U.K.

Printed in the United States of America

21 20 19 18 17 16 15   7 6 5 4 3 2 1

Library of Congress Cataloging-in-Publication Data

Porter, Stanley E., 1956-
John, his Gospel, and Jesus: in pursuit of the Johannine voice / Stanley E. Porter.
pages   cm
Includes bibliographical references and index.
ISBN 978-0-8028-7170-1 (pbk.: alk. paper)
1. Bible. John — Criticism, interpretation, etc.
2. Jesus Christ — Person and offices.   I. Title.

BS2615.52 .P76
226.5′06 — dc23

2015019219

www.eerdmans.com

Contents

Preface

This volume reflects my continuing and abiding interest in John's Gospel and Jesus over the course of the last nearly twenty years. My work in John's Gospel began with a single paper that I wrote at the invitation of a good friend. At that time, more of my efforts were beginning to be devoted to the study of the Synoptic Gospels, and in particular, focused upon Jesus. Now that I look back on it, the progression from the Synoptic Gospels to John's Gospel was a natural one. After beginning to dig deeply into matters related to the Synoptic Gospels, including issues surrounding questions of the historical Jesus, it was a matter of course that I would extend my interest to the Gospel of John. The papers in this volume are at least some of the results of that interest. Once I decided to concentrate efforts on John's Gospel, I realized that I wished to focus upon various distinctive topics within John's Gospel — what I have called in the subtitle to this book the Johannine voice — and their relationship to Jesus. Two of the chapters have been published before, but they are thoroughly revised here in the light of my overall intention to explore the relationship of John's Gospel and Jesus. These two published papers include my first paper on John's Gospel and a second one, written to honor another friend. All of the other papers were delivered at conferences over the years. Each year for a number of years, when an invitation for papers was extended at a particular conference, I returned to John's Gospel, each time exploring a different dimension of this Gospel. Sometimes more of the emphasis is upon John's Gospel, and sometimes less, but the focus has always been upon the distinctly Johannine voice, especially as it represents, presents, and treats Jesus. When all is said and done regarding the similarities and differences among the four Gospels, it is still Jesus who stands at the heart of what these early testimonies to his life and work represent and wish to convey.

Along the way, in order to better equip me for the work of writing these essays, I also engaged in extensive bibliographic work on the Johannine writings, especially John's Gospel. I wish to thank my former teaching and research assistant Andrew Gabriel for sharing the burden of preparing this bibliography. This bibliography is now in print, as a suitable prelude to this volume. Those interested in pursuing the research related to topics in this monograph may wish to consult Stanley E. Porter and Andrew K. Gabriel, *The Johannine Writings and Apocalyptic: An Annotated Bibliography* (JOST 1; Leiden: Brill, 2013).

I wish also to thank Christopher Land, at the time also my teaching and research assistant and now my faculty colleague, for his close editing of this manuscript. I appreciate his unswerving attention to detail and argumentation. I also thank Wally V. Cirafesi, also a former teaching and research assistant, for his bringing the bibliographic references up to date and also providing editorial expertise. Both of them did more than just check punctuation and spelling but also rewrote sentences, added numerous passages and references, and called attention to a number of errors and mistakes. I appreciate their active role and participation in this project, which has made it a much finer and more cohesive work. I finally wish to thank Bryan Dyer, Dave Yoon, and Woojin Chung, also at various times my teaching and research assistants, for their significant help, especially with ch. 8. Dave Yoon and Wendy Porter also read through the entire manuscript at the final stages and made many helpful suggestions.

Thanks are extended for permission to reprint the two previously published chapters in this volume. They are chapter 8, "Jesus, the Passover Theme, and John's Gospel," which originally appeared as "Can Traditional Exegesis Enlighten Literary Analysis of the Fourth Gospel? An Examination of the Old Testament Fulfilment Motif and the Passover Theme," in *The Gospels and the Scriptures of Israel* (ed. Craig A. Evans and W. Richard Stegner; Studies in Scripture in Early Judaism and Christianity 3; JSNTSup 104; Sheffield: Sheffield Academic Press, 1994), 396-428; and chapter 9, "Jesus and the Ending of John's Gospel," which first appeared as "The Ending of John's Gospel," in *From Biblical Criticism to Biblical Faith: Essays in Honor of Lee Martin McDonald* (ed. Craig A. Evans and William Brackney; Macon, GA: Mercer University Press, 2007), 55-73. These have been used with the permission of the publishers and/or editors of the volumes. They have also been adapted for this volume (esp. the former) and brought up to date in significant ways.

I also thank McMaster Divinity College, where I have the great privilege of being president and dean, as well as professor of New Testament, for having bestowed upon me the Roy A. Hope Chair in Christian Worldview. It may seem strange for a professor of New Testament to hold a chair in Christian worldview, but I would say that, for those interested in Jesus and the world around them, it makes eminently good and natural sense.

Lastly, it is my honor to thank my wife, Wendy, for her unstinting support in all ways. She never ceases to amaze me, and to love me.

Abbreviations

AB	Anchor Bible
ABRL	Anchor Bible Reference Library
AJEC	Ancient Judaism and Early Christianity
APF	*Archiv für Papyrusforschung*
AThANT	Abhandlungen zur Theologie des Alten und Neuen Testaments
ATRSup	Anglican Theological Review Supplement
BBR	*Bulletin for Biblical Research*
BDAG	F. W. Danker, W. Bauer, W. F. Arndt, and F. W. Gingrich, *Greek-English Lexicon on the New Testament and Other Early Christian Literature*
BECNT	Baker Exegetical Commentary on the New Testament
BETL	Bibliotheca Ephemeridum Theologicarum Lovaniensium
Bib	*Biblica*
BibSac	*Bibliotheca Sacra*
BIS	Biblical Interpretation Series
BJRL	*Bulletin of the John Rylands University Library of Manchester*
BLG	Biblical Languages: Greek
BNTC	Black's New Testament Commentaries
BT	*Bible Translator*
BZ	*Biblische Zeitschrift*
CBET	Contributions to Biblical Exegesis and Theology
CBNTS	Coniectanea Biblica: New Testament Studies
CBQ	*Catholic Biblical Quarterly*
CBR	*Currents in Biblical Research*
CRLM	Cambridge Readings in the Literature of Music
EBib	Études bibliques

ECC	Eerdmans Critical Commentary
EPRO	Études préliminaires aux religions orientales dans l'empire romain
ETL	*Ephemerides Theologicae Lovanienses*
EvQ	*Evangelical Quarterly*
ExpTim	*Expository Times*
FFNT	Foundations and Facets: New Testament
FRLANT	Forschungen zur Religion und Literatur des Alten und Neuen Testaments
GCT	Gender, Culture, Theory
GRRS	Graeco-Roman Religion Series
HBT	*Horizons in Biblical Theology*
HDR	Harvard Dissertations in Religion
HNT	Handbuch zum Neuen Testament
HTR	*Harvard Theological Review*
ICC	International Critical Commentary
JBL	*Journal of Biblical Literature*
JETS	*Journal of the Evangelical Theological Society*
JGRChJ	*Journal of Greco-Roman Christianity and Judaism*
JÖB	*Jahrbuch der Österreichsichen Byzantinistik*
JOST	Johannine Studies
JSHJ	*Journal for the Study of the Historical Jesus*
JSNT	*Journal for the Study of the New Testament*
JSNTSup	Journal for the Study of the New Testament Supplement Series
JSOTSup	Journal for the Study of the Old Testament Supplement Series
JTS	*Journal of Theological Studies*
KEK	Kritisch-exegetischer Kommentar über das Neue Testament
LBS	Linguistic Biblical Studies
LCL	Loeb Classical Library
LNTS	Library of New Testament Studies
MNTS	McMaster New Testament Studies
MPER	Mitteilungen aus der Papyrussammlung der Nationalbibliothek in Wien (Papyrus Erzherzog Rainer)
NAC	New American Commentary
NCB	New Century Bible
Neot	*Neotestamentica*
NICNT	New International Commentary on the New Testament
NOHM	New Oxford History of Music
NovT	*Novum Testamentum*

NovTSup	Novum Testamentum Supplement Series
NSBT	New Studies in Biblical Theology
NTG	New Testament Guides
NTL	New Testament Library
NTM	New Testament Monographs
NTOA	Novum Testamentum et Orbis Antiquus
NTS	*New Testament Studies*
NTT	New Testament Theology
NTTS	New Testament Tools and Studies
OGIS	*Orientis Graeci inscriptiones selectae*
PBMS	Paternoster Biblical Monograph Series
PBTM	Paternoster Biblical and Theological Monographs
PGM	*Papyri Graecae Magicae*
PNTC	Pillar New Testament Commentary
RB	*Revue biblique*
SBG	Studies in Biblical Greek
SBL	Society of Biblical Literature
SBLDS	Society of Biblical Literature Dissertation Series
SBLMS	Society of Biblical Literature Monograph Series
SBLRBS	Society of Biblical Literature Resources for Biblical Study
SBLTT	Society of Biblical Literature Texts and Translations
SBT	Studies in Biblical Theology
SJT	*Scottish Journal of Theology*
SNTSMS	SNTS Monograph Series
SPCK	Society for Promoting Christian Knowledge
STAC	Studien und Texte zu Antike und Christentum
StBL	Studies in Biblical Literature
SympS	Symposium Series
TDNT	*Theological Dictionary of the New Testament*
TENT	Texts and Editions for New Testament Study
TR	*Theologische Rundschau*
TrinJ	*Trinity Journal*
TSAJ	Texte und Studien zum antiken Judentum
TW	Theologie und Wirklichkeit
TynBul	*Tyndale Bulletin*
UBSGNT	*United Bible Societies Greek New Testament*
VE	*Vox Evangelica*
VT	*Vetus Testamentum*
WBC	Word Biblical Commentary

WMANT	Wissenschaftliche Monographien zum Alten und Neuen Testament
WUNT	Wissenschaftliche Untersuchungen zum Neuen Testament
ZNW	*Zeitschrift für die neutestamentliche Wissenschaft und die Kunde der älteren Kirche*
ZPE	*Zeitschrift für Papyrologie und Epigraphik*

Introduction

This monograph is primarily about John's Gospel and its distinctive Johannine voice, but it cannot be understood fully without considering how John's Gospel relates to Jesus. Hence, the title of this volume is *John, His Gospel, and Jesus: In Pursuit of the Johannine Voice.* In one sense, the title could perhaps be better formulated as "Jesus and John's Gospel," but ultimately that title will not quite work, because we begin and end with John and his Gospel, and it is John's Gospel with which I am concerned throughout. The chapters included here are, in that sense, essays or attempts at solutions to enduring problems in the study of John's Gospel and hence essays (in the sense of attempts) to discover and uncover elements of the unique Johannine voice. Nevertheless, no matter what issues one tackles in John's Gospel, in one way or another, they all (at least the ones that matter) end up coming back to Jesus in some way. This is entirely appropriate and right, as it is Jesus who stands as the cornerstone of the Christian faith and what Christianity from its earliest days was truly about — confessing Jesus. It is Jesus that the Gospel writers, no matter what one's view is regarding what they are trying to accomplish, are so eager and concerned to proclaim, from the earliest days of his life or earthly ministry to his death and resurrection. Even if John does so in a way that one can argue is stylistically, historically, and theologically different from the way it is done in the Synoptic Gospels, that is, in his own unique Johannine voice — and I make no comment on these issues here, for I fear that the differences have been greatly exaggerated to make a point and at the expense of the issues themselves — John's Gospel too is concerned with the incarnate Word, Jesus, who ministered through word and deed until his arrest, crucifixion, and then resurrection, as well as final earthly appearances.

1

In this volume, however, I am concerned virtually exclusively with John's Gospel, especially the way in which it addresses a number of important issues that continue to be discussed in Johannine scholarship, as well as a few that have been neglected and that seem important to me. John's Gospel has generated an enormous amount of discussion within recent New Testament scholarship. Such discussion is more than warranted, as scholars attempt to answer a variety of questions that have been either neglected or relegated to the category of "assured results" by previous research. I dare say that the amount of scholarship generated far exceeds the capacity of any single individual to appreciate fully and to grasp in its entirety. Hence, I have chosen to focus on issues that have come into my purview as being of recurring and abiding significance, first, for understanding John and his Gospel, and second, for understanding the Jesus who stands tall within this Gospel from his first appearing as the incarnate *logos* to his final charge to his closest followers.

Although this monograph is primarily about John and his Gospel and attempts to enter the recently generated discussion at a number of different points, it is also about Jesus, as I have indicated. For many people, even or especially scholars, John's Gospel and Jesus are more often juxtaposed than integrated. This volume is an attempt at coordination rather than disentanglement. Most, if not all, of the issues of importance in Johannine studies ultimately have bearing on the question of who Jesus is, who he claimed to be, how he is depicted in the varying early Christian sources, especially the New Testament, and how these New Testament authors respond and react to him in their respective writings. The same could be said of all of the Gospel accounts, but it is especially true of John's Gospel. This observation about Jesus may not at first seem evident, in the light of the kinds of discussions in which Johannine scholars often engage. I need not recount these here in detail, but they include, among others, (1) the tendency to denigrate the historicity of John's Gospel; (2) the positing of various levels of Johannine exposition, to the point where the original historical context is ignored in favor of the context of the contemporary Johannine community; (3) the emphasis upon literary features and even a literary orientation at the expense of the realities that they purport to convey; (4) the cleverness of the Gospel's author, in relation to either his literary proclivities or his theological agenda, to the point of overlooking more obvious features that link the Gospel account with other Gospels and its own appropriate historical context; and (5) the finding of conceptual categories supposedly in the Gospel that are then declared to be late and therefore suspect. I do not wish to juxtapose John's Gospel and Jesus. I wish instead to examine a number of important issues in Johannine studies, viewing them as windows into John's understanding of Jesus, the central (and, yes, historical) figure of his account.

I would like to make clear how each of the chapters in this monograph contributes to the agenda that I have outlined above. In some ways, many of these studies are preliminary ones, at least as much designed to spur further discussion as to finally answer questions. As I have stated, these are essays in pursuit of the Johannine voice — with no final claim to having actually arrived at the conclusion; no doubt, much more could be said on virtually all of these topics.

The first chapter of this volume is concerned with John's Gospel and other, competing Gospel accounts. I refer here in particular to P.Egerton 2, one of the best-known and most widely discussed noncanonical early church accounts of the activities and teaching of Jesus. This fragmentary Gospel has recently aroused much discussion. I am not concerned here with much of that discussion, but as I make evident in the chapter, I have engaged in such discussion elsewhere and have made my opinion on P.Egerton 2 very clear. I do not downplay its importance. To the contrary, I believe that it is a very important document in tracing the development of early Christianity, though perhaps not as important as some other scholars have posited. P.Egerton 2 has often, and especially recently, been linked to the early Johannine Gospel fragment P.Rylands Greek 457 (also known as $\mathfrak{p}^{52}$), and it is their relationship that I wish to discuss here, because I do not follow the trend of much of the latest discussion. The relationship of P.Egerton 2 and P.Rylands III Greek 457, especially our ability to date these papyri, is directly related to the question of the dating of John's Gospel. Implicitly contained within this discussion of the date of these papyri is the possibility of reentering a period of previous scholarship when the date for John's Gospel was held as wide open, and many have argued for a date well into the second century. I argue against such a hypothesis. In this chapter I do not spend as much time discussing the implications for Jesus, except to say that the determination of date has implications for how John's Gospel relates to other possible influences, such as Gnosticism. Instead, I think that the establishment of a firm early date for the composition of John's Gospel reinforces the path (even if a narrow one) of current scholarship, which is seeing a closer relationship between John's Gospel and the Synoptic Gospels and drawing lines of connection closer between the Jesus depicted in all of them.

The second chapter, John's public proclamation and Jesus, in direct contrast to the first chapter, is directly concerned with John's Gospel and Jesus. I contend that John's Gospel was designed from the outset as a public proclamation of the gospel, that is, of who Jesus is. There has been much discussion in recent times about the original audience of the Gospels. The traditional view has been that the Gospels were written in relative isolation and specifically for individual communities. This includes John's Gospel, which has often been seen as a sectarian document. Some recent research has shifted this understanding, arguing that John's Gospel, like the other Gospels, was written not to a small original audience but for a much wider readership. It was not written for some Christians but for all Christians, to paraphrase the title of one recent book on this topic. I wish to take this assertion even further and argue that the very narrative structure and fiber of John's Gospel is designed to make it a public proclamation of who Jesus is — in other words, not just for all Christians, but for everyone, Christian and non-Christian alike. In order to do so, I must briefly trace much of the narrative of the Gospel itself. I begin with the prologue, where three concepts linked to particular words are used: *word, light,* and *world.* The interplay of these three concepts sets the stage for who Jesus is: the enfleshed Word, who brings light to the world. Thus, from the outset, John in his Gospel is concerned with a public proclamation of Jesus. This pattern is developed further in a number of individual episodes within the Gospel. These include (1) Jesus' proclamation by John the Baptist; (2) his encounter with Galileans in John 1–2; (3) Jesus' encounter with Jews in John 3, in particular, Nicodemus, in an episode that deals with moving from darkness to light, and in John 11, in the episode with Lazarus; (4) the Samaritans of the first half of John 4, beginning with the woman at the well and extending to others; (5) the physically infirm of John 5, with the man at the pool of Bethesda, and of John 9, with the man healed from his blindness; (6) the second half of John 4, with the official who has an ill son (the emphasis is upon the official, not the healing); (7) the political leaders of John 18–19, including both Pontius Pilate and the Jewish leaders as they engage in a tangled dialogue regarding Jesus; (8) Jesus' own words to his disciples, including his "I am" statements and his farewell discourse in John 14–16; and, finally, (9) John 21, where the Gospel ends with a final public declaration of Jesus. Rather than John's Gospel being a sectarian or even simply Christian Gospel, it is structured and presented as a public proclamation of Jesus and his gospel of salvation.

In the next chapter, on the sources of John's Gospel, I venture more boldly into questions about Jesus in relation to John's Gospel. Along the way, I raise questions about the history of discussion of the sources of John's Gospel and begin with the not-very-encouraging observation that there has been plenty of generalization — to the point of possibly even misrepresentation — of the history of discussion. As a result, a number of stereo-types have formed about John's Gospel in relationship to the Synoptics, especially around the issue of utilizing or sharing common sources. Until fairly recently this result has had a direct effect on the issue of the historical reliability of John's Gospel, to the point of virtually excluding much discussion about the Jesus of John's Gospel within historical Jesus research. In examining some of the recent work, I note that there are four broad positions regarding the source relationships between John's Gospel and the Synoptics. Two of these positions may be considered extreme. These include the view that John's Gospel is entirely dependent upon or entirely independent of the Synoptics and/or their sources or traditions. These viewpoints are fairly easily dismissed. I am more interested in mediating positions that see the possibility of some kind of overlap between the Synoptic Gospels and John's Gospel. In order to explore this possible relationship more fully, I offer a list of twenty-three episodes that have some type of relations among all the Gospels, and I examine them briefly, which leads to making a number of observations about these episodes when the four Gospels are compared with each other. The result of this investigation is to categorize the kinds of relationships that I find within the Gospels. Perhaps the most important result is that I identify a number of sections where John's Gospel seems, in relation to the Synoptics, to reflect an independent common tradition. That is, John's Gospel appears to be recounting the same episode as found in the Synoptic Gospels, but it also seems to have access to an independent source or sources in its own retelling. The number of such passages is larger than one might at first expect. Having established that there appears to be common independent material in John's Gospel, I then draw upon the traditional criteria of authenticity in historical Jesus research to see whether John's Gospel can add anything to this discussion. I draw on these criteria (aware that they have come under attack), as an appropriate step when engaging in the traditional exercise of historical Jesus research. By using the criteria of multiple attestation, coherence or consistency, embarrassment, and rejection and execution, I find that John's Gospel can speak to questions of historical authenticity at a number of points. These include especially the passion narrative, where John's Gospel seems to be able to attest to a number of elements not found in the other Gospel accounts. In this way, examining the possible sources of John's Gospel aids our knowledge not only of the Johannine Jesus but the Jesus of the Synoptic Gospels and historical Jesus research as well.

The fourth chapter concerns the Johannine prologue. Some may wonder whether anything new can be said about this well-known and, more important, well-studied passage of John's Gospel. It indeed is a memorable passage, even said to be "hymnic," which many of the most insightful New Testament scholars have examined over the years from a number of angles, as they attempt to trace the course of its argument regarding the *logos* and Jesus. If it is a hymn, an approach I consider in this chapter, it seems to be one about how the *logos* became Jesus, or God-in-the-flesh. Rather than attempting a new and novel interpretation of this familiar passage, I go back and examine how it has been treated by some of the most well-known approaches in New Testament studies. I then also examine it from the standpoint of two less common approaches. I start with form criticism. The prologue to John's Gospel has been a rich feeding ground for a variety of form critics through the years. From the days of at least Eduard Norden, at the turn of the twentieth century, to the present, various proposals have been made regarding the form of the prologue. Some try to encompass all of the prologue, while others — it appears to be the majority — are selective in the passages included, indicating to many that they believe they have found the underlying original form of the prologue itself. After discussing the shortcomings of form-critical approaches, I turn to source criticism. Source criticism also has proved to be a productive ground for examination of the Johannine prologue, from the times of the history-of-religion school to the present, including the New Tübingen school. The history of source-critical analyses of this passage encompasses most of the major proposals regarding the background influences on the New Testament — but unfortunately with the same lack of consensus that was found in form criticism. At this point, I turn to two more recent and innovative approaches in examining the prologue: musical-liturgical criticism and what I call functional criticism. The former approach, a relatively recent innovation, attempts to place the Johannine prologue within the context of the use of music within the incipient and developing early Christian liturgy. Appreciating the prologue's possible Hellenistic and Jewish origins, though noting the difficulty of establishing them, musical-liturgical criticism examines the prologue as an instance of how the early church enshrined its worship of Jesus within a liturgical form. The latter approach, functional criticism, rejects the types of criticism that look simply to form or background as sufficient explanation of the use of a passage. Instead, functional criticism explores the function that a passage performs in and of itself and within the context of the larger work of which it is a part. Even though many of the scholars examined in this section would not have recognized that they were performing a type of functional criticism, the results of their interpretations show that they have — they define the prologue according to its use and then trace its implications and influences throughout the rest of the Gospel. As a result, we see that how John conceived of the *logos* becoming Jesus functioned as a paradigm for the entire Gospel, which ends up being a testimony to Jesus as the Christ.

In chapter 5 I turn to another approach that examines the whole of John's Gospel, this time to explore its Christology. There is little doubt that John has a high Christology, one that I explore in varying ways in other chapters in this monograph. Here, however, I go into more detail regarding the christological perspective of John and his Gospel. There have been many ways of exploring the Christology of John's Gospel, especially by examining Jesus' various titles. In this chapter, however, I take a different approach, looking closely at the thirty-five occurrences of "I am" in the Gospel. This construction has been examined in several different ways by scholars, the intent often being to discover its conceptual background in order to explain its meaning in the Gospel itself. I analyze the issues differently. Here I take the "I am" statements as a primary means by which the author of John's Gospel structures the christological development of the Gospel itself. The first task is to define the three different variations of the "I am" construction: absolute, predicate, and locative. The first is the use of the simple statement "I am." In the second, a predicate is attached, such as "I am the bread of life." The third use involves adding a locative adjunct, such as "I am from above." With these categories, it is relatively easy to sort out the various instances of "I am," which fall into a number of interesting patterns throughout the Gospel, beginning with John the Baptist's *denial* that he is the Christ and moving on to Jesus' early affirmation to the Samaritan woman that he *is* the Christ. Thereafter in the Gospel, the "I am" statements are used to define further what the messiahship of Jesus means. A number of predicate uses of the construction create various metaphors to describe Jesus' messianic character, such as "the bread of life," "the light of the world," "the true shepherd," and "the way, truth, and life." A number of locative uses are also employed to describe where Jesus is from (from above, not from this world) and where he is going (to where those who are not his followers cannot come). Besides the introductory uses in John 1 and 4, the absolute construction is used in two other significant places. In John 8 Jesus defines himself as being before Abraham, a usage that links to the prologue and defines Jesus as temporally and hierarchically before Abraham and with the Father. In John 18, just before his arrest, Jesus affirms three times to those around him, "I am." This invocation of his messianic claim closes his earthly ministry with a strong affirmation of his messianic character. As the narrative unfolds, the author of John's Gospel expands the notion of Messiah by linking Jesus as Messiah with a variety of other functions, such as Savior, King, and Son of the Father. The use of "I am" statements in John's Gospel is a significant means by which the author develops his expansive view of Jesus as Messiah.

The next chapter tackles one of the most difficult and emotion-laden topics in contemporary Johannine research — the question of "the Jews" and the apparent blanket condemnation they receive in this Gospel. In the eyes of some, this supposed censure justifies rejecting the Gospel as being outright anti-Jewish. This is a strong claim, no doubt exacerbated in the light of the post-Holocaust environment in which we now do New Testament studies. Nevertheless, these charges need to be examined in clear light. In fact, they were thoroughly examined at a major conference in 2000 that explored this topic in great detail and resulted in publication of a major reference work on the subject. Despite these efforts, issues surrounding this important topic still await resolution. I begin this chapter by examining a number of the most widely repeated analyses of the Gospel, as a means of gaining a platform for examining its use of the phrase "the Jews." This examination illustrates the unsatisfactory nature of many, if not most, of the proposals, whether for or against John's alleged anti-Jewishness. I then categorize the uses of "the Jews" within the Gospel itself. The resulting categories, while helpful in exposing weaknesses of previous proposals, do not solve the major interpretive issues. Recently, some New Testament scholars have proposed that the distinction between sense and reference might solve this problem. Even here, however, there appears to be significant confusion over these concepts. Nevertheless, they do appear to provide a way forward in differentiating the types of meanings that are conveyed by use of the word group "the Jews." I conclude that "the Jews" has the sense of identifying the Jewish religious-ethnic group as a whole, but that this singular sense is modulated within the varying Johannine contexts to identify more narrowly the Jews that belong to a particular group, such as the chief priests, the Pharisees, or other leaders. Whereas what the term "the Jews" is used to refer to is still important, the referential use is mediated through the sense of the term, which is the focus of my exploration here. Besides the frequent meaning of the Jews as a whole (often in nonemotive contexts), the term "the Jews" is often used within the varied Johannine contexts to indicate the various leaders of the Jews in their activities. I therefore believe that it is clearly wrong to criticize overall the usage of "the Jews" in John's Gospel as being anti-Jewish, for the meaning of this term varies significantly according to context. In those instances where the language often seems the harshest, such usage is confined to a select few of the Jews who were involved in particular acts, especially against Jesus. A number of implications follow from these findings. The most important relate to what they indicate regarding Jesus and the Judaism of his day. On the basis of my findings, I suggest some possible conclusions regarding the parting of the ways between Judaism and Christianity — in particular, that this parting transpired early on. In fact, it possibly began with the conflicts between Jesus and the Jewish leaders and escalated, leading to a relatively early separation between the two groups.

In chapter 7 I examine the notion of truth in John's Gospel. This concept has been examined before by a number of scholars and in a variety of ways, but I think that the significance of the concept as it is manifested through use of ἀληθ-words merits further discussion. I would say that other scholars have generally failed to grasp the significance of the use of truth language for framing both the conceptual and the structural organization of the entire Gospel. Truth is a topic dealt with in roughly half of the chapters in John's Gospel, and it is presented in two major ways: both in relational and in propositional terms. The relational usage concerns God/Father, the Son, and the Spirit, as well as humanity. In this chapter I thus divide the relational treatment of truth according to how it enlightens discussion of each of these major figures within the Gospel, and then I attempt to integrate them together into a whole. I find that God is seen as the origin of truth; the Son is seen to be the embodiment of the truth, mediating between God and humanity; and the Spirit, also known as the Paraclete, is the one sent to continue the work of the Son after his departure. These relate to each other in a hierarchy, in which God is seen as being in the realm above, while humanity is in the realm below. This gap between heaven and earth is mediated by Jesus, the Son. Each of these — Father, Son, and Spirit — is a representative of, or bearer of witness to, the truth. Truth originates with God but is found in Jesus and the Spirit — who is known as the Spirit of truth — so that humans can come to knowledge of the truth. In some areas of recent theology, there has been a major emphasis upon the propositional nature of truth. This is not the place for a broad discussion of such an approach. On occasion, however, John's Gospel depicts truth as having a propositional dimension, that is, truth as not merely part of the relational configuration that I have outlined above. Instead, truth is treated as an abstract topic. Even these statements, however, once we examine the larger context in which they are made, have a relational element to them, in that they too are part of the larger conceptual framework that the Gospel expounds — with God above and humans below, and the gap between them that keeps humans from God's truth broached by the mediator Jesus and his surrogate, the Spirit of truth. The passage in which Pilate asks Jesus, "What is truth?" (John 18:38), often attracts the most attention regarding the question of John's depiction of truth. As I point out, however, this question comes at the conclusion of an episode near the end of the Gospel and shows that Pilate is the only one at this point who does not already know the answer to the question. The divine foundation of truth, within God, the Son, and the Holy Spirit, is established at the outset of the Gospel, within the prologue itself, and forms a conceptual and structural framework for the entire Gospel. The final reference to this framework occurs in John 21:24, where the author himself attests that he has borne witness to the truth.

Chapter 8, on the notion of Passover in John's Gospel, argues that the Passover theme — the author seeing Jesus as the Passover lamb slain for the sins of his people — forms a major part of the Gospel structurally and conceptually. This chapter is a thoroughly revised and updated form of a chapter that was first published a number of years ago. At the time, the Passover theme was not so widely recognized in Johannine scholarship, including writers of commentaries, who often avoided drawing out the significance of any Passover elements. Since then, perhaps in part because of this earlier chapter, the theme has been more widely examined and seen as an important part of the conceptual and even theological structure of John's Gospel. Most scholars have recognized clear Passover motifs in John 1, especially vv. 29 and 36 (with John the Baptist's acclamation of Jesus as the Lamb of God, who takes away the sin of the world), and John 19, especially vv. 13-42 (with its several Old Testament quotations and depictions of the time and manner of Jesus' death). In addition, however, a structural principle is at play whereby the organization of passages cited from the Old Testament helps shape the Gospel and its presentation of Jesus. Within this framework, several key episodes make further explicit and implicit references to Passover. In this chapter I argue that a number of major passages spaced throughout the Gospel — besides John 1 and 19 — also make clear that the Johannine author saw Jesus as the sacrificial Passover lamb who dies on behalf of his followers. Many of these passages are structured around the feasts in John's Gospel, especially Passover, as one might expect; others simply make various Passover references. The five other relevant passages that I examine are the following:

2:13-25, Jesus' cleansing of the temple, with the event occurring around Passover and Jesus seen as inaugurating a new sacrificial system;

ch. 6, especially vv. 1-14 and 22-71, with the account of the feeding of the
   five thousand and with allusions to Moses, both reflecting Christian
   Passover ideas;

8:31-47, a passage I did not treat in the original article but add here in
   the light of recent research suggesting that this passage also at least
   alludes to Passover;

11:47–12:8, the words of Caiaphas regarding the death of one substitut-
   ing for the destruction of the nation, and several other references
   to Passover;

chs. 13–17, Jesus' final meal with his disciples, a commemoration of Passover, before his death.

These five, along with the verses cited above from John 1 and 19, constitute
seven significant passages within John's Gospel. They combine a variety of
elements to indicate that the author sees Jesus as the Passover lamb and
wishes to depict Jesus as such to his readers. John the Baptist announces
that Jesus inaugurates a new sacrificial order; Jesus himself feeds his people
like a new Moses, and he participates in a final Passover meal with his closest followers, before he himself is slaughtered like a Passover lamb — all in
fulfillment of Old Testament quotations that the Johannine author cites to
underscore the significance of the event.

The final chapter of this volume deals with the final chapter of John's
Gospel. John 21 is a notoriously problematic chapter in the history of Johannine scholarship, almost as contentious in its own way as Mark 16:9-20 and
John 7:53–8:11 were to a previous era of New Testament scholarship. The
vast majority of critical scholarship sees John 21 as a later addition to the
Gospel by a now-unknown author. A few writers think that it may have been
written by the same author as the rest of the Gospel, but that it was written
separately from the Gospel and appended at some time after the completion
and distribution of the Gospel itself. I originally published this chapter as a
defense of the authenticity and integrity of John 21. In this volume, I have
taken the opportunity to reexamine the arguments and to place them within
the larger context of the implications of this chapter for John's Gospel and
what it says about Jesus. I begin first by examining three major arguments
that the chapter is not authentic. The first includes language arguments,
including grammar and vocabulary. Many scholars have assumed that such
arguments are overwhelmingly persuasive, though in actuality, they are surprisingly inconclusive. The next argument that I examine concerns the unity
of John 21. Many have argued that John 21 is disunified, with two separate

incidents concerning Peter and the Beloved Disciple. The incident with Peter and the fishing trip is often linked to Luke 5:1-11, with some arguing that the Petrine passage in John 21 is derived from this Synoptic source. Again, the arguments regarding disunity are not as strong as some might think; in fact, other scholars make strong claims for textual unity. The third argument concerns the supposed two endings of John. This is a recent proposal that argues that there were originally two endings to John: one at the end of John 20, and the other including John 21, with the two being brought together early on. Examination of this hypothesis inevitably involves discussion of John 20:30-31, a passage that has been the subject of persistent debate over a number of issues. I find that much of this debate is motivated by particular theological or ideological views and often reflects a lack of understanding of some of the major linguistic issues involved. Rather than supporting two closings to John's Gospel, the evidence points to there being a single Gospel ending at the end of John 21. This unity and authenticity allow us to see how the figure of Jesus continues his actions and teachings in John 21 as well.

Each of the studies that I include here is, of necessity, a preliminary exploration of John's unique perspective on Jesus and other attendant issues. The preliminary nature of these studies is explained in part by the grandness of the Gospel that I examine and by the overwhelming greatness of its major character, Jesus the Christ. I also realize that John's Gospel continues to generate huge quantities of secondary literature, as scholars continue their own explorations of this marvelous Gospel. I am satisfied if I have examined afresh a number of interesting and potentially productive topics regarding John, his Gospel, and Jesus, all in pursuit of the Johannine voice.

CHAPTER 1

John's Gospel, Competing Gospels, and Jesus

1. Introduction

A number of revisionist developments in recent research have had a direct impact upon our understanding of John's Gospel and, with it, how we understand its presentation of Jesus. These developments include a desire to date a number of noncanonical documents as early as or even earlier than the canonical Gospels, including John's Gospel; a reassessment of the notion of Gnosticism, including the presence of early gnostic gospels; and a redefinition within these documents of the notions of orthodoxy and heterodoxy. Each of these developments challenges the traditional view of John's Gospel within the canon, and with it the presentation it makes of Jesus.[1] If some of these noncanonical documents are earlier, then perhaps their depiction of Jesus is more authentic. If Gnosticism was an early phenomenon, our view of Jesus will no doubt be different from the one we see on the basis of our canonical Gospels, including John's Gospel.[2] If notions of orthodoxy and heterodoxy are fluid concepts, then we perhaps need to rethink the reliability we place upon our biblical accounts, including the place of John's Gospel within the New Testament canon.[3]

1. I return to this topic in more detail in ch. 3, on the sources of John's Gospel and Jesus, especially in relationship to the Synoptic Gospels.
2. I have addressed some of these issues in S. E. Porter and G. L. Heath, *The Lost Gospel of Judas: Separating Fact from Fiction* (Grand Rapids: Eerdmans, 2007), which concentrates on one document that raises such issues.
3. See S. E. Porter, *How We Got the New Testament: Text, Transmission, and Translation* (Grand Rapids: Baker, 2013), esp. ch. 2; and Porter, "Canon: New Testament," in *The Oxford*

The evidence that would need to be surveyed in order to address fully all of these developments is far beyond what could be presented in a single book. In any case, my immediate goal is something much more modest, but nevertheless important. In the course of my investigation of this broad-ranging and important topic regarding the reception of John's Gospel and how it has fared in comparison with other Gospels, canonical and otherwise, I have discovered that a number of subtle currents are developing, especially with regard to the issue of dating the Gospel, as a result of the revisiting of a number of issues regarding second-century papyri. These trends have strong implications for how we view John's Gospel, as well as how we view Jesus and the events surrounding him. A relatively recent volume that focuses upon the Johannine corpus addresses some of the papyrological issues but seems to assume the results of much current scholarly discussion.[4] Most of the essays in my monograph focus on issues that are internal to the Gospel of John itself, but I wish in this chapter to focus upon the relation of John's Gospel to some papyrological evidence in order to investigate further the question of this Gospel's relation to others.

2. Noncanonical Documents and the Gospel of John

I first deal briefly with the date of composition of John's Gospel according to scholarly opinion. Then, with this information as a backdrop, I examine two papyrological discoveries that have a bearing on this date and that have been the subject of recent discussion. The first is a papyrus of John's Gospel itself, but one that has recently aroused significant controversy. The second is a papyrus of an unknown gospel, the so-called Egerton papyrus. These two papyri have been linked in scholarly discussion ever since they were first published, each in 1935. By discussing these two papyri together and then independently, I believe that we can better understand the relationship of John's Gospel to at least some other gospels.

Encyclopedia of the Books of the Bible (ed. M. D. Coogan; 2 vols.; Oxford: Oxford University Press, 2011), 1:109-20.

4. C. E. Hill, *The Johannine Corpus in the Early Church* (Oxford: Oxford University Press, 2004), 148-54. In his volume Hill addresses a number of issues and argues that the Johannine writings were accepted early on in the church, not as gnostic but as what amounts to orthodox.

a. The Date of John's Gospel

The Gospel of John is generally thought to be the latest written of the four canonical Gospels. Agreement on this point, however, has not prevented the forming of considerable difference of opinion on the date of its composition. The range is probably broader than that for any other Gospel and has a clear bearing on the relationship of John to other gospels, canonical or otherwise. The following dates have been proposed:[5]

> before A.D. 70: Wüttig, Küppers, Wilms, Gebhardt, Cribbs,[6] Robinson,[7] Morris,[8] Wallace[9]
> 70-85: Wittichen, Alford, Reithmayr, Bleek, Kysar[10]
> 75-140: Boring[11]
> 80-90: Ewald, Godet, Bisping, Westcott, Clames, Zahn, Beasley-Murray (around 80),[12] Carson,[13] Köstenberger (after 81)[14]
> 85-95: Camerlynck, Lindars[15]

5. The basic set of dates and proponents is provided by J. Moffatt, *An Introduction to the Literature of the New Testament* (3rd rev. ed.; Edinburgh: T&T Clark, 1918), 580-82, but I have changed the arrangement slightly and added later proponents. For early scholars, see also F. Godet, *Commentary on the Gospel of John* (trans. M. D. Cusin; 3 vols.; Edinburgh: T&T Clark, 1899), 1:184-85.

6. F. L. Cribbs, "A Reassessment of the Date of Origin and the Destination of the Gospel of John," *JBL* 89 (1970): 38-55.

7. J. A. T. Robinson, *Redating the New Testament* (Philadelphia: Westminster, 1975), 254; Robinson, *The Priority of John* (ed. J. F. Coakley; London: SCM Press, 1985).

8. L. Morris, *The Gospel according to John* (NICNT; Grand Rapids: Eerdmans, 1971), 35 (rev. ed., 1995, 30); Morris, *Studies in the Fourth Gospel* (Carlisle: Paternoster, 1969), 283-92, esp. 291.

9. D. B. Wallace, "John 5,2 and the Date of the Fourth Gospel," *Bib* 71 (1990): 177-205.

10. R. Kysar, *John: The Maverick Gospel* (rev. ed.; Louisville, KY: Westminster John Knox, 1993), 25.

11. M. E. Boring, *An Introduction to the New Testament: History, Literature, Theology* (Louisville, KY: Westminster John Knox, 2012), 633 (a pretty wide range!).

12. G. R. Beasley-Murray, *John* (2nd ed.; WBC 36; Dallas: Word, 1990), lxxviii.

13. D. A. Carson, *The Gospel according to John* (PNTC; Grand Rapids: Eerdmans; Leicester: InterVarsity Press, 1991), 85; cf. D. A. Carson, D. J. Moo, and L. Morris, *An Introduction to the New Testament* (Grand Rapids: Zondervan, 1992), 167 (2nd ed., 2005, 267).

14. A. J. Köstenberger, *John* (BECNT; Grand Rapids: Baker, 2004), 8; cf. Köstenberger, "The Destruction of the Second Temple and the Composition of the Fourth Gospel," in *Challenging Perspectives on the Gospel of John* (ed. J. Lierman; WUNT 2.219; Tübingen: Mohr Siebeck, 2006), 69-108, who ties the date of composition with the date of the temple destruction.

15. B. Lindars, *The Gospel of John* (NCB; Grand Rapids: Eerdmans, 1972), 42.

90-100:[16] Mangenot, Batifoffol, B. Weiss, McNeil,[17] Wikenhauser,[18] Harrison (80-100),[19] Harrington,[20] Kümmel,[21] Beilner and Ernst,[22] McDonald and Porter,[23] Keener,[24] D. Martin,[25] Hagner[26]

90-110: Guthrie,[27] Brown[28]

90-120: Jackson

100: Lightfoot, Weizsäcker, Reynolds, Harnack (after 95), Cornely, Lepin (before 100), Bultmann,[29] Barrett,[30] R. Martin[31]

16. As Robinson notes (*Redating*, 261, citing evidence), this date has probably become the most common in research over the last century.

17. A. H. McNeile, *An Introduction to the Study of the New Testament* (Oxford: Clarendon Press, 1927), 275 (2nd ed., 1953, 293), whose dates stay the same regardless of $\mathfrak{p}^{52}$ (see below).

18. A. Wikenhauser, *New Testament Introduction* (New York: Herder & Herder, 1958), 319.

19. E. F. Harrison, *Introduction to the New Testament* (Grand Rapids: Eerdmans, 1964), 206.

20. W. J. Harrington, *Record of the Fulfillment: The New Testament* (Chicago: Priory, 1965), 392.

21. W. G. Kümmel, *Introduction to the New Testament* (trans. H. C. Kee; Nashville: Abingdon, 1973), 246.

22. W. Beilner and M. Ernst, *Unter dem Wort Gottes* (Thaur, Austria: Kulturverlag, 1993), 601-2.

23. L. M. McDonald and S. E. Porter, *Early Christianity and Its Sacred Literature* (Peabody, MA: Hendrickson, 2000), 306.

24. C. S. Keener, *The Gospel of John: A Commentary* (2 vols.; Peabody, MA: Hendrickson, 2003), 1:142.

25. D. B. Martin, *New Testament History and Literature* (New Haven: Yale University Press, 2012), 164.

26. D. A. Hagner, *The New Testament: A Historical and Theological Introduction* (Grand Rapids: Baker, 2012), 291.

27. D. Guthrie, *New Testament Introduction* (4th rev. ed; Downers Grove, IL: InterVarsity Press, 1970), 297.

28. R. E. Brown, *An Introduction to the Gospel of John* (ed. F. J. Moloney; New York: Doubleday, 2003), 215; cf. Brown, *An Introduction to the New Testament* (New York: Doubleday, 1997), 334, where he is open to A.D. 80-110.

29. R. Bultmann, *Das Evangelium des Johannes* (KEK 2; Berlin: Evangelische Verlagsanstalt, 1963 [1941]), 203 n. 4, with reference to P.Egerton 2. However, in the introduction to the English translation (Bultmann's original German does not include an introduction), Walter Schmithals, although purportedly reflecting the "literary and historical results" found in the commentary (p. 3), gives a span of A.D. 80-120 for composition and redaction of John's Gospel (p. 12; see introduction to *The Gospel of John: A Commentary*, by R. Bultmann [trans. G. R. Beasley-Murray et al.; Oxford: Blackwell, 1971], 3-12).

30. C. K. Barrett, *The Gospel according to St. John* (2nd ed.; Philadelphia: Westminster, 1978), 128.

31. R. P. Martin, *The Four Gospels* (vol. 1 of *New Testament Foundations;* Grand Rapids: Eerdmans, 1975), 282.

100-110: Renan, Schenkel, Knopf[32]
100-125: O. Holtzmann, J. Réville, Jülicher, W. Bauer
130-140: Hilgenfeld, Keim, Thoma, Lützelberger, A. Réville, Schmiedel
140-155: Bretschneider (ca. 150), Schwegler, Zeller, Volkmar, Tayor, Pfleiderer (before 135-40), van Manen, Kreyenbühl, Erbes, Schwartz (ca. 150), Meyer,[33] Loisy (150-60)[34]
160-170: Baur, Scholten, Bruno Bauer

Debate still continues regarding the earliest dating for the Gospel of John (as well as for the latest!). Proponents of an early date often cite two pieces of supposed evidence. The first is the Gospel's failure to mention the fall of Jerusalem (but cf. John 2:19-20, where, according to some scholars, Jesus refers to destruction of "this temple").[35] This argument is not sufficient, however, since the events depicted in the Gospel do not demand that the fall of Jerusalem be mentioned; all of the events refer to the life and ministry of Jesus. After all, the closing episode of the Gospel occurs just after Jesus' resurrection. Moreover, if one were to consistently apply this argument, one would need to explain several other passages that have often been cited as reflecting later events — in particular, the passages regarding exclusion from the synagogue (e.g., John 9:22; 12:42; 16:2). Admittedly, these passages are explainable on lines other than simply late composition,[36] but the problem they raise indicates that putting weight on a text's reference (or lack of reference) to a particular event can cut both ways.

The second line of evidence cited by proponents of an early date concerns John 5:2 and the supposed use of the "present tense" form of the verb to refer to the pool by the Sheep Gate. It is claimed that this "present tense"

---

32. R. Knopf, *Einführung in das Neue Testament: Bibelkunde des Neuen Testaments Geschichte und Religion des Urchristentums* (New York: Ökumenischen Rates der Kirchen, 1929), 121

33. E. Meyer, *Ursprung und Anfänge des Christentums* (3 vols.; Stuttgart: Cotta'sche Buchhandlung, 1921-23), 1:331; but later (3:47 n. 2 and 650-51) he rejects this date and argues for the first two decades of the second century.

34. A. Loisy, *The Birth of the Christian Religion* (trans. L. P. Jacks; London: Allen & Unwin, 1948), 52.

35. Suggested by R. B. Edwards, *Discovering John* (London: SPCK, 2003), 47.

36. See, e.g., R. Kimelman, "Birkat ha-Minim and the Lack of Evidence for an Anti-Christian Jewish Prayer in Late Antiquity," in *Jewish and Christian Self-Definition* (vol. 2 of *Aspects of Judaism in the Greco-Roman Period;* ed. E. P. Sanders; London: SCM Press, 1981), 226-44.

indicates that the Gospel was written while the pool was still in use.[37] There are two problems with this position. The first is that the form is not a present tense-form; it is simply the unaugmented form of εἰμί, a verb that lacks any significant contrast between present and aorist tense-forms and is instead aspectually vague. The second is that the present tense-form in Greek is not necessarily a present-time marker.[38] I can respect the desire to establish an early date for the Gospel, as it places the writing of the book closer to the events in Jesus' life that it purports to depict. If the early date is correct, however, it needs to be established along lines other than these.

Given the inconclusive nature of the arguments just presented, most scholars attempt to date the Gospel of John by drawing links to other historical events or processes, such as the rise of Gnosticism and the development of the early church.

b. Two Important Papyrological Discoveries

Arguments for later dates of John's Gospel are more complex and cannot be so easily correlated with historical events or processes as mentioned above. These later dates need to be seriously revised in the light of publication in 1935 of two important papyrus documents. The first is P.Egerton 2 (P.Lond. Christ. 1), which was quickly recognized as a noncanonical gospel, and the other is P.Rylands Greek 457 ($\mathfrak{P}^{52}$), a fragment of the Gospel of John itself.[39]

P.Egerton 2, a manuscript found in Egypt but now housed in the British Library, was published as a fragment of an unknown gospel in four parts. Its publication caused quite a bit of excitement, as the manuscript contains very Gospel-like episodes involving Jesus.[40] The first major episode in particular

37. E.g., see Wallace, "John 5,2."

38. Both issues are discussed in S. E. Porter, *Verbal Aspect in the Greek of the New Testament, with Reference to Tense and Mood* (SBG 1; New York: Peter Lang, 1989), ch. 2 and 442-47.

39. These two important manuscripts are discussed in more detail in S. E. Porter, "Recent Efforts to Reconstruct Early Christianity on the Basis of Its Papyrological Evidence," in *Christian Origins and Greco-Roman Culture: Social and Literary Contexts for the New Testament* (ed. S. E. Porter and A. W. Pitts; TENT 10; Early Christianity in Its Hellenistic Context 2; Leiden: Brill, 2013), 71-84. See also Porter, *How We Got the New Testament*, 103-6.

40. The two major publications are H. I. Bell and T. C. Skeat, *Fragments of an Unknown Gospel and Other Early Christian Papyri* (London: Trustees of the British Museum, 1935); and anonymous, *The New Gospel Fragments* (London: Trustees of the British Museum, 1935; rev. eds., 1951, 1955). The most recent thorough treatment is by T. Nicklas in T. Kraus,

sounds very Johannine in nature, for it describes Jesus confronting lawyers, challenging them to search the Scriptures (see John 5). For this reason, dating the papyrus in relation to John's Gospel became an item of importance.

The dating of literary papyrus manuscripts is admittedly quite complex, as the basis of such dating — when there is no date written on the papyrus, as one might have for a documentary text — is primarily comparison of handwriting with other manuscripts, as well as use of any factual data, such as where the manuscript was found in relation to other documents. As a result, there is often considerable difference of opinion, usually by at least as much as twenty-five years. For the purpose of dating P.Egerton 2, comparison was drawn by the editors to three dated manuscripts on the basis of similarity of handwriting: P.Berolinensis ined. 6854 (written in the reign of Trajan, who died in A.D. 117; this manuscript was later published as BGU I 22 and dated to 114), P.London 130 (a horoscope from the early years of the second century); and, purportedly the most similar, P.Fayum 110 (dated to 94).[41] The editors contended that these manuscripts provided the most constructive points of comparison. As a result, the editors suggested a date of ca. 150 (later revised to 140-60) for this particular manuscript, with original composition of the text to around 110-30.[42] (It is not entirely clear how they arrived at this later date on the basis of the comparisons, except possibly out of hesitation because few biblical or biblical-like manuscripts had been dated to the second century, then or since.) From the start, the editors also noticed that numerous canonical Gospel passages were apparently cited or reflected by this papyrus, including the following, roughly in order of their appearance in the papyrus: John 5:39; 9:29; 8:59; 10:31; 7:30, 44; 10:39; Luke 4:30; Matt 8:2-4 // Mark 1:40-44 // Luke 5:12-14; Luke 17:14; Matt 22:16; Luke 6:46; John 3:2; Luke 18:19; John 10:25; Matt 15:7-8; Mark 7:6-7.[43] In other words, all of the canonical Gospels are represented, with John's Gospel represented especially heavily. Initial discussion led to the conclusion that, despite some possibilities (such as the *Gospel of Peter*, later pretty well dismissed), this unknown gospel was not a portion of any known nonca-

---

M. Kruger, and T. Nicklas, *Gospel Fragments* (Oxford: Oxford University Press, 2009), 9-120. See also S. E. Porter, "Der Papyrus Egerton 2 (P.Egerton 2/P.Lond.Christ 1)" and "Der Papyrus Köln VI 255 (P.Köln VI 255)," in *Antike christliche Apokryphen in deutscher Übersetzung*, vol. 1, part 1 (ed. C. Markschies and J. Schröter; Tübingen: Mohr Siebeck, 2012), 360-65, 366-67.

41. Bell and Skeat, *Fragments*, 1-2.
42. Bell and Skeat, *Fragments*, 5; anonymous, *New Gospel Fragments*, 17.
43. Taken from the parallels arranged by Bell and Skeat, *Fragments*, 27.

nonical gospel. More important, scholars concluded that it may have been independent of the Synoptic Gospels and even possibly a source of John's Gospel.[44] Later discussion (published also in 1935) revised this conclusion by rejecting the idea that P.Egerton 2 was as early as the canonical Gospels and instead concluded that the author probably knew the Synoptic Gospels (though perhaps used them from memory), but that, because John's Gospel is (as thought at the time, see above) late (they suggest a date as late as 120-30), the author of Egerton and John's Gospel were both using a common source.[45] For fifty or so years, the discussion of P.Egerton 2 has pretty much revolved around these fundamental issues.

The second papyrological publication of significance regarding John's Gospel also occurred in 1935, when the papyrologist C. H. Roberts published a fragment from a codex (an early form of book, in which sheets of papyrus or parchment are folded and bound together) with John 18:31-33 and 37-38 on its two sides.[46] The fragment, which has become identified as the earliest fragment of a New Testament manuscript, is P.Rylands Greek 457. When Roberts published this fragment, he made use of the recently published P.Egerton 2 in his own analysis. Like P.Egerton 2, P.Rylands Greek 457 was not dated, and its date of composition had to be determined by means of comparative paleography. In discussing the date of the document, Roberts drew comparisons to several other manuscripts. He began with two undated literary documents, P.Berolinensis 6845 (a fragment of Homer's *Iliad* dated to the late first or early second century A.D.)[47] and P.Egerton 2

---

44. Bell and Skeat, *Fragments*, 38.

45. Anonymous, *New Gospel Fragments*, 27, 28. I find it interesting that this publication does not refer to P.Rylands Greek 457 in any of its revised forms. However, C. H. Dodd concluded the next year, after publication of P.Rylands Greek 457, that P.Egerton 2 made use of John's Gospel ("A New Gospel," in his *New Testament Studies* [Manchester: Manchester University Press, 1953], 12-52, esp. 45; originally published in 1936). P.Egerton 2 is misidentified by G. M. Burge as a Johannine fragment ("Gospel of John," in *The Bible Knowledge Background Commentary: John's Gospel, Hebrews–Revelation* [ed. C. A. Evans; Colorado Springs, CO: Cook, 2005], 38).

46. C. H. Roberts, *An Unpublished Fragment of the Fourth Gospel in the John Rylands Library* (Manchester: Manchester University Press, 1935); repr. with corrections in *BJRL* 20 (1936): 45-56; and in the *Catalogue of the Greek and Latin Papyri in the John Rylands Library Manchester* (vol. 3; Manchester: Manchester University Press, 1938), 1-3, with supplementary bibliography.

47. Roberts (*Unpublished Fragment*, 14) notes that the German papyrologist Wilhelm Schubart revised his opinion of this papyrus to late first century (W. Schubart, *Griechische Palaeographie* [Berlin: Beck, 1925], 117-18).

(mid-second century). Of the dated manuscripts, Roberts drew attention to
P.Fayum 110 (A.D. 94), P.London 2078 (reign of Domitian, 81-96), P.Oslo II
22 (127), and P.Berolinensis ined. 6854 (before 117; now BGU I 22, dated to
114). The one major difference that Roberts noted between P.Rylands Greek
457 and P.Egerton 2 is that there are no *nomina sacra* in the former, while
there are a number of them in the latter. (I return to this major point below.)[48] Roberts concluded that the fragment is to be dated to the first half of
the second century. Almost immediately after Roberts's publication, several
other scholars attempted to refine the dates, such as to the reign of Hadrian
(117-38), and more particularly 117-20; and possibly to the reign of Trajan
(98-117).[49] Recent discussion by papyrologists and New Testament textual
critics has settled on the date of ca. 125, give or take twenty-five years.[50] The
result of this dating of P.Rylands Greek 457 was to render any date for the
composition of John's Gospel later than around 100, and at the latest 110,
highly problematic because the later papyrus copy could not, of course,
predate the composition of the Gospel itself. In fact, in most introductions
to John's Gospel, many of which I have noted above, the date of P.Rylands
Greek 457 is used to establish the latest date for the composition of John's
Gospel. This is easily seen in the fact that most of the later dates, such as in
the second century, are held by scholars writing before the publication of
P.Rylands Greek 457.

48. Roberts, *Unpublished Fragment*, 17-18. Nomina sacra (singular: *nomen sacrum*) are
special ways of writing important biblical words, such as Ἰησοῦς (Jesus), κύριος (Lord),
θεός (God), and Χριστός (Christ), with some letters dropped out and usually a line drawn
over the remaining letters.

49. The first and third opinions are attributed to A. Deissmann, "Ein Evangelienblatt
aus den Tagen Hadrians," *Deutsche allgemeine Zeitung* 564 (3 December 1935) [English
translation in *British Weekly*, 12 December 1935, 219]; and the second to U. Wilken, "Die
Bremer Papyrus Sammlung," *Forschungen und Fortschritte* 12 (1936): 89 (cited in Roberts,
Catalogue, 1-2).

50. See, e.g., J. Finegan, *Encountering New Testament Manuscripts* (London: SPCK,
1975), 85-90 ("end of the first or beginning of the second century, at all events hardly later
than A.D. 125" [85]); K. Aland and B. Aland, *The Text of the New Testament: An Introduction
to the Critical Editions and to the Theory and Practice of Modern Textual Criticism* (trans. E. F.
Rhodes; 2nd ed.; Grand Rapids: Eerdmans, 1989), 84-87 ("the consensus has come in recent
years to regard 125 as representing the later limit, so that 𝔓⁵² must have been copied very
soon after the Gospel of John was itself written in the early 90s A.D." [85]); B. M. Metzger,
Manuscripts of the Greek Bible (Oxford: Oxford University Press, 1981), 62 (A.D. 100-150);
P. W. Comfort, *Early Manuscripts and Modern Translations* (Grand Rapids: Baker, 1990), 55
(A.D. 110-25); P. W. Comfort and D. P. Barrett, *The Text of the Earliest New Testament Greek
Manuscripts* (Wheaton, IL: Tyndale, 2001), 365 (A.D. 100-125).

c. Recent Developments regarding These Two Papyri

Since the original publication of these papyri, however, several scholarly discussions have tended to push the date of the copying (though not necessarily the composition) of both P.Egerton 2 and P.Rylands Greek 457 to a later time — with the possible implication that both the Egerton gospel and the Gospel of John are later compositions. I wish to analyze these arguments in more detail.

The first line of argument revolves around the date for P.Egerton 2. Since the original discovery and publication of this fragment, a small piece of what appears to be the same manuscript has been discovered and published (P.Köln VI 255). Michael Gronewald, its editor, argues for a date of at the earliest 200, on the basis of a single feature: an apostrophe between two consonants in recto line 4 — ανενεγʼκον.[51] Gronewald cites the papyrologist Eric Turner as indicating that this apostrophe is frequent only in the third century A.D. From his conclusion, Gronewald draws several implications. One is that the earlier date allowed Bell and Skeat to conclude that the Egerton gospel and John used a common source, but that the late date shows that reconstructions based upon such a scenario, such as that of Mayeda,[52] are compromised, and that the following conclusion of Jeremias in Hennecke and Schneemelcher's volume is no doubt correct. Jeremias concludes as follows:

> There are contacts with all four Gospels. The juxtaposition of Johannine . . . and Synoptic material . . . and the fact that the Johannine material is shot through with Synoptic phrases and the Synoptic with Johannine usage, permits the conjecture that the author knew all and every one of the canonical Gospels. Only he had no one of them before him as a written text. On the contrary the above-mentioned digressions . . . show that the material has been reproduced from memory. Consequently we may have before us an instance of the overlapping of written and oral tradition:

51. M. Gronewald, "Köln VI, no. 255: Unbekanntes Evangelium oder Evangelienharmonie (Fragment aus dem 'Evangelium Egerton')," in *Kölner Papyri*, vol. 6 (ed. M. Gronewald et al.; Papyrologica Coloniensia 7; Cologne: Westdeutscher Verlag, 1987), 136-45 (137). However, he also notes that the use of the verb form is attested in B. Mandilaras, *The Verb in the Greek Non-Literary Papyri* (Athens: Hellenic Ministry of Culture and Sciences, 1973), par. 683(2), where Mandilaras shows that the form is known from the early second century A.D.
52. G. Mayeda, *Das Leben-Jesu-Fragment Papyrus Egerton 2 und seine Stellung in der urchristlichen Literaturgeschichte* (Bern: Paul Haupt, 1946).

although the tradition was already fixed in writing, it was still widely re-
produced from memory and in this way, enriched with extra-canonical
material . . . , found new expression in writing. The text shows no historical knowledge that carries us beyond the canonical Gospels.[53]

Gronewald's later dating of P.Egerton 2 has been accepted by, among others,
Udo Schnelle[54] and Helmut Koester, although they draw other implications
from this dating that Gronewald did not. Schnelle broaches the subject of
whether the date for P.Rylands Greek 457 should be reevaluated, and with
it the date of the composition of John's Gospel.[55] I will return to this argument below. Koester states that Gronewald "cites convincing arguments for
a date of the style of the handwriting rather closer to Papyrus Bodmer II
(= NT $\mathfrak{P}^{66}$), i.e., to about the year 200 CE."[56] Here is what Gronewald actually says with regard to P.Bodmer II: "Nach Bekanntwerden des Johannesevangeliums P.Bodmer II wurde P.Egerton 2 wegen der paläographischen
Verwandtschaft mehrfach herangezogen, um eine Datierung für P.Bodmer
II zu gewinnen. H. Hungers Datierung von P.Bodmer II auf die Mitte des
zweiten Jahrhunderts stiess auf den Widerstand von E. G. Turner, der den
Anfang des dritten Jahrhunderts für wahrscheinlicher hielt."[57] The major
argument used by Gronewald is the use of the apostrophe in P.Egerton 2, not
the correspondence to P.Bodmer II. In any case, this does not stop Koester
from positing that P.Egerton 2 reflects pre-Johannine material, a point to
which I will return below.

Gronewald's argument needs to be reassessed, however. The evidence
he cites regarding the apostrophe is not entirely convincing. He cites a footnote by Turner in his *Greek Manuscripts*. In this note Turner says, "In the first
decade of iii A.D. this practice [the use of the apostrophe] suddenly becomes
extremely common and then persists."[58] He then goes on to note examples

53. J. Jeremias, "An Unknown Gospel with Johannine Elements (Pap. Egerton 2)," in
New Testament Apocrypha (ed. E. Hennecke and W. Schneemelcher; 2 vols.; London: Lutterworth, 1963), 1:95 (Gronewald cites the German, 1:59).

54. U. Schnelle, *The History and Theology of the New Testament Writings* (trans. M. E.
Boring; Minneapolis: Fortress Press, 1998), 477 and n. 119.

55. He is joined in this opinion by, e.g., C. Tuckett and C. Hill (see below, nn. 69 and
72).

56. H. Koester, *Ancient Christian Gospels: Their History and Development* (Philadelphia:
Trinity Press International, 1990), 206.

57. Gronewald, "Köln VI, no. 255," 136.

58. E. G. Turner, *Greek Manuscripts of the Ancient World* (ed. P. J. Parsons; 2nd ed.;
London: Institute of Classical Studies, 1987), 11 and n. 50.

not from the third century but from the second century, including BGU III 715.5 (A.D. 101), P.Petaus 86.11 (184/85), and SB XIV 11342.11 (193). One can hardly say that the one instance in P.Egerton 2 is an extremely common use — especially when there are other places where an apostrophe could have been used and where one is used in P.Bodmer II. The use of the apostrophe may point to nothing more than that the manuscript was written in the second half of the second century, say around 180 or 190. This conclusion is in fact consistent with the majority opinion regarding the date of P.Bodmer II, with proposals ranging from before 150 (Hunger, and now Comfort and Barrett), around 150 (Cavallo), around 200 (Martin, the editor), to the opening of the third century (Turner).[59] The lack of frequency of the apostrophe and the general dating of P.Bodmer II point to this middle to late second-century date.

This line of thought raises the question of the relevance of the manuscripts that were used by Bell and Skeat for comparison. My own comparison of photographs of these manuscripts indicates that the ones that were originally suggested are perhaps not the most fitting.[60] I believe that they are earlier, based upon the formation of the letters. P.Bodmer II is a more fitting comparison, as is P.Oxyrhynchus L 3533 (late second century; a fragment of Menander) and P.Oxyrhynchus III 473 (an honorary decree, A.D. 138-60).[61] If these comparisons are accurate, a likely date for P.Egerton 2 would be in the mid to late second century.

This line of inquiry regarding P.Egerton 2 leads directly to concerns regarding P.Rylands Greek 457, since the fortunes of P.Rylands Greek 457 are often linked to those of P.Egerton 2. For example, Schnelle emphasizes that Roberts linked P.Egerton 2 with P.Rylands Greek 457, with the implication that, if the one is dated later, the other should be dated later

59. See J. van Haelst, *Catalogue des Papyrus littéraires Juifs et Chrétiens* (Paris: Publications de la Sorbonne, 1976), loc. cit.; Comfort and Barrett, *Text*, 376.

60. I recognize the complexities in establishing the dates for undated manuscripts, having worked with such manuscripts over a number of years and having faced the difficulties involved. Some of this work resulted in the following publications: S. E. Porter and W. J. Porter, "P.Vindob. G 26225: A New Romanos Melodus Papyrus in the Vienna Collection," *JÖB* 52 (2002): 135-48 with plate; and *New Testament Greek Papyri and Parchments: New Editions* (2 vols.; MPER, n.s., 30, 31; Berlin: Walter de Gruyter, 2008).

61. There are also some similarities to P.Oxyrhynchus IV 656 (redated to the second century by most scholars; fragment of Genesis), P.Oxyrhynchus L 3523 ($\mathfrak{p}^{90}$, second century; fragment of John), and P.Rylands Greek 5 ($\mathfrak{p}^{32}$, perhaps redated to the second century on the basis of similarity to P.Oxyrhynchus IV 656, both originally dated to the third century by Hunt; fragment of Titus).

as well.[62] Furthermore, Andreas Schmidt has argued that P.Rylands Greek
457 more closely resembles P.Chester Beatty III and X and thus should be
dated to around 170 (±25 years).[63] However, the most sustained reassessment of P.Rylands Greek 457 has been made by Brent Nongbri.[64] I use the
word "sustained" because of its length, not necessarily its decisiveness.
In fact, much of Nongbri's assessment is simply not germane, including
his ad hominem arguments against Roberts on the basis of Roberts's age
and experience, his questioning the process by which the papyrus was
published, and his simply disagreeing with the most recent consideration
of all of the early papyri by Comfort and Barrett.[65] Nongbri is responding
to Georg Strecker's call for a new analysis of the papyrus[66] — or at least
one that agrees with the conclusions he seems to want. Nongbri provides
photographs of some of the papyri that have previously been brought into
the discussion and adds several new ones to be considered, on which he
comments. He believes that he has established that, while there may be
similarities between P.Rylands Greek 457 and some early manuscripts —
in particular P.Berolinensis 6845, P.Fayum 110, P.London inv. 2078 (= SB
V 7987), P.Florence I 1, and P.Egerton 2, which he uncritically accepts
as dated to ca. 200 on the basis of Gronewald's statements (but note my
comments above that call this into question) — there are a number of later
manuscripts that also have similar features. These include P.Michigan inv.
5336 (= SB XXII 15782, A.D. 152), P.Amherst II 78 (184), P.Oxyrhynchus
LI 3614 (200), P.Oxyrhynchus LII 3694 (after 200), and P.Oxyrhynchus
XLI 2968 (190).

In considering the various arguments regarding P.Rylands Greek 457,
I wish to deal with the manuscript similarities first. Examination of photo-

62. Schnelle, *History and Theology*, 477 n. 119.

63. A. Schmidt, "Zwei Anmerkungen zu Ryl. III 457," *APF* 35 (1989): 11-12. Schmidt
also entertains the idea that P.Rylands Greek 457 was a text that combined John 18:31 and
19:7 (see recto). It is true that two of the same words appear in these verses, but there is
nothing else to support this claim.

64. B. Nongbri, "The Use and Abuse of P52: Papyrological Pitfalls in the Dating of the
Fourth Gospel," *HTR* 98.1 (2005): 23-48.

65. Nongbri, "Use," 27 n. 13, 30, 25-26 n. 9, 31-32. He does not object, e.g., to the fact
that Skeat, who coedited P.Egerton 2 with Bell, was a very young man at the time; the
process by which noteworthy manuscripts are published first is usual, and was followed by
those who published P.Egerton 2; and Nongbri offers no substantive rebuttal of Comfort
and Barrett — apart from apparently not liking their results.

66. G. Strecker, *The Johannine Letters: A Commentary on 1, 2, and 3 John* (trans. L. M.
Maloney; Minneapolis: Fortress Press, 1996), xli n. 28.

graphs of P.Rylands Greek 457 and P.Chester Beatty III (Revelation) and X (Daniel) indicate that these are not in fact close and should not be used as a comparison for dating. P.Chester Beatty III is characterized by thick and heavily drawn letters, with several letters that drop significantly below the line, including phi and iota. It also has a number of *nomina sacra* (to which I will return below). The letters rarely touch and are written independently, apart from a couple of instances of iota following alpha or epsilon. P.Chester Beatty X is more lightly drawn, with lettering that is less regular and compact. The phi is less likely to extend below the line, and virtually no iotas do so. The alpha is more regular and compact. The hand of P.Rylands Greek 457 is also thick, but not evenly so (there are blobs of ink at the bottoms of some vertical strokes), and the letters are larger and less compact. There is more space on a line. The iota does not extend significantly below the line (there is no example of phi). The two different types of alpha are written much more freely, and the eta has both vertical lines fully extended. The delta is also more compact. I am thus not convinced by Schmidt's comparison.

I am likewise suspicious of a number of Nongbri's supposed parallels. I agree with Nongbri's assessment of P.London inv. 2078 (= SB V 7987, A.D. 81-96) — which has many inscription-like features and more angular lines to such letters as kappa — as probably being too early. Likewise, I agree with Roberts's (and Nongbri's) questioning of P.Florence I 1, as it has some similarities but generally is quite different from P.Rylands Greek 457. I would go further, however, and question the pertinence of most of the new manuscripts that Nongbri introduces. The first is P.Michigan inv. 5336 (= SB XXII 15782). There are some similarities, as he notes, but there are also a number of distinctions, including the use of the tilted lunate sigma and the increased use of ligatures, which are both signs of later writing. Similarly, P.Amherst II 78 (A.D. 184), though put forward by Turner, has a more compact and squashed appearance. P.Oxyrhynchus LI 3614 (200) is much more cursive, with several letters that go above and then below the line. By the time Nongbri gets to P.Oxyrhynchus LII 3694 (after 200) and XLI 2968 (190), the similarities are even fewer. It is unclear to me what Nongbri is actually trying to prove, but the parallels he musters do not make his case that the date of P.Rylands Greek 457 is later than has previously been thought. If anything, the texts that he admits have similarities indicate a date between 94 and 150, exactly the range that was put forward by Roberts.

Comparison of P.Rylands Greek 457 with a number of manuscripts previously suggested, however, is more helpful. P.Berolinensis 6845 (late first or early second century)[67] has a number of similarities with the Rylands fragment, although it might be that P.Rylands Greek 457 is a little later on the basis of its being a little freer, with less inscriptional forms of letters. Of the dated manuscripts, P.Fayum 110 (A.D. 94) is very close in appearance, including formation of epsilon, upsilon, delta, eta, and two types of alpha. P.Oslo II 22 (127) writes the eta, mu, and iota similarly, but the turned-down lunate sigma is probably later, as is the looser hand. P.Berolinensis ined. 6854 (before 117), now BGU I 22 (114), is even more spacious in some ways, with greater unevenness of letters, with some letters tending toward a later date.

The comparison of photographs and of the manuscripts themselves has led me to conclude that P.Egerton 2 and P.Rylands Greek 457 have no especially close ties with each other. In fact, they display more similarities to other manuscripts than they do to each other. Once this linkage is severed, it is important to establish the dates independently, and in fact, if possible, to create a sequence. On the basis of these comparisons, as well as the pertinent evidence that Nongbri marshals, I would hold firm to the early second century date of P.Rylands Greek 457, placing it around 100-120. P.Egerton 2, as stated above, should be dated to the mid to late second century. This reestablished early date for P.Rylands Greek 457 — admittedly on the basis of comparison of manuscripts, although in this case with some dated ones — also reaffirms a date for composition of the Gospel before the turn of the first century.

d. Nomina Sacra

I now turn to one last piece of evidence regarding the dating of these two papyri and their relationship to John's Gospel: the *nomina sacra*. These special forms have been an item of renewed interest in recent times. Early studies have shown that Christian manuscripts tended to use special forms (often mistakenly called abbreviations) for such words as Ἰησοῦς (Jesus), κύριος (Lord), θεός (God), and Χριστός (Christ). Later forms developed as well.[68]

---

67. On the late first century, see n. 47 above.

68. The best contemporary survey of *nomina sacra* is L. W. Hurtado, "The Origin of the *Nomina Sacra*: A Proposal," *JBL* 117.4 (1998): 655-73; he draws upon this survey in his *The Earliest Christian Artifacts: Manuscripts and Christian Origins* (Grand Rapids: Eerdmans, 2006), 95-134; cf. also Hurtado, "The Earliest Evidence of an Emerging Christian Material and Visual Culture: The Codex, the Nomina Sacra, and the Staurogram," in *Text and Artifact in the Religions of Mediterranean Antiquity* (ed. S. G. Wilson and M. Desjardins; Waterloo, ON: Wilfrid Laurier University Press, 2000), 271-88.

The important issue here is whether *nomina sacra* were used in P.Rylands Greek 457. This small fragmentary text does not have any of the early words that were written in a suspended form, so we cannot tell directly from examination of the manuscript. However, there are several places on the lines that are no longer extant where a *nomen sacrum* could have been used, including the possibility of three instances of the use of "Jesus" (recto lines 2, 5, and 7). Roberts, when he first published the papyrus, did not include *nomina sacra* in his reconstruction.[69] Several recent editions of the papyrus, however, have reconstructed it with *nomina sacra*.[70] In fairly recent discussion, Christopher Tuckett has argued that the line spacing indicates that *nomina sacra* were not used.[71] Charles Hill and Larry Hurtado, apart from each other's knowledge, have independently argued in response that they believe that there is slightly greater probability that they were used.[72]

Hill's arguments merit attention, as he has gone to great lengths to determine the potential use of *nomina sacra* in P.Rylands Greek 457. He marshals five arguments, but in effect they are all dependent upon the first one, which claims that, when writing the relevant *nomen sacrum*, the scribe of P.Rylands Greek 457 would have used the "long contracted form"[73] with three letters.[74] Hill arrives at this conclusion on the basis of the fact that $\mathfrak{P}^5$, $\mathfrak{P}^{22}$, $\mathfrak{P}^{39}$, $\mathfrak{P}^{90}$, $\mathfrak{P}^{106}$, and $\mathfrak{P}^{108}$ all use this three-letter form, although he admits that the two-letter form is used by $\mathfrak{P}^{28}$, $\mathfrak{P}^{45}$, $\mathfrak{P}^{66}$, and $\mathfrak{P}^{75}$.[75] Hill's argument unfortunately must be rejected for several reasons. The first is that the earlier New Testament manuscripts tend to use the two-letter form, not the three-letter form. These include $\mathfrak{P}^{66}$ and $\mathfrak{P}^{75}$ (apart from $\mathfrak{P}^{90}$, but with only one example of the two-letter form), as well as P.Egerton 2, which has five instances of the two-letter

69. Later comments by Roberts have indicated to some that he later thought that *nomina sacra* were used, although his statements are not directed specifically to this manuscript but only to the use of *nomina sacra* in general. See C. M. Tuckett, "P52 and *Nomina Sacra*," *NTS* 47.4 (2001): 544-48, here 545 and n. 8.

70. E.g., D. C. Parker and W. J. Elliott, *The Gospel according to John,* vol. 1: *The Papyri* (vol. 4 of *The New Testament in Greek;* Leiden: Brill, 1995), loc. cit.; Comfort and Barrett, *Text,* 367-68.

71. Tuckett, "P52," 548.

72. C. E. Hill, "Did the Scribe of P52 Use the *Nomina Sacra*? Another Look," *NTS* 48.4 (2002): 587-92; L. W. Hurtado, "P52 (P.Rylands Gk. 457) and the Nomina Sacra: Method and Probability," *TynBul* 54.1 (2003): 1-14.

73. Hill, "Scribe," 587 n. 4. Hurtado ("P52," 9 n. 27) prefers the term "long suspended."

74. Hurtado, "P52," 9.

75. Hill ("Scribe," 588) differentiates between the two-letter forms, which I do not believe is necessary here.

form of Jesus' name. The second reason is that the vast majority of instances of *nomina sacra* are of the two-letter type (there are only thirteen examples in the manuscripts he cites, compared with far more than that in p[66] alone, to say nothing of the five examples in P.Egerton 2). This means that all of Hill's estimates for the individual lines and for the entire passage on each side should be calculated on the basis of the fewer number of letters. This results in a greater discrepancy in terms of line length. Once this argument has been modified, the other arguments fall into line correspondingly. Hill also attempts to extend the number of letters on some of the lines, for example, based upon spaces around any iota with diaeresis, and the spacing of *nomina sacra*.[76] The issue of spaces around any iota with diaeresis does not actually help Hill's case. There are three instances of an iota with diaeresis (recto lines 1-2 and verso line 2). The first one has no noticeably increased space either before or after the iota, the third has no space after but some extra space before, and the second has extra space on both sides. This makes it impossible to tell whether there would or would not have been extra space in any other instances. Hill also accepts Roberts's observation regarding the tendency of scribes to separate *nomina sacra* from their surrounding words by addition of space.[77] There is no doubt that this is a tendency in some cases, but it is not a universal one. In fact, in P.Egerton 2 it occurs in roughly half the instances (seven of thirteen, on the basis of my observation of photographs). My selective observation of a number of photographs of pages of p[66] and p[75] indicates that the number is no more than this, and perhaps even fewer. A further factor that Hill does not take into account is the possibility that other words in the passage perhaps would have been written with a *nomen sacrum* (e.g., βασιλεύς twice, which is written as a *nomen sacrum* in P.Egerton 2, but not seen as plausible by Hurtado),[78] and thus there would have been even fewer letters on the page and thus fewer letters on a line (by as many as 1.5 letters per line). The cumulative effect of all of these considerations is to render Hill's calculations suspect, leaving as the more plausible scenario the suggestion that there were no *nomina sacra* used in this manuscript — or at least that we cannot be sure that any were used. This is thus a further piece of evidence in support of the early date of the manuscript. It is just possible that P.Rylands Greek 457 is a manuscript that indicates a stage before *nomina*

76. Hill, "Scribe," 589, 591.
77. Hill, "Scribe," 589, citing C. H. Roberts, *Manuscript, Society, and Belief in Early Christian Egypt* (London: British Academy, 1979), 35 n. 2, 38 n. 2.
78. Hurtado, "P52," 6.

sacra were widely used, possibly even used at all — which was probably around 100.[79] A parallel has been observed in P.Oxyrhynchus IV 656 (second century; Genesis), where this manuscript does not have any *nomina sacra*, even though the word θεός (God) is used.

3. Implications of Comparison of Gospels

A number of implications can be drawn from the above discussion of P.Rylands Greek 457, P.Egerton 2, and the other manuscripts mentioned in the light of John's Gospel.

a. Timeline of Development

As almost every scholar who works with ancient manuscripts admits, the dating of manuscripts is extremely difficult when all one has is undated manuscripts for comparison. Nevertheless, the development of a timeline or trajectory is necessary. The evidence that I have analyzed above indicates that the order of writing of the manuscripts discussed above was as follows:

> the canonical Gospel of John, probably 70-90, which would ensure that there was enough time for it to be circulated, copied, and transmitted to Egypt, where it was then used and copied further;
> then P.Rylands Greek 457 around 100-120, although the absence of the *nomina sacra,* if they were introduced around 100, may possibly push the date even earlier;
> and then P.Egerton 2 copied sometime from the mid to late second century, perhaps around 170.

b. Early Date of John's Gospel

If the timeline I have just articulated is correct, and if a reasonable time for transmission of a document was thirty years (this seems to be a rule of thumb used by a number of scholars),[80] then it is worth reconsidering the date of

---

79. Hurtado, "P52," 4.
80. In discussion when this paper was first delivered, one participant suggested that

composition for John's Gospel. I cannot go into detail here, but the sequence would fit both ends of the trajectory noted above. Beginning with the latest date, if P.Rylands Greek 457 was copied around 120, then a reasonable date of the composition of John's Gospel would be around 90. So far, this conclusion matches the standard and usual dates for the composition of the two documents, as indicated above. If P.Rylands Greek 457 was copied around 100, however, then the date of composition of John's Gospel might have been as early as 70. This scenario also would fit within the parameters of some of the suggested dates for John's Gospel mentioned above. If we were to be highly speculative and posit a date for copying of P.Rylands Greek 457 that was earlier than 100, then that would quite possibly, even if not necessarily, push the date of composition of John's Gospel even earlier, possibly even earlier than the fall of Jerusalem. Even though the usual arguments for such an early date are not convincing, as noted above, an argument from the surrounding manuscript data may just make such a hypothesis at least worth considering and not dismissing too easily. I will note that there is no early papyrological or transmissional evidence that stands in the way of an early dating. In fact, the timeline above might well encourage such a recalculation.

c. P.Egerton 2 Dependent upon John's Gospel

There are two arguments to consider here regarding P.Egerton 2. The first is the one from chronology. Even when the early date of P.Egerton 2 as a manuscript is accepted, its composition is said to be around 110-30. This would mean, by the reckoning that I have presented above, that P.Egerton 2 was written after the composition of John's Gospel and contemporary with the copying of P.Rylands Greek 457. Koester, however, has argued that, even if P.Egerton 2 is dated later, the tradition represented is earlier than that of John. Koester considers especially P.Egerton 2 fragment 1 (verso lines 7-20) in arriving at the conclusion that Egerton has language that is "not yet" as Johannine as the Gospel itself. His evidence includes the following: the term νομικοί, a Lukan word in a document that, Koester contends, has "very little else that would suggest dependence upon Luke";[81] the use of "life" rather

---

the period may be shorter, on the basis of the view suggested by R. Bauckham regarding the spread of the gospel. See Bauckham, "John for Readers of Mark," in *The Gospels for All Christians: Rethinking the Gospel Audiences* (ed. R. Bauckham; Grand Rapids: Eerdmans, 1998), 147-71. These times of course are all relative — but nevertheless suggestive.

81. Koester, *Ancient Christian Gospels,* 208. A somewhat similar view has been argued

than "eternal life," "more typical" (he says) for John;[82] and the phrasing "Jesus answered and said" (ἀποκριθεὶς καὶ εἶπεν), which (he claims — see below) is "never used" in John's Gospel.[83] We can dispense with the last reason
immediately, as Koester appears to be confused at this point. The phrasing
"Jesus answered and said" is indeed used about twenty times in John's Gospel, but the Greek construction is not ἀποκριθεὶς καὶ εἶπεν ("answering and
he said"), which is pretty close to nonsense, but ἀπεκρίθη καὶ εἶπεν ("he
answered and said") in John — and ἀποκριθεὶς εἶπεν ("answering, he said")
in the Synoptic Gospels, which P.Egerton 2 has. In any case, P.Egerton's use
of ἀποκριθεὶς εἶπεν in no way demands that we see John's Gospel as a later
development. Koester's other reasons are no more persuasive. For example,
there is other evidence in P.Egerton 2 of use of Luke, besides the phrasing
ἀποκριθεὶς εἶπεν noted already. Fragment 1 recto lines 40-41 perhaps reflects
Luke 17:14, and fragment 2 recto lines 51-52 reflects Luke 6:46. Next, the
term "eternal life" is not more typical of John than is "life," with "life" appearing a few more times than the phrase "eternal life." Thus, when Koester
says that John's Gospel has expanded P.Egerton 2, one must reject such a
conclusion.[84] Similar estimations have been reached regarding the Synoptic material in P.Egerton 2, contrary to Koester's protestations.[85] Instead,
like other early noncanonical gospel-like texts, P.Egerton 2 should be seen
as a literarily creative expression of the early church, reflecting "a creative
retelling of a number of Gospel stories from the Synoptics and John, woven
together into a new series of communally inspired episodes."[86]

---

by Francis Watson in the recent *Gospel Writing: A Canonical Perspective* (Grand Rapids:
Eerdmans, 2013), 286-340.

82. Koester, *Ancient Christian Gospels,* 209.

83. Koester, *Ancient Christian Gospels,* 209.

84. Koester also states (*Ancient Christian Gospels,* 208) that ἐραυνᾶτε translated as an
imperative ("search") is "preferable for Egerton 2 to the indicative ('you search') of John's
Gospel," but when he offers the P.Egerton 2 phrasing in his reconstruction he translates it
"you search" (p. 209) — further evidence that Koester is simply confused on a number of
the more technical points.

85. E.g., F. Neirynck, "Papyrus Egerton 2 and the Healing of the Leper," *ETL* 61 (1985):
153-60, repr. in his *Evangelica II, 1982-1991: Collected Essays* (ed. F. Van Segbroeck; BETL 99;
Leuven: Peeters/Leuven University Press, 1991), 773-83; contra Koester, *Ancient Christian
Gospels,* 211-13.

86. S. E. Porter, "What Do We Know and How Do We Know It? Reconstructing
Early Christianity from Its Manuscripts," in *Christian Origins,* 41-70, here 56 (see 54-56 on
P.Egerton 2, and 57-59 on several other such manuscripts).

d. Nomina Sacra

Whereas the dating of P.Rylands Greek 457 is not precise, there is nothing in the reconstruction offered above that refutes the idea that there was a relatively fast and early development of the use of the *nomina sacra* in the manuscripts of the New Testament. By considering the other early Johannine manuscripts, we see what amounts to a trajectory of roughly 100 years from the time of composition of John's Gospel to the full development of the use of such terms. P.Rylands Greek 457 would occur in the first half of such development and not yet reflect the use of such *nomina sacra*. However, by the time of P.Egerton 2, and then the other Johannine manuscripts, such as P.Bodmer II, $\mathfrak{p}^{75}$, and $\mathfrak{p}^{90}$, as well as the early third-century manuscripts, the *nomina sacra* were in widespread use. Whereas discussion of the *nomina sacra* in P.Rylands Greek 457 has usually been used for reconstructive purposes, when used for the purposes of dating the manuscript, the findings may well aid in our reconstruction of the textual history of early Christianity, in particular the possible dating of John's Gospel.

e. Development of the Codex and Canon

Finally, I note that the evidence from P.Rylands Greek 457 and P.Egerton 2 indicates that the codex was indeed an early Christian development that went hand in hand with the development of the Christian canon.[87] P.Rylands Greek 457 is clearly a piece of a codex, with continuous writing on both sides, so far as we can determine. Estimates are that the page would have been 21 cm. high by 20 cm. wide, with 18 lines of text on a page. There would have been about 130 pages, or roughly 65 or (with title page) 66 leaves folded in half to make the manuscript. At this stage, the manuscript likely contained only John's Gospel. By the end of the second century, if not earlier, however, some manuscripts would have included multiple Gospels (e.g., Tatian's *Diatessaron*). By the time of the writing of $\mathfrak{p}^{45}$, probably around the early third century, the four canonical Gospels were being gathered together, as this four-Gospel manuscript indicates.[88] All of the evidence we possess,

---

87. On the development of the Gospel writings into a recognized canon, see Porter, *How We Got the New Testament*, 84-106.

88. There is the possibility that $\mathfrak{p}^4$, $\mathfrak{p}^{64}$, and $\mathfrak{p}^{67}$, if they are from the same manuscript, may have been a fourfold Gospel codex, dated to the late second century. For discussion, see Porter, *How We Got the New Testament*, 95-99.

however, suggests that only the canonical Gospels were gathered into such groupings.

To be sure, P.Egerton 2 indicates that early noncanonical documents were written in codex form as well. In fact, many of the apocryphal gospel fragments are in codex form, including P.Oxyrhynchus V 840 (although there is debate over whether it is a miniature codex or an amulet).[89] What P.Egerton 2 tells us, however, is that, by the time P.Egerton 2 was written, the four canonical Gospels were already recognized, since there is evidence for the use of all four of them. There may be other noncanonical gospels cited in P.Egerton 2 (unknown to us because we have not yet discovered them), but lacking such evidence, we must take seriously the fact that P.Egerton 2 does cite the four canonical Gospels, and especially John's Gospel — and citation is what I believe it is, as Koester's arguments simply have no persuasive or evidential power. Moreover, we must consider that P.Egerton 2 intertwines the four Gospels together, drawing upon each one, in a way that indicates that these four were in some way recognized as having canonical and quotable status within the early church. This in fact was the conclusion of Jeremias, who, as noted above, concluded that "the juxtaposition of Johannine . . . and Synoptic material and the fact that the Johannine material is shot through with Synoptic phrases and the Synoptic with Johannine usage, permits the conjecture that the author knew all and every one of the canonical gospels."[90] The effect of this argument may be to push the date of composition of P.Egerton 2 to later, that is, to closer to the time of the copying of this manuscript. In any event, it does nothing to diminish the recognition of John's Gospel as early. In fact, the apparent organization of $\mathfrak{P}^{45}$, with the Gospels ordered as Matthew, Luke, John, and Mark, perhaps reinforces recognition of the prominence of John's Gospel.[91]

89. However, one of the other very early apocryphal documents, the Fayum fragment (P.Vindobonensis G. 2325), is written on one side of the sheet only and may well reflect a single sheet or scroll.

90. Jeremias, "Unknown Gospel," 1:95. This is cited by Koester, who opines that, "if this conclusion were true, Papyrus Egerton 2 would appear to be, even with a date of ca. 200 CE, a spectacularly early piece of evidence for the establishment of the four-gospel canon of the New Testament" (*Ancient Christian Gospels,* 207). However, he goes on to say that "Jeremias's observation . . . is not quite accurate" (p. 207). Hill ("Scribe," 305-6) appears to have taken Koester's comment as an endorsement of the conclusion, failing to note that he believes it inaccurate.

91. This organization also makes use of such terminology as "Fourth Gospel" for John's Gospel somewhat suspect, as it is not the fourth Gospel but the third. There was such variation among collections of the Gospels in the early centuries, possibly regionally determined

34

f. Implications for John's Gospel and Jesus

So far, much of our attention has been given to treating P.Egerton 2 and P.Rylands Greek 457, two important early documents for studying John's Gospel. Rather than linking these two documents together, so that the fortunes or misfortunes of one have a direct effect on the other, I believe, as indicated above, that they should be separated from each other and evaluated individually and on their own merits. When that is done, I think that the evidence leads to a reestablishment of what might be called the traditional date for both of them, but independently of each other. These are important findings in their own right. However, they have greater implications for the study of John's Gospel and Jesus. I believe that there is possibly a subtle, hidden agenda of other scholars involved in the redating of these early documents, so as to open up the possibility again of John's Gospel being written sometime within, perhaps well into, the second century. As noted above, those who argued for a late date for John's Gospel all pretty much predate the discovery of P.Rylands Greek 457. I cannot help but think that those who are arguing for a late date for this Johannine fragment also have in mind the reversion to a late date for the Gospel. One of the many and several consequences of this late dating was a denigration of the Gospel as to its significance in relation to the Synoptic Gospels. However, on the basis of my own research presented here, I think that an early date of both P.Rylands Greek 457 and John's Gospel can be maintained. As a result, I would argue that there is no need to pull John's Gospel away from the Synoptics. To the contrary, I believe that John's Gospel probably needs to be more fully integrated into the kinds of discussions that regularly go on regarding the Synoptics, including matters regarding the historical Jesus, the historicity of particular events, and the authenticity of various sayings of Jesus. In that sense, this chapter is eminently about Jesus, as much as it is about John's Gospel. The trajectory that I have outlined regarding the composition of John's Gospel in relation to P.Rylands Greek 457 and P.Egerton 2 indicates that the Jesus of John's Gospel belongs within the environment of the first century and just as much a part of the discussion of the Jesus of the Synoptics as their Jesus does. This is not the place to tease out all of the implications of such a statement, except to say that it brings a recognizable unity and cohesiveness (indeed, coherence)

---

and reflecting the period before a fixed order was established. Codex Bezae (D) apparently had the order Matthew, John, Luke, Mark. See Porter, *How We Got the New Testament,* 87-88.

to the discussion of Jesus in relation to the larger field of Gospel studies, by means of John's Gospel.[92]

4. Conclusion

Over the last one hundred years, the dating of John's Gospel has been linked to that of several Johannine-like gospel manuscripts, including P.Rylands Greek 457, which is an admittedly small fragment of the Gospel, and P.Egerton 2, which is a noncanonical gospel that draws heavily upon John's Gospel, among the other now-canonical Gospels. Recent discussion of these later gospel-related manuscripts has raised questions regarding John's Gospel. The more we investigate these manuscripts, whether they are fragments of John's Gospel or later church compositions of a gospel sort, the more insight they can perhaps offer us into the history of early Christianity and, more important, even the compositional history and timeline regarding John's Gospel. In the discussion above, we saw that, once we examined a number of other ancient manuscripts, some of them biblical and some of them not, some of them dated and others not, we were able to disassociate P.Rylands Greek 457 from P.Egerton 2 regarding their respective dates of composition. Comparison of these other manuscripts also provided for the opportunity to revisit the question of the date of each of these important documents. As a result, we were able to posit a variety of possible scenarios concerning the copying of these individual documents, which have implications for the composition of John's Gospel. I believe that a plausible case can be made that the determination of the timeline of copying of these gospel-like documents not only helps to account for their development but allows us to examine more closely the possible date of composition of John's Gospel. This process has resulted in positing the possibility of an early composition for John's Gospel relative to these gospel-like documents, and clarifies the trajectory of early Christian writings.

---

92. An apparently similar agenda is being explored by the group that produced the John, Jesus, and History volumes, although I think that they perhaps have not been as willing to question some fundamental assumptions but wish to work within the established paradigm in respect to many of the major questions in Johannine studies. See P. N. Anderson, F. Just, and T. Thatcher, eds., *John, Jesus, and History*, vol. 1, *Critical Appraisals of Critical Views;* vol. 2, *Aspects of Historicity in the Fourth Gospel* (Atlanta: Society of Biblical Literature, 2007-9).

CHAPTER 2

Public Proclamation of Jesus in John's Gospel

1. Introduction

One of the major issues surrounding John's Gospel — especially within the last decade or so — has been the question of the Gospel's original audience.[1] There has been much discussion regarding the original audience of all of the canonical Gospels. The traditional viewpoint, as is widely known and usually recognized, is that the four Gospels were each written for specific ecclesial audiences.[2] A number of scholars have recently argued that there was a more widespread audience in mind when the Gospels were first written.[3] In this chapter, I go beyond both of these views — at least, with regard to John's Gospel — by arguing that John's Gospel was originally written as a "public" Gospel with public proclamation in mind. In other words, I contend that it was originally written, not for a particular ecclesial community (whether in Ephesus or elsewhere), but as a full and public declaration to all people of who the Messiah, who is also the Son of God, is: Jesus (John 20:31). This

1. The most recent monograph-length treatment of the topic is E. W. Klink III, *The Sheep of the Fold: The Audience and Origin of the Gospel of John* (SNTSMS 141; Cambridge: Cambridge University Press, 2007).

2. Most commentaries identify a particular audience for the individual Gospels. E.g., Matthew's Gospel is usually said to have been written for a Jewish audience after the fall of Jerusalem and destruction of the temple. For a discussion of this proposal, as well as similar proposals relating to the other Gospels, see L. M. McDonald and S. E. Porter, *Early Christianity and Its Sacred Literature* (Peabody, MA: Hendrickson, 2000), 285-309 and notes.

3. The most significant work in this respect is R. Bauckham, ed., *The Gospels for All Christians: Rethinking the Gospel Audiences* (Grand Rapids: Eerdmans, 1998). Cf. also E. W. Klink III, ed., *The Audience of the Gospels: Further Conversation about the Origin and Function of the Gospels in Early Christianity* (LNTS 353; New York: T&T Clark, 2010).

account of the Gospel's composition, I believe, fully accounts for its unique combination of both historical and theological content.

A public declaration concerning the Messiah is accomplished through a number of distinct features of John's Gospel. These include the structure of the narrative, which begins with the prologue and works its way through various episodes to its close; the vocabulary selected and utilized throughout; the characters introduced and developed; and, lastly, the final statement regarding the identity of Jesus, already cited above. Before discussing these particular features of the Gospel, all of which contribute to making it a public proclamation of the Messiah, I briefly analyze contending theories regarding the origin of John's Gospel.

2. Theories Regarding the Origin of John's Gospel

There are numerous theories, some more plausible than others, regarding the origin of John's Gospel. Such theories almost inevitably raise the question of the authorship of the Gospel. This is certainly not the place to discuss all of them, except to note that I have not found a single, concise but comprehensive discussion of these issues.[4] The reason, no doubt, is that the question of the origin of John's Gospel of necessity deals with a relatively large number of distinct yet closely related issues — authorship, date of composition, audience, sources, communities of origin, and the like. I offer here a brief summary of over one hundred years of discussion of such issues for the simple purpose of helping to establish what I believe is the origin of John's Gospel. The rest of this chapter is devoted to exemplifying and supporting this proposal by discussion of the Gospel as a public proclamation of the Messiah, Jesus.

The traditional claim for John's Gospel is that John, the son of Zebedee and one of Jesus' disciples, was the author of John's Gospel.[5] This position was held for centuries, basically until the rise of German higher criticism, culminating in the results of form criticism.[6] This distinctly German type of

---

4. Those interested may find useful bibliographic references on these and related topics in S. E. Porter and A. K. Gabriel, *Johannine Writings and Apocalyptic: An Annotated Bibliography* (JOST 1; Leiden: Brill, 2013).

5. The earliest claims regarding authorship by John the son of Zebedee are those of Papias (cited by Eusebius, *Hist. eccl.* 3.39.4-5) and Irenaeus (*Haer.* 3.1.2).

6. Rejection of John the son of Zebedee as author of John's Gospel apparently began with David Friedrich Strauss (*The Life of Jesus Critically Examined* [trans. Georg Eliot from

criticism,[7] at least at its outset, had widespread effects on Johannine scholarship and severely eroded any confidence in apostolic authorship, as well as in an early date of composition. These results were due to form-critics placing the composition of the Gospel at a time far removed from both apostolic origins and an early date. Rudolf Bultmann is best known for his theory of the three sources of John's Gospel:[8] a signs/miracles source, a sayings/discourse source, and a passion source. From the time of Bultmann, various other form-critical solutions have been proposed, their best-known promoters including Robert Fortna and Urban von Wahlde,[9] among a number of others. Interpretation of the relationships among and origins of these various sources has led to various hypotheses about the original audience of the Gospel. These proposals have revolved around the question of whether the Gospel was addressed to a Hellenistic, a Jewish, or a Christian audience, with the Gospel often seen as a response to other forms of sectarianism, such as early Gnosticism. J. Louis Martyn proposed an early, middle, and late period of development of an essentially Jewish Johannine community that was in conflict with the synagogue.[10] Oscar Cullmann's proposal regarding

---

4th German ed.; London: George Allen, 1848 (1835)], 71-73, 365-86; *A New Life of Jesus* [2 vols.; London: Williams & Norgate, 1879 (1865)], 77-101); Ernest Renan (*The Life of Jesus* [London: Watts, 1935 (1863)], 10-16); and Ferdinand Christian Baur (*The Church History of the First Three Centuries* [trans. Allan Menzies; 3rd ed.; 2 vols.; London: Williams & Norgate, 1878-79], 1:177-81). For a brief history of earlier discussion, see J. Moffatt, *An Introduction to the Literature of the New Testament* (3rd rev. ed.; Edinburgh: T&T Clark, 1918), 567-70, 580-82.

7. A concise, recent discussion of form criticism, especially as a distinctly German type of criticism, and some of the implications of its use are found in K. Sparks, "Form Criticism," in *Dictionary of Biblical Criticism and Interpretation* (ed. S. E. Porter; London: Routledge, 2007), 111-14. The individual form critics merit their own attention to appreciate the nuances of their respective positions.

8. R. Bultmann, *Das Evangelium des Johannes* (KEK 2; Göttingen: Vandenhoeck & Ruprecht, 1941); ET *The Gospel of John: A Commentary* (trans. G. R. Beasley-Murray et al.; Oxford: Blackwell, 1971).

9. E.g., R. Fortna, *The Gospel of Signs: A Reconstruction of the Narrative Source Underlying the Fourth Gospel* (SNTSMS 11; Cambridge: Cambridge University Press, 1970); R. Fortna, *The Fourth Gospel and Its Predecessor: From Narrative Source to Present Gospel* (Philadelphia: Fortress Press, 1988); U. C. von Wahlde, *The Earliest Version of John's Gospel: Recovering the Gospel of Signs* (Wilmington, DE: Michael Glazier, 1989). Von Wahlde has put forth his form-critical solution in his recent full-scale commentary: *The Gospel and Letters of John* (3 vols.; ECC; Grand Rapids: Eerdmans, 2010).

10. J. L. Martyn, *History and Theology in the Fourth Gospel* (3rd ed.; Louisville, KY: Westminster John Knox, 2003 [1968]).

a Johannine circle responding to the influences of heterodox Judaism has been influential and has led to other community-authorship hypotheses.[11]

A significant turning point in Johannine scholarship occurred with an article by Wayne Meeks on the sectarian nature of John's Gospel.[12] His proposal led to increased emphasis on the Gospel as a document written for a particular type of community. As a result, a variety of proposals were developed and put forth regarding this specific community. Several are worth noting. Georg Richter proposed four particular communities represented by the Gospel's theological development: the Mosaic-prophet Christians, the Son-of-God Christians, the docetic Christians, and the antidocetic redaction. Wolfgang Langbrandtner also proposed three periods: the foundational writing, the redaction, and the letters. Raymond Brown proposed four stages: before the Gospel, when the Gospel was composed, when the Johannine letters were written, and after the letters were written.[13] These theories are dependent upon a number of different factors, several of which include the presumption that Christianity had developed sufficiently within a relatively short amount of time to create a number of significant and identifiable subgroups such as are depicted, one of which accounted for the Gospel's origins. This scenario required, furthermore, that a late date be posited for the time of composition, so as to allow for incremental and periodic development within the early church. This approach also led to various proposals regarding the relationship of John's Gospel to the other Gospels. Opinions on this relationship have varied through the last fifty or so years, from John's Gospel having no connection with the Synoptics to its author being familiar with one or more of the Synoptics.[14]

More recent Johannine research, however, has rejected much of the hypothesis regarding various Johannine schools and communities and has sought to reintroduce a text-immanent author as the writer of the book. As a result, various proposals have been put forward, such as that apostolic authorship of John's Gospel is defensible, that the Gospel itself points to the

11. O. Cullmann, *The Johannine Circle* (trans. J. Bowden; London: SCM Press, 1976); followed by, e.g., R. E. Brown, *The Community of the Beloved Disciple* (New York: Paulist Press, 1979).

12. W. Meeks, "The Man from Heaven in Johannine Sectarianism," *JBL* 91 (1972): 44-72.

13. These several views noted above are taken from R. E. Brown, *Introduction to the Gospel of John* (ed. F. Moloney; New York: Doubleday, 2003), 7-76.

14. For a summary of such positions, see F. Neirynck, "John and the Synoptics: 1975-1990," in *John and the Synoptics* (ed. A. Denaux; Leuven: Leuven University Press, 1992), 3-62. See also my ch. 3 in this volume for further discussion.

Beloved Disciple as its author, that the Gospel has connections to the Synoptics and has some accounting of historical facts within it, and even that a date of composition at least as early as the Synoptics is possible.[15] This significant swing in perspective on John's Gospel is reflected in recent discussion of the nature not only of John's Gospel but of all of the Gospels. It has been argued that all of the Gospels show signs that they were not written simply for their own sectarian communities but for the wider Christian church of the time. Rather than John's Gospel having been composed for insiders and reflecting the internal workings of a specific community, the Gospel is seen as written to Christians beyond such narrow confines. Thus Richard Bauckham, followed by Edward Klink on John's Gospel, assuming that this is the case for all the Gospels, posits how John's readers would have thought of the Gospel in relation to Mark's Gospel, which they would have probably known.[16] Similarly, Stephen Barton argues, against Meeks, that there are many images and concepts in John's Gospel that are deeply rooted in the biblical tradition and therefore can hardly be addressed to a sectarian context.[17] Yet despite these recent efforts, the argument for John's Gospel being more than a circumstantially constrained composition continues to lack sustainable substance and interpretive power in many, if not most, critical circles.

I believe, however, that the proposal that the Gospels are essentially documents for widespread circulation beyond a single or restricted sectarian sphere is almost assuredly correct.[18] The literary relations that are shared among the Synoptics and also with John, the history of transmission of the

15. E.g., R. Bauckham, *Jesus and the Eyewitnesses: The Gospels as Eyewitness Testimony* (Grand Rapids: Eerdmans, 2006), 358-411; J. A. T. Robinson, *The Priority of John* (ed. J. F. Coakley; London: SCM Press, 1985).

16. R. Bauckham, "John for Readers of Mark," in *Gospels for All Christians,* 153-61. See also his more recent treatment, "The Fourth Gospel as the Testimony of the Beloved Disciple," in *The Gospel of John and Christian Theology* (ed. R. Bauckham and C. Mosser; Grand Rapids: Eerdmans, 2008), 120-39. Klink is cited in notes 1 and 3 above. See also W. V. Cirafesi, "The Johannine Community Hypothesis (1968–Present): Past and Present Approaches and a New Way Forward," *CBR* 12.2 (2014): 173-93.

17. S. Barton, "Early Christianity and the Sociology of the Sect," in *The Open Text* (ed. F. Watson; London: SCM Press, 1993), 140-62. Barton's argument that both fundamentalists and others have readily turned to John's Gospel is hardly compelling in discussing its original audience and origins. C. E. Hill has provided plausible evidence that this connection is not the case in his *The Johannine Corpus in the Early Church* (Oxford: Oxford University Press, 2006).

18. I am rather surprised that it has taken the scholarly world so long to acknowledge such a fact — when many "ordinary" readers of the Gospels have long recognized that there is more to the Gospels' provenance than sectarian interests.

Gospels, and the clear, common portrait of Jesus Christ that emerges in each of them all indicate a recognizable shared knowledge, one that is best (possibly, only) explained by some type of knowledge of each other. I wish to argue something even stronger here, however. Rather than asserting or attempting to prove that John's Gospel was another of the Gospels written for a wider audience, I wish to argue that there is much evidence in John's Gospel itself that the book was written as more than a sectarian, Jewish, Hellenistic, or even Christian document,[19] but that it was written as a public proclamatory Gospel. In other words, the Gospel of John was written with the intention of being a public and widespread declaratory statement and witness to the work of God through Jesus Christ, and it was composed in a way that declared this intention openly. The kind of evidence that points in this direction goes beyond the simple selection of lexical items, but includes the entire narrative stance of the Gospel, the structure of its presentation of characters, and the nature of the dialogue it contains. The best proof for this perspective is found within the Gospel itself. I turn now to a brief account of this evidence.

3. The Public Nature of John's Gospel

A number of indicators of the public nature of John's Gospel revolve around the structure of the narrative.[20] In brief, the unfolding of the narrative pattern of the Gospel occurs as follows. Written to both Jews and Gentiles, the Gospel opens beyond the mundane human realm (John 1:1-18) and develops, through a variety of scenes, what it means that God's anointed was the

19. I differ here from the contention of Bauckham and company. Bauckham extends the audience of the Gospels to the broad *Christian* community (cf. Bauckham, "For Whom Were the Gospels Written?" in *Gospels for All Christians*, 9-10) and contends that they were not meant for non-Christians. I think the audience, at least for John, is even broader and extends to the wider public, including Christian and non-Christian communities. Bauckham admits that his thesis is simply taken for granted, by appealing to scholarly consensus, but here in this chapter I will attempt to show how the audience of John's Gospel includes both Christians and non-Christians.

20. At this point, many would expect a discussion of the "signs" in John's Gospel, about which there are numerous discussions (e.g., W. J. Bittner, *Jesu Zeichen im Johannesevangelium* [WUNT 2.26; Tübingen: Mohr Siebeck, 1987]), but I take a different approach. For a discussion of the Johannine signs, with bibliography, see A. J. Köstenberger, "The Seventh Johannine Sign: A Study in John's Christology," *BBR* 5 (1995): 87-103, esp. n. 1, although one need not accept his proposal of the temple cleansing as the seventh sign.

incarnate Jesus and that he strides the earth as God's public representative. Jesus' ministry includes revealing his nature and identity in clear and obvious ways to people in all walks of life, including Galileans (chs. 1 and 2), Jews (chs. 3 and 11), Samaritans (ch. 4), the physically infirm (chs. 5 and 9), nobility (ch. 4), and Roman political leaders (chs. 18–19) — in other words, the height and breadth of society.[21] The revelation of Jesus' nature and identity takes place by means of Jesus' own words (chs. 10, 14–16, 17), but also through the Gospel's closing (ch. 21). The Gospel closes with Peter and the Beloved Disciple continuing this broad, public, and inclusive ministry of Jesus. In what follows, I take up several of these key episodes in support of this thesis regarding the public character of John's Gospel. Several of these key episodes are also treated in more detail in other chapters in this monograph.

a. John's Prologue (1:1-18)

The prologue of John's Gospel is probably the single most expressive statement that indicates the public character of the book. The prologue sets the stage for this public character through the introduction and development of three key concepts, linked here to three particular lexical items: *word (logos), light/illumination,* and *world.*[22]

The prologue begins with a declaration that in the beginning was "the word." *Logos*-language (or perhaps, better, "word-language") is well known from the Old Testament, including the creative word of God in Genesis 1 (esp. vv. 3, 5, 6, 8, 9, 10, 11, 14, 20, 22, 24, 26, 28, and 29, in which words for "say," "call," and "bless" are all used), and the words of God declared by

---

21. It is perhaps noteworthy that many of these events and discourses are unique to John's Gospel.

22. See also R. H. Gundry, *Jesus the Word according to John the Sectarian* (Grand Rapids: Eerdmans, 2002), 1-50, who offers a more expansive treatment of what he calls Word Christology in John's Gospel. I wrote the first draft of this chapter before seeing his book, so have resisted changing my approach, although I am very sympathetic to his analysis — as well as his manifesto. For a focused treatment of John's prologue, see my ch. 3 in this volume. A recent treatment of many of the issues in John's prologue, handled in a method compatible with mine below, appears in P. M. Phillips, *The Prologue of the Fourth Gospel: A Sequential Reading* (LNTS 294; London: T&T Clark, 2006). In my identification of these concepts with particular lexical items, I am not thereby simply equating words and concepts. I realize that these concepts might be found using other language, and that the treatment I am offering is not exhaustive. I use "word" and *logos* somewhat interchangeably.

many in the Old Testament, including Israel's leaders and prophets.[23] It is also well known from the surrounding Greco-Roman culture — in which the principle of rationality was important in Platonic, Neoplatonic, and then especially Stoic thought.[24] As rightly captured in Louw and Nida's semantic domain 33, communication words are often used in such overt expressions of thoughts and ideas.[25] John's prologue opens with the related statements that the *logos* was in the beginning, the *logos* was face to face with God (πρὸς τὸν θεόν; note the declaratory stance),[26] and the *logos* was God. That is, this *logos* was in the beginning face to face with God (in a stance of declaration from the beginning). All things came about through this *logos,* and apart from it nothing came about. What came into being in or by the *logos* was life, and the life was the light of humanity (John 1:1-4). The opening four verses are overt, declarative, and public in their stance regarding the *logos*. The *logos* is the divine word of communication, existent with God in a stance of face-to-face relation from the beginning, and responsible for creation itself, being the embodiment of light and then the illumination for all of humanity. There is a correlation here between the *logos* as creative and as declarative, and the ensuing result of illumination of all of humanity. As John 1:5 states, "The light shines in darkness and the darkness did not overcome [or comprehend] it."

23. E.g., Exod 4:22; 5:1; 7:17; 8:1, 20; 9:1, 13; 10:3; 11:4; 32:27; Josh 7:13; 24:2; Judg 6:8; 1 Sam 10:18; 15:2; 2 Sam 7:5, 8; 12:7, 11, 12; 1 Kgs 11:31; 12:2; 13:2, 21; 14:7; 17:14; 20:13, 14, 28, 42; 21:19; 22:11; 2 Kgs 1:4, 6, 16; 2:21; 3:16, 17; 4:43; 7:1; 9:3, 6, 12; 19:6, 20, 32; 20:1, 4, 12, 15, 16, 18; 1 Chron 17:4, 7; 21:10, 11; 2 Chron 11:4; 12:5; 18:10; 20:15; 21:12; 34:23, 24, 26, as well as Isaiah, Jeremiah, Ezekiel, Amos, Obadiah, Micah, Nahum, Haggai, and Zechariah — 418 times in all.

24. There is much scholarly discussion of the conceptual background of *logos*-language. I cannot hope to resolve all the issues here — nor do I think that that is necessarily appropriate to do, given John's Gospel and its context. Representative views are found in, e.g., C. H. Dodd, *The Interpretation of the Fourth Gospel* (Cambridge: Cambridge University Press, 1954), 263-85; R. E. Brown, *The Gospel according to John* (2 vols.; AB 29, 29A; Garden City, NY: Doubleday, 1966-70), 1:519-24; T. W. Manson, "The Johannine Logos Doctrine," in his *On Paul and John: Some Selected Theological Themes* (ed. M. Black; SBT 38; London: SCM Press, 1963), 136-59; J. Ronning, *The Jewish Targums and John's Logos Theology* (Peabody, MA: Hendrickson, 2010); and for a recent survey, Phillips, *Prologue of the Fourth Gospel,* 73-141. For exegetical implications of such choices, see S. E. Porter and K. D. Clarke, "What Is Exegesis? An Analysis of Various Definitions," in *Handbook to Exegesis of the New Testament* (ed. S. E. Porter; NTTS 25; Leiden: Brill, 1997), 3-21, esp. 3-4.

25. See J. P. Louw and E. A. Nida, *Greek-English Lexicon of the New Testament: Based on Semantic Domains* (2nd ed.; 2 vols.; New York: United Bible Societies, 1989).

26. See S. E. Porter, *Idioms of the Greek New Testament* (2nd ed.; BLG 2; Sheffield: Sheffield Academic Press, 1994), 172-73.

Many scholars have repeated the claim that *logos*-language is not used in the rest of John's Gospel. This is only partially correct. The lexeme itself, λόγος, is used forty-two times in the Gospel, with thirty-eight of those occurring outside of the prologue, so in that sense *logos*-language is used elsewhere in John's Gospel. Nevertheless, the same specific technical sense as is found in the prologue, with its possible Old Testament and philosophical connotations, is not found in the rest of the Gospel. A number of instructive instances of usage, however, make it clear that the author wishes to maintain the declarative sense of the Gospel as established in the prologue through *logos* language.

As examples of such declaration, the following instances are worth noting. John 2:22 says that, after his resurrection, Jesus' disciples remembered that Jesus had spoken about the temple, and "they believed the Scripture and the word [λόγος] that Jesus had spoken." Here Jesus' word, his spoken word, is put on the same authoritative level as Scripture, thus approaching, if not outright approximating, the sense in which the Old Testament prophets proclaimed the creative word of God. John 4:41 states that many more "believed on account of his [i.e., Jesus'] word [λόγος]." Jesus' word, John says, had the power to persuade and bring people to belief. I will return below to the episode in John 4:46-54 regarding the healing of the official's son, but in v. 50, John's Gospel says that Jesus spoke to the official and he "believed the word [λόγος] that Jesus had spoken to him." The word of Jesus is believed and has its source in the one able to heal. In John 5:24 Jesus states that "the one hearing my word [λόγος] and believing in the one who sent me has eternal life." Here the word of Jesus is placed in parallel to the one who sent him, that is, God, and both together are able to effect eternal life. By contrast, as John 5:38 states, there are those who do not believe Jesus, because they do not have God's "word [λόγος]" in them. There is a discernible linkage between Jesus' word and God's word in John's Gospel. John 7:40 records that some of the crowd heard Jesus' words (λόγοι) and, on this basis, declared that he was the prophet. Jesus' words and a prophet's words, spoken on behalf of God, are equated. In John 8:31 Jesus states to believing Jews, "If you remain in my word [λόγος], you are truly my disciples." There is something about Jesus' "word [λόγος]" that provides the condition for being a true disciple. Similarly, in John 8:37 Jesus tells those seeking to kill him that "my word [λόγος] does not dwell in you." They are not responsive to, or have not internalized, Jesus' proclamation. John 8:43 states that those who are not God's children are those who "are not able to hear my word [λόγος]." In John 8:51 and 52 Jesus states, "If someone keeps my word [λόγος]," that person will not see or taste death. This outcome is based upon Jesus himself keeping God's "word [λόγος]" (8:55). The word was with God and is now with the people. It is the "word [λόγος] of God" (10:35) that they must ultimately obey (whether transmitted by Jesus or by Isaiah the prophet; 12:38). Nevertheless, this word (λόγος) of Jesus (12:48) is seen to be the word (λόγος) that judges, which must be kept by those who love Jesus (14:23) and want to be loved by God (14:24). This word (λόγος) of Jesus has cleansing power (15:3). In Jesus' farewell prayer for his disciples, he recounts that he had made God known and that they had kept God's word (λόγος, 17:6), which he had given to them (17:14), because God's word (λόγος) is truth (17:17). This true word (λόγος), whether from Scripture or from the mouth of Jesus, is to be fulfilled (18:9, 32). There is certainly enough common language here, supported by how it functions within the narrative and dialogue, to indicate that the theme of the effectual and abiding word, introduced in the prologue, continues to be proclaimed and powerful in the rest of the Gospel. The *logos*-language is but one of the three concepts introduced in John's prologue and promoted throughout the rest of the Gospel.

The illumination theme is also developed further in the Gospel. As we noticed in John 1:4, the *logos* ("word") led to life, and this life was the light (φῶς) of humanity, illuminating the darkness. The notion of this illuminating light is developed further in the prologue itself, however, before spreading to the rest of the Gospel. John 1:6-8 states that John the Baptist was one sent by God, but that he was not the "light [φῶς]" but a witness to the light. The true light (φῶς) was the one that illuminates the entire world (1:9). Reference is made to this light in John 3:19, when John says that "the light [φῶς] is come into the world," but humans love darkness more. Jesus picks up the concept again in John 8:12, with reference to himself as the "light [φῶς] of the world," and with reference to the truth that he continues to be "the light [φῶς] of the world" (9:5; cf. 11:9), at least for a little while (12:35). The reason that Jesus came as "light [φῶς] into the world" (12:46) was so that those who believe in him would not remain in darkness but would be enlightened and out in the open light.

A third motif that promotes the public, proclamatory nature of John's Gospel relates to the audience for the *logos* ("word") and its illumination. This is "the world [κόσμος]." The notion of the world appears frequently in the Gospel, providing the stage upon which the word and the light move. The light, when it comes into the world, enlightens every human (John 1:9), but the light, though in the world and bringing the world about, was not known by the world (1:10). The sphere in which the *logos*/word and Jesus are to function is a broad and inclusive one. As John says, Jesus came to take away the sins of the world (κόσμος, 1:29). It was because of God's love for the world (κόσμος, 3:16) that he sent his unique, or one and only, son. The purpose of his coming was not to judge the world (κόσμος) but so that it might be saved (3:16, 17). As a result, a number of people do proclaim him as the Savior of the world (κόσμος, 3:17; 4:42).

The prologue is thus the place that introduces three key ideas, linked to three particular lexical items: *word (logos), light,* and *world.* The word is seen to be at the beginning and with God, and this word has an illuminating power that then shines into the entire world. All three of these vocabulary items are introduced in the prologue and then continue to be used in this way throughout the Gospel. The *logos,* first as God's word or expression and then as Jesus' word, is a concept that continues to be developed throughout the Gospel — to the point of the word itself becoming the flashpoint for human behavior, both good and bad, faithful and not. This word is the equivalent of Scripture, the word of God, and obedience to it is the condition of eternal life. Similarly, the light enters and illumines, pointing the way to the "unique" or even "uniquely begotten" (μονογενής, 1:14, 18).[27] Finally, the world is the object of this word and light.

The word *(logos)* is introduced as being in relation with God and the one that enlightens humanity as the true light. Not until John 1:14, however, does the author states that the *logos* became flesh and lived among humans. This verse is important because it describes the enfleshment of the *logos* in an animate form, Jesus Christ. Whereas to this point the *logos*/word is the public spokesperson or proclaimer for God, at the point of incarnation, Jesus then becomes the public speaker of God's word. This Jesus then becomes the spokesman for and within John's public, proclamatory Gospel.

b. Galileans (chs. 1–2)

The first group of people who are participants in the public Gospel include those from the region of Galilee.[28] There is some question about how John the Baptist fits this particular scenario, as he appears to be his own public,

---

27. I do not dismiss too quickly the rendering of μονογενής as "uniquely begotten," based upon verbal transparency.

28. Besides the usual commentaries, see B. M. Stovell, *Mapping Metaphorical Discourse in the Fourth Gospel: John's Eternal King* (LBS 5; Leiden: Brill, 2012), 135-70, even though she emphasizes different features of the discourse for different purposes.

proclamatory figure. In fact, there is no doubt that John the Baptist is a public figure. John's Gospel states that priests and Levites were sent from Jerusalem to ask him who John the Baptist is (1:19). He answers by pointing away from himself and to the Christ (1:20). When Jesus comes to John to be baptized (1:29), John publicly announces Jesus as "the lamb of God who takes away the sin of the world," as one of higher rank who baptizes in the Spirit, and as the Son of God (1:33, 34). This encounter between John the Baptist and Jesus contains a number of features that are worth noting, especially in the development of John's Gospel as a public, proclamatory Gospel. John the Baptist is a public figure, but he turns attention away from himself and to Jesus. Although John himself is involved in public proclamation, he makes it clear that he is awaiting and recognizing a greater public figure than he. Although John is in the desert, he attracts an inquisitive crowd that includes those in authority from Jerusalem. In his observations about Jesus, he draws attention to several important features. One is Jesus as the lamb of God. This is the first of several Passover references within the Gospel used to capture and describe the sacrificial nature of Jesus' ministry and death.[29] A second is John the Baptist's use of "son of God" language (see also 1:49; 3:18; 5:25; 10:36; 11:4, 27; 19:7; and, finally, 20:31, where "son of God" language is used of Jesus by others in John's Gospel).[30] The use of "son of God" language resonates not only in a Jewish context to describe those who are God's children but, even more so, within a Greco-Roman context. There was a tradition of Hellenistic kings being divinized, from the time of Alexander the Great until the time of the Romans. The Romans themselves had an increasing tendency to wish to divinize at first past, and then present, caesars. The so-called Priene calendar inscription (or inscriptions) from Asia Minor, erected in 9 B.C. to commemorate Augustus's birthday, in fact uses "son of God"–type language of Caesar. Here John the Baptist proclaims Jesus as the "Son of God," language used of him throughout John's Gospel. In his invoking this directly confrontational

---

29. On the Passover as a major theme in John's Gospel, see ch. 8 in this volume.

30. There is a textual variant in John 1:34 between "son of God" and "elect of God." However, there is very strong proto-Alexandrian and Byzantine support for "son of God," and more restricted support for "elect of God." Some commentators look too much at the Jewish background of the term and miss the implications within a Roman context. See, e.g., A. J. Köstenberger, *John* (BECNT; Grand Rapids: Baker, 2004), 71; J. F. McHugh, *John 1–4* (ICC; London: T&T Clark, 2009), 141-42; J. R. Michaels, *John* (NICNT; Grand Rapids: Eerdmans, 2010), 132-33. For extended recent discussion, see T.-M. Queck, "A Text-Critical Study of John 1:34," *NTS* 55 (2009): 22-34.

language with respect to a Roman audience, John is saying that there is another besides Caesar who is the (true) Son of God — that is, pointing away from John the Baptist and to Jesus (see esp. 20:31) in a public and proclamatory way.[31]

A number of Galileans, however, are included within the group of Jesus' followers. These include the disciples and those at the wedding in Cana. John 1:43 opens with Jesus intending to depart for the area of Galilee.[32] Jesus finds Philip, who was from Bethsaida, the same city as Andrew and Peter (see 1:40). Technically, Bethsaida was in the Gaulinitis area on the other side of the Sea of Galilee (on the east), but it was considered in the region of Galilee. Philip then brings his brother Nathanael to Jesus. Nathanael is skeptical, not about a Galilean, but about one from Nazareth — a small village of little repute. When Jesus tells Nathanael about seeing him sitting under a fig tree, Nathanael is impressed — though Jesus tells him he will see many greater things. However, Nathanael does make two very important proclamations that follow directly from what we have already heard. He declares Jesus to be "Son of God" and "King of Israel." As already noted above, "son of God" language was intentionally confrontational in a Roman context, for it was used of the emperor in a variety of inscriptions and other references. Caesar was seen to be the apotheosis of the divine, being on earth for a particular time and purpose (e.g., the Priene calendar inscription[s] describe[s] Caesar in terms of giving thanks to the gods for their son as savior who has brought good news). This Johannine passage goes further, however, and links the "son of God" language with being the "king of Israel." On the one hand, the

---

31. For a version of the Priene inscription, see V. Ehrenberg and A. H. M. Jones, *Documents Illustrating the Reigns of Augustus and Tiberius* (2nd ed.; Oxford: Clarendon Press, 1955), 81-84. For the argument that the entire Gospel is a direct confrontation of Rome, based in its Christology, see T. Thatcher, *Greater than Caesar: Christology and Empire in the Fourth Gospel* (Minneapolis: Fortress Press, 2009). For a marshaling of the evidence regarding Greco-Roman divinization, and how to interpret it in relation to the New Testament, especially Paul, see S. E. Porter, "Paul Confronts Caesar with the Good News," in *Empire in the New Testament* (ed. S. E. Porter and C. L. Westfall; MNTS; Eugene, OR: Pickwick Publications, 2011), 164-96, esp. 168-89.

32. I interpret John 1:35-42 as indicating that Jesus traveled northward from the area north of the Dead Sea, where John the Baptist was preaching, stopping off along the way. Then, John 1:43 opens with Jesus intending to depart (wherever he was) and go into the area of Galilee. Some commentators debate whether the subject of the verb of intention in v. 43 is Andrew (e.g., Köstenberger, *John*, 78, though he opts for Jesus). This interpretation is highly unlikely, as the implied subjects of opening verses of subunits in John's Gospel are — where they are to be inferred — virtually always the major agent of the action.

reference to "son of God" would have been seen by a Roman audience as proclaiming Jesus as a rival to Caesar. This in itself would have been seen to be provocative and confrontational. On the other hand, the link between the rival to Caesar and being king of Israel would have inflamed the situation even further by suggesting a rival king to Caesar. Here the nature of the rival king is named in respect to the nation of Israel. Jesus not only is said to be a rival to Caesar (as Son of God) but is said to possess his own rival throne (as King of Israel). Jesus closes the section by saying to Nathanael that he will see the heavens opened and the angels of God ascending and descending upon the son of man. This language resonates with Dan 7:13 and directly suggests that Jesus is the heavenly being revealed from heaven as God's agent in judgment of the earth. Nathanael and others will see this visible manifestation of the son's and king's power.

The second Galilean scene involves the wedding at Cana. In some ways, this scene is one in which Jesus appears at first to back away from a public acknowledgment of who he is. Our Gospel author, however, makes clear that this episode is a turning point in which the public dimension of the Gospel becomes more fully known. After Jesus initially declines to act on his mother's indirect suggestion that he do something in the wedding feast, he then enters into the goings-on of the feast by telling the servants to fill the water pots. Once it is recognized that Jesus has provided the best wine last, the author of our public Gospel lets us know that this was the beginning of the signs that Jesus did. This sign does two things: it manifests Jesus' glory by showing what he is capable of, and it persuades his disciples because they have directly seen him do it. The beginning of Jesus' ministry is seen as a means both of introducing the public nature of his ministry and of developing further the public nature of John's Gospel as a Gospel about Jesus Christ. His first arena of public declaration is a wedding in Galilee.

c. Jews (chs. 3, 11)

Galileans are already included within the ambit of the Gospel as public witnesses and proclaimers of its message, within the larger scope of John's Gospel's own public proclamation of who Jesus is. The author of the Gospel now turns to the Jews.[33] John 3 contains the account of the visit of Nicodemus, a Pharisee, to Jesus. Much has been made of this encounter, especially of the

---

33. The topic of "the Jews" in John's Gospel is treated more fully in ch. 6 of this volume.

fact that it takes place at night (John 3:2).[34] Certainly, this time does not seem commensurate with the idea that John's is a public Gospel or that he wishes to make a public proclamation. However, two things are not often noticed about this nocturnal encounter. The first is that Jesus' response is stated as a public declaration, and the second is that the following discourse, which moves seamlessly from Jesus to the narrator/author, is offered as one of public witness. When Jesus responds to Nicodemus, he does so in several ways. One distinct way is his use of kingdom-of-God language. In both of his first two responses (3:3, 5), Jesus speaks of seeing or entering the kingdom of God. This language, reminiscent of language already used in relation to Jesus, immediately pushes from the private to the public. There is nothing more public than a kingdom and its king, especially when they are being proclaimed. Then Jesus invokes the language of natural phenomena, such as the wind blowing (3:8). These too are public expressions. Despite Nicodemus's confusion, this dialogue leads to the language of testimony and witness. Jesus exhorts Nicodemus to recognize that we "bear witness" to that "which we have seen" (3:11). This is no longer private discourse but public testimony. The shift in emphasis is clearly now on public phenomena. The capstone of this encounter is found in John 3:13, when Jesus brings in the very public display and image that he used in John 2: "No one has ascended into heaven but he who descended from heaven, the son of man," to which he adds the example of Moses lifting up the serpent in the wilderness as attesting to the son of man being lifted up — both public and proclamatory acts of witness and testimony.

Jesus (or the narrator) then continues to speak.[35] John 3:16-21 is a passage full of the public language that is first introduced in the prologue, especially language regarding light and the world. God loved the world in this way: he gave his unique son. He did so not to judge the world but to save it, through belief in the Son of God. The light, Jesus, has come into the world, and those who *practice* the truth love light, unlike those who prefer darkness. After the prologue, perhaps, this is one of the most theologically dense passages in the Gospel, especially as it "illuminates" the public nature of the message regarding Jesus and the public character of the Gospel itself.

---

34. For excellent treatments of this episode, but with different goals, see F. P. Cotterell, "The Nicodemus Conversation: A Fresh Appraisal," *ExpTim* 96 (1984-85): 237-42; and Stovell, *Mapping Metaphorical Discourse*, 181-219.

35. I am not sure that one needs to decide whether it is Jesus or the narrator who now speaks. Everything the Gospel author says is in one sense what God wishes to say by means of Jesus and others, and so the transition from Jesus to the narrator as spokesperson for God is natural and understandable.

John 11 includes a similar kind of episode, one that involves both public manifestation of Jesus and his relationship to the Jews.[36] This scene revolves around the raising of Lazarus from the dead. In a narrative parallel to the wedding at Cana, Jesus at first resists acting on the information that he receives regarding the situation. This time he explains his motive, not with reference to his hour not yet being present, but with regard to how his delaying action will bring glory to the Son of God (11:4). Right from the start, even though Jesus' actions appear confusing to his immediate followers, they are presented as being glorifying to God and to the Son of God. Although his disciples do not respond directly to the potential Roman threat, they do recognize tensions with the Jews and warn Jesus not to go to Bethany. Jesus uses this opportunity to speak of the contrast between light and dark. A person walks in the day so as not to stumble, because one sees the light of this world (11:9). Jesus' coming to Bethany is a coming that is seen and realized even before he arrives (11:20). His arrival thus provides the narrator with an opportunity to set the stage for Jesus' subsequent actions. In Jesus' discussion with Martha regarding the resurrection, she appears to have an informed theology of the resurrection and, furthermore, of who Jesus is, even to the point of declaring that she is one who believes (note the use of the stative aspect, πεπίστευκα) that Jesus is the Christ, the son of God, the one who has come into the world (11:27).[37] This is a linguistically and conceptually powerful statement of public affirmation.

The Johannine account notes not only that the disciples fear the Jews who want to kill Jesus, but that there are Jews there in Bethany as part of the mourning process (John 11:31, 33, 36, 37). They offer commentary on the scene through reaffirming the reality of death (11:33), acknowledging the amount of love Jesus shows for his now-dead friend Lazarus (11:36), and, provocatively, asking whether Jesus could have done anything to prevent Lazarus's death (11:37). Jesus then raises Lazarus from the dead, commenting upon the event in language of seeing the glory of God (cf. 11:4). Lazarus then comes out of the grave, with the result that some Jews believe in Jesus, while others go to the Pharisees and report what Jesus has done. What looks like a mixed result in fact is part of the proclamatory nature of the Gospel.

36. See Stovell, *Mapping Metaphorical Discourse*, 171-74.

37. See S. E. Porter, *Verbal Aspect in the Greek of the New Testament, with Reference to Tense and Mood* (SBG 1; New York: Peter Lang, 1989), 245-70, esp. 255, building upon what has been recognized by, e.g., C. K. Barrett, *The Gospel according to St. John* (2nd ed.; Philadelphia: Westminster, 1978), 306; contra Köstenberger, *John*, 336 n. 71.

Early on in his ministry, Jesus is depicted by the author of John's Gospel as confronting the Jews — or at least some of them (to be discussed further in ch. 6). The encounter with Nicodemus is an occasion for the Gospel author to extend Nicodemus's comments regarding being born again into an intense passage about the love of God for the world, which motivated the sending of his Son so that humans might believe. Later, in the episode surrounding Lazarus, the Jews respond both positively and negatively. The negative response is not entirely negative for the purposes of the Gospel, however, as the negative response results in word of Jesus' activities making its way to Jerusalem, where the Pharisees begin to plot Jesus' demise (John 11:53). In other words, the events of Jesus' ministry are seen to be those that collide head on with the religious establishment. Jesus' public ministry has now met with public resistance.

d. Samaritans (ch. 4)

Galileans, Jews, and now Samaritans are included within the wide ambit of John's public Gospel. In the beginning of John 4, Jesus passes through Samaria as he goes between Judea and Galilee.[38] On the way, he stops at Jacob's well, where he asks a Samaritan woman to give him a drink. In the course of their conversation, Jesus makes clear to her a number of important truths: that he does not care about artificial divisions between Jews and Samaritans, or even between men and women; that physical water, though vital for daily life, does not satisfy the need for eternal life; and that he knows far more about her than she is comfortable admitting. The combination of these factors — in many ways parallel to Jesus' earlier encounter with Nathanael — leads the woman to return to Sychar and to bring out the men of the village to see the one who has publicly spoken what she thought were private matters.

The author uses this episode as a way of declaring, proclaiming, and illustrating the public nature of the Gospel. Whereas the Samaritan woman had been expecting the Messiah, when she returned they were asking whether Jesus himself was the Messiah. The result is that many believed that he was, on the basis of Jesus demonstrating that he knew the private

---

38. I do not address here the geographic issues concerning this trip. There are many potential ways of addressing them. One is to note that the author wishes for Jesus to visit the Samaritans early in Jesus' ministry.

things of her life. When they hear Jesus, they declare that he is the Savior of the world (4:42). What began as a private conversation has been transformed into yet another example of the public nature of the Gospel, and in this way the author of John makes clear that he is writing for more than sectarian or private interests; rather, the Gospel proclaims that Jesus is the Savior of the world.

e. The Physically Infirm (chs. 5, 9)

Jesus also heals a number of people who are physically infirm. The Gospel's author uses these episodes to indicate further the public nature of the gospel message and to create a public Gospel.

One of these healings involves a man at the pool of Bethesda (John 5). Here is a person who had virtually no status within the social structure of the times. He had been ill for thirty-eight years without anyone to put him in the pool when the waters were troubled, and he was destined to remain there until he died — perhaps the only surprising element is that he was still alive. John says that, when Jesus saw the man, he knew that this person had already been there a long time (5:6), which indicates that the man's situation was obvious. Then Jesus circumvents the entire process. Rather than asking for help from his disciples to lift the man in, or lifting him in himself, or even anointing him with water from the pool, Jesus simply speaks his healing into existence: "Arise, take up your pallet and walk" (5:8). It is not all simple, however, as Jesus has healed him on the Sabbath. This fact leads to a direct confrontation over whether healing on the Sabbath is permitted. When the now-healed lame man is asked who healed him, he points to Jesus. This detail gives Jesus an occasion to speak of his work as the work of his Father (5:19-47). Jesus as the Son does the work of the Father, who shows him all things and empowers him for what he does. Jesus then turns this comment into an appropriate response to his words. One who hears his word and believes has eternal life (John 5:24). The scene ends with Jesus making a public declaration of what is to happen: an hour is coming when there will be an obvious public response to Jesus when the dead arise and judgment is executed.

John 9 depicts another healing, this one of a blind man. The disciples presume that the blind man's illness is the result of either his or his parents' sin. Jesus denies this idea, saying that his blindness is in order that the works of God might be displayed in him (9:3). At first (and perhaps even at second or third) glance, this statement strikes one as a poor reason for a person to be ill — until we realize what the author is trying to do in his Gospel. Individual episodes, such as these healings, are all occasions to illustrate that the gospel is to be proclaimed publicly through all possible means. Jesus states that the reason for this man's illness is to display the works of God. Jesus, as God's emissary, is at work while it is day, that is, while there is light. In fact, Jesus says, he is the light of the world (9:4-5). Directly after this proclamation, he heals the man. This healing miracle immediately becomes news to the man's neighbors, some of whom recognize him while others do not, and then scandal to the Pharisees. Their interrogation of the blind man leads to a number of public declarations about who Jesus is. He is a prophet (9:17), he is the Christ (9:22), he is from God (9:30), and he is the son of man (9:35, 38). Jesus concludes by noting that he came into the world to judge humanity, so that those who do not see might see, but that those who do not see might be blind (9:39).

f. Nobility (ch. 4)

In the second half of John 4, after the episode with the Samaritan woman, we have a depiction of Jesus' confrontation with a royal official.[39] Although this episode might be related by the author as an instance of healing, the healing does not involve the royal official directly. Instead, he is another person to be a recipient of and respondent to Jesus.

The royal official has a son who is ill, and he goes to Jesus and requests that Jesus come and heal this son, who is about to die. In an inversion of what might be expected, Jesus counters by pointing out that people are always expecting signs and wonders, when belief is all that is required (4:48). Jesus tells the official to go away, because his son will recover. John reports that the man "believed the word Jesus spoke to him" (4:50). Upon the official's return to his house, his servants greet him to tell him of his son's recovery, which had occurred at the time Jesus had spoken and he had believed (4:53). As a result, his entire household believes (4:53), with the boy's healing acting as a public demonstration and confirmation of Jesus' power and identity. A private illness leads to a public proclamation.

---

39. See my account of this episode from a Synoptic perspective in S. E. Porter, *Criteria for Authenticity in Historical-Jesus Research: Previous Discussion and New Proposals* (JSNTSup 191; Sheffield: Sheffield Academic Press, 2000), ch. 4.

g. Roman Political Leaders (chs. 18–19)

The most prominent political figure in the narrative of John's Gospel is Pontius Pilate. He too becomes a witness to the public nature of John's Gospel.

After Jesus is arrested, he is taken before Pilate in the Praetorium (18:33). Pilate begins to interrogate him regarding his identity. He asks Jesus, "You are the king of the Jews?" (18:33). As noted above regarding Rome and competing kingdoms, this is a question that any Roman official would have wanted answered. Jesus' response is that his kingdom is not from this world. If it were from this world, Jesus says, his servants would fight (18:36). Pilate responds, "So, then, are you a king?" as he attempts to confirm that Jesus is claiming to be at least a type of king, even if an inactive one in this world. Jesus clarifies that he is a king who has come into the world to bear witness to the truth. He is a proclaimer of truth.[40] Such a king Pilate does not find particularly troublesome, perhaps because the pronouncement of ideas seems far less threatening than the wielding of a sword. Pilate proposes that Jesus be released. However, the Jewish leaders, by this time very frustrated in their dealings with Jesus throughout the Gospel account, are not content to have him released but demand more. Pilate emerges from the shadows of his ambivalent answer into the more public space of confrontation with the Pharisees (18:38; 19:4). When Pilate is alone in private with Jesus, he is sympathetic (see 19:12), but when he emerges into the public sphere, he is swayed negatively by the Jewish leaders (see 18:40; 19:5-6, 13). They reject his offer of a release of Jesus and demand the release instead of Barabbas, a thief. Then they call into question Pilate's own loyalty to Caesar by accusing him of being sympathetic to an enemy of Caesar. A combination of movement in both temporal and spatial locations — the shifting from casual to imminent around Passover (18:39), and the moving from inside to outside — makes the condemnation of Jesus emerge as a particularly public and overt act by Pilate and the Jewish leaders, but also makes it erupt onto the scene as a public declaration of the Gospel. Jesus is led out before the crowd by Pilate, and the crowd demands his death. The author also notes that it was the day of preparation for the Passover. The public holiday becomes a public execution. As his final act, Pilate places an inscription over Jesus with the words "Jesus the Nazarene, the King of the Jews" (19:19). The dramatic irony is unavoidable.[41] What Pilate writes as a means of derogating the Jew-

---

40. The issue "what is truth" is explored in more detail in ch. 7 of this volume.
41. See P. D. Duke, *Irony in the Fourth Gospel* (Atlanta: John Knox Press, 1985), 136-37,

ish leaders becomes a fixed, public declaration of the truth that the entire Gospel has been declaring from the prologue to the end: that Jesus is God's appointed person to bring the message of salvation.

h. Jesus' Own Words (chs. 10, 14–16, 17)

Before I conclude with the closing section of the Gospel, I turn to several of the discourses of Jesus, which offer still further evidence of the public nature and proclamation of the Gospel. The author uses these discourses as a means of making clear the public nature of Jesus' ministry, and hence the public nature of the Gospel as a work that is not for a single or confined group but for the world.

A number of "I am" speeches and one extended discourse, the farewell discourse (John 14–16), illustrate what I am arguing. I first address one of the "I am" speeches, the one found in John 10 regarding the good shepherd.[42] Jesus begins by talking about the thief who enters the sheepfold by climbing over the fence, rather than entering by the door (10:1). The shepherd enters by the door (10:2), and the sheep will respond to the shepherd, but not to the stranger. When his listeners do not understand what he is saying (10:6 calls this a παροιμία, or figurative saying), Jesus expands upon it. He uses a number of metaphors to describe himself: he is the door of the sheep (10:7), the door (10:9), and the good shepherd (10:11, 14). He contrasts himself in all of these characterizations with those who try to usurp the rightful place and role that he assumes. One of the key attitudes he anticipates is his willingness to lay down his life for his sheep (10:11, 15, 18). These sheep include sheep of this fold, presumably those of his immediate audience, consisting of Pharisees and other Jews (cf. 9:40), and other sheep not of this fold, presumably others who will hear and respond to him. All of these sheep, he says, will become one flock with one shepherd. The other sheep are presumably those already depicted in the Gospel who are not of the Jewish fold, that is,

---

and on irony in general (esp. its revelatory character, as in this episode), see G. R. O'Day, *Revelation in the Fourth Gospel: Narrative Mode and Theological Claim* (Philadelphia: Fortress Press, 1986), 11-32. The use of irony is greatly overlooked in New Testament studies. On irony, see the classic study by S. Kierkegaard, *The Concept of Irony, with Constant Reference to Socrates* (trans. L. M. Capel; Bloomington: Indiana University Press, 1965). On dramatic irony, see G. G. Sedgewick, *Of Irony: Especially in Drama* (2nd ed.; Toronto: University of Toronto Press, 1948), esp. 3-27. Irony in the Gospel is also noted in ch. 7, again with Pilate.

42. The "I am" sayings are discussed in more detail in ch. 5 of this volume.

Samaritans and Gentiles of various kinds. The Gospel itself depicts Jesus as declaring himself to be the shepherd of a flock much larger than simply one group — in fact, a flock of all humanity. He declares this message to those around him, who are within his existing fold, as an anticipatory proclamation to those not yet in the fold.

The second passage I consider here is the farewell discourse of John 14–16. This speech is clearly addressed to Jesus' closest followers. At the outset, after he has said he is going away (13:33), Peter asks Jesus where this is (13:36) and whether he can follow (13:37). In response, Jesus addresses this discourse to his disciples. In many respects, because the discourse is addressed to his closest followers, it does not have the same public dimension as other discourses have in John. However, I believe that there are pronounced indicators that John's Gospel is addressed to a larger public, and that such indicators can be found even in the farewell discourse. At first, Jesus addresses his words directly in response to Peter's comments about where Jesus is going (14:1-7). Then the rest of the disciples seem to want to enter into the discussion with their own related questions (e.g., 14:8, 22) regarding Jesus' relation to the Father, the leaving of the Spirit, and when these things will occur. As noted already above, in John 14:23-24 Jesus states that the one who loves him will keep his word and that the one who does not love him will not keep his word. At this point, Jesus seems to summarize what he has been saying by pointing to his previous comments as things that he has already told them (14:25). He now wishes to tell them new things.

The first new thing is about the Holy Spirit/Paraclete (John 14:26-31).[43] Then Jesus uses the metaphor of being the true vine as a way of connecting the disciples to himself and to the Father. This teaching constitutes a call both to decision and to constancy (15:1-8). On the basis of this constancy, he calls the disciples his friends (15:14). He frames their friendship with him in terms of the world and its opposite response to him and to them. He tells them, "If the world hates you, you know that it has hated me before" (15:18). They are not to be of the world; they have been chosen out of the world (15:19). The glimpses that Jesus has given of how the disciples relate to the world are now, in chapter 16, put in a context of direct confrontation with those outside their circle. Jesus notes particularly that they will be kicked out of the synagogue (16:2). There is a noticeable progression to the unfolding of the discourse: from the disciples as a group in themselves, to their being a group that has been distinguished from the world, to becoming a group that

---

43. The Paraclete is discussed in ch. 7 of this volume, as part of the discussion of truth.

is exiled from the synagogue. This sequence appears — contrary to my initial comments above — to be heading in a direction that makes the disciples increasingly sectarian rather than more public in their witness and the witness of the Gospel. This is not necessarily the case. The key to understanding the passage is the disciples being depicted as interacting with the world (cf. 17:15) and then with the synagogue. They did not choose to be excluded, but it is nevertheless the result, Jesus says. He tells them that they will be exiled from the synagogue and, furthermore, that some will kill them (16:2), that their hour (of trial, judgment, and condemnation) will come (16:4). The context of even this private discourse thus includes the information that the mission of the disciples takes place within the larger scope of those who will hate and persecute them.

i. Gospel Closing (ch. 21)

The final passage I mention as a support for my argument that the audience of John's Gospel is a wider public is John 21. There is frequent scholarly discussion, especially in commentaries, of whether this chapter was originally part of John's Gospel. In ch. 9 below I treat this issue in greater detail. I conclude that the arguments from vocabulary and grammar are not compelling in the argument that it should be seen as distinct or as a later addition. When this lack of argument is combined with the fact that there is no text-critical evidence for the chapter ever being separate from the rest of the Gospel, as well as the fact that there have been a number of plausible scenarios created for the integration of chapter 21 with the rest of the Gospel, I believe that we are on very firm ground in seeing John 1–21 as being the original form of the Gospel.

In the light of this conclusion, I believe that it makes good sense for us to look at John 21 as in many ways the mirror equivalent to the prologue to the Gospel. Whereas the prologue lays out many of the ideas that we have seen developed in the Gospel concerning its public focus and witness, a number of features of John 21 extend this scenario in a similar programmatic way. Some scholars have contended that any Gospel must end with a missionary thrust.[44] However, because that hypothesis is based on the longer ending of

---

44. E.g., D. Rhoads, J. Dewey, and D. Michie, *Mark as Story: An Introduction to the Narrative of a Gospel* (2nd ed.; Minneapolis: Fortress Press, 1999), 61-62, 140; P. L. Danove, *The End of Mark's Story: A Methodological Study* (Leiden: Brill, 1993), 220-28.

Mark (16:9-20, which is a later composite addition), it is doubtful that we can make that feature one that distinguishes a Gospel. Nevertheless, we do see a missionary thrust in the ending of John's Gospel. John 21 consists of three major parts, preceded by the purpose statement of the Gospel. This purpose statement — John 20:30-31 — gives an indication of what to expect in the concluding chapter. John says that Jesus performed many other signs in the presence of his disciples, but that the ones in the Gospel were written so that the reader may believe that the Christ, the Son of God, is Jesus, and that by believing may have life in his name.[45]

The first of the two concluding episodes is a fishing story. Peter and some of the other disciples decide to go fishing. They have no luck until Jesus meets them on the shore and instructs them to let their nets down on the other side. They have a huge catch, then come to shore and eat together, at which time Jesus breaks bread with them. John says that this is the "third time that Jesus was manifested to the disciples, as raised from the dead" (John 21:14). The two previous times that Jesus had been seen by the disciples were (1) after the resurrection, when the doors were shut tight and the disciples were inside in fear of the Jews (20:19), and (2) when Jesus appeared to Thomas eight days later, again when they were inside (20:26). The fact that the third time of his appearance is in an open and public place, rather than inside, points to a movement away from the fear and isolation that may have originally attended the ignominy of the crucifixion of Jesus. Just as Peter and the other disciples moved outside to go fishing, so Jesus meets them there, outside in a public place, in a third and confirmatory appearance, which marks the transition from the time of the crucifixion to the time of the raised Jesus. He is now alive again, and the disciples are meant to be public witnesses to the work that Jesus has done, as evidenced by this third and final confirmatory appearance of the risen Jesus.

The second episode is the rehabilitation of Peter after his denial. Jesus asks Peter three times whether he loves Jesus.[46] Peter replies each time that Jesus knows that he does. The third time Jesus changes the word for "love" from ἀγαπάω to φιλέω, the word that Peter uses each time in answering

45. There has been much misguided discussion regarding John 20:30-31, especially use of the tense-form of πιστεύ[σ]ητε. For a good summary of the issues, see D. A. Carson, "Syntactical and Text-Critical Observations on John 20:30-31: One More Round on the Purpose of the Fourth Gospel," *JBL* 124 (2005): 693-714, and the discussion in ch. 9 below.

46. On the nature of Jesus' questions to Peter, see D. Estes, *The Questions of Jesus in John: Logic, Rhetoric, and Persuasive Discourse* (BIS 115; Leiden: Brill, 2013), 87-89, where he classifies them as "test questions" not designed to elicit information.

him. Φιλέω love is related to relational love, while ἀγαπάω love is concerned with deeper levels of esteem. I do not believe that these words are true synonyms or that the variation is merely stylistic.[47] Again, we have a tripartite structure. Here it is probably used to reinforce the fact that Peter is at a point of offering φιλέω love, which essentially means that he truly likes Jesus, but he needs to aspire to offering ἀγαπάω love, a love that holds Jesus in higher esteem than any other. Before his colleagues, as well as before Jesus, Peter offers a public proclamation of who Jesus is. He is not able to fully proclaim the kind of love that Jesus asks him to, but he offers a public proclamation nonetheless. Peter's rehabilitation is well on its way by his proclamation of Jesus as the recipient of his φιλέω love, as a step along the way to ἀγαπάω love.

The third episode concerns the Beloved Disciple, who has explicitly appeared only a few times in the Gospel.[48] He is the one who is seated closest to Jesus at the Last Supper (John 13:23), he is standing near to Jesus' mother when Jesus is crucified (19:26), he is the one who recognizes Jesus on the shore (21:7), and he is the one about whom Peter inquires in the closing episode. John's Gospel closes by affirming that this disciple bears witness to these things and wrote these things. Many more things could have been written (so much so that they would have exceeded the books available; 21:25), but the ones that were written serve as a witness and testimony to the things that Jesus did. The Beloved Disciple has borne witness to what Jesus did and said and wrote them down as a form of public proclamation as to who Jesus is. He could have written much more, because Jesus did and said much more. Instead, he has let this proclamation suffice. The Gospel thus concludes with a resounding proclamation of Jesus in the depiction of the Beloved Disciple.

---

47. See K. L. McKay, "Style and Significance in the Language of John 21:15-17," *NovT* 27 (1985): 319-33; D. Shepherd, "'Do You Love Me?' A Narrative-Critical Reappraisal of Ἀγαπάω and Φιλέω in John 21:15-17," *JBL* 129 (2010): 777-92, who uses Peter's expressed love for Jesus in previous episodes as a means of explaining the use of "love" language in John 21; and S. E. Porter, "Study of John's Gospel: New Directions or the Same Old Paths?" in *Linguistic Analysis of the Greek New Testament: Studies in Tools, Methods, and Practice* (Grand Rapids: Baker, 2015), 297-301.

48. On the function of the Beloved Disciple in John 21, see Bauckham's interesting comments in *Jesus and the Eyewitnesses*, 407-8. See also R. Bauckham, *The Testimony of the Beloved Disciple: Narrative, History, and Theology in the Gospel of John* (Grand Rapids: Baker, 2007), 73-91. Cf. J. H. Charlesworth, *The Beloved Disciple: Whose Witness Validates the Gospel of John?* (Valley Forge, PA: Trinity Press International, 1995).

4. Conclusion

John's Gospel is not just a Gospel written for a small group of early Christians as a sectarian tract, or even for a broader range of Christians at large. It is a Gospel written for a wider public. In this chapter, I have tried to demonstrate that a wide range of episodes and encounters within John's Gospel point to the Gospel as a public, proclamatory document. That is, the Gospel was not written with a small private community in mind. All of its contents are presented as part of a wider witness and testimony. A common pattern that we have seen in several of the episodes is a movement from a particular case or instance — an encounter with a particular man, a conversation with a specific woman — to an episode or statement with much larger proclamatory implications. A singular encounter often grows to include others not previously included in the encounter. A few words of conversation often grow into an entire discourse. When these episodes or discourses grow and develop, they often include statements that move beyond the confines of the episode to take the gospel of Jesus Christ, as Son of God, King of Israel, Messiah, and more, to a much larger group. Jesus himself is clearly depicted as encouraging this movement through both his words and his deeds. These episodes and statements, however, encompass more than simply Jesus; they are a part of the narrative structure and fiber of the entire Gospel. John's Gospel, therefore, is more than a Gospel of a sectarian group or even of one dimension of early Christianity. It is not simply a Gospel to the Jews or to the Greeks or to the early Christians; rather, it is a public proclamation of the Gospel, written for the wider world in which Jesus lived. It is written for the *whole* world, which it calls upon to hear his words and to respond in personal belief.

CHAPTER 3

The Sources of John's Gospel and Jesus

1. Introduction

The tendency in the Johannine scholarship of the last century was progressively to distance John's Gospel from the Synoptic Gospels and, as a result, to distance it from authentic Jesus source material. Sources and historicity were often discussed as separate issues in Johannine scholarship. This is a problem that I mentioned briefly in chapter 1 above, "John's Gospel, Competing Gospels, and Jesus," to which I now return. To my mind, however, it is inevitable that the two issues of sources and historicity should be considered together, since the reliability of a narrative is directly related to the reliability of the sources that its author used. In this chapter, I briefly examine the history of discussion regarding the sources underlying John's Gospel and its relations with the Synoptic Gospels. I then develop some notions that have been emerging in recent Johannine scholarship. First, I will addresses the fact that there are significant indications at a number of places in John's Gospel that the author knew of an earlier Jesus tradition of the same sort as that used by the Synoptic writers. I consider a number of passages that seem to suggest possible source relations between the Synoptics and John's Gospel. Second, I will argue that it is plausible to believe that much of this material goes back to Jesus himself. I thus continue a recent trend in Johannine scholarship that gives full credit to the historical plausibility of John's Gospel. I believe that the entire discussion, however, could benefit from more methodological rigor, which I will try to provide through use of several of the standard criteria for historical Jesus research.

2. John, the Synoptics, and Other Sources

Many scholars have recounted the development of source theories regarding John's Gospel, as well as the relationship between John and the Synoptics.[1] The standard viewpoint follows a three-stage discussion, well summarized by Thomas Brodie, who recounts the theological period of the eighteenth century and before, the historical period of the nineteenth and twentieth centuries, and the literary period of the twentieth century.[2] To briefly summarize the major tendencies in this discussion: once emphasis was placed upon the question of the historicity of the sources lying behind John's Gospel — that is, once there was movement beyond emphasis upon the theological dimensions of John's Gospel — the first stage of the discussion was to accept the idea that a relation existed between John's Gospel and the Synoptics, especially, but not exclusively, a relationship with Mark's Gospel. This assumption was purportedly shifted in 1938 by the work of Percival Gardner-Smith, who argued for the independence of John's Gospel from the Synoptic Gospels.[3] With John's Gospel severed from the other Gospels, there was a need to posit hypothetical sources that lay behind this Gospel. This period of examination of the sources of John's Gospel apart from the Synoptics was initiated, according to most scholars, by Rudolf Bultmann in his 1941 commentary on John, which inaugurated source criticism of John's Gospel and from which virtually all later work has taken its cue.[4] Bultmann differentiated three purported sources: a signs/miracles source, a sayings/discourse source, and a passion source.[5] Many have disagreed with the Bultmannian

1. A reasonably recent treatment is C. L. Blomberg, *The Historical Reliability of John's Gospel: Issues and Commentary* (Downers Grove, IL: InterVarsity Press, 2001), 44-49; cf. his "The Historical Reliability of John: Rushing In Where Angels Fear to Tread?" in *Jesus in Johannine Tradition* (ed. R. T. Fortna and T. Thatcher; Louisville, KY: Westminster John Knox, 2001), 71-82.

2. T. Brodie, *The Gospel according to John: A Literary and Theological Commentary* (New York: Oxford University Press, 1993), 3-9.

3. P. Gardner-Smith, *Saint John and the Synoptic Gospels* (Cambridge: Cambridge University Press, 1938).

4. R. Bultmann, *Das Evangelium des Johannes* (KEK 2; Göttingen: Vandenhoeck & Ruprecht, 1941); ET *The Gospel of John: A Commentary* (trans. G. R. Beasley-Murray et al.; Oxford: Blackwell, 1971).

5. Closely related to this theory, and reflecting a recent surge of renewed interest, is the work of those who argue for various editions of John's Gospel. See, e.g., H. C. Waetjen, *The Gospel of the Beloved Disciple: A Work in Two Editions* (New York: T&T Clark, 2005); F. Siegert, *Das Evangelium des Johannes in seiner ursprünglichen Gestalt: Widerherstellung und*

source analysis (esp. with regard to the signs source), but it continues to be influential in Johannine criticism — with the proviso that there has been a revival of interest in finding connections between the Synoptics and the Synoptic-like tradition in John's Gospel. So the standard scenario.

One of the significant factors that I have noted during the course of my investigation, however, is that many of these recountings of the standard theory of Johannine sources are not entirely accurate, and in fact run the risk of being somewhat misleading. As a result, I wish to begin with an assessment of some of the developments in the history of discussion regarding John's Gospel, the Synoptics, and other sources, especially where they vary from the standard scenario.

Discussion of sources in John's Gospel, including so-called hypothetical sources (the term is Craig Blomberg's, but it is possibly misleading, since each of the sources is established in relationship to textual evidence, such as the use of words like "sign," and not in that sense hypothetical), clearly precedes the work of Bultmann. For example, one can find a rudimentary identification of the same types of sources in the work of R. H. Strachan from 1917. In the first edition of his *The Fourth Gospel,* Strachan differentiates, among other features of the Gospel, (1) miracle/sign material on the basis of the use of the word "sign" and (2) discourses as features that differentiate John's Gospel from the Synoptics.[6] His definition of the miracle/sign material as focusing upon use of the word "sign" is still often used in discussions and definitions of this supposed source. To these miracles/signs he links the discourses. I have not done a thorough enough study to speak definitively, but I would venture that Strachan was not the first to consider such categories.[7]

A further issue to note is that Gardner-Smith was not nearly so independent-minded as some have construed him to be. It is true that Gardner-Smith thought that John's Gospel was literarily independent of the

---

Kommentar (Göttingen: Vandenhoeck & Ruprecht, 2008); U. C. von Wahlde, *The Gospel and Letters of John* (3 vols.; ECC; Grand Rapids: Eerdmans, 2010).

6. R. H. Strachan, *The Fourth Gospel: Its Significance and Environment* (London: SCM Press, 1917), esp. 1-2. The third edition (1941) is different in its presentation (see 1ff.).

7. Another person attributed with introducing the "signs" source before Bultmann is A. Faure, "Die alttestamentlichen Zitate im 4. Evangelium und die Quellenscheidungshypothese," *ZNW* 21 (1922): 99-121, where he mentions a *Wunderbuch* (this reference is found in F. Neirynck, "The Signs Source in the Fourth Gospel: A Critique of the Hypothesis," in F. Neirynck, *Evangelica II, 1982-1991: Collected Essays* [ed. F. Van Segbroeck; BETL 99; Leuven: Peeters/Leuven University Press, 1991], 651-78, here 652 n. 3).

final forms of the Synoptics. However, he did not believe that John's Gospel was "a wholly 'independent' account" (a view he attributes to the "irresponsible circles which produced the Apocryphal Gospels").[8] Instead, he posits that John's Gospel shares a number of sources, as do all of the Synoptic Gospels, and that John shares a stream of tradition with the author of Luke's Gospel. The bulk of the substantive traditions used by the Gospel writers, including John, go back to primitive apostolic traditions.[9]

A further feature to note is that Bultmann himself was apparently not the one to define systematically the sources that are attributed to him. When his commentary appeared in 1941, it did not have an introduction. An introduction was provided to the English edition of 1971 by Walter Schmithals, which "brings together the literary and historical results of the Commentary."[10] This introduction appears to be the source of the more systematic treatment of the supposed three sources. Bultmann himself in the commentary proper appears to introduce, but not define at length, two primary sources: the "sign" source and the "discourse" source. He also treats a set of miscellaneous sources and the passion narrative as a separate source, but he attributes the latter to the work of Martin Dibelius.[11]

There has also been less of a consensus around the signs source than has often been thought. Robert Fortna wrote two significant monographs that argued rigorously for a signs source.[12] However, from relatively early on, a number of scholars have challenged, questioned, or at least proposed modifications to the signs-source hypothesis. Two well-known scholars in this regard are C. K. Barrett and Raymond Brown. Barrett, for example, more fundamentally disagrees with the depiction of Johannine studies as rejecting the use of the Synoptics and endorsing a reconstructed discourse source. Instead, Barrett believes that the unity of John's Gospel indicates that the only sources we can speak of confidently are those that are known to have

---

8. Gardner-Smith, *Saint John,* 90.

9. See Gardner-Smith, *Saint John,* appendix b.

10. Bultmann, *John,* 3. This feature is not recognized by a number of scholars, although it is appreciated by Neirynck ("Signs Source," 652).

11. Bultmann, *John,* 635 n. 1, citing M. Dibelius, *Die Formgeschichte des Evangeliums* (2nd ed.; Tübingen: Mohr Siebeck, 1933; repr. ed. G. Iber, 1971), 179-80; ET *From Tradition to Gospel* (trans. B. L. Woolf; London: Ivor Nicholson & Watson, 1934), 179-80.

12. R. Fortna, *The Gospel of Signs: A Reconstruction of the Narrative Source Underlying the Fourth Gospel* (SNTSMS 11; Cambridge: Cambridge University Press, 1970); Fortna, *The Fourth Gospel and Its Predecessor: From Narrative Source to Present Gospel* (Philadelphia: Fortress Press, 1988). Fortna's efforts have not gone uncriticized.

an independent existence. In this category, he includes the Synoptics and related traditions, a signs source, discourses, a Judean source, and a passion narrative.[13] Brown creates his own variation on the source hypothesis by isolating five layers of tradition, which are compatible with his community hypothesis for the development of the Gospel.[14]

Lastly, a neglected area of recent discussion is the possibility that John's Gospel, if not in its final form, at least in some form and quite possibly in some of its traditions, was concurrent with or even preceded the Synoptics. This hypothesis proves to be so challenging to the standard paradigm of New Testament studies that it has been virtually dismissed without further ado — despite no less a scholar than John Robinson being its primary advocate.[15]

What this brief corrective survey shows is that the Johannine discussion regarding its sources and relations to the Synoptics has been far more convoluted far longer than the standard scenario depicts. There has been a recognition for much longer than is usually posited, and especially among scholars who are not antagonistic to finding a substantial historical basis in John's Gospel, that the Gospel used sources, some of which we may now have access to through the Synoptic Gospels, and some of which we may now only have access to through reconstructions from the Gospel itself. In other words, the discussion of Johannine sources has been a complex one, in which there has been a lack of clarity and even forthrightness about how both known and reconstructed sources have (rightly) been treated together as a means of gaining access to the traditions that stand behind John's Gospel.

3. John's Knowledge of the Jesus Tradition

The predominant and widely held view is that the author of John's Gospel knew very little of the Jesus tradition. In fact, whereas many earlier commen-

13. C. K. Barrett, *The Gospel according to St. John* (2nd ed.; Philadelphia: Westminster, 1978), 15-21. Barrett maintained this position also in the first edition (1955), when perhaps he was more in tune with current scholarship.

14. R. E. Brown, *The Gospel according to John* (2 vols.; AB 29, 29A; Garden City, NY: Doubleday, 1966-70), 1:xxxiv-xxxix. Cf. his *The Community of the Beloved Disciple* (New York: Paulist Press, 1979).

15. One could speculate that Bishop Robinson would have had more success with his hypothesis if he had lived to promote it more actively after the appearance of his book *The Priority of John* (ed. J. F. Coakley; London: SCM Press, 1985).

tators and authors on John's Gospel devoted at least some space to discussing the relation of John to the Jesus tradition, this notion has virtually disappeared from much recent scholarship. The focus now is upon discussing the possible sources of the Gospel, with an apparently implicit belief that John's Gospel gives little access to authentic Jesus tradition.

At least four theories regarding the sources of John's Gospel are currently on the table for discussion, although some are more popular than others.[16] The first is that John's Gospel relies primarily upon the Synoptic Gospels, especially Mark's Gospel, but possibly on one or more of the others as well. This is a theory of what might best be called restricted dependence. This theory has been widely promoted for a number of years by such advocates as E. F. Scott, Benjamin Bacon, V. Stanton, B. H. Streeter, W. F. Howard, R. H. Lightfoot, and, more recently, J. A. Bailey, Frans Neirynck, Richard Bauckham, and Manfred Lang, among others.[17]

A second theory regarding John's Gospel and the Synoptics is that both have access to commonly available material, reliable oral and written traditions that possibly "interlock," or help to explicate each other, with regard to the Jesus tradition, neither one having complete independence or knowledge of the tradition. This is a theory of flexible dependence. Leon Morris was apparently the first to propose what D. A. Carson has called interlocking tradition (although it was anticipated by Edwyn Hoskyns and Francis Noel

---

16. Cf. T. Thatcher, "Introduction," in *Jesus in Johannine Tradition* (ed. R. T. Fortna and T. Thatcher; Louisville, KY: Westminster John Knox, 2001), 1-9, who offers four theories that concentrate on the means of transmission: oral tradition, written source, Synoptic dependence, and developmental theory. I wish to emphasize the dependent vs. independent elements. Cf. R. Kysar, *The Fourth Evangelist and His Gospel: An Examination of Contemporary Scholarship* (Minneapolis: Augsburg, 1975), 13-66.

17. E. F. Scott, *The Fourth Gospel: Its Purpose and Theology* (Edinburgh: T&T Clark, 1908), 29-45; B. W. Bacon, *The Fourth Gospel in Research and Debate* (London: Fisher Unwin, 1910), 356-84; V. H. Stanton, *The Gospels as Historical Documents*, vol. 3: *The Fourth Gospel* (Cambridge: Cambridge University Press, 1920), 209-76, esp. 219-20; B. H. Streeter, *The Four Gospels: A Study of Origins* (London: Macmillan, 1930), 393-426; W. F. Howard, *The Fourth Gospel in Recent Criticism and Interpretation* (rev. C. K. Barrett; 4th ed.; London: Epworth, 1955 [1931]), 128-43; R. H. Lightfoot, *History and Interpretation in the Gospels* (London: Hodder & Stoughton, 1935), esp. 206-25; J. A. Bailey, *The Traditions Common to the Gospels of Luke and John* (NovTSup 7; Leiden: Brill, 1963), 103-14 (though not for all parallel passages); F. Neirynck, "John 4,46-54: Signs Source and/or Synoptic Gospels," *ETL* 60 (1984): 367-75 (repr. in Neirynck, *Evangelica II*, 679-88); R. Bauckham, "John for Readers of Mark," in *The Gospels for All Christians: Rethinking the Gospel Audiences* (ed. R. Bauckham; Grand Rapids: Eerdmans, 1998), 147-71; M. Lang, *Johannes und die Synoptiker* (Göttingen: Vandenhoeck & Ruprecht, 1999). Clearly this theory is making a significant comeback.

Davey in their commentary on John),[18] and he has been followed by Carson and Blomberg.[19]

A third theory of Gospel relationships is that there are a variety of oral and written historical sources that John uses, including ones that the Synoptics used, as well as a variety of other sources that possibly go back to earlier tradition. This is a theory of semi-independence. Gardner-Smith proposed this approach, followed in various forms by Barrett, J. Louis Martyn, Brown (two are dependent and three independent of his five layers of tradition), Barnabas Lindars, and others.[20] Several of these theories have a developmental component to them, as can be seen in their being linked to the levels and traditions proposed by Martyn and Brown.

A final proposal regarding John's Gospel and the Synoptics is that the author of John uses a number of oral or written sources, but that these sources are neither inherently historical in nature nor directly related to the Synoptic traditions. This is a theory of full independence. Bultmann, Fortna, Urban von Wahlde, Robinson, D. Moody Smith, and others have proposed this approach.[21]

Theories of complete or virtually complete dependence or independence encounter numerous problems and have probably rightly been rejected in recent discussion. Despite the efforts of someone like Brodie or Neirynck to limit what is found in John's Gospel to what is found in the Synoptics, there clearly is material that is found only in John's Gospel. For example, numerous scholars have noted how the discourses of Jesus in John's Gospel (e.g., John 6, 17) are unparalleled in the Synoptics, and how even

---

18. E. Hoskyns and F. N. Davey, *The Fourth Gospel* (2nd ed.; London: Faber & Faber, 1947), 65-85.

19. See L. L. Morris, *Studies in the Fourth Gospel* (Exeter: Paternoster, 1969), 15-63; D. A. Carson, *The Gospel according to John* (PNTC; Grand Rapids: Eerdmans; Leicester: InterVarsity Press, 1991), 49-58; Blomberg, *Historical Reliability*, 53-54.

20. Gardner-Smith, *Saint John*, 88-97; Barrett, *John*, 15-21; J. L. Martyn, *History and Theology in the Fourth Gospel* (3rd ed.; Louisville, KY: Westminster John Knox, 1979 [1968]); Brown, *John*, 1:xxxiv-xxxix; B. Lindars, *The Gospel of John* (NCB; Grand Rapids: Eerdmans, 1972), 25-28, 46-54.

21. Bultmann, *John*; Fortna, *Fourth Gospel*; U. C. von Wahlde, *The Earliest Version of John's Gospel: Recovering the Gospel of Signs* (Wilmington, DE: Glazier, 1989); Robinson, *Priority of John*; D. M. Smith, *Johannine Christianity: Essays on Its Setting, Sources, and Theology* (Edinburgh: T&T Clark, 1984), 37-172; cf. D. M. Smith, *The Fourth Gospel in Four Dimensions: Judaism and Jesus, the Gospels, and Scripture* (Columbia: University of South Carolina Press, 2008), 81-111, 133-43; and D. M. Smith, *John among the Gospels* (2nd ed.; Columbia: University of South Carolina Press, 2001 [1992]), which surveys previous research.

vocabulary is clearly what we would identify as Johannine (i.e., definitely not Synoptic),[22] to say nothing of the unique position of the prologue (John 1:1-18).[23]

In contrast, such episodes as the feeding of the five thousand and the clear parallels between various episodes of the passion narrative illustrate that full independence is not plausible either. Many scholars, before the wave of skepticism hit Johannine studies, recognized a number of common episodes between John's Gospel and the Synoptics. These include, among others, at least the following:

John the Baptist (Matt 3:1-6 // Mark 1:2-6 // Luke 3:1-6 // John 1:19-23);

John's preaching (Matt 3:11-12 // Mark 1:7-8 // Luke 3:15-18 // John 1:24-28);

Jesus' baptism (Matt 3:13-17 // Mark 1:9-11 // Luke 3:21-22 // John 1:29-34);

calling of the disciples (Matt 4:18-22 // Mark 1:16-20 // Luke 5:1-11 // John 1:35-51);

haul of fish (Luke 5:1-11 // John 21:1-11);

healing at Capernaum (Matt 8:5-13 // Luke 7:1-10 // John 4:46b-54);

feeding of the five thousand (Matt 14:13-21 // Mark 6:32-44 // Luke 9:10b-17 // John 6:1-15);

walking on the Sea of Galilee (Matt 14:22-33 // Mark 6:45-52 // John 6:16-21);

healing at Gennesaret (Matt 14:34-36 // Mark 6:53-56 // John 6:22-25);

Peter's confession (Matt 16:13-20 // Mark 8:27-30 // Luke 9:18-21 // John 6:67-71);

triumphal entry (Matt 21:1-9 // Mark 11:1-10 // Luke 19:28-40 // John 12:12-19);

cleansing of the temple (Matt 21:12-13 // Mark 11:15-17 // Luke 19:45-46 // John 2:14-22);

anointing of Jesus by a woman (Matt 26:6-13 // Mark 14:3-9 // Luke 7:36-50 // John 12:1-8);

warning regarding betrayal (Matt 26:21-25 // Mark 14:18-21 // John 13:21-30);

22. Barrett, *John*, 5-7.

23. Brodie's supposition that John's prologue reflects Acts 1:1-5 is implausible at best. See T. L. Brodie, *The Quest for the Origin of John's Gospel: A Source-Oriented Approach* (New York: Oxford University Press, 1993), 170.

Last Supper (Matt 26:17-29 // Mark 14:12-25 // Luke 22:7-20 // John 13:1-20);[24]

warning regarding Peter's denial of Jesus (Matt 26:30-35 // Mark 14:26-31 // Luke 22:31-34 // John 13:36-38);

Jesus' betrayal and his arrest, including Peter's resistance (Matt 26:36-56 // Mark 14:32-52 // Luke 22:39-53 // John 18:1-12);

Jesus' trial before the high priest and Peter's denial (Matt 26:57-75 // Mark 14:53-72 // Luke 22:54-71 // John 18:13-27);

Jesus' trial before Pilate (Matt 27:11-14 // Mark 15:2-5 // Luke 23:2-5 // John 18:29-38);

choice of Barabbas (Matt 27:15-23 // Mark 15:6-14 // Luke 23:17-23 // John 18:39-40);

Jesus' crucifixion and burial (Matt 27:24-26, 31b-37, 45-54, 57-61 // Mark 15:15, 20b-26, 33-39, 42-47 // Luke 23:24-25, 26-34, 44-48, 50-56 // John 19:16-30, 38-42); and

empty tomb (Matt 28:1-8 // Mark 16:1-8 // Luke 24:1-12 // John 20:1-13).[25]

To say the least, this is a significant list of events common to both the Synoptic Gospels and John.

Theories of flexible dependence or semi-independence thus seem to have the only reasonable chance of being shown to be correct. In reality, there is, I believe, little distinction between these two theories, except for emphasis. As a result, I wish to show that their explanations of the data are the most plausible, and that they provide a means of reintroducing the issue of using John's Gospel as a source in historical Jesus research.

The interlocking-material hypothesis would appear to offer a plausible solution to the relationship between John's Gospel and the Synoptics, and

24. Here we perhaps could also list the Bread of Life episode in John 6. See ch. 8 below for further discussion of this episode.

25. This is a list based upon Howard, *Fourth Gospel,* 129, but expanded. Cf. also Streeter, *Four Gospels,* 398-99 n. 2. Streeter notes that there are a number of places where John and the Synoptics appear to have parallel individual sayings apart from the episodes above. These appear in Mark 6:4 // John 4:44; Mark 8:35 // John 12:25; Mark 9:37 // John 13:20; and Matt 10:24 // Luke 6:40 // John 13:16 // John 15:20. These parallelisms merit separate attention. However, it is worth considering whether, if the limited independence of John can be established, these are independent versions of words of Jesus. Their plausibility rests on the fact that they are aphoristic in nature, yet significantly different in actual wording. See E. K. Broadhead, "The Fourth Gospel and the Synoptic Sayings Source: The Relationship Reconsidered," in *Jesus in Johannine Tradition,* 291-301.

it has in fact commended itself to a number of recent scholars. However, I do not believe that interlocking tradition is a satisfactory explanation in and of itself, without having already shown a plausible relationship between the individual accounts. Blomberg discusses a number of examples where John seems to know of Synoptic or Synoptic-like material. This point is widely agreed upon by a number of scholars today and so does not in and of itself prove interlocking tradition but could simply indicate John's use of the Synoptics. Likewise, the instances where John's Gospel answers the question of why certain events took place could simply reveal the later Johannine author filling in noticeable gaps in the Synoptic tradition. Examples might include why Jesus went to Jerusalem in Mark 10:1 (Lazarus's illness, John 11); why Peter had access to the courtyard in Mark 14:54 (through the unnamed disciple, John 18:15-16); why false charges were brought in Mark 14:58-59 (Jesus' prediction of the temple's destruction, John 2:19); and the reason for Jesus being sent to Pilate in Mark 15:1-3 (the Jews did not have the right to inflict the death penalty, John 18:31). In other words, the interlocking tradition explanation could be used to support a theory that shows how the Johannine and Synoptic traditions relate to each other, but it cannot of itself establish the relationship between the bodies of material.

Rather than analyzing in detail each of the episodes that the Synoptics and John's Gospel have in common to attempt to determine which ones reveal direct dependence and which ones reveal independence, I wish to make a few brief observations on the respective traditions in order to establish that there appears to be a quantifiable and recognizable level of appeal in John's Gospel to material known or shared in common, to which the Synoptics also had access. I concentrate upon the episodes that involve Jesus directly (a still substantial number), since my goal here is to find a means of using Johannine material in the historical Jesus discussion. Most analyses of the Gospels confine themselves to the Synoptics. Besides Blomberg, who makes comments regarding relationships between John and the Synoptics, the only recent work that I know of that treats all four of the Gospels is Darrell Bock's book on Jesus, but he does not compare them systematically.[26] He is content to treat most of the episodes with an account in John's Gospel as distinct from the Synoptics. Furthermore, he is not attempting to determine whether

---

26. D. L. Bock, *Jesus according to Scripture: Restoring the Portrait from the Gospels* (Grand Rapids: Baker, 2002). C. Keener's fairly recent volume *The Historical Jesus of the Gospels* (Grand Rapids: Eerdmans, 2009) is somewhat similar to Bock's in terms of its goals, but it also does not compare the Gospels systematically.

the four Gospel accounts constitute evidence regarding the historical Jesus, since he is trying to create an amalgamated portrait through the Gospels of Jesus. In other words, he is attempting to do much of the opposite of what I am trying to do here.

The following are the episodes that I believe are worth examining:

1. John the Baptist (Matt 3:1-6 // Mark 1:2-6 // Luke 3:1-6 // John 1:19-23). This episode reveals independent traditions from a common body of material. There is little verbal correlation or overlap between the Synoptic and Johannine traditions, apart from the agreement that John the Baptist's message, a quotation of Isa 40:3, was that he was "the voice of one crying in the desert, make straight the way of the Lord" (found in John, Matthew and greatly expanded in Luke, but not found in Mark).

2. John's preaching (Matt 3:11-12 // Mark 1:7-8 // Luke 3:15-18 // John 1:24-28). The relationship of the traditions in this episode is highly complex. Some elements reveal triple tradition (e.g., Matt 3:11 // Mark 1:7 // Luke 3:16), while other portions indicate common sayings material in Matthew and Luke (Matt 3:12 and Luke 3:17). There is also uniquely Lukan material that John seems to follow in some wording, as well as in syntactic ordering (Luke 3:15-16 and John 1:24-26), regarding the nature of John's ministry. It appears that at least two traditions may be involved, Mark and so-called Q, with John either knowing Luke or possibly reflecting a third independent source that relies upon common tradition.

3. Jesus' baptism (Matt 3:13-17 // Mark 1:9-11 // Luke 3:21-22 // John 1:29-34). This episode reveals largely independent, common tradition for John's Gospel in distinction from the Synoptics, but it is conveyed with uniquely Johannine elements. Mark and Luke follow a common introductory formula, apparently altered by Matthew. John's introduction (1:29) does not share any major features, except mention of Jesus. The baptism is common to all of the authors, and reference to water is shared between John, Mark, and Matthew, but the phrasing appears to be independent. There is further common reference to the Holy Spirit as a dove. Again, the phrasing of the Synoptics reveals commonality that is not found in John's Gospel (e.g., heavens opening). The difference is more than simply placing the episode in the mouth of John the Baptizer. One might argue for Johannine dependence, since the mention is of the Spirit descending as a dove, elements common to all four Gospels. However, not only is the phrasing in John's Gospel different, but John does not mention the voice from heaven (as do the Synoptics, for which

there would be no reason to exclude it); instead, John's Gospel returns to John's relation to Jesus as the one baptizing. This episode reveals a common independent tradition and establishes the fact that certain elements were considered established in the tradition — John the Baptist's involvement, that Jesus was baptized, and that the Spirit descended as a dove. John's unique material revolves around seeing Jesus as the lamb of God, one of John's distinctive concepts,[27] and his further development of the relation of John the Baptist to Jesus. The other Gospel that develops its own ideas is Matthew, but he does so with his own emphasis upon righteousness.

4. Calling of the disciples (Matt 4:18-22 // Mark 1:16-20 // Luke 5:1-11 // John 1:35-51 [cf. below on v. 42]). The calling of the disciples contains independent, common tradition between John and the Synoptics, along with unique Johannine material. The relationship of the Synoptics is a complex one that indicates independent traditions known to Luke and Mark/Matthew. Nevertheless, John has little to nothing in common with the Synoptics, apart from the mention of Simon Peter and Andrew (the latter mentioned in Mark and Matthew). John's Gospel also has unique material, including the initial reference to Jesus as the lamb of God and the Philip and Nathanael story. This episode reveals that there was a common tradition of the calling of disciples, and they included Simon Peter and Andrew.

5. Naming of Peter (Matt 16:17-18 // Mark 3:16 // Luke 6:14 // John 1:42). The Gospels all agree that Jesus named Simon as Peter. However, they do it in three different ways. Mark and Luke appear to share a tradition, but Matthew and John have more developed explanations. The three accounts are possibly related around knowledge of Peter being the son of John (Bariona), but only John's Gospel refers to him as Cephas, subordinating the name Peter. This appears to reflect an earlier or at least an independent tradition that differs from what is found in Matthew.

6. Haul of fish (Luke 5:1-11 // John 21:1-11). The possible relation of these episodes is complex, not least because of the temporal dislocation of one or the other. However, I am not concerned here with that issue but with the possible common or independent tradition. It is possible that a common tradition, or even the Synoptic episode, has been utilized in the later Johannine context. The lack of common linguistic elements, however, makes this possibility unlikely. Apart from words necessary

27. See ch. 8 in this volume for a fuller exposition of the Passover theme.

to indicate that it is an episode that involves fishing (e.g., lake [though different words are used] and net [used differently in singular and plural]), there is virtually nothing in common.

7. Healing at Capernaum (Matt 8:5-13 // Luke 7:1-10 // John 4:46b-54). I have treated this episode elsewhere in greater detail.[28] Nevertheless, the main point is worth repeating. In this account, John's Gospel seems to reflect an independent tradition; that is, both John and the Synoptics draw independently upon a common pool of material. The relation between the Matthean and Lukan accounts is problematic, in that Matthew records Jesus as conversing with a centurion, while Luke has "elders of the Jews" coming as emissaries to Jesus — although the core of the episode regarding healing and authority seems to reflect common material. John refers to a "commander" and shares very little else in common, especially at the point that Matthew and Luke do. It is likely that Matthew's version is the origin of Luke's, but it appears that John's is independent.[29]

8. Feeding of the five thousand (Matt 14:13-21 // Mark 6:32-44 // Luke 9:10b-17 // John 6:1-15). The feeding of the five thousand is the one miracle common to all four Gospels. The Synoptics are clearly related, with Mark the likely source. Even this relationship is complex, however, since there are a number of points where Matthew and Luke differ from Mark but agree with each other (e.g., "the crowds followed"). The Johannine version, however, is clearly different from that of the Synoptics. The introductory verse shares only one word with the Synoptics. There are a number of common words as the account unfolds (e.g., buy [John 6:5], the proposed amount to purchase [6:7], the five loaves and two fish [6:9, although a different word for fish is used], and the quantity gathered [6:13]), but many of the significant details are apparently independent (e.g., Philip's specific involvement, the actual

---

28. S. E. Porter, *Criteria for Authenticity in Historical-Jesus Research: Previous Discussion and New Proposals* (JSNTSup 191; Sheffield: Sheffield Academic Press, 2000), ch. 4; cf. also C. M. Tuckett, "The Fourth Gospel and Q," in *Jesus in Johannine Tradition*, 281-90, esp. 283-86, where he recognizes elements of the Johannine account that may be earlier than those of the Synoptics. See also ch. 2 above, where the Johannine story is treated as part of the public proclamatory nature of John's Gospel.

29. A conclusion supported by J. D. G. Dunn, *Jesus Remembered* (vol. 1 of *Christianity in the Making;* Grand Rapids: Eerdmans, 2003), 216; contra F. Neirynck, "John 4,46-54: Signs Source and/or Synoptic Gospels," who argues that the Johannine account is dependent upon the Synoptics.

process of seating the people, and blessing and dividing the food). It appears that John's common, independent tradition has the essential details of the incident, including the amount of food divided and the huge quantity gathered, but little else in common with the Synoptic accounts.[30]

9. Walking on the Sea of Galilee (Matt 14:22-33 // Mark 6:45-52 // John 6:16-21). In this instance, John's Gospel may well share a tradition in common with the Synoptics and quite possibly Mark as a source, since there are a number of specific verbal similarities that correlate with Mark's account.

10. "Healing" at Gennesaret (Matt 14:34-36 // Mark 6:53-56 // John 6:22-25). The Johannine episode gives an account of activities on the other side of the lake (the eastern side), with no mention of a healing. The episode is either a Johannine creation to get the crowd to Jesus, who had walked across the sea, or it is an independent tradition to which John had access. It clearly is not a variation on the Synoptic account, since it has virtually nothing in common with that account.

11. Peter's confession (Matt 16:13-20 // Mark 8:27-30 // Luke 9:18-21 // John 6:67-71). I have discussed the relation of the Synoptic passages elsewhere, where I showed that there is reasonable possibility that Matthew represents an independent source from the other two Gospel accounts.[31] The Johannine account also seems to reflect independent, common tradition. This is indicated by the complete divergence — apart from the use of "he said" and "he answered" — of the wording of what the Johannine participants say from what is said in the other Gospels, while retaining the participants as Jesus and Peter. The affirmation by Peter is also distinct in John, having Peter declare that Jesus is "the holy one of God," rather than "the Christ" (Mark), "the Christ of God" (Luke), or "the Christ, the Son of the living God" (Matthew).

---

30. This passage has recently been studied in great detail in S. A. Hunt, *Rewriting the Feeding of Five Thousand: John 6.1-15 as a Test Case for Johannine Dependence on the Synoptic Gospels* (StBL 125; New York: Peter Lang, 2011). Hunt concludes that his "findings are at least suggestive of John's direct dependence on the Synoptics" (282). His study merits further attention, but I do not think that his analysis is convincing. This is because what he calls "direct dependence" also requires a high level of redactional activity by the Johannine author — leaving plenty of ambiguity regarding what exactly he is finding. In some ways, however, we are arguing similarly. Hunt wishes to avoid positing an unknown and unrelated source for John's Gospel.

31. Porter, *Criteria for Authenticity*, 160.

12. Triumphal entry (Matt 21:1-9 // Mark 11:1-10 // Luke 19:28-40 // John
    12:12-19). The Synoptic Gospels appear to reflect a broad common tra-
    dition for this pericope, but John's Gospel appears to be independent,
    though reflecting something of that common tradition. The introduc-
    tory verse shares only the mention of Jesus entering Jerusalem. John's
    Gospel includes no reference at all to the events surrounding the secur-
    ing of the animal for Jesus' entry (as do Mark and Luke). Instead, the
    Johannine narrative continues with the crowd taking up branches and
    crying out. Although these events are the same as those in the Synop-
    tics, the wording is different. The proclamation of the crowd, which is
    a quotation of Ps 118:25-26, is virtually identical with Mark's wording —
    "Hosanna, blessed is the one coming in the name of the Lord," to which
    Matthew adds, "Hosanna to the son of David," reflecting a Matthean
    theme regarding the sonship of David (Luke omits "Hosanna"). Each
    of the Synoptic accounts then continues the quotation, often including
    enhancement of it (Mark adds a parallel line not found in the psalm, and
    Luke changes the last line to "in heaven peace, and glory in the highest,"
    rather than "Hosanna in the highest"). John enhances his quotation sim-
    ilarly, adding the line "and the king of Israel."

13. Cleansing of the temple (Matt 21:12-13 // Mark 11:15-17 // Luke 19:45-
    46 // John 2:14-22). Difficulties clearly surround the placement of this
    episode in the Synoptic and Johannine chronologies. A directly related
    issue is that of whether there was one or two cleansings of the temple.
    When I originally examined these passages, I thought that the episodes
    recorded in the Synoptic and Johannine accounts seemed to indicate
    that there was a common episode. The Synoptic accounts seemed to
    derive directly from a common source (mediated through Mark?), but
    John seemed to reflect an independent, common source, rather than a
    separate incident.[32] The reasons for this conclusion were that the refer-
    ence to the "temple" used similar vocabulary, the progression of events
    for those selling was the same, and similar reference was made to those
    who were sitting at tables and dealing in doves. In other words, the
    incidental details, though conveyed differently, were consonant. The
    words that Jesus uttered were not identical, but there was wording in
    common, referring to "making the house" into something other than it
    should be. Upon further thought, however, the incidental details seem

32. Cf. Blomberg, *Historical Reliability,* 87-91; M. A. Matson, "The Temple Incident: An
Integral Element in the Fourth Gospel's Narrative," in *Jesus in Johannine Tradition,* 145-53.

to indicate that these are two separate incidents, but both related to the temple. John's account has only six words in common with the Synoptic accounts. These are the initial "and," reference to the temple, "the sellers," and another "and." The Johannine account is sufficiently different that it has very little in common with the Synoptic accounts, apart from essential features to establish that this event occurred in the temple and involved those selling. The incidental details are exactly what one might expect with a temple event; they do not identify this as a single temple occurrence but instead indicate two separate events. The Synoptics record one of these, and John's Gospel the other.[33]

14. Anointing of Jesus by a woman (Matt 26:6-13 // Mark 14:3-9 // Luke 7:36-50 // John 12:1-8). This episode is highly problematic, since there are such radical differences between the Synoptic and the Johannine accounts. Matthew and Mark seem to be derived from a common source (probably mediated through Mark?), but Luke has a number of significant variants regarding what actually happened, suggesting the possibility of a separate episode (e.g., Simon the Pharisee vs. Simon the leper, most likely two different people, and a different location). The Johannine account seems to record an incident similar to that of Matthew and Mark, and even Luke, although the wording and focus are again different, with the attention being paid not to the response of the host as in Luke or the disciples as in Matthew and Mark, but to that of Judas. There are also a number of distinctly Johannine elements, including placing the event in the home of Lazarus, with his sister Martha serving. The Johannine event closes with the same exact wording as is found in Mark and Matthew — "you do not always have me." It is possible that this represents two entirely different accounts, but the settings and conclusion are so similar as to possibly argue against this. It is therefore more probable that, because of the accounts having such little verbal similarity throughout, we have here an independent tradition attesting to a common event, but one that has been placed by John within his distinctive context.

15. Warning regarding betrayal (Matt 26:21-25 // Mark 14:18-21 // John 13:21-30). This incident seems to reflect a common, dependent tradi-

---

33. This problem is discussed in more detail but for other purposes in S. E. Porter, "Study of John's Gospel: New Directions or the Same Old Paths?" in *Linguistic Analysis of the Greek New Testament: Studies in Tools, Methods, and Practice* (Grand Rapids: Baker, 2015), 294-97.

tion. The setting is described similarly, and the language of Jesus has many similarities within the accounts. For example, Jesus says "Truly [or, "truly, truly" in John] I say to you that one of you will betray me." The description of that one as the one who will dip is also similar. John's account is fuller in detail, which is because it includes distinctly Johannine material related to the Beloved Disciple.

16. Last Supper (Matt 26:17-29 // Mark 14:12-25 // Luke 22:7-20 // John 13:1-20). The accounts of the Last Supper are significantly different in the Synoptics and John's Gospel, with the Synoptics recording preparation for the meal and John recording the footwashing. As a result, scholars — including Synoptists — often distinguish them from each other.[34] I believe that there is a basis for placing the footwashing scene with the other Last Supper accounts.[35] If this is the case, then it is clear that we have common, independent traditions.[36] There is so little that reflects verbal agreement between the Synoptics and John, however, that it is difficult to know how to analyze them, except that some scholars are inclined to think that John's Gospel gets the timing of the event correct (John 13:1),[37] in which case there is basis for thinking of an independent reliable tradition used by John.

17. Warning regarding Peter's denial of Jesus (Matt 26:30-35 // Mark 14:26-31 // Luke 22:31-34 // John 13:36-38). Matthew and Mark appear to share a common tradition throughout this episode. Luke seems to be independent at a number of places, especially in the dialogue with Peter. The account in John's Gospel is similarly independent, except that it has a slight possibility of some relationship with the Lukan account (John 13:37 and Luke 22:33, concerning Peter following Jesus). All four accounts agree, however, on the general words that Jesus uttered to Peter regarding

---

34. This approach appears in the synopsis by K. Aland, *Synopsis of the Four Gospels* (6th ed.; Stuttgart: United Bible Societies, 1983), 279-82.

35. This is also the approach taken in the synopsis of W. A. Stevens and E. D. Burton, *A Harmony of the Gospels for Historical Study* (New York: Scribners, 1904), par. 133.

36. The strongest case for a common episode is J. Jeremias, *The Eucharistic Words of Jesus* (NTL; London: SCM Press, 1966), 56-82, esp. 81. See ch. 8 of this volume for a more detailed discussion of these issues.

37. The strongest advocates for two calendars being in use in Palestine are A. Jaubert, *La date de la cène: Calendrier biblique et liturgie chrétienne* (EBib; Paris: Gabalda, 1957); Jaubert, "The Calendar of Qumran and the Passion Narrative in John," in *John and the Dead Sea Scrolls* (ed. J. H. Charlesworth; New York: Crossroad, 1990), 62-75; and E. Ruckstuhl, *Chronology of the Last Days of Jesus: A Critical Study* (trans. V. J. Drapela; New York: Desclee, 1965).

his denial. The alternatives are that there are at least two independent sources here (Matthew and Mark vs. Luke and John), or, possibly more likely, three, with Luke and John independent of each other.

18. Jesus' betrayal and his arrest, including Peter's resistance (Matt 26:36-56 // Mark 14:32-52 // Luke 22:39-53 // John 18:1-12). John's Gospel records only that Jesus went with his disciples to the other side of the Kidron valley, an account not found in the Synoptics, who record the Gethsemane episode. In the episode of Jesus' arrest, the Synoptics are clearly derived from a common source. Even though John's Gospel records the same basic event, including the incident with the sword, the wording is independent at most places. For example, John records different details regarding Judas, does not mention Judas identifying Jesus with a kiss, and records a different dialogue between Jesus and Judas, revolving around the theme of seeking and finding.

19. Jesus' trial before the high priest and Peter's denial (Matt 26:57-75 // Mark 14:53-72 // Luke 22:54-71 // John 18:13-27). These accounts reflect two independent, common traditions. Both report the basic details of Jesus being interrogated by the high priest and Peter's denial, but at the points of comparison there is little verbal correlation (e.g., when Peter denies Jesus, he is seated [the Synoptic account] vs. standing [John's account]). The Johannine account has numerous expansive details not found in the Synoptic account.

20. Jesus' trial before Pilate (Matt 27:11-14 // Mark 15:2-5 // Luke 23:2-5 // John 18:29-38). I have analyzed this episode elsewhere, where I concluded that there are two independent, common accounts.[38] The common material records that Jesus was interrogated by Pilate. Both the Synoptics and John record the question of Pilate ("You are the king of the Jews?") and Jesus' answer ("You say"). However, there is little else in common. For example, the wording of the speech margins, or introductory words of saying, in the Synoptics and in John is dissimilar. John's account also has much greater development.

21. Choice of Barabbas (Matt 27:15-23 // Mark 15:6-14 // Luke 23:17-23 // John 18:39-40). There appear to be two independent, common sources of the Barabbas incident, with Matthew and Mark reflecting a common source, and Luke and John reflecting another. The points of correlation between Luke 23:18 and John 18:40 regarding the crowd crying out are striking, including verbal choice and syntactic ordering.

38. Porter, *Criteria for Authenticity*, 204-7.

22. Jesus' crucifixion and burial (Matt 27:24-26, 31b-37, 45-54, 57-61 // Mark 15:15, 20b-26, 33-39, 42-47 // Luke 23:24-25, 26-34, 44-48, 50-56 // John 19:16-30, 38-42). There is so little that actually overlaps in significant ways between the Synoptic and Johannine crucifixion and burial accounts — apart from the necessary facts, such as the incident involving Jesus, the place of the skull, his crucifixion and that of two others, and the offering of wine-vinegar — that it is difficult to deny the independence of the material. The points of correlation are often confined to only a few words, and there is no section where there is a large amount of close overlap.

23. Empty tomb (Matt 28:1-8 // Mark 16:1-8 // Luke 24:1-12 // John 20:1-13). There appears to be a common, dependent tradition between the Synoptics and John regarding the empty tomb.[39] The common elements include the phrasing regarding the first day of the Sabbath in Mark, Luke, and John (note the slight variation in Matthew), reference to Mary Magdalene in Matthew and John, and reference to the tomb in Mark, Luke, and John.

As a result of this survey, admittedly not in the detail that the material warrants but sufficient to be suggestive, I believe that the following conclusions can be drawn. It can be established that:

1. A number of sections of material are unique to John's Gospel, regardless of what one posits as to a source. (No scholar seriously denies this point.)

2. In a number of passages that John's Gospel shares with the Synoptics, it is clear that John's Gospel is dependent upon Synoptic or Synoptic-like material:
   a. walking on the Sea of Galilee (Matt 14:22-33 // Mark 6:45-52 // John 6:16-21);
   b. warning regarding betrayal (Matt 26:21-25 // Mark 14:18-21 // John 13:21-30); and
   c. empty tomb (Matt 28:1-8 // Mark 16:1-8 // Luke 24:1-12 // John 20:1-13).

3. In a few passages John's Gospel appears to share a dependent, common tradition with one but not all of the Synoptic Gospels:

---

39. See F. Neirynck, "John and the Synoptics: The Empty Tomb Stories," *NTS* 30 (1984): 161-87 (repr. in Neirynck, *Evangelica II*, 571-600).

a. John's preaching (Matt 3:11-12 // Mark 1:7-8 // Luke 3:15-18 // John 1:24-28);

b. warning (possibly) regarding Peter's denial of Jesus (Matt 26:30-35 // Mark 14:26-31 // Luke 22:31-34 // John 13:36-38); and

c. choice of Barabbas (Matt 27:15-23 // Mark 15:6-14 // Luke 23:17-23 // John 18:39-40).

4. Perhaps most interestingly, in a number of passages John's Gospel appears to reflect independent, common tradition that narrates the same basic event but utilizes a source (in some cases, perhaps his own eyewitness testimony) different from that found in the Synoptics:

a. John the Baptist (Matt 3:1-6 // Mark 1:2-6 // Luke 3:1-6 // John 1:19-23);

b. Jesus' baptism (Matt 3:13-17 // Mark 1:9-11 // Luke 3:21-22 // John 1:29-34);

c. calling of the disciples (Matt 4:18-22 // Mark 1:16-20 // Luke 5:1-11 // John 1:35-51);

d. naming of Peter (Matt 16:17-18 // Mark 3:16 // Luke 6:14 // John 1:42);

e. haul of fish (Luke 5:1-11 // John 21:1-11);

f. healing at Capernaum (Matt 8:5-13 // Luke 7:1-10 // John 4:46b-54);

g. feeding of the five thousand (Matt 14:13-21 // Mark 6:32-44 // Luke 9:10b-17 // John 6:1-15);

h. Peter's confession (Matt 16:13-20 // Mark 8:27-30 // Luke 9:18-21 // John 6:67-71);

i. triumphal entry (Matt 21:1-9 // Mark 11:1-10 // Luke 19:28-40 // John 12:12-19);

j. cleansing of the temple (Matt 21:12-13 // Mark 11:15-17 // Luke 19:45-46 // John 2:14-22, even if this is possibly two separate events);

k. anointing at Bethany (Matt 26:6-13 // Mark 14:3-9 // Luke 7:36-50 // John 12:1-8);

l. Last Supper (Matt 26:17-20 // Mark 14:12-17 // Luke 22:7-18 // John 13:1-20);

m. Jesus' betrayal and his arrest, including Peter's resistance (Matt 26:36-56 // Mark 14:32-52 // Luke 22:39-53 // John 18:1-12);

n. Jesus' trial before the high priest and Peter's denial (Matt 26:57-75 // Mark 14:53-72 // Luke 22:54-71 // John 18:13-27);

o. Jesus' trial before Pilate (Matt 27:11-14 // Mark 15:2-5 // Luke 23:2-5 // John 18:29-38); and

p. Jesus' crucifixion and burial (Matt 27:24-26, 31b-37, 45-54, 57-61

// Mark 15:15, 20b-26, 33-39, 42-47 // Luke 23:24-25, 26-34, 44-48, 50-56 // John 19:16-30, 38-42).

These findings show that there are numerous episodes that John's Gospel and the Synoptics both recount, but that they are not dependent upon the same sources.[40]

4. John and Authentic Jesus Tradition

As of late, questions regarding the historical Jesus are once again becoming a part of Johannine scholarship, although not without some resistance.[41] The work of the John, Jesus, and History group at the Society of Biblical Literature stands behind a large amount of the research headed in this direction.[42] As the recounting of scholarship above makes clear, however, much of the scholarly work on John's Gospel through the years has not raised such questions as frequently or seriously. Even several recent scholars who have raised questions about the historical reliability of John's Gospel, such as Blomberg, do not integrate their findings with the results of recent historical Jesus research. The same can be said of mainline historical Jesus research itself. Scholars have apparently been so highly influenced by the majority conclusions of Johannine scholarship, especially regarding historicity, that they have given little to no place to the results of inquiry regarding John's Gospel when considering such issues. As a result, the standard criteria used in historical Jesus research are rarely brought to bear on the Johannine material in relation to the Synoptic material.

There are admittedly problems with the standard criteria used in historical Jesus research,[43] including, among others, the development and rise

40. F. J. Moloney ("The Fourth Gospel and the Jesus of History," in his *The Gospel of John: Text and Context* [BIS 72; Leiden: Brill, 2005], 45-65; originally in *NTS* 46 [2000]: 42-58) has suggested that John's Gospel might provide a basic framework for the life of Jesus.

41. See P. Foster, "Memory, Orality, and the Fourth Gospel: Three Dead-Ends in Historical Jesus Research," *JSHJ* 10 (2012): 191-227. For a response to Foster, see S. E. Porter and H. T. Ong, "Memory, Orality, and the Fourth Gospel: A Response to Paul Foster with Further Comments for Future Discussion," *JSHJ* 12 (2014): 143-64.

42. See, e.g., P. N. Anderson, F. Just, and T. Thatcher, eds., *John, Jesus, and History*, vol 1: *Critical Appraisals of Critical Views*; vol 2: *Aspects of Historicity in the Fourth Gospel* (Atlanta: SBL, 2007-9); P. N. Anderson, *The Fourth Gospel and the Quest for Jesus: Modern Foundations Reconsidered* (LNTS 321; London: T&T Clark, 2006).

43. On this point, see the essays in T. Holmén and S. E. Porter, eds., *The Handbook*

of these criteria in relationship to form criticism, the kinds of assumptions that are often linked to such criteria, the question of whether they accomplish what they purport to do, and the minimalistic results that are often found. These are telling criticisms. However, if we agree that these criteria have some validity — or at least are valid within the terms of historical Jesus research — insofar as showing the likelihood that a given tradition has some kind of claim to authenticity (as that term is defined in historical Jesus research),[44] then it is worth considering which of the criteria might be relevant to John's Gospel. I cannot here discuss all of the criteria, but I wish to posit that the criterion of multiple attestation, along with the criteria of coherence or consistency, embarrassment, and rejection and execution (this latter group relying in some way upon or originating from the criterion of multiple attestation), has relevance for discussing the relation of John's Gospel to the Synoptics in relation to the historical Jesus.

a. Multiple Attestation

The criterion of multiple attestation affirms that, where there are multiple independent traditions attested, an episode has a higher claim to authenticity.[45] The exercise in the section above was one in establishing the plausibility of seeing independent, though common, traditions in John's Gospel. These were established by analyzing two competing factors. The first is that John's Gospel attests to the basic components of incidents recorded in the Synoptic Gospels, most of them found in Mark and attested by at least one other Gospel. The second is that, usually apart from basic vocabulary needed to establish the nature of the incident and from mention of pivotal events, the wording of John's Gospel is often distinct from that of the Synoptic Gospels and does not necessarily show a redactional tendency in conformity with its style elsewhere. Sometimes this particular wording reflects Johannine emphases, but often it does not, with distinctly

---

for the Study of the Historical Jesus, vol. 1: *How to Study the Historical Jesus* (Leiden: Brill, 2011), part 1. Many such questions, already raised by others, are found in Porter, *Criteria for Authenticity,* 63-123. See also S. E. Porter, "How Do We Know What We Think We Know? Methodological Reflections on Jesus Research," in *Jesus Research: New Methodologies and Perceptions; The Second Princeton-Prague Symposium on Jesus Research* (ed. J. H. Charlesworth, with B. Rhea and P. Pokorný; Grand Rapids: Eerdmans, 2014), 82-99.

44. See Porter, *Criteria for Authenticity,* 144 n. 38.

45. See Porter, *Criteria for Authenticity,* 82-89, for discussion.

The Sources of John's Gospel and Jesus

Johannine elements often being confined to sections where there is not a clear Synoptic parallel.

Several examples from the discussion above are worth noting in support of this claim and the perspective that I am arguing for. For instance, analysis of John's Gospel in various episodes of the passion account confirms that the passion narrative is not simply a single source, but that it is a set of independent sources that go back to a common tradition. This is well exemplified in the above sections 18, 19, 20, and 22, where I discuss the betrayal and arrest of Jesus, his trial before the Sanhedrin and Pilate, and his crucifixion. This is an important finding. We now see confirmatory evidence through the multiple independent traditions of a number of key elements of the accounts, including the actual wording between Pilate and Jesus.[46] This evidence includes elements of the passion account in John's Gospel alongside the Synoptics. A further result is that the example discussed in section 6 regarding the haul of fish is bolstered in its claim to authenticity by the use of multiply attested Johannine material. In other words, the Lukan account can now be confirmed through multiple attestation by the Johannine account. This conclusion adds another potentially authentic episode to the Jesus material of the Gospels.

The examples in which John and one of the Synoptic Gospels seem to reflect a common, independent source, as opposed to the other Synoptic Gospels, provide support for including John's Gospel in discussion of questions regarding the historical Jesus. For example, the episode of the choice of Barabbas (section 21) appears, in the light of our discussion, to be supported by two independent sources, the one found in Matthew and Mark, and the other in Luke and John.

b. Coherence, or Consistency

I turn now from the criterion of multiple attestation to that of coherence, or consistency. The criterion of least distinctiveness was an older criterion used by scholars such as Dibelius and Bultmann to distinguish the authentic part of a tradition on the basis of its least distinctive features (the distinctive features being attributed to secondary accretion). The criterion of least distinctiveness has been shown, at least for the Synoptic Gospels, to be invalid,

---

46. I have argued elsewhere that this conversation probably occurred in Greek as well. See Porter, *Criteria for Authenticity*, 126-80, 181-208 passim.

since there are no set patterns for development of the traditions.[47] If this is the case, then once John's Gospel is entered into the equation regarding questions of authenticity in Jesus tradition, it not only may well satisfy the criterion of multiple attestation, but it may also satisfy other criteria. In many instances, the Johannine tradition is longer or more fully developed than that in the Synoptic Gospels. In some instances, this may well reflect development by the author of John's Gospel. In some instances, however, it may well reflect independent common tradition. The question is what the basis of this perceived Johannine development is, and whether the development may be coherent, or consistent, with other authentic material. If the uniquely Johannine material within a Johannine independent source is coherent with other authentic material, then there is the presumption that this material may be authentic as well.[48]

An example may be the naming of Peter (section 5), where John notes that his name was Cephas. This is consistent with what is found elsewhere in the New Testament, including Paul (Gal 1:18; 2:9, 11, 14; 1 Cor 1:12; 3:22; 9:5; 15:5). The criterion of coherence gives credibility to the account found in John's Gospel. Another example — if it is to be considered the same episode — might be the cleansing of the temple (section 13), where John includes mention of the things that were being sold in the temple, something not specified in the Synoptic Gospels. Even if they are two separate episodes, the coherence of John's account with that of the Synoptics might not prove a second temple cleansing, but it might at least establish the credibility of the Johannine account as an account of such an incident.

c. Embarrassment

The criterion of embarrassment argues that material that cannot be readily explained as created by the early church has a probability of authenticity.[49] There are a number of limitations to this criterion, but there is also the possibility of using it with the Johannine material. Some of the common episodes that John recounts are already classified by some scholars as embarrassing. These include the baptism of Jesus by John the Baptist (section 3), where

47. Porter, *Criteria for Authenticity*, 77-79. The invalidity of this criterion has been most trenchantly shown, even if it is still often neglected, by E. P. Sanders, *The Tendencies of the Synoptic Tradition* (SNTSMS 9; Cambridge: Cambridge University Press, 1969).
48. See Porter, *Criteria for Authenticity*, 79-82.
49. Porter, *Criteria for Authenticity*, 106-10.

the event seems to place Jesus in a subordinate position to John. Another might include the Last Supper incident in John's Gospel, where, instead of being depicted as eating the final meal together, Jesus is seen as washing the disciples' feet. This footwashing account is unparalleled in the Synoptic Gospels but is depicted as itself causing embarrassment on the basis of the reaction of Peter (John 13:8).

d. Rejection and Execution

The criterion of rejection and execution argues that authentic tradition contains the motivation for Jesus' rejection and execution at the hands of the Romans and Jews.[50] The triumphal entry (section 12) and the cleansing of the temple (section 13) are two instances that potentially fulfill this criterion. The triumphal entry as depicted in John's Gospel has the same central focus as does the Synoptic account, namely, the passage from Ps 118:25-26. However, John's Gospel provides an explanation that may well help further explain what is not explicated in Mark's Gospel. For example, Mark's Gospel depicts Jesus entering triumphantly but then going to the temple, surveying the scene and retiring to Bethany, to return again the next day. No explanation is given of this turn of events. John's Gospel says that the quotations that are being used to explain Jesus' mission (including also Zech 9:9) were not understood by his disciples until after Jesus was glorified. This comment could account for why the triumphal entry seems to dissipate so quickly in the eyes of the initially jubilant and welcoming crowd. In the episode of the cleansing of the temple, a similar scenario may be in place. In the Synoptic account, Jesus rebukes those selling in the temple for making it a cave of thieves. In the Johannine account, Jesus refers to the temple as the "house of my Father," which is being turned into a house of merchandising. Again, the Johannine author notes that the disciples realized only later the significance of Jesus' depiction, in the light of the passage from Ps 9:9, that "zeal for my Father's house will consume me." This explanation of the Johannine temple cleansing would apply whether this event is the same as the one depicted in the Synoptics or a separate incident.

50. Porter, *Criteria for Authenticity*, 110-12.

5. Conclusion

It is noteworthy that, until recently, John's Gospel has not figured largely in historical Jesus research. At one time there was serious discussion of the historical value of John's Gospel, but with the rise of form criticism, development of the criteria for authenticity, and rejection of the "theological" Gospel, this discussion was abandoned. The result has been that, in most discussions of the Synoptic Gospels and issues regarding the historical Jesus, John's Gospel is not given serious attention on the same level. Instead, John's Gospel is often depicted as being something unique and standing apart from the other Gospels. There are indeed unique elements in John's Gospel, which should not be denied. However, to say that John's Gospel has unique elements does not mean that it is unique in its entirety, or that it is unique to the point of being incredible or unreliable, or that it is uniquely without historical antecedent, or even that it is without relationship to the Synoptic Gospels. Discussions of the sources of John's Gospel have varied over the years, from those who saw it as consciously utilizing one or more of the Synoptic Gospels or their traditions to those who rejected such dependence and have seen it as independent (and often of no historical value, although this does not necessarily follow from independence). At the places where John's Gospel also depicts material found in the Synoptics, I believe that it is at least worth considering whether John's Gospel provides independent attestation of authenticity. In a number of places it appears that an independent line is being pursued, yet depiction of the same event is occurring, suggesting that an independent yet shared or related tradition is being used.[51] Once we recognize this common dependence on a single event, the result can be utilized along with the traditional historical criteria of authenticity in order to enhance our historical portrait of the Jesus of the Gospels.

---

51. F. Mussner (*The Historical Jesus in the Gospel of St John* [trans. W. J. O'Hara; Freiburg: Herder; London: Burns & Oates, 1965]) sees the "Johannine problem" as "chiefly a hermeneutical one" (8). Based upon the work of Martin Heidegger and Hans Georg Gadamer, Mussner tries to understand what it means that the Johannine author "saw" Jesus through different interpretive lenses. My conclusion above is sympathetic to Mussner's perspective. On these major philosophical/hermeneutical figures, see S. E. Porter and J. C. Robinson, *Hermeneutics: An Introduction to Interpretive Theory* (Grand Rapids: Eerdmans, 2011), 57-73 and 74-104.

CHAPTER 4

John's Gospel Prologue and Jesus

1. Introduction

The prologue to John's Gospel (John 1:1-18) has been intensively studied over the last one hundred years, as an examination of any commentary from this period well illustrates. One of the recurring questions is the nature of this passage, which appears quite different from the beginning of any other Gospel, and in many ways even stands out from the rest of John's Gospel (e.g., in its cosmic perspective, in which *logos* is personified).[1] There is widespread agreement that this prologue is ultimately about the enfleshment or, perhaps more theologically, the incarnation and public appearance of the *logos* as a human being, Jesus Christ. This enfleshed *logos*, Jesus Christ, then lived within the human realm, his glory was seen by others, he was announced by John the Baptist, and he was identified as being in unique relationship with God. This is the beginning of Jesus Christ's own ministry in the world. In other words, the movement of the prologue traces how the *logos* became Jesus and was recognized as God. Such a powerful and unique statement within the Gospels about who Jesus Christ is and where he came from is bound to have aroused a response — even (or perhaps especially) among critical scholars, as they attempt to determine how exactly to think about such a passage. This unique combination of expressive features as found

1. This does not mean, however, that the prologue is totally independent of the rest of John's Gospel, as some scholars have argued. See P. J. Williams, "Not the Prologue of John," *JSNT* 33.4 (2011): 375-86, for discussion of the issue of segmenting the prologue. See my discussion in ch. 2 of this volume regarding the programmatic nature of the prologue for the rest of the Gospel, especially as it establishes who the incarnate Word is. Ch. 2 also includes other bibliography regarding the prologue.

in the prologue has raised a number of questions regarding its provenance and nature, especially the sense in which it may reflect an early, preformed hymnic section of the New Testament.[2] Hymns in the ancient world were distinguished by both formal and content features. That is, they had a hymnic structure, and they had a focus on particular addressees. Hymns in the ancient world were poetically structured passages that were addressed to gods. In this case, the question is whether the prologue to John's Gospel — which clearly focuses upon and exalts the enfleshed *logos,* Jesus Christ, as God — is a hymn, or whether it is best described as something else. That is, many scholars have posited that, in some ways, one can determine that this passage was once a preformed unit that — while perhaps not directly addressed to a god (as hymns in the ancient world were) — had enough other characteristics, such as formulaic composition or particular conceptual background, to merit such a designation.[3]

Depending upon the critical mood of the time, the perspectives on this passage have varied considerably. Early in the last century, the Greek or Hellenistic background of the prologue was often emphasized, with scholars finding similarities with various Greek concepts, such as occur in Stoic and Hermetic doctrine. In the middle of the century, the mood shifted to finding the background in the Jewish concept of the divine, creative Word. No doubt because of the failure to reach a clear consensus, a number of scholars argued that the prologue must be examined primarily in relation to its function within the Gospel, anticipating its major themes (e.g., "witness") — a view

---

2. See, e.g., the treatment of the prologue within this context in R. N. Longenecker, *New Wine into Fresh Wineskins: Contextualizing the Early Christian Confessions* (Peabody, MA: Hendrickson, 1999), esp. 111-14.

3. For a good, concise definition of "hymn," see W. K. C. Guthrie, "Hymns," in *The Oxford Classical Dictionary* (ed. N. G. L. Hammond and H. H. Scullard; 2nd ed.; Oxford: Clarendon Press, 1970), 534. For the sake of this chapter, I am not differentiating between hymns, creeds, or confessional statements, since by all accounts they overlap significantly in meaning for the New Testament. See Longenecker, *New Wine,* 8-23. That there is more work to be done on this issue is reflected by the fact that L. W. Hurtado places John 1:1-18 within the portions commonly seen as hymnic (*At the Origins of Christian Worship* [Carlisle: Paternoster, 1999], 86), while T. L. Brodie argues that the prologue should be interpreted in its final form, not as a hymn (*The Gospel according to John: A Literary and Theological Commentary* [New York: Oxford University Press, 1993], 143). B. Lindars is perhaps closest to the latest consensus with his view that the language is distinct but fully a part of the Gospel (*John* [NTG; Sheffield: JSOT Press, 1990], 73-74), repr. in B. Lindars, R. B. Edwards, and J. M. Court, *The Johannine Literature,* with an introduction by R. A. Culpepper (Sheffield: Sheffield Academic Press, 2000), 85-86.

that I myself have explored elsewhere in this volume, but not for source-critical purposes. A number of scholars on the fringe of the discussion have also explored various musical-liturgical characteristics of this passage.

In this chapter I return to the question of the background and use of this passage within John's Gospel by examining it from four critical perspectives that to varying degrees have been brought to bear upon the discussion of its "hymnic" characteristics: form criticism, source criticism, musical-liturgical criticism, and functional criticism.[4] I am not interested in proving one of these methods correct (i.e., that the passage categorically is or is not a hymn or has a particular background or can be understood only in a particular way) or in disproving others, so much as opening up the kinds of insights that each can contribute in the light of previous research and discussion.[5] I think that we can still learn something from utilizing a variety of critical perspectives to interpret this important passage.

2. Form Criticism

The classic work of Eduard Norden, *Agnostos Theos,* has still not been superseded as the basic guide to form-critical analysis of supposed hymnic passages within the New Testament.[6] In his work, Norden attempts to define

4. Other methods could be used as well. A fairly recent attempt at feminist criticism of the prologue is found in A. Jasper, *The Shining Garment of the Text: Gendered Readings of John's Prologue* (JSNTSup 165; GCT 6; Sheffield: Sheffield Academic Press, 1998); and a "sequential reading," combining literary theory, rhetoric, and sociolinguistics, is found in P. M. Phillips, *The Prologue of the Fourth Gospel: A Sequential Reading* (LNTS 294; London: T&T Clark, 2006). I briefly analyze these works in S. E. Porter, "Study of John's Gospel: New Directions or the Same Old Paths?" in *Linguistic Analysis of the Greek New Testament: Studies in Tools, Methods, and Practice* (Grand Rapids: Baker, 2015), 277-306. See also (though it arrived too late for consideration) A. J. Akala, *The Son-Father Relationship and Christological Symbolism in the Gospel of John* (LNTS 505; London: Bloomsbury, 2014).

5. Although there has been a tendency in much criticism to argue for interpretive dominance, some recent work has shown that interpretive frameworks, even with their manifest weaknesses, can profitably coexist. For example, see the varied approaches represented in S. E. Porter, ed., *Handbook to Exegesis of the New Testament* (NTTS 25; Leiden: Brill, 1997), and the hermeneutical stances noted in S. E. Porter and B. M. Stovell, eds., *Biblical Hermeneutics: Five Views* (Downers Grove, IL: InterVarsity Press, 2012), where several of the proponents see hermeneutical and exegetical coexistence as not only possible but desirable; and in S. E. Porter and J. C. Robinson, *Hermeneutics: An Introduction to Interpretive Theory* (Grand Rapids: Eerdmans, 2011).

6. E. Norden, *Agnostos Theos: Untersuchungen zur formengeschichte religiöser Rede*

the formal characteristics that distinguish a passage as hymnic. Many works have been written before and even more since, many of the later ones surprisingly ignorant of Norden's work (some mention it, but show little sign of having engaged with it in any serious way).[7] One of the major changes since the time of Norden, however, has been the growth and development of form criticism as a theologically motivated interpretive tool. This has no doubt hindered much form-critical analysis, since to use the method seems to be tantamount to accepting a particular critical agenda.[8] I do not believe that this is necessarily the case. Rather, one can use form criticism by looking at formal criteria to identify literary forms, instead of using such features to reconstruct a determinative *Sitz im Leben*.[9]

On the basis of formal criteria, Norden defined the characteristics of an-

(Leipzig: Teubner, 1913; repr., Darmstadt: Wissenschaftliche Buchgesellschaft, 1956), esp. 144-276, with appendixes 4 (347-54), 5 (355-64), 6 (365-66), and 8 (380-87); cf. Norden, *Die Antike Kunstprosa vom VI. Jahrhundert v. Chr. bis in die Zeit der Renaissance* (repr., Stuttgart: Teubner, 1995 [1898]), 2:810-29.

7. Works notable for their form-critical worth include J. Kroll, *Die christliche Hymnodik bis zu Klemens von Alexandria* (Königsberg: Harlung, 1921); E. Stauffer, *Die Theologie des Neuen Testaments* (Geneva: Oikumene Verlag, 1941), 322 (ET *New Testament Theology* [trans. J. Marsh; London: SCM Press, 1955], 237); G. Schille, *Frühchristliche Hymnen* (Berlin: Evangelische Verlagsanstalt, 1962); R. Deichgräber, *Gotteshymnus und Christushymnus in der frühen Christenheit* (Göttingen: Vandenhoeck & Ruprecht, 1967); M. Lattke, *Hymnus: Materialien zu einer Geschichte der antiken Hymnologie* (NTOA 19; Göttingen: Vandenhoeck & Ruprecht, 1991); G. Kennel, *Frühchristliche Hymnen? Gattungskritische Studien zur Frage nach den Leidern der frühen Christenheit* (WMANT 71; Neukirchen-Vluyn: Neukirchener Verlag, 1995); C. Stettler, *Der Kolosserhymnus* (WUNT 2.131; Tübingen: Mohr Siebeck, 2000); as well as a number of smaller studies and responses to these writers.

8. For examination of form criticism in its major New Testament application (Gospel and historical Jesus research), see S. E. Porter, *The Criteria for Authenticity in Historical-Jesus Research: Previous Discussion and New Proposals* (JSNTSup 191; Sheffield: Sheffield Academic Press, 2000), 63-69. I am pleased to see the growth of what is being called the new form criticism, which is less concerned with the *Sitz im Leben,* and more with the location within the text. See, e.g., three works by M. J. Buss: *Biblical Form Criticism in Its Context* (JSOTSup 274; Sheffield: Sheffield Academic Press, 1999); *The Concept of Form in the Twentieth Century* (Sheffield: Sheffield Phoenix Press, 2008); and *The Changing Shape of Form Criticism: A Relational Approach* (ed. N. M. Stipe; Hebrew Bible Monographs 18; Sheffield: Sheffield Phoenix Press, 2010), where relationships between early types of form criticism (promoted by, e.g., Hermann Gunkel) and notions of context, such as context of culture and situation (e.g., in the work of Bronislaw Malinowski and J. R. Firth), are duly noted.

9. Even S. Fowl, who is (rightly) highly critical of much previous work on so-called hymnic passages, grants that form-critical distinctions can be made. See his *The Story of Christ in the Ethics of Paul: An Analysis of the Function of the Hymnic Material in the Pauline Corpus* (JSNTSup 36; Sheffield: JSOT Press, 1990), 16-17, 45.

cient hymnic forms, illustrating each one with a number of significant examples from ancient literature. As a result, he distinguished between Greek and Semitic forms of hymnic passages. The Greek characteristics include either (1) a "you" (singular) style,[10] including such features as the use of apostrophe,[11] strophe, and antistrophe,[12] in which there is an invocation of the god, a recounting of his deeds, and an actual request;[13] or (2) a "he" style, where the speaker announces his intent to praise the god, a description of the god's nature, and an epilogue with salutation or perhaps request;[14] (3) meter based upon vowel length (not stress), although this feature had changed in Christian circles by perhaps the time of the New Testament and certainly by the fifth century;[15] (4) a participle style of predication;[16] and (5) a relative pronoun style.[17] A number of later scholars, such as Ernst Käsemann, picked up on only a few of these stylistic characteristics and made them preeminent in New Testament analysis.[18] The Jewish characteristics include (1) parallelism,[19] whether synonymous, antithetical, or synthetic; (2) the unhellenistic forms of "you are," "I am," and "he is";[20] and (3) the attributive use of participles and predication.[21] One notices immediately that differentiation of these categories is problematic in itself, since there is a certain amount of overlap of features. There is more difficulty than this, however, as Norden himself

10. This feature was recognized by Plato in *Cratylus* 400E-401A. For examples, see Pindar, *Olympian Odes* 4; Euripides, *Daughters of Troy*, 884-88.

11. E.g., *Homeric Hymn to Hermes.*

12. E.g., Sophocles, *Antigone* 781-94, 1115-45.

13. E.g., Cleanthes, *Hymn to Zeus:* invocation (lines 1-6), recounting of deeds (lines 7-31), and request (lines 32-39).

14. Aristides, *Speech* 43. Norden notes that the praise of a god does not always need direct address in the second person, but the praise expresses the god's virtues in the form of a third person statement (*Agnostos Theos*, 163).

15. On classical Greek meter, see M. L. West, *Greek Meter* (Oxford: Clarendon Press, 1982). On the later, stress meter of the great Christian poet Romanus Melodus, see P. Maas and C. Trypanis, *Sancti Romani Melodi Cantica: Cantica Genuina* (Oxford: Clarendon Press, 1963), 511-16.

16. Sophocles, *Oedipus the King* 200-202; Julian, *Fifth Speech,* introduction.

17. Homer, *Iliad* 1:37-38; Sophocles, *Electra* 175-76; Aristophanes, *Thesmophorae* 315-16; *Orphic Hymn to Pluto;* and many later Christian writers.

18. See E. Käsemann, "A Primitive Christian Baptismal Liturgy," in his *Essays on New Testament Themes* (trans. W. J. Montague; London: SCM Press, 1964), 149-68.

19. E.g., 2 Macc 1:23; Poimandres, Tract 5.

20. E.g., second person: Poimandres, Prayer I (to Hermes) and Ps 85:10; first person: Gen 17:1; third person: P.Lond. 46:135-39 (fourth century).

21. E.g., Isa 45:6-7; *Odes Sol.* 22; *PGM* 3009-19.

realized. For example, some scholars believe that what is so conveniently and traditionally referred to as Semitic poetic parallelism is only as ancient as the eighteenth-century invention of it by Robert Lowth.[22] There is the further difficulty that some of the features associated with one or the other — Greek or Jewish — are found in prominent texts from the other group. For example, Aristides uses the "he is" style in his purely Hellenistic writing, and an obelisk to Horus in Egypt uses the articular participle, as does the Rosetta Stone, not usually thought of as Semitic in style. Norden himself had noted that Greek and Semitic parallelism had much in common.[23]

When it comes to analysis of the prologue to John's Gospel, the difficulties with form-critical analysis become even more pronounced, as many scholars have noted. Most recent scholars question whether the prologue to John's Gospel can be considered a hymn at all, certainly as it is now found within the Gospel itself, since there do not appear to be any uses of the predicate participle, and there is no parallelism (except perhaps in John 1:3).[24] Many scholars go even further and consider that the vocabulary, syntax, and style of the prologue are thoroughly Johannine in their current form.[25]

Despite such recent pronouncements, a number of scholars in the past saw a variety of hymnic features in the prologue. Often these analyses began with claiming to have discovered parts of the prologue that belonged to the original hymn. For example, as Jack Sanders recounts, Rudolf Bultmann, Käsemann, and Rudolf Schnackenburg, among others, have analyzed the various sections of the prologue, and the consensus among this group seems to be that John 1:1-4/5 and vv. 9-11 or 10-12 belonged to the original hymn, but with much uncertainty regarding whether v. 4 or v. 5 ends the first poetic section.[26] This lack of certainty has led some scholars to a skeptical conclu-

---

22. C. K. Barrett, *The Gospel according to St. John* (2nd ed.; Philadelphia: Westminster, 1978), 150. Barrett notes that those in the New Testament period did not seem to know of Lowth's Semitic parallelism, nor did Josephus, Philo, or the translators of the Septuagint. See R. Lowth, *De sacra poesie Hebraeorum: Praelectiones academicae* (Oxford: Clarendon Press, 1821), lecture 19 (ET *Lectures on the Sacred Poetry of the Hebrews* [trans. G. Gregory; London: Chadwick, 1847]). Barrett's comments are expanded in his "The Prologue of St. John's Gospel," in his *New Testament Essays* (London: SPCK, 1972), 26-48.

23. Norden, *Antike Kunstprosa*, 2:816-19; but cf. Norden, *Agnostos Theos*, 355-64, where a contrast is drawn between Greek and Semitic Christian parallelism.

24. J. T. Sanders, *The New Testament Christological Hymns: Their Historical Religious Background* (SNTSMS 15; Cambridge: Cambridge University Press, 1971), 21.

25. C. A. Evans, *Word and Glory: On the Exegetical and Theological Background of John's Prologue* (JSNTSup 89; Sheffield: JSOT Press, 1993), 185.

26. Sanders, *New Testament Christological Hymns*, 21-23, citing R. Bultmann, *The Gos-*

sion: what confidence can we have in this approach if this is all the better we can do in identifying such basic literary types?[27]

Nevertheless, a number of outlines of this passage attempt to come to terms with its structure, being more concerned with form than prehistory. I have found at least seven major different outlines, although I am sure that there are probably many more. I summarize here the major approaches.

One approach is to try to find supposed instances of Semitic parallelism and to divide the prologue into poetic strophes. C. F. Burney was one of the earliest to take this approach, and he did so with a vengeance.[28] One of Burney's major thrusts was to find the Aramaic origin of John's Gospel, including its prologue. As a result, he placed great emphasis upon co-ordination by means of the use of the Greek conjunction καί ("and"). He divided the hymn into eleven parallel couplets, with interspersed comments by the writer of the Gospel. For the couplets, he determined whether they were indicating what he called climactic, synonymous, or antithetical parallelism. His results are as follows:

1. John 1:1ab, synonymous
2. vv. 1c-2, synonymous
3. v. 3ab, antithetical (with a break after γέγονεν)
4. v. 4ab, climactic
5. v. 5ab, climactic
6. v. 10bc, antithetical
7. v 11ab, climactic
8. v. 14ab, synonymous
9. v. 14cd, climactic
10. vv. 14e-16a, climactic
11. v. 17ab, antithetical

---

pel of John: A Commentary (trans. G. R. Beasley-Murray et al.; Oxford: Blackwell, 1971), 16-17; E. Käsemann, "The Structure and Purpose of the Prologue to John's Gospel," in his *New Testament Questions of Today* (Philadelphia: Fortress Press, 1969), 138-67, esp. 139-52; R. Schnackenburg, *The Gospel according to St. John* (trans. K. Smyth et al.; 3 vols.; London: Burns & Oates, 1968-82), 1:224-29. The disagreement over whether the first section ended with v. 4 or with v. 5 was one of the major disagreements between Bultmann and Käsemann. The most important work to argue against disunity of John's Gospel, including the prologue, is E. Ruckstuhl, *Die literarische Einheit des Johannesevangeliums* (NTOA 5; Freiburg: Universitätsverlag; Göttingen: Vandenhoeck & Ruprecht, 1988 [1951]).

27. See Barrett, *John*, 150-51.

28. C. F. Burney, *The Aramaic Origin of the Fourth Gospel* (Oxford: Clarendon Press, 1922), 40-42.

The interjections occur between couplets 5 and 6 (vv. 6-10a), 7 and 8 (vv. 12-13), 10 and 11 (v. 16b), and after 11 (v. 18). Burney is rigorous in applying his poetic criteria to find regular patterns of parallelism in two-line strophes. However, although the legacy of Burney's attempt to find an Aramaic origin remains strong in some ways,[29] virtually everyone has dismissed his proposal for the form of the prologue.[30]

The great Latinist J. H. Bernard[31] finds what he calls a "logos hymn," with couplets, triplets, and single lines. He thinks of this section as being a Hebraic style of hymn, but one using phrases familiar in Greek-speaking society, perhaps something like the *Odes of Solomon*, which he sees as similar. Bernard's strophes consist of:

> John 1:1, three lines
> v. 2, one line
> v. 3, two lines
> v. 4, two lines
> v. 5, two lines
> v. 10, three lines
> v. 11, two lines
> v. 14ab, two lines
> v. 14cd, two lines
> v. 14e, one line
> v. 18, three lines

In this accounting, John 1:6-9, 12-13, and 15-17 were not part of the original hymn, as most readily seen in the difference between vv. 6-7 and vv. 1-5.

John Painter adopts the same analytical method but tries to create what he sees as originally a Wisdom hymn, in which the hymn has John 1:1-3a,

---

29. See, e.g., the acceptance by the Aramaic advocate M. Black, in *An Aramaic Approach to the Gospels and Acts* (3rd ed.; Oxford: Clarendon Press, 1967), 143. C. K. Barrett (*The Gospel of John and Judaism* [London: SPCK, 1975], 20-31) refutes Burney point by point.

30. An exception is Bultmann, who accepted the Aramaic background (*John*, 18).

31. J. H. Bernard, *A Critical and Exegetical Commentary on the Gospel according to St. John* (ed. A. H. McNeile; 2 vols.; ICC; Edinburgh: T&T Clark, 1928), 1:cxliv-cxlv. R. Fortna (*The Gospel of Signs: A Reconstruction of the Narrative Source Underlying the Fourth Gospel* [SNTSMS 11; Cambridge: Cambridge University Press, 1970], 162) claims that "there has emerged a consensus (not quite unanimous, to be sure) to the effect that in writing the Prologue John made use of an earlier Logos-hymn which can be reconstructed, despite some uncertainties." While most scholars may recognize some idea of *logos* behind the prologue, it is difficult to see a consensus on a reconstructable *logos*-hymn.

4-5, 10-12ab, and 14a-c, all with parallels in Wisdom, Proverbs, and Sirach, among other sources.[32] He connects these together to create a continuous hymn in which he sees vv. 6-9 and 13 as not original, and with vv. 14d-18 as comment on the original hymn, as indicated by the non-Johannine vocabulary used in them. The Evangelist has added these comments, along with a few other passages, and has replaced the word "wisdom" with *logos,* and introduced the theme of incarnation in v. 14.

More recently, Sanders[33] is less concerned to find the rigid patterns of Burney or even of Bernard. Instead, he finds six strophes of unequal length, consisting of:

John 1:1-2, four lines
vv. 3-4, four lines
v. 5, two lines
v. 9, three lines
v. 10, three lines
v. 11, two lines

Note that Sanders deletes John 1:6-8 and vv. 12-18 as later additions and not part of the original structure of the hymn. These several attempts to find the formal structure of the hymn have concentrated upon the individual lines and stanzas, working from the smaller to the larger units.

A number of analyses have taken a larger perspective and worked down to the individual units. For example, Raymond Brown finds four strophes, with interjections on John the Baptist.[34] Brown's strophes consist of the following:

John 1:1-2   The Word with God
vv. 3-5   The Word and Creation
vv. 10-12a   The Word in the World

---

32. J. Painter, *The Quest for the Messiah: The History, Literature, and Theology of the Johannine Community* (Edinburgh: T&T Clark, 1991), 107-28, esp. 116.

33. Sanders, *New Testament Christological Hymns,* 20.

34. R. E. Brown, *The Gospel according to John* (2 vols.; AB 29, 29A; Garden City, NY: Doubleday, 1966-70), 1:3-36, esp. 3-4. Cf. J. Weiss, *Earliest Christianity: A History of the Period A.D. 30-150* (ed. R. Knopf; trans. F. C. Grant; 2 vols.; repr., Gloucester, MA: Peter Smith, 1970), 2:790, who apparently proposed a four-strophe structure; and J. D. G. Dunn, *Christology in the Making* (Philadelphia: Westminster, 1980), 240, who contends that he is presenting a "not too controversial" outline, but one that deletes vv. 6-8, 13, 15, and 17-18.

vv. 14, 16   The Community's Share in the Word-become-Flesh

The first interlude is on John the Baptist's Witness to the Light in John 1:6-9, a clarifying reason in vv. 12b-13, a parenthesis on John's testimony to the preexistence of Jesus in v. 15, and a concluding comment in vv. 17-18.

Joachim Jeremias, C. K. Barrett, and George Beasley-Murray[35] take a similar approach but do not delete any of the material, finding four major sections:

John 1	Jeremias	Barrett	Beasley-Murray
1-5	The Logos of God	The Cosmos	The Word and Creation
6-8	The Witness Pointing to Him	The Witness of John	The Witness to the Word by John the Baptist
9-13	The Fate of the Logos in the World	The Coming of the Light	The Reactions to the Word in the World
14-18	The Confession of the Believing Community	The Economy of Salvation	The Confession of the Word by the Church

Beasley-Murray's treatment is noteworthy in that he believes that he can subsume all of the material into his outline, without positing later additions or extraneous material.

Alan Culpepper goes even further in working with the material as found within the prologue by finding a complex chiastic structure, with v. 12b as the pivot: "He gave them authority to become the children of God." The following is Culpepper's structure of John 1:1-18:[36]

35. J. Jeremias, *The Central Message of the New Testament* (London: SCM Press, 1965), esp. 72-73 (though with sympathies for Burney); Barrett, *John*, 149-50; G. R. Beasley-Murray, *John* (WBC 36; Waco, TX: Word, 1987), 4-5.

36. R. A. Culpepper, "The Pivot of John's Prologue," *NTS* 27 (1980-81): 1-31, esp. 2-6, for previous studies (including chiastic ones), and 16 for his chiastic outline. See also P. Lamarche, "The Prologue of John" (1964), in *The Interpretation of John* (ed. J. Ashton; 2nd ed.; Edinburgh: T&T Clark, 1997), 47-65; R. Kysar, *The Maverick Gospel* (Atlanta: John Knox, 1976), 26; C. H. Giblin, "Two Complementary Literary Structures in John 1:1-18," *JBL* 104 (1985): 87-103; J. Staley, "The Structure of John's Prologue," *CBQ* 48 (1986): 241-64, esp. 249; and A. J. Köstenberger, *John* (BECNT; Grand Rapids: Baker, 2004), 19-22, who cites additional literature. Unfortunately for chiastic theories of the New Testament, there is little to no basis for this category of macro-chiasm or type of analysis in ancient usage, only among determined New Testament scholars (and piling on advocates fails to strengthen the argument!). See S. E. Porter and J. T. Reed, "Philippians as a Macro-Chiasm and Its Exegetical Significance," *NTS* 44 (1998): 213-31, esp. 213-21.

A   vv. 1-2, The Word with God

   B   v. 3, Creation Came through the Word

      C   vv. 4-5, We Have Received Life through the Word

         D   vv. 6-8, John the Baptist Is Sent to Testify

            E   vv. 9-10, Incarnation and the Response of the World

               F   v. 11, The Word and His Own (Israel)

                  G   v. 12a, Those Who Accepted the Word

                     H   v. 12b, Authority to Become Children of God

                  G′   v. 12c, Those Who Believed the Word

               F′   v. 13, The Word and His Own (Believers)

            E′   v. 14, Incarnation and the Response of the Community

         D′   v. 15, The Testimony of John the Baptist

      C′   v. 16, We Have Received Grace from the Word

   B′   v. 17, Grace and Truth Came through the Word

A′   v. 18, The Word with God

One needs to ask what exactly, if anything important, we have found from this brief survey of form-critical analyses. One finding is that there is in fact very little firm agreement. Some believe that Semitic parallelism exists (e.g., Burney, Bernard, Painter, and Sanders) and that the "he" style is used (e.g., Bernard and Painter, who find Logos or Wisdom hymns), but otherwise there is very little specific consensus. Other scholars are able to find competing structures, some of them more comprehensive in their analysis, without needing to find sets of parallelism that require the positing of later added material. To my mind, when one posits the adding of later material to make a hypothetical structure work, there is always the question whether one is actually finding what was there before or creating something to fit a theory. These proposals do nothing to mitigate this unease. Nevertheless, one cannot help but remark that most, if not all, of the scholars who have analyzed the passage, whether or not they think it was written by the author of the Gospel, find some sort of parallelism to the passage. Most claim that the parallelism is Semitic, but given the instances of Greek parallelism, this feature cannot be assumed. We may not be able to say that the prologue to John's Gospel fits a strict definition of "hymn" as defined by Norden, that is, exemplifying the range of characteristics that he posited, but it is undeniable that there is a poetic quality to the passage that demands acknowledgment and further attention.

3. Source Criticism

Much source criticism of the New Testament reflects the legacy of the history-of-religion approach, with all of the strengths and shortcomings that this method implies. Such scholars as Paul Wendland, Richard Reitzenstein, Wilhelm Bousset, and Norden,[37] as well as many later followers, believed that all religion, including Christianity, followed the evolutionary model of the day, and that comparative studies were useful in determining origins (apart from theological interests). As Norden says in his *Agnostos Theos,* Israelite religion was simply the youngest of the ancient Near Eastern religions, and earlier religions in Sumeria, Assyria, Babylon, and Egypt had many of the same characteristics, such as the "I" and "you" styles.[38] During the first half of last century, history-of-religion research fell on hard times in much of New Testament studies (although it continued to be practiced in some hymnic research),[39] no doubt because of some of its abuses and eccentricities. For example, some scholars imbued source-critical conclusions with ontological substance, read much later sources back into earlier documents, or simply piled on parallels without adequate explanation. These kinds of approaches inevitably led to a reaction, seen especially in the biblical theology movement,[40] but a reaction that itself perhaps hindered rather than

37. See P. Wendland, *Die Hellenistisch-Römische Kultur in ihren Beziehungen zu Judentum und Christentum: Die urchristlichen Literaturformen* (Tübingen: Mohr Siebeck, 1912); R. Reitzenstein, *Die hellenistischen Mysterienreligionen: Nach ihren Grundgedanke und Wirkungen* (repr., Darmstadt: Wissenschaftliche Buchgesellschaft, 1966 [1910]); R. Reitzenstein and H. H. Schaeder, *Studien zum antiken Synkretismus aus Iran und Griechenland* (repr., Darmstadt: Wissenschaftliche Buchgesellschaft, 1965); W. Bousset, *Kyrios Christos: A History of the Belief in Christ from the Beginnings of Christianity to Irenaeus* (trans. J. E. Steely; Nashville: Abingdon, 1969 [1913]); Norden, *Agnostos Theos;* Norden, *Antike Kunstprosa.* For a brief conspectus on the history-of-religion movement, see W. Baird, *History of New Testament Research,* vol. 2: *From Jonathan Edwards to Rudolf Bultmann* (Minneapolis: Fortress Press, 2003), 222-53.

38. Norden, *Agnostos Theos,* 207-23.

39. See Sanders, *New Testament Christological Hymns,* which is essentially a source-critical study that attempts to find a common "myth of origins" behind the hymns of the New Testament; and K. Wengst, *Christologische Formeln und Lieder des Urchristentums* (Gütersloh: Mohn, 1972).

40. On this movement, see B. S. Childs, *Biblical Theology in Crisis* (Philadelphia: Westminster, 1970). It is well known that these were the kinds of things James Barr was reacting to in his *The Semantics of Biblical Language* (Oxford: Oxford University Press, 1961) and *Biblical Words for Time* (London: SCM Press, 1962) regarding simple equation of word and concept and positing unique linguistically determined mind-sets for various ethnic groups.

encouraged more recent and pertinent discussion of the origins of thought and expression in the New Testament. With the tendency to find the origins of the New Testament almost exclusively in a form of later rabbinic Judaism, only recently corrected to appreciate Judaism's own diversity in the first century, important insights about the religious complexity of the New Testament world have been overlooked. Recent work has been referred to as a new history-of-religion approach, led by such scholars as Martin Hengel and the New Tübingen school,[41] that has attempted to find the relation of Christianity to the Greco-Roman world, of which Judaism was a part. This approach certainly merits further investigation, since it does not fall victim to the easy disjunctive thinking of so much previous work in the nineteenth and early twentieth centuries but attempts the more difficult task of assessing Christianity in relation to a number of different religious systems, including Judaism (if "systems" is the right word to use).

Source criticism of the hymnic and credal passages in the New Testament has traditionally looked to a number of different sources for what is found. One of these is the Old Testament, especially places in the Old Testament that have liturgical significance, such as the Psalms, and the prayers found in, for example, 2 Maccabees. In 1914 one scholar found that there were at least 196 songs, hymns, and prayers in the Old Testament,[42] which could have formed the background for the New Testament writers. Another source, as already mentioned, is ancient Near Eastern religions. There are some very interesting hymns to gods from, for example, Sumeria, Babylon, Assyria, and Egypt, in which a god is directly addressed and praised for his power or beneficence.[43] A third source often cited is other religious cults that address a god or gods. Today some of these might be seen as philosophies, such as Stoicism, with its praise of Zeus in, for example, Cleanthes' *Hymn to Zeus*.[44] Other possible religious cults that have been cited are the Hermetic

---

41. What distinguishes Hengel's history-of-religion approach is his marshaling of important material from the Hellenistic world, such as is found in M. Hengel, *Hellenism and Judaism* (trans. J. Bowden; 2 vols.; Philadelphia: Fortress Press, 1974), as well as a number of other works. See also C. Fletcher-Louis, *Luke-Acts: Angels, Christology, and Soteriology* (WUNT 2.94; Tübingen: Mohr Siebeck, 1997).

42. C. F. Kent, *The Songs, Hymns, and Prayers of the Old Testament* (London: Hodder & Stoughton, 1914).

43. See F. A. Vanderburgh, *Sumerian Hymns from Cuneiform Texts in the British Museum* (New York: Columbia University Press, 1908; repr., 1966); C. G. Cumming, *The Assyrian and Hebrew Hymns of Praise* (New York: Columbia University Press, 1934; repr., 1966).

44. See S. van Arnim, *Stoicorum veterum fragmenta* (4 vols.; Stuttgart: Teubner, 1964), 1:121-22 (no. 537), for Cleanthes' hymn.

literature (of which Reitzenstein's view concerning its Greco-Egyptian origins has essentially been confirmed in recent work),[45] the Homeric and Orphic hymns,[46] and even gnostic and Mandaean texts.[47] A fourth source, which stems from the heyday of the history-of-religion research but has experienced a recent revival, is religious rituals in which hymns are addressed to humans as to gods. These are associated with various religious groups, from even before the time of Alexander, when Oriental cults often venerated their human rulers as gods. Alexander encouraged this kind of worship, and it was used as a source of power by the Hellenistic kings (see the Rosetta Stone, lines 1-5; *OGIS* 90). This same convention was used by the Roman emperors, and by the end of the first century, emperor worship had spread from the East to the West.[48] Other sources sometimes mentioned, although they have not figured as prominently in the discussion, are various syncretistic religious systems, as, for example, reflected in the magical papyri, where any and all means of divine help are sought; Jewish synagogue and possibly temple worship; and early Christian rituals and beliefs in which various rituals or liturgy would have been present, such as baptism, Passover, and other worship ceremonies.

When we turn to the prologue of John's Gospel, we can see that the same fate of an abundance of widely varying sources as has been offered for other ancient documents also applies here. In much previous discussion, there has been a host of proposals regarding the source of this supposed Johannine hymn. Among recent commentators, however, two major tendencies attempt to avoid source-critical questions. One current of thought

45. See R. Reitzenstein, *Poimandres: Studien zu griechisch-ägyptischen und frühchristlichen Literatur* (repr. ed.; Darmstadt: Wissenschaftliche Buchgesellschaft, 1966); cf. B. P. Copenhaver, *Hermetica* (Cambridge: Cambridge University Press, 1992), xlv-lix. The most sustained study of the Hermetic literature in relation to the New Testament is C. H. Dodd, *The Bible and the Greeks* (London: Hodder & Stoughton, 1934), 99-248; cf. also his *Interpretation of the Fourth Gospel* (Cambridge: Cambridge University Press, 1953), 10-53.

46. See H. G. Evelyn-White, *Hesiod, the Homeric Hymns, and Homerica* (LCL; London: Heinemann; Cambridge, MA: Harvard University Press, 1950), 285-463; A. N. Athanassakis, *The Orphic Hymns: Text, Translation, and Notes* (SBLTT 12; GRRS 4; Atlanta: Scholars Press, 1977).

47. See J. M. Robinson, ed., *The Nag Hammadi Library in English* (New York: Harper & Row, 1988); and B. Layton, *The Gnostic Scriptures* (London: SCM Press, 1987).

48. A still important study of the ancient sources is A. Deissmann, *Light from the Ancient East* (trans. L. R. M. Strachan; 4th ed.; London: Hodder & Stoughton, 1927), 338-78. See also L. J. Kreitzer, *Striking New Images: Roman Imperial Coinage and the New Testament World* (JSNTSup 134; Sheffield: Sheffield Academic Press, 1996), 69-98.

is to believe that the prologue did not originate with another source, but that it was composed by the author of the Gospel (see, e.g., Craig Evans, D. A. Carson, and Craig Keener, among others);[49] the other is to study only the text we have (e.g., R. H. Lightfoot, J. N. Sanders and B. A. Mastin, C. K. Barrett, Leon Morris, G. R. Beasley-Murray, Mark Stibbe, and Thomas Brodie, among many others).[50] In order to appreciate this reaction against previous scholarship, however, it is worth considering some of these previous source-critical views. Some of them have points of contact with some of the form-critical analyses already mentioned above.

I cite three major source-critical positions that have been argued for John's prologue.[51] Of those that may still merit some attention, the first emerged directly from the history-of-religion discussion but has generally been dismissed in recent thought. This is the idea that the source of the prologue was the Greek *logos* doctrine, possibly transmuted through Philonic or Alexandrian Judaism.[52] The *logos* doctrine appears first in the pre-Socratic thinker Heraclitus,[53] a fifth-century B.C. philosopher, probably from Ephesus. He has proved to be an enigmatic thinker; some scholars are skeptical

---

49. See Evans, *Word and Glory,* 185 n. 3; D. A. Carson, *The Gospel according to John* (PNTC; Grand Rapids: Eerdmans; Leicester: InterVarsity Press, 1991), 111-12; C. S. Keener, *The Gospel of John: A Commentary* (2 vols.; Peabody, MA: Hendrickson, 2003), 1:333-34 (even if added later by John).

50. R. H. Lightfoot, *St. John's Gospel: A Commentary* (ed. C. F. Evans; Oxford: Clarendon Press, 1956), 78; J. N. Sanders and B. A. Mastin, *A Commentary on the Gospel according to St. John* (BNTC; London: A&C Black, 1968), 67; Barrett, *John,* 151; L. Morris, *The Gospel according to John* (rev. ed.; NICNT; Grand Rapids: Eerdmans, 1995 [1971]), 71; Beasley-Murray, *John,* 5; M. Stibbe, *John* (Readings: A New Bible Commentary; Sheffield: JSOT Press, 1993), 22-31; Brodie, *John,* 143. On this point, E. E. Ellis seems to be confused (*The Making of the New Testament Documents* [BIS 39; Leiden: Brill, 1999], 165-68).

51. See Sanders, *New Testament Christological Hymns,* 29-57, who offers finer gradations of theories, but there are numerous conceptual overlaps between them.

52. Many commentaries have sections on the *logos* idea, although many include it simply to argue against it. For a survey, see E. Harris, *Prologue and Gospel: The Theology of the Fourth Evangelist* (JSNTSup 107; Sheffield: Sheffield Academic Press, 1994), 196-201, esp. 196 n. 2. See also E. Krebs, *Der Logos als Heiland im ersten Jahrhundert: Ein religions- und dogmengeschichtlicher Beitrag zur Erlösungslehre* (Freiburg: Herder, 1920); R. G. Bury, *The Fourth Gospel and the Logos-Doctrine* (Cambridge: Heffer, 1940); E. K. Lee, *The Religious Thought of St. John* (London: SPCK, 1950), 74-108; and Phillips, *Prologue,* 73-141, who in the end dismisses it.

53. See H. Diels, *Die Fragmente der Vorsokratiker* (3 vols.; Berlin: Weidmannsche Buchhandlung, 1912), 1:67-113.

that he even had a *logos* doctrine,[54] but most think that he had a metaphysics at least of sorts.[55] As J. Adam states:

> In Heraclitus the three conceptions, Logos, Fire, and God, are fundamentally the same. Regarded as the Logos, God is the omnipresent Wisdom by which all things are steered; regarded in his physical or material aspect, that is to say, as Fire, he is the substance which creates, sustains, and in the end perhaps reabsorbs into himself the world; and in both of these aspects at once, he is the ever-changing and yet forever changeless unity in which all multiplicity inheres.[56]

After being forgotten by Plato and Aristotle, Heraclitean thought was revived by the Stoics. They adopted belief in the unitary eternal word, as Cleanthes notes in his *Hymn to Zeus* line 21.[57] This eternal word communicated, explained, and was common to all; that is, it directed all things, providing the basis of Stoic ethics in the concept of humanity and the world living consistently with the *logos* (ὁμολογουμένως).[58] As Adam again states: "By the Stoics the Heraclitean concept of Logos was further elaborated, but the elements of pantheism and materialism still remained. From the Stoics the doctrine passed to Philo, who under Platonic influence clearly separates the Logos from the supreme God, letting pantheism give place to theism."[59]

"At the same time," Adam continues, "the Logos is frequently personi-

54. See J. Barnes, *The Presocratic Philosophers* (London: Routledge & Kegan Paul, 1979), 57-60, with specific reference to fragment 1 (Diels).

55. See fragments 30, 32, 67 (Diels). This position is generally endorsed by J. Adam, *The Religious Teachers of Greece* (Edinburgh: T&T Clark, 1909), 212-40; P. Wheelwright, *Heraclitus* (Oxford: Clarendon Press, 1959); G. S. Kirk, J. E. Raven, and M. Schofield, *The Presocratic Philosophers* (2nd ed.; Cambridge: Cambridge University Press, 1983), 186-212.

56. Adam, *Religious Teachers*, 233. Note that Heraclitus also believed in a final conflagration. See Adam, *Religious Teachers*, 228-29. Cf. P. van der Horst, "'The Elements Will Be Dissolved with Fire': The Idea of Cosmic Conflagration in Hellenism, Ancient Judaism, and Early Christianity," in his *Hellenism-Judaism-Christianity: Essays on Their Interaction* (Leuven: Peeters, 1998), 271-92; F. H. Sandbach, *The Stoics* (London: Chatto & Windus, 1975), 74.

57. See Cleanthes, *Hymn to Zeus*, line 21: "So that there might be one eternally existing Word." See Adam, *Religious Teachers*, 218.

58. See A. A. Long, *Hellenistic Philosophy: Stoics, Epicureans, Sceptics* (2nd ed.; London: Duckworth, 1986), esp. 145-47. See also T. Enberg-Pedersen, "*Logos* and *Pneuma* in the Fourth Gospel," in *Greco-Roman Culture and the New Testament: Studies Commemorating the Centennial of the Pontifical Biblical Institute* (ed. D. E. Aune and F. E. Brenk; NovTSup 143; Leiden: Brill, 2012), 27-48.

59. Adam, *Religious Teachers*, 239.

fied" — for example, as divine Word,[60] firstborn or eldest son of God,[61] God's vice-regent in the world,[62] the intermediary between God and humanity,[63] and eternal or preexistent,[64] and so forth. In this regard, the link between Greek philosophy and Christianity is explicitly made by John's Gospel in the prologue. It has even been suggested that the author of John's Gospel, writing from Ephesus, was perhaps intentionally invoking his Ephesian predecessor, Heraclitus, by using *logos* language.[65] Despite this scholarship on the relation between the *logos* in the New Testament and in other Greek thought of the time,[66] much of this comparative work has been dismissed for a number of reasons. The major one is the problem of positing parallels in thought and actually finding a cause-and-effect relationship between them. Furthermore, many believe that Philo had no articulated doctrine of the *logos* in which there is a concept of preexistence, especially before the time of the New Testament — besides there being a lack of exact parallels in Philo with the New Testament references.[67] As a result, this position is not strongly propounded today.

A second source of the Johannine prologue is often identified in the Jewish Sophia or Wisdom tradition, especially as found in the Wisdom writings of the Old Testament.[68] This position begins with recognition of the creative

60. Philo, *QG* 2:62, where the *logos* is referred to as a "second God" in the likeness of God; *Her.* 119.

61. Philo, *Agr.* 51; *Conf.* 146.

62. Philo, *Cher.* 36, where the *logos* is referred to as the ruler and steersman of all; *Conf.* 146.

63. Philo, *Her.* 2-5; *QE* 2:13, 94; *Deus* 138; *Sacr.* 119.

64. Philo, *Plant.* 18; *Conf.* 41, 147; *Leg.* 2:86.

65. Adam, *Religious Teachers*, 240, citing W. R. Inge, *Christian Mysticism* (London: Methuen, 1899), 47; Norden, *Antike Kunstprosa*, 2:473-74. Cf. also E. F. Scott, *The Fourth Gospel: Its Purpose and Theology* (2nd ed.; Edinburgh: T&T Clark, 1908), 145-75; W. L. Knox, *Some Hellenistic Elements in Primitive Christianity* (Schweich Lectures; London: British Academy, 1944), 43.

66. Note that Justin Martyr had Stoic sympathies but parted company over the issue of God (*Dial.* 2). See T. R. Glover, *The Conflict of Religions in the Early Roman Empire* (London: Methuen, 1909), esp. 72.

67. See, e.g., Dunn, *Christology in the Making*, 220-30, where he notes confusion over Philo's view of *logos* as unexpressed and expressed thought, its immaterial nature compared to the Stoics, and its intermediate function. However, note his conclusion: "In the end of the day the Logos seems to be nothing more for Philo than God himself in his approach to man, God himself insofar as he may be known by man" (228).

68. A classic study of this Wisdom approach is J. R. Harris, *The Origin of the Prologue to St John's Gospel* (Cambridge: Cambridge University Press, 1917), 1-66; repr. in A. Falcetta,

Word of God in the Old Testament, such as is found in Gen 1,[69] as well as in such places as the Psalms and the prophets.[70] There seems to have been a development in later biblical thought regarding this Word, so much so that many scholars see a hypostatization, in which in the Wisdom literature the figure of Wisdom becomes the active intermediary that performs God's tasks in the world.[71] As a result, parallels in a number of texts are often found which seem to support a preexistent and personalized Wisdom, seen to be God's partner in creation and seeking to dwell upon earth among humanity.[72] Some have even cited verbal parallels in this Wisdom literature to various parts of the Johannine prologue: for example, "in the beginning was the word" (// Prov 8:22-26; Sir 1:1-19; 24:3-4),[73] "the word was with God" (// Wis 8:3; 9:4, 9; Prov 8:30).[74] Dodd went so far as to find parallels to virtually every verse in the prologue, this kind of parallelism coming out of normative Judaism of the time.[75] This hypothesis has commanded more assent than most others and is probably the most widely held today, especially the first regarding a *logos* doctrine.[76] There is a question, however, whether it should command such assent, since it relies just as much on a set of posited parallels as the *logos* position. This point seems to be overlooked because the appeal is more directly to a Jewish rather than to a Greek background. However, we have the major difficulty of how the Wisdom figure became the *logos* figure in John's Gospel, and then became located in Christ. At this point, Dodd suggests that there are parallels not only to the Wisdom tradition but to Philo, indicating that what he would characterize as "normative" Judaism was in fact Hellenistic Judaism, including the kind of thought found in Philo, an Alexandrian Jew. The coming together of the Old Testament and Wisdom and Greek philosophical traditions in Alexandria, or elsewhere around the

---

ed., *James Rendel Harris: New Testament Autographs and Other Essays* (NTM 7; Sheffield: Sheffield Phoenix Press, 2006), 117-84, with notes by Harris for a second edition.

69. Cf. also Gen 15:1; Deut 5:5; Josh 8:27; 2 Sam 7:4; 1 Kgs 13:20.

70. E.g., Ps 33:6; 107:20; 147:15, 18; Isa 9:8; 55:10-11.

71. E.g., Wis 9:1-2, 17; 18:14-16.

72. E.g., Sir 24:1-11; Prov 1:20-32; 8:27-30; Job 28:25-27.

73. But cf. Philo, *Virt.* 62.

74. But cf. Philo, *Ebr.* 30; *Leg.* 2:49; *Cher.* 48-50; *Fug.* 50.

75. Dodd, *Interpretation of the Fourth Gospel*, 263-85, esp. 274-75, 276-77.

76. See, e.g., O. Cullmann, *The Christology of the New Testament* (trans. S. C. Guthrie and C. A. M. Hall; 2nd ed.; London: SCM Press, 1963), 248-69; J. Ashton, "The Transformation of Wisdom: A Study of the Prologue of John's Gospel," in his *Studying John: Approaches to the Fourth Gospel* (Oxford: Clarendon Press, 1994 [1986]), 5-35; M. Scott, *Sophia and the Johannine Jesus* (JSNTSup 71; Sheffield: JSOT Press, 1992), esp. 94-115.

Mediterranean, has presented a third or mediating view in trying to find the most plausible explanation of the conceptual origins of the prologue to John's Gospel. The idea is not that one must find a single individual responsible for the conceptual shift from *logos* to Wisdom and from Wisdom to incarnation (John 1:14), but that these kinds of issues were being frequently debated and discussed in the Hellenistic Judaism of the time.[77]

These two previous major views are the most often referred to today regarding the origin of John's prologue. However, a number of other positions have been introduced through the years. One that, it seems to me, is no longer worth arguing is that the prologue reflects a gnostic and possibly even Mandaean background, including that of a heavenly redeemer. This idea was first proposed by Bultmann and later endorsed by James Robinson, among others,[78] who claim that there was a pre-Christian gnostic myth that influenced Christian thought. This hypothesis has been thoroughly disproved by a number of scholars, including the detailed treatment of Evans, who briefly surveys previous discussion.[79] The major and decisive argument against Bultmann and his followers' position is that the documents used (if they are gnostic at all) either are much later (Mandaean and Hermetic literature) or have been shown in a number of crucial instances to have been influenced by Christian thought (e.g., *Odes of Solomon*). Attempts to establish the earliness of the traditions fail to account for the clearly derivative features. As to the myth of a heavenly redeemer, Bultmann, acknowledging the difficulty, believed that the myth was older, going so far as to imply that various forms of this myth all seemed to originate with a common myth. No such myth has ever been found.

In the light of the revival or rejuvenation of the history-of-religion

---

77. This view is argued by Knox, *Some Hellenistic Elements,* 44 (cf. W. L. Knox, *St. Paul and the Church of the Gentiles* [Cambridge: Cambridge University Press, 1939], 55-89); Harris, *Prologue and Gospel,* 197-98. Dunn rejects both traditions above (*Christology in the Making,* 215-30), for the reason that he wishes to argue that the notion of preexistence is found for the first time in John 1:1-18. Not only does he seem to think disjunctively about the evidence (i.e., because a clear incarnated being is not found in Philo or Old Testament thought, there is no conception of preexistence), but he seems to have overlooked or radically minimized other New Testament evidence (e.g., Phil 2:6-11; Col 1:15-20).

78. E.g., R. Bultmann, "The History of Religions Background of the Prologue to the Gospel of John" (1923), in *The Interpretation of John,* 27-46; Bultmann, *John,* 14-18; J. M. Robinson, "The Johannine Trajectory," in *Trajectories through Early Christianity,* by J. M. Robinson and H. Koester (Philadelphia: Fortress Press, 1971), 232-68, esp. 252-66.

79. Evans, *Word and Glory;* his is simply the latest in a number of studies that have shown the bankruptcy of the hypothesis. Cf. Phillips, *Prologue,* 96-106.

school, and perhaps having learned from the work that has been modeled by Hengel, I think that there is plenty of scope for further exploration of a number of other complex stories of origin to be brought to bear on this passage. I also think it is fair to say now, however, that the state of discussion seems a bit exhausted, with not much progress having been made since early last century. The primary reason is probably that the marshaling of parallels can be frustrating without some kind of larger framework for evaluation to see whether the parallels are indeed true parallels. So far, most of them have not withstood critical scrutiny, let alone commanded assent.

4. Musical-Liturgical Criticism

Musical-liturgical criticism may be unfamiliar to most scholars, because it is a relatively newly fashioned criticism that draws upon our knowledge of music, worship, and liturgy in the ancient world, including that of the New Testament, to analyze how texts and practice interrelated.[80] In this instance, musical-liturgical criticism examines the prologue as an instance of how the early church enshrined its worship of Jesus within a liturgical form. In some ways, musical-liturgical criticism may prove to be one of the most productive

---

80. Some of the most important research on music in the ancient world, including that of the New Testament and liturgy, includes E. Wellesz, ed., *Ancient and Oriental Music* (NOHM 1; London: Oxford University Press, 1957), with specialist articles on the Bible by C. H. Kraeling (283-312), postbiblical Judaism by E. Werner (313-35), ancient Greek music by I. Henderson (336-403), and Roman music by J. E. Scott (404-20); E. Wellesz, "Early Christian Music," in *Early Mediaeval Music up to 1300* (ed. D. A. Hughes; rev. ed.; NOHM 2; London: Oxford University Press, 1955), 1-13; M. L. West, *Ancient Greek Music* (Oxford: Clarendon Press, 1992); E. Werner, *The Sacred Bridge: The Interdependence of Liturgy and Music in Synagogue and Church during the First Millennium* (2 vols.; vol. 1: London: Dobson; New York: Columbia University Press, 1959; vol. 2: New York: Ktav, 1984); J. Quasten, *Music and Worship in Pagan and Christian Antiquity* (trans. B. Ramsey; Washington, DC: National Association of Pastoral Musicians, 1980 [1930]); W. S. Sheppard, *Musical Aspects of the New Testament* (Amsterdam: Ten Have, 1962); D. G. Dix, *The Shape of the Liturgy* (Westminster: Dacre Press, 1954); J. McKinnon, ed., *Music in Early Christian Literature* (CRLM; Cambridge: Cambridge University Press, 1987); C. Hannick, "Christian Church, Music of the Early," in *New Grove Dictionary of Music and Musicians* (ed. S. Sadie; 20 vols.; London: Macmillan, 1980), 4:363-71; P. F. Bradshaw, *The Search for the Origins of Christian Worship: Sources and Methods for the Study of Early Liturgy* (Oxford: Oxford University Press, 1992); P. Bradshaw, ed., *The New Westminster Dictionary of Liturgy and Worship* (Louisville, KY: Westminster John Knox, 2002); and C. Jones, G. Wainwright, and E. Yarnold, eds., *The Study of Liturgy* (rev. ed.; New York: Oxford University Press, 1992 [1978]).

areas of current investigation of John's prologue (and other passages), since there appear to be so many as yet unresolved questions regarding worship in the early church, including how hymns figured into that worship. There has been much work on early Christian liturgy, especially as it relates to the New Testament.[81] In much of this study, however, it is commonly assumed that the music and liturgy of the Jewish temple were taken over by early synagogues and then became the music and liturgy of the early Christian church. In other words, the idea is that a single historical thread connected Judaism to Christianity. The major problems with this assumption begin with the fact that the Hebrew people did not have a continuous uninterrupted history themselves, to say nothing of the modifying effect of their manifest cultural assimilation in Babylon, Persia, the Greek world, and the Roman world. The influence of Hellenism is clearly established by the time of the New Testament, so much so that one cannot speak of Judaism apart from Hellenistic Judaism, whether inside or outside of Palestine, as Hengel has shown. Furthermore, the music and liturgy of the temple were professional, whereas the liturgy of the synagogue was not used for similar purposes, and perhaps did not even involve music. The influence of the destruction of the temple in A.D. 70 marks a decisive shift in Jewish-Christian relations, but one already affected by the shift from Christianity being a Jewish sect to being a Gentile religion, especially through the missionary ventures of Paul.[82] The destruction of the temple seriously affected Judaism as well, and it is not clear that there was a simple transference from temple to synagogue in

81. See, among others, N. Micklem, ed., *Christian Worship: Studies in Its History and Meaning* (Oxford: Clarendon Press, 1936); O. Cullmann, *Les premières confessions de foi chrétiennes* (Paris: Presses Universitaires, 1943); Cullmann, *Early Christian Worship* (SBT 10; London: SCM Press, 1953); Martin, "Aspects of Worship in the New Testament Church," *VE* 2 (1963): 6-32; Martin, *Worship in the Early Church* (2nd ed.; London: Marshall, Morgan & Scott, 1978); M. Hengel, "The Song about Christ in Earliest Worship," in his *Studies in Early Christology* (Edinburgh: T&T Clark, 1995), 227-91; P. F. Bradshaw and L. A. Hoffman, eds., *The Making of Jewish and Christian Worship* (Notre Dame: University of Notre Dame Press, 1991); D. Peterson, *Engaging with God: A Biblical Theology of Worship* (Grand Rapids: Eerdmans, 1992); Hurtado, *At the Origins;* J. F. White, *Introduction to Christian Worship* (3rd ed.; Nashville: Abingdon, 2000 [1980]); M. D. Stringer, *A Sociological History of Christian Worship* (Cambridge: Cambridge University Press, 2005); G. Wainwright and K. B. Westerfield Tucker, eds., *The Oxford History of Christian Worship* (Oxford: Oxford University Press, 2006); and G. L. Borchert, *Worship in the New Testament: Divine Mystery and Human Response* (St. Louis: Chalice, 2008).

82. See S. E. Porter and B. W. R. Pearson, "Why the Split? Christians and Jews by the Fourth Century," *JGRChJ* 1 (2000): 82-119, who trace the early separation of Christianity and Judaism.

ritual and practice.[83] Even if lines of continuity could be established, we still have the pressing problem that there are few certainties about early music or liturgy, whether Jewish or Christian. Recent liturgical studies now doubt the notion of a single Urtext to the Jewish liturgy, instead believing that there were multiple patterns of worship.[84] Later rabbinical documents are to be seen, therefore, as prescriptive documents that attempt to control the later liturgical situation. (The Mishnah list of five worship activities includes recitation, blessing, and readings — but not music.)

Concerning music specifically, our knowledge is very fragmentary, for Jewish music did not develop a notation system until the tenth century. Scholars still assume, however, that psalmody was the music of the early church. It may have been, but there are no documents that say so, including early recountings of early Christian worship services (e.g., Justin, *1 Apol.* 67), although Pliny in his letter to Trajan (10:96) mentions "singing about Christ as to a god."[85] We also know that Paul mentions using "psalms, hymns, and spiritual songs" (Eph 5:19; Col 3:16), but there is much scholarly dispute over what these terms actually mean, and how or whether they are to be distinguished. Some scholars, since the time of Heinrich Schlier in the 1930s, believe that they are synonyms,[86] but my inclination is to think, along with Egon Wellesz,[87] that, while they may semantically overlap, they are distinct terms and not complete synonyms. In any case, much of the evidence for music and liturgy in the early church is late (third to fourth century) and has been influenced by the discussion in the Roman Empire of the time, which was concerned with issues such as Constantine's conversion and tensions between East and West.[88]

In any case, we are discussing the prologue to John's Gospel in relation

83. For helpful essays on Judaism before and after the destruction of the temple, see D. R. Schwartz and Z. Weiss, eds., *Was 70 CE a Watershed in Jewish History? On Jews and Judaism before and after the Destruction of the Second Temple* (AJEC 78; Leiden: Brill, 2012).

84. Bradshaw, *Search for the Origins*, 4-13.

85. This lack of evidence was early on recognized by H. Lietzmann, *The Beginnings of Christianity* (trans. B. L. Woolf; London: Lutterworth, 1949 [1937]), 147-48.

86. H. Schlier, "ᾄδω, ᾠδή," *TDNT* 1 (1964): 163-65, esp. 164.

87. E. Wellesz, "Early Christian Music," in *The New Oxford History of Music*, vol. 2: *The Early Middle Ages to 1300* (ed. R. Crocker and D. Hiley; rev. ed.; London: Oxford University Press, 1955), 2:2; cf. his *A History of Byzantine Music and Hymnography* (2nd ed.; Oxford: Clarendon Press, 1961), 33-34.

88. On the above, see esp. W. J. Porter, "Music," in *Dictionary of New Testament Background* (ed. C. A. Evans and S. E. Porter; Downers Grove, IL: InterVarsity Press, 2000), 711-19.

to its possible hymnic qualities. In this light, it is appropriate to ask what we know about the use of music in the ancient world, especially in Christian circles. We have hypotheses from a number of scholars on what Jewish music may have been like during this time. Their hypotheses are that the music was probably responsorial, in which the leader intoned the verse and the congregation repeated it.[89] However, we do not have any evidence supporting this hypothesis. What we do have are some instances of Greek music. We have about fifty extant ancient Greek musical documents.[90] One of the most important of these is a fragment of Euripides' *Orestes,* with musical notation from the chorus, dating to about 200 B.C. We also have two hymns to Apollo, carved on stone, fragments representing oral performances at Delphi in 127 B.C. The earliest Christian hymn, P.Oxyrhynchus XV 1786, was probably copied in the late third century A.D. and has excited much discussion. Some believe that it reflects Greek influence, while others believe that it is more Jewish — depending upon the orientation of the particular scholar examining the manuscript.[91] These and similar documents seem to indicate that singing did take place in the ancient world and probably in the early church, but that it was probably unison singing (and later than the New Testament). If an instrument was involved in early church singing (and there is serious question whether instruments were used), it probably either played the melody or was used to play a single drone note.[92] This singing may well have been antiphonal or responsorial, with a leader singing and the congregation following, either repeating the line or singing the second part as a response.

An interesting phenomenon to note is the development of ekphonetic notation.[93] In about the sixth century or so, basic accentuation marks ap-

89. A. Z. Idelsohn, *Jewish Music in Its Historical Development* (New York: Tudor, 1948 [1929]), 20-21.

90. See West, *Ancient Greek Music,* where the texts are presented.

91. E. Werner, "Music," in *Interpreter's Dictionary of the Bible* (ed. G. A. Buttrick; 4 vols.; Nashville: Abingdon, 1962), 3:457-69, esp. 467-68; M. L. West, "Analecta Musica," *ZPE* 92 (1992): 1-54, esp. 47, citing E. Pöhlmann, *Denkmähler altgriechischer Musik: Sammlung Übertragung und Erläuterung aller Fragmente und Fälshungen* (Nuremberg: Verlag Hans Carl, 1970), 106-9. The latest and most complete study is C. Cosgrove, *An Ancient Christian Hymn with Musical Notation: Papyrus Oxyrhynchus 1786; Text and Commentary* (STAC 65; Tübingen: Mohr Siebeck, 2011), who believes that the hymn reflects the ancient Greek tradition of creation falling silent as humanity "hymns" the god.

92. See Cosgrove, *Ancient Christian Hymn,* 127-28.

93. See Wellesz, *Byzantine Music,* esp. 246-310; W. J. Porter, "The Use of Ekphonetic Notation in Vienna New Testament Manuscripts," in *Akten des 23. Internationalen Papyrologenkongresses: Wien, 22-28. Juli 2001* (ed. B. Palme; Vienna: Verlag der Österreichischen

parently began to be placed upon ancient manuscripts, some at the time of copying but most later in a different hand. These marks, or what came to be a full system of notation called *neumes,* developed into a complex system of marking. Many of the diacritical marks are based upon the basic accentuation and punctuation marks that are commonly used in printed New Testament Greek texts, but the system became far more complex. This notational system indicated to the reader of the text how the text was supposed to be intoned for musical-rhetorical liturgical purposes. This system is often found especially on minuscule manuscripts from the tenth century and later, although intermediate systems of notation are found on some majuscule manuscripts of this approximate time as well. A major hindrance in this discussion has been that classical scholars, New Testament scholars, and Byzantinologists have often not communicated together in their findings, leaving major gaps in our knowledge.

As noted above, most recent scholarship has disagreed with the idea that the prologue to John's Gospel is a hymn, arguing instead that it is a thoroughly Johannine composition. There have been other proposals regarding its possible liturgical use, however. For example, Aileen Guilding, in a neglected study, sees John 1 as "unmistakably a Christian meditation on the first chapter of Genesis."[94] Relying upon some of the arguments noted above regarding Semitic parallelism, Guilding sees the *logos* language as reflecting the language of Genesis and God's creative actions. She even attempts to place the prologue specifically within the Hebrew liturgical calendar. Cullmann is not so specific but sees the prologue as serving a sacramental purpose revolving around the opposition of "seeing and believing" (v. 14).[95] Cullmann wants to label this passage a "confession formula," one that has common features with others in the New Testament. John's Gospel, according to Cullmann, has a chief concern with connecting sacramental belief and practice in the early church with the historical life of Jesus, which is found from the start in the prologue, with its discussion of the incarnate *logos.*

It is difficult to establish a firm musical-liturgical context for the prologue to John's Gospel, but several of the comments above might indicate a way forward in the discussion. Perhaps the term "hymn" as it is usually conceived is too restrictive, if we think solely of a fixed-form composition

Akademie der Wissenschaften, 2007), 581-86; J. A. Smith, *Music in Ancient Judaism and Early Christianity* (Farnham, UK: Ashgate, 2011), 227.

94. A. Guilding, *The Fourth Gospel and Jewish Worship: A Study of the Relation of St. John's Gospel to the Ancient Jewish Lectionary System* (Oxford: Clarendon Press, 1960), 48.

95. Cullmann, *Early Christian Worship,* 40-42.

addressed directly to a god. We may know that music was a part of the early church, but we know very little about its formal characteristics or how it would have related to an early document such as John's Gospel. As Guilding and Cullmann make us aware, however, there is perhaps room for some flexibility without necessarily abandoning the concept of hymn altogether. One of the documents that Wendy Porter and I have edited for publication is a portion of John's Gospel containing John 7.[96] This document was given a form of ekphonetic notation so as to aid the reader in intoning it. It is entirely possible — although it certainly cannot be proved — that the prologue to John's Gospel need not have had its origins in a hymn in the strict sense of the term, but that it was used as part of the liturgy of the early church with the same purpose as a traditional hymn. That is, it could have been an intoned passage that enshrined the early church's attestation of the movement of the *logos* into human form, that is, Jesus, who was recognized as God come in the flesh. Since we know that early Christians used Scripture as the source of their reading and recitation, it is entirely possible, if not probable, that some of the earliest texts that they intoned in musical chant style, after the Psalms and similar texts, were forms of their earliest documents, such as the opening of John's Gospel.

5. Functional Criticism

Functional criticism grew out of frustration with the other forms of criticism described above.[97] Functional criticism recognizes that imprecise criteria have been used in previous discussion of the so-called hymnic passages in the New Testament, resulting in some plausibilities but many uncertainties.[98]

96. See S. E. Porter and W. J. Porter, *New Testament Greek Papyri and Parchments: New Editions* (MPER, n.s., 29; Berlin: Walter de Gruyter, 2008), no. 40. See also W. Porter, "Use of Ekphonetic Notation," 581-86; and S. E. Porter, "What Do We Know and How Do We Know It? Reconstructing Early Christianity from Its Manuscripts," in *Christian Origins and Greco-Roman Culture: Social and Literary Contexts for the New Testament* (ed. S. E. Porter and A. W. Pitts; TENT 10; Early Christianity in Its Hellenistic Context 2; Leiden: Brill, 2013), 41-70, esp. 66-69.

97. See Fowl, *Story of Christ*, esp. 19, 20, who notes, regarding passages in the Pauline letters, that "little attention has been devoted to understanding these passages within the context of the epistles in which they appear" and that even commentators have not "explored the role that each of these hymnic passages plays in the argument of their respective epistles."

98. Phillips utilizes some elements of a functional approach but attempts too much by seeking to integrate a variety of possibly contradictory critical stances into a single sequen-

These results have often come about because of a concentration on what might be considered peripheral issues, such as forms or sources. A related question is the problem of how to weigh various Greek and Jewish factors, in a milieu in which separating the two is virtually impossible, and perhaps not even desirable. As a result, locating influence and sources is much more complex than simply noting parallels, which can be accounted for along several different lines, without necessarily establishing influence. At the end of the day, it might well be argued, there remains the question of the significance of such a discussion. One must wonder what has been proved, if it can be shown that a particular form or a particular source has been used, especially when such estimations sometimes involve highly complex and highly questionable reconstructions (note the deleting or reconfiguring of lines and wording in the form-critical proposals noted above). Nevertheless, in several passages often cited as hymns in the New Testament, including the prologue to John's Gospel according to a number of scholars, there are hymnic or poetic features to be noted. One of the difficulties with such features, however, is that they clearly do not point in the direction of either Jewish or Greek hymnology, at least as traditionally conceived, so it is difficult to establish a norm against which to judge these stylistic features.

As a result, a functional approach to such material has been developed. Such an approach revolves not around the form, source, or other origin of a passage, but around the important factor of how the material is used by the author in his argument. Stephen Fowl's investigation of the hymnic passages in Paul is one of the best functional approaches to the material that is currently available. He agrees that the passages he is examining are hymnic in the limited sense of their being poetic accounts of the nature and/or activity of a divine figure already held in esteem by the audience to which the book is addressed. However, this itself is a narrower view of function in this context than I believe is necessary. Fowl performs his functional analysis in relation to how the passages present stories about Christ to use them for ethical, rather than christological, purposes. I do not believe that functional criticism needs to focus on Christology (or not) or ethics. Functional criticism can serve its purpose if it simply focuses upon textual function. In that regard, functional criticism has a number of obvious similarities with literary criticism and forms of rhetorical criticism. These relations cannot be explored here, except to say that, as Frank Kermode

---

tial reading. The result seems to be more of a composite of interesting and potentially useful insights than it is a single or even functional critical stance. See Phillips, *Prologue*, 143-220.

has shown,[99] literary texts, ancient and modern, must be concerned with fundamental structures. Such structures shape an unfolding argument or story and merit further attention.[100]

Although functional criticism as a criticism per se is of recent articulation, there have been a number of what still might be called (even if they do not style themselves in this way) functional analyses of the prologue to John's Gospel. In one sense, every commentator has at least an ostensible claim to being a functional critic, since the passage is (purportedly) treated within the context of the developing argument of the book. In principle, this terminology might be correct, but in fact many commentators lose sight of the overall argument in their attention to individual details, especially if and as they proceed verse by verse rather than movement by movement. In this discussion, I cite several representative examples of criticism that moves beyond this basic stance to arrive at what might truly be called functional criticism.

The first functional-critical analysis of John's prologue that I examine was proposed by Bernard, whom I noted above for his outline of the passage in form-critical terms. His argument is that the "hymn" provides the philosophical rationale of the main thesis of John's Gospel.[101] The hymn begins with proclamation of the Word as preexistent and divine. Then Old Testament notions of the Word as creative, life-giving, and light-giving (John 1:3-5) are introduced. The whole universe, including humanity (vv. 10-11), is unconscious of God's omnipresent energy, but God became incarnate as the abiding and visible exhibition of the divine glory in the form of the Son, who exhibits the Father (v. 14; Thompson goes even further and sees v. 14 as the theme of the entire Gospel).[102] The Word as incarnate reveals the invisible God (v. 18), which the rest of the Gospel then elaborates. The strength of such a functional analysis as presented by Bernard depends upon the merit given to its important philosophical background. As of now, this particular theory has received renewed support from Marianne Meye Thompson's analysis, although it must be said that the history of discussion is one of changing fortunes for background theories. Nevertheless, perhaps through this type of functional criticism it is again appropriate to ask questions re-

99. F. Kermode, "St. John as Poet," *JSNT* 28 (1986): 3-16.

100. See S. E. Porter, "Literary Approaches to the New Testament: From Formalism to Deconstruction and Back," in *Approaches to New Testament Study* (ed. S. E. Porter and D. Tombs; JSNTSup 120; Sheffield: JSOT Press, 1995), 77-128.

101. Bernard, *John,* esp. 1:cxlv.

102. M. M. Thompson, *The Humanity of Jesus in the Fourth Gospel* (Philadelphia: Fortress Press, 1988), 50-51.

garding background, rather than opting for only one approach or one that excludes consideration of background issues.

Whereas Bernard tries to link the prologue to wider philosophical discussion, especially Old Testament imagery and thought, a number of scholars see the prologue as serving as some type of formal introduction to the ideas or themes of the rest of the Gospel. For example, Beasley-Murray sees the prologue of John's Gospel as providing "a directive to the reader how the entire Gospel should be read and understood."[103] Carson states it this way: "The Prologue is a foyer to the rest of the Fourth Gospel . . . simultaneously drawing the reader in and introducing the main themes."[104] A number of scholars use the term "overture" to describe the function of the prologue. Bultmann himself used this language,[105] followed apparently by such scholars as Sanders and Mastin, who compare the prologue to the overture of a Wagner opera.[106] Steven Smalley, however, is content with the term "prologue," using it with reference to an unfolding drama.[107] I am not sure that the analogy of the overture is entirely appropriate, since not every theme of an opera is always introduced in the overture (this is in fact limited even in operas, Wagner being one of the few to do so).[108] In any event, all of these commentators and scholars are attempting to see the prologue as integral to what the Gospel presents, even if some of the language (e.g., the use of *logos;* but cf. ch. 2 above) is unique to the prologue. Carson sees the prologue as opening with a riveting account that invites readers to read the story for themselves, and as using terminology and categories that would have appeal to Jews, Christians, pagans, Hellenists, and Easterners alike. Carson then goes on to note the themes of the prologue that are mentioned later in the Gospel. These include preexistence (John 1:1-2; 17:5), "in him was life" (1:4; 5:26), the life is the light of the world (1:4, 9; 8:12), the light is rejected by darkness (1:5; 3:19), the light is not quenched by dark-

---

103. Beasley-Murray, *John,* 5, quoting H. Thyen, "Aus der Literatur zum Johannesevangelium," *TR* 39 (1975): 53-69, 222-52, here 223. Cf. Stibbe, *John,* 24.

104. Carson, *John,* 111. Cf. D. Tovey, *Narrative Art and Act in the Fourth Gospel* (JSNTSup 151; Sheffield: Sheffield Academic Press, 1997), 99.

105. Bultmann, *John,* 13, but who also states that "it is not necessary for anything to follow."

106. Sanders and Mastin, *John,* 67. Cf. R. G. Maccini, *Her Testimony Is True: Women as Witnesses according to John* (JSNTSup 125; Sheffield: JSOT Press, 1996), 38, who seems to get his metaphors confused, when he says that he thinks the term "overture" fits a drama better.

107. S. Smalley, *John — Evangelist and Interpreter* (Exeter: Paternoster, 1978), 92.

108. See J. Warrack and E. West, "Overture," in *The Oxford Dictionary of Opera* (Oxford: Oxford University Press, 1992), 531-32, where it is noted that this is not altogether true of Wagner.

ness (1:5; 12:35), the light is coming into the world (1:9; 8:12), Christ was not received by his own (1:11; 4:44), the world did not believe (1:11; 12:41; 16:8-11), being born of God and not of flesh (1:13; 3:6; 8:41-42), glory was manifested (1:14; 2:11; 12:41), there is the one and only Son (1:14, 18; 3:16), truth is in Jesus Christ (1:17; 14:6), the only begotten is given in incarnation and death (1:18; 3:16), and no one has seen God except the one from God (1:18; 6:46).[109] For Carson, the declaration of the purpose of the Gospel in 20:30-31 is connected to 1:14 through the reality of the incarnation of the *logos* in humanity. Warren Carter has performed a similar analysis. He states, "While more recent scholarship has observed similarities of style, vocabulary and content between Prologue and Gospel, it has not pressed the questions considered here — the Prologue's function and contribution in relation to (1) the document of which it is a part, and (2) the situation which that document addressed and by which it was shaped."[110] Carter selects themes less specific than ones Carson chooses, but ones that are interrelated in the Gospel: "(1) the origin and destiny of Jesus the *logos*, (2) Jesus' role as the revealer, (3) responses to Jesus, and (4) the relationship of Jesus the *logos* to other figures."[111] Thus, Carter posits that the Gospel reinforces Christology in a context of competing figures. Again, we see a possible line of continuity between this form of criticism and some of the traditional criticisms, as thematic issues are used as a means of discussing situation.

A third proposal regarding the function of the prologue is that it serves as the prologue to a source called "the book of signs." This source-critical analysis was first posed in detailed form by Bultmann and has since been developed by a number of scholars. The book of signs is one of the two major conceptual sources of John's Gospel, the first being the book of signs in John 1–12, and the second the discourse source in John 13–21, although Bultmann thought there may have been a separate passion source as well, and perhaps some Synoptic traditions.[112] Without necessarily accepting the

---

109. Carson, *John*, 111, based upon J. A. T. Robinson, "The Relation of the Prologue to the Gospel of St. John," *NTS* 9 (1963): 120-29; repr. in Robinson, *Twelve More New Testament Studies* (London: SCM Press, 1984), 65-76, here 68.

110. W. Carter, "The Prologue and John's Gospel: Function, Symbol, and the Definitive Word," *JSNT* 39 (1990): 35-58, here 37; and Carter, *John: Storyteller, Interpreter, Evangelist* (Peabody, MA: Hendrickson, 2006), 51-53. Cf. D. Deeks, "The Structure of the Fourth Gospel" (1968), in *The Gospel of John as Literature: An Anthology of Twentieth-Century Perspectives* (ed. M. W. G. Stibbe; NTTS 17; Leiden: Brill, 1993), 77-101.

111. Carter, "Prologue," 37.

112. See Bultmann, *John*, 6-7. His theory has been picked up and developed mostly by

source-critical hypothesis in its entirety, Gary Burge has used it as a constructive framework for discussing the structure of John's Gospel and the place of the prologue in relation to it. According to Burge's analysis,[113] the book of signs in John 1–12 is introduced by the prologue in 1:1-18, followed by four further sections:

> Jesus and the Baptist (1:19-51);
> Jesus and the Jewish institutions (2:1–4:54), in which Jesus replaces each one, such as purification vessels at Cana (1:1-12), the temple in Jerusalem (2:13-25), a rabbi in Jerusalem (3:1-21), and a sacred well in Samaria (4:1-42);
> Jesus and the Jewish festivals (5:1–10:42), including Sabbath (5:1-47), Passover (6:1-71), Tabernacles (festival of water and light; 7:1-52), and Dedication (Hanukkah; 10:1-39); and
> foreshadowings of Jesus' death and resurrection (11:1–12:50), including Lazarus on death and life (11:1-57) and Jesus, anointed for death, entering Jerusalem to die (12:1-50).

The Gospel then moves to what Burge calls "the book of glory" in chs. 13–21. Burge's analysis has the strength of recognizing some of the findings of source criticism regarding John's Gospel, by attempting to integrate the prologue into that scheme. Rather than arguing that the prologue controls the entire Gospel, he sees it functioning in relation to one of the two major sources. Of course, in the light of recent criticism of such source theories, Burge's theory may suffer the same loss of credibility.

In some ways, the functional approach utilizes and incorporates the findings of other forms of criticism in its analysis. This is most obvious in the third view above, in which the source-critical findings regarding the book of signs and the book of glory provide the foundation for the functional analysis of the prologue. In another distinct sense, however, the functional approach has left behind the findings of other forms of criticism as unnecessary to the

---

R. Fortna (*The Gospel of Signs* and *The Fourth Gospel and Its Predecessor: From Narrative Source to Present Gospel* [Philadelphia: Fortress Press, 1988]), who combines the discourse and passion source into a single source. Many have questioned aspects of this analysis, if not the entire enterprise. For summaries, see Smalley, *John*, 103-13; Painter, *John*, 80-93.

113. See G. M. Burge, *Interpreting the Gospel of John* (Grand Rapids: Baker, 1992), 76-79. Cf. U. C. von Wahlde, *The Earliest Version of John's Gospel: Recovering the Gospel of Signs* (Wilmington, DE: Michael Glazier, 1989), and vol. 1 of his recent three-volume commentary *The Gospel and Letters of John* (ECC; Grand Rapids: Eerdmans, 2010).

interpretive task. It is as if the result is a recognition that these other forms of criticism, even though they may have been enlightening on various points, have failed to prove their cases convincingly, and so, rather than continue the same tired quest, one abandons it and turns to another form of criticism, functional criticism. The results of much of this functional criticism have many similarities to other forms of criticism much in vogue in current interpretation, including types of literary and rhetorical criticism, as noted above. A major contribution of functional criticism is its emphasis, at least in its treatment of the Johannine prologue, upon the character of Jesus. This is seen in both how Jesus is described within the prologue and how ideas introduced in the prologue are seen to be developed further within the rest of the Gospel. Other forms of criticism, as observed above, tend to concentrate simply upon the so-called hymnic passage itself in their attempts to define the structure, background, or uses of the particular passage. Functional criticism seems to require that one move beyond the prologue itself. Some of what it means to be a functional account of the passage is to serve as a link between the prologue and the rest of the Gospel, in an attempt to see the functional consequences, even the paradigmatic implications, of the incarnate Jesus Christ.

6. Conclusion

In the past, critical methods have gone in and out of fashion, with the tendency being to focus upon and use one method at a time. One of the major findings of the current investigation of John 1:1-18, the prologue to John's Gospel, is that there has been much misunderstanding of these critical perspectives, resulting in some confusion over how they can and should be used. To say, for example, that a passage reflects a particular form, reflects a theological perspective similar to that of other thought of the time, or functions in a particular way can constitute a legitimate conclusion, but such a finding does not mean that the author is not also creatively employing the passage for his own purposes. As a result, in relation to John 1:1-18, I believe that it is not contradictory to say that this passage can be analyzed with profit from each perspective in order to see that its balanced formal features, which at least in part reflect the theological framework of the Hellenistic Judaism of the time (whether emphasis is placed more on the Greek or Jewish side, if such a distinction is even appropriate), create an introduction to the Gospel that, in its lofty tone, sets the tenor for the rest of the work, especially as that focuses upon the ministry of Jesus Christ.

CHAPTER 5

Jesus and the "I Am" Sayings in John's Gospel

1. Introduction

An underdeveloped feature in determining the christological portrait of Jesus in John's Gospel is the role that the "I am" sayings play (ἐγώ εἰμι or variants).[1] Much important work has discussed the origin and background of the

---

1. I do not mean that there has been a lack of studies of the "I am" statements. There have been many. They just have not all been as productive as they might have been. As examples of such studies, whether freestanding or as part of larger wholes, see E. Schweizer, *Ego Eimi: Die religionsgeschichtliche Herkunft und theologische Bedeutung der johanneischen Bildreden, zugleich ein Beitrag zur Quellenfrage des vierten Evangeliums* (FRLANT 56; Göttingen: Vandenhoeck & Ruprecht, 1939); R. Bultmann, *The Gospel of John: A Commentary* (trans. G. R. Beasley-Murray et al.; Philadelphia: Westminster, 1971 [1941]), 225-26; D. Daube, "The I Am of the Messianic Presence," in his *The New Testament and Rabbinic Judaism* (London: Athlone, 1956), 325-29; H. Zimmermann, "Das absolute 'ego eimi' als die neutestamentliche Offenbarungs-formel," *BZ* 4 (1960): 54-69, 266-76; R. E. Brown, "Ego Eimi — 'I Am,'" in his *The Gospel according to John* (2 vols.; AB 29, 29A; Garden City, NY: Doubleday, 1966-70), 1:533-38; W. Manson, "The *Ego Eimi* of the Messianic Presence in the New Testament," in his *Jesus and the Christian* (London: James Clark, 1967), 174-83; R. Schnackenburg, *The Gospel according to St. John* (trans. K. Smyth et al.; 3 vols.; London: Burns & Oates, 1968-82), 2:79-89; P. B. Harner, *The 'I Am' of the Fourth Gospel* (Philadelphia: Fortress Press, 1970); C. K. Barrett, *The Gospel according to St. John* (2nd ed.; Philadelphia: Westminster, 1978), 291-93; L. Morris, "The 'I Am' Sayings," in his *Jesus Is the Christ: Studies in the Theology of John* (Grand Rapids: Eerdmans, 1989), 107-25; G. M. Burge, "'I Am' Sayings," in *Dictionary of Jesus and the Gospels* (ed. J. B. Green, S. McKnight, and I. H. Marshall; Downers Grove, IL: InterVarsity Press, 1992), 354-56 (for bibliography); D. M. Ball, *"I Am" in John's Gospel: Literary Function, Background, and Theological Implications* (JSNTSup 124; Sheffield: Sheffield Academic Press, 1996); C. H. Williams, *I Am He: The Meaning and Interpretation of 'Anî Hû' in Jewish and*

"I am" sayings,[2] and several important studies have examined the meaning of these sayings individually in the Johannine context.[3] Such discussions often rely upon a posited distinction between the so-called predicate (e.g., "I am the light of the world") and nonpredicate (e.g., "I am") uses of the construction.[4] However, there has been relatively little significant work on how the author uses the "I am" sayings to shape the messianic christological disclosure of Jesus in the Gospel.[5] In this chapter, I first survey recent work on the "I am" sayings. This review will show that, whereas there has been much useful discussion,[6] some of the most important aspects of this particular linguistic structure have yet to be fully appreciated. Then I survey several proposals regarding the structure and organization of John's Gospel. Once these have been assessed, I demonstrate that the "I am" sayings are a major

---

Early Christian Literature (WUNT 2.113; Tübingen: Mohr Siebeck, 2000), esp. 255-303; Williams, "'I Am' or 'I Am He'? Self-Declaratory Pronouncements in the Fourth Gospel and Rabbinic Tradition," in *Jesus in Johannine Tradition* (ed. R. T. Fortna and T. Thatcher; Louisville, KY: Westminster John Knox, 2001), 343-52 (which summarizes the results of her monograph); Williams, "'I Am' Sayings," in *Dictionary of Jesus and the Gospels* (ed. J. B. Green, J. K. Brown, and N. Perrin; 2nd ed.; Downers Grove, IL: InterVarsity Press, 2013), 396-99; cf. G. Braumann and H.-G. Link, "I Am," in *New International Dictionary of New Testament Theology* (ed. C. Brown; 3 vols.; Grand Rapids: Zondervan, 1975), 2:278-83; F. Büchsel, "εἰμί, ὁ ὤν," *TDNT* 2 (1964): 398-400. For a brief history of earlier research, see R. Kysar, *The Fourth Evangelist and His Gospel: An Examination of Contemporary Scholarship* (Minneapolis: Augsburg, 1975), 119-22.

2. E.g., C. H. Dodd, *The Interpretation of the Fourth Gospel* (Cambridge: Cambridge University Press, 1953), 93-96, 349-50; Williams, *I Am He,* who examines the Hebrew Bible, ancient versions, Targumim, and rabbinic writings.

3. E.g., Williams, *I Am He,* 257-99; R. Bauckham, "Monotheism and Christology in the Gospel of John," in his *The Testimony of the Beloved Disciple: Narrative, History, and Theology in the Gospel of John* (Grand Rapids: Baker, 2007), 243-50.

4. The nonpredicate use is sometimes called an "absolute" use. Burge, following others, further differentiates between predicate uses that are explicit and predicate uses with an uncertain (i.e., apparently implicit) predicate ("'I Am' Sayings," 354-55). See also Williams, "'I Am,'" 343, but who disputes the implicit predicate use; cf. also Williams, *I Am He,* 299-303; Williams, "'I Am' Sayings," 398-99.

5. For a negative response to the christological interpretations, see K. L. McKay, "'I Am' in John's Gospel," *ExpTim* 107 (1996): 302-3.

6. In some ways I am very sympathetic to what Catrin Williams is trying to do in her *I Am He,* as she arrives at a distinctly theological interpretation of the "I am" sayings. However, I believe that she relies far too heavily upon the supposed background in a variety of sources and uses than is necessary (and uses virtually all Jewish sources), and whereas she does interpret many of the same passages, she does not see the "I am" sayings as a structuring device for the Gospel in the same way that I do.

JOHN, HIS GOSPEL, AND JESUS

means by which the author structures an expansive messianic-christological revelation of who Jesus is in the Gospel itself.

2. The Meaning of the "I Am" Sayings in John's Gospel

Johannine studies as a (sub)discipline have generally reflected the same alternation of emphasis between Jewish and Hellenistic background as has been characteristic of other areas of New Testament studies. This cyclic repetition does the discipline a grave disservice, if for no other reason than that it creates the impression that linear progress is being made, yet it amounts to nothing more than a Hegelian dialectic.[7] We are right now in a period of emphasis upon the Jewish background of the New Testament, which has an impact upon interpretation of many New Testament passages, especially several in the Gospels and in John's Gospel in particular. Without attempting to offer a full-scale analysis of the data, I wish here to survey quickly the last hundred years of scholarly discussion concerning John's "I am" sayings in an attempt to bring some clarity to the current discussion. In many ways, David Ball's study provides the fullest and clearest account, and so I use his study as a starting point for the discussion below.[8] Nevertheless, his study has a number of limitations, not least that he wishes to see all uses of the "I am" sayings as Jewish in background (whereas I read some of the data and the discussion differently).[9] In addition, he confines himself only to instances in which the "I am" saying is on the lips of Jesus, thereby excluding other instances of importance (see below). This is a serious shortcoming, in that it fails to recognize a number of important uses of Johannine "I am." Finally, Ball does not deal with what he calls "related" phrases, which, as I will argue below, should be treated together with the more formulaic instances.[10]

---

7. I am referring to the idea that there is a posited thesis (e.g., Jewish background), then a reactive antithesis (e.g., Hellenistic background), which results in a supposed synthesis (e.g., some kind of modified Jewish background involving some Hellenistic elements), before beginning the process again.

8. Ball, "I Am." More recent works are of course to be added to his list, including the important work by Williams, I Am He, which fits conveniently within the Jewish background discussion and provides an excellent survey of previous discussion in this area, as well as discussion of the evidence. She extends the usual discussion to the Targumim and rabbinic writings.

9. Ball, "I Am," 20.

10. Ball, "I Am," 21-22.

a. Greco-Roman Background

Scholarly discussion of the "I am" sayings in John's Gospel has been colored by the fact that, early in the last century, a number of scholars appealed to later sources that cannot rightly be treated as part of the background to the Johannine use of the construction. These later sources included the Mandaean documents, made popular in discussion through the unbelievably large (and even continuing) influence of Rudolf Bultmann, and the gnostic sources, which, though interesting, are clearly later and derivative.[11]

More important are some parallels from the inscriptional materials that were made widely available by Adolf Deissmann in his *Light from the Ancient East*.[12] The examples of predicate structure in Isis texts are minimized by Ball, since Deissmann himself shows similarities in usage to that of the Septuagint.[13] I am not sure that it is so easy to dismiss these examples, however, when they are found in extrabiblical religious texts that predate the New Testament. It may well reflect the influence of Judaism on other religions, but it may also help to explain why the Septuagint renders particular linguistic structures as it does. By the late first century B.C., the religious conventions of Judaism were intermixed with those of other religions. In any case, an example of the absolute use of "I am" has apparently not been found in nonbiblical literature.

b. Jewish Background

Despite the use of the predicate structure in extrabiblical texts, most scholars look to the Old Testament and to the expression *ani hu* as the interpretive

---

11. For a discussion of attempts to relate John's Gospel to Mandaean or gnostic writings, see E. M. Yamauchi, "Jewish Gnosticism? The Prologue of John, Mandaean Parallels, and the Trimorphic Protennoia," in *Studies in Gnosticism and Hellenistic Religions: Presented to Gilles Quispel on the Occasion of His Sixty-Fifth Birthday* (ed. R. van den Broek and M. J. Vermaseren; EPRO 91; Leiden: Brill, 1981), 467-97. The article where Bultmann first laid out his theory is "Die Bedeutung der neuerschlossenen mandäischen und manichäischen Quellen für das Verständnis des Johannesevangeliums," *ZNW* 24 (1925): 100-146.

12. A. Deissmann, *Light from the Ancient East* (trans. L. R. M. Strachan; 4th ed.; London: Hodder & Stoughton, 1927), 138-42, with numerous examples, including an Isis inscription cited by Diodorus Siculus 1.27, an Isis inscription from Ios, and a part of the London magical papyrus 46.145ff.

13. Deissmann is not referred to by Williams, if her index or bibliography is to be believed.

framework for the use of "I am" in John's Gospel. This Hebrew usage is particularly prominent in so-called Deutero-Isaiah and in some of the Wisdom literature, and it seems to be used in some contexts where the Hebrew "I am YHWH" is rendered by "I am" in the Septuagint. Of the 180 or so instances of "I am" occurring in the Septuagint, the vast majority are predicate constructions, especially the statement "I am the Lord." The absolute usage occurs relatively few times compared to the predicate construction. Although many previous discussions of the "I am" constructions have found similarities between the Old Testament and Johannine uses of the predicate construction,[14] the fact that this construction is also paralleled in some Greco-Roman religious texts means that the Septuagint cannot be treated as determinative for its background.

c. Other Possible Backgrounds

A number of scholars have proposed other possible backgrounds for the development and meaning of the "I am" constructions in John's Gospel. These include attention to the Synoptic usage, usage in parousia passages, and a variety of other instances.[15] Most of these explanations are attempts to find a comprehensive set of categories that links usage in John with other New Testament usage, rather than convincingly explaining the origin of the construction.

d. Reconsiderations and Reformulations

As Ball points out, some scholars opt for an exclusive background in order to explain the Johannine "I am" usage. Ball and Williams wish to find the Old Testament and Jewish usage as determinative.[16] As I have briefly pointed out

---

14. Perhaps most prominently in Williams, *I Am He,* 15-54; Bauckham, "Monotheism and Christology," 243-50.

15. See, e.g., P. N. Anderson, "The Origin and Development of the Johannine *Ego Eimi* Sayings in Cognitive-Critical Perspective," *JSHJ* 9 (2011): 139-206. Not all are convinced, as in P. Foster, "Memory, Orality, and the Fourth Gospel: Three Dead-Ends in Historical Jesus Research," *JSHJ* 10 (2012): 191-227, esp. 212-25. For a critique of Foster, see S. E. Porter and H. T. Ong, "Memory, Orality, and the Fourth Gospel: A Response to Paul Foster with Further Comments for Future Discussion," *JSHJ* 12 (2014): 143-64.

16. Ball, *"I Am,"* 258; Williams, *I Am He,* 304.

above, however, such an exclusive attempt at an explanation leaves much unexplained. It is preferable at this point to recognize that the world out of which John's Gospel emerged was complex, in which the Greco-Roman milieu provided the framework for a number of religious cults to flourish. Their flourishing brought them into inevitable contact, so that at least their conceptual worlds and forms of expression had a possible influence on each other.

3. The Structure of John's Gospel

Before returning to the "I am" sayings in John's Gospel, I wish to discuss the overall structure of the Gospel. I then bring these two together in an explanation of the use of the "I am" sayings as a christological structuring device used by John. A number of different organizing principles have been suggested for this Gospel. Here, I am not concerned with the kinds of conceptual and theological outlines that are so often found in commentaries, but with structural outlines that rely upon noting particular textual features. I consider two such plans here.

a. Signs and Passion

A number of scholars have found a signs source lying behind the Gospel of John, although the dimensions and shape of this signs source are debated.[17] C. H. Dodd originally proposed that the Gospel consists of three distinct parts: the Proem (John 1), the Book of Signs (John 2–12), and the Book of the Passion (John 13–20/21).[18] His scheme has been modified a number of times, with some scholars perceiving the signs source to include John 2–11,

---

17. E.g., R. Fortna, *The Gospel of Signs: A Reconstruction of the Narrative Source Underlying the Fourth Gospel* (SNTSMS 11; Cambridge: Cambridge University Press, 1970); Fortna, *The Fourth Gospel and Its Predecessor: From Narrative Source to Present Gospel* (Philadelphia: Fortress Press, 1988); U. C. von Wahlde, *The Earliest Version of John's Gospel: Recovering the Gospel of Signs* (Wilmington, DE: Michael Glazier, 1989). For an evaluation of the signs-source hypothesis, see F. Neirynck, "The Signs Source in the Fourth Gospel: A Critique of the Hypothesis," in his *Evangelica II, 1982-1991: Collected Essays* (ed. F. Van Segbroeck; BETL 99; Leuven: Peeters, 1991), 651-78.

18. C. H. Dodd, *Interpretation of the Fourth Gospel* (Cambridge: Cambridge University Press, 1953), 289 and throughout.

with ch. 12 serving as a transition to the passion account.[19] Craig Evans's discussion of the quotation formulas reinforces this outline, in that it observes a shift in quotation formula that occurs in 12:38, from "as it is written" to "so that it might be fulfilled."[20] This theory has great staying power, and its strength lies in its link to the form-critical agenda. This is also its major weakness, however, since there are a number of competing theories on the composition and shape of the signs source. The result is that the theory looks more like a source theory that attaches other parts to it, something reminiscent of Bultmann's proposal regarding three sources (sayings, signs, passion).[21]

b. Signs, Discourses, and "I Am"

Stephen Smalley has proposed that the Gospel is organized around a combination of signs, discourses, and "I am" sayings.[22] In Smalley's analysis, there are seven signs, each linked to a discourse, and correlated with an "I am" saying. The seven "I am" sayings share the emphasis on the theme of life.[23] Smalley is to be commended for drawing the "I am" sayings into the analysis, but the difficulties with his account are several. One is that the "I am" sayings themselves within the Gospel are separated from their respective signs and discourses, and in fact in Smalley's analysis do not occur in the order in which they are presented in the Gospel itself. Furthermore, even the discourses do not necessarily follow their respective signs (water into wine in John 2 with new life in John 3; official's son in John 4 with water of life in ch. 4; sick man in John 5 with the life-giving son in John 6; feeding the five thousand in John 6 with bread of life in ch. 6 and spirit of life in ch. 7; blind man in John 9 with light of life in John 8; Lazarus raised in John 11 with the life-giving shepherd in John 10; and catch of fish in John 21 with life as a disciple in John 14-16). A final difficulty is that Smalley confines himself to the predicate uses

---

19. E.g., R. Fortna, "Jesus Tradition in the Signs Gospel," in *Jesus in Johannine Tradition* (ed. R. Fortna and T. Thatcher; Louisville, KY: Westminster John Knox, 2001), 199.

20. C. A. Evans, "On the Quotation Formulas in the Fourth Gospel," *BZ*, n.s., 1 (1982): 79-83. See ch. 8 of this volume, where I use Evans's proposal with regard to the Passover theme in John's Gospel.

21. Bultmann, *John*.

22. Smalley's proposal has many similarities to Bultmann's, already noted above.

23. S. S. Smalley, *John: Evangelist and Interpreter* (Exeter: Paternoster, 1983), 86-92.

only (15:1; 14:6; 10:7; 6:35; 8:12; 11:25 and 10:11), disregarding the absolute or other uses.

It is clear that, although a consistent tradition has found a signs source in the Gospel, and even though this source has been used in conjunction with the "I am" sayings to describe the structure of the Gospel, no single analytical plan proves entirely convincing.

4. The "I Am" Sayings in John's Gospel as Structuring Johannine Christology

In this section, I examine the "I am" sayings in the Gospel of John and demonstrate that their use — predominantly, though not only, by Jesus — both reveals and affirms the Christology of the book, that is, the author's view of who Jesus is. This Christology is essentially that Jesus is the Messiah, understood in an expansive way as God's (the Father's) preexistent emissary on earth.[24] He is then further described using a variety of christological language, which informs readers about who this Messiah is and where he is from and going.

There are thirty-five instances of "I am" sayings in John's Gospel. They have been categorized according to a number of different schemes. One of the most common is the predicate vs. predicateless, or nonpredicate, distinction. This is a basic formal distinction, but it has difficulty describing such usage as in those instances with prepositional phrases (e.g., John 8:23, "I am not from this world"). I would argue that there are more categories of usage than simply the two, although the attempt to be formally rigorous is to be commended and followed so far as possible. Another scheme is the pictorial vs. nonpictorial pattern.[25] This scheme, the most recent to be proposed, is less useful than the one above, for a number of reasons. One of its limitations is that the categories are not formally based, a requirement when one is dealing with a linguistic pattern such as the "I am" statements. Another difficulty

---

24. For a recent treatment of some similar ideas (received too late for more detailed consideration), see A. J. Akala, *The Son-Father Relationship and Christological Symbolism in the Gospel of John* (LNTS 505; London: Bloomsbury, 2014).

25. On pictorial patterns, see R. A. Culpepper, *Anatomy of the Fourth Gospel: A Study in Literary Design* (Philadelphia: Fortress Press, 1983); R. Zimmermann, "Imagery in John: Opening Up Paths into the Tangled Thicket of John's Figurative World," in *Imagery in the Gospel of John: Terms, Forms, Themes, and Theology of Johannine Figurative Language* (ed. J. Frey, J. van der Watt, and R. Zimmermann; WUNT 200; Tübingen: Mohr Siebeck, 2006), 5-6.

is that it is difficult to draw firm boundaries between the two categories of pictorial and nonpictorial, since imagistic language is associated with most if not all examples of the use of "I am." I would contend that a formally based classification scheme is warranted, and that the instances fall into three definable categories. These categories are the following:

1. absolute usage, in which the "I am" construction stands on its own, as a class without adjuncts, modifiers, or adverbial modification (thus, "I am");
2. locative usage, in which the "I am" construction has adjunctive attachments, or is part of an adverbial/locative structure (thus, "I am not from this world"); and
3. predicate usage, in which the "I am" construction is part of a predicate structure with a predicate complement (thus, "I am the light of the world").

To anticipate my conclusions: absolute constructions are used in their Johannine context to affirm boldly that Jesus is the Messiah (the Christ), made especially clear in contrast to John the Baptist, who affirms equally boldly that he is not the Christ. Predicate constructions are used to elucidate the messianic Christology by appealing to examples (often vividly pictorial) that enlighten the notion of a messianic figure. Locative constructions are used to draw distinctions in place between God and humanity, such that the Messiah is the one who mediates between these two spheres, the divine and the human.[26]

My analysis indicates that, within John's Gospel, the essential revelation of who Jesus is occurs by means of Jesus' own utterances of the absolute usage in three significant groupings in the Gospel (John 4:26 and 6:20; 8:24, 28, 58; and 18:5, 6, 8). The stage is set for these revelatory instances by two instances of the predicate construction uttered by John the Baptist in anticipation of Jesus' own self-revelation (1:20; 3:28). Interspersed between the major scenes of revelation are scenes of development and specification using both predicate (6:35, 41, 48, 51; 8:12, 18; 10:7, 9, 11, 14; 11:25; 14:16; 15:1, 5) and locative (7:34, 36; 8:23; 12:26; 14:3; 17:14, 16, 24) constructions. The "I am" phrasing is used to make a very clear and consistent christological presentation throughout the Gospel, namely, that Jesus is indeed the Christ,

---

26. I thus reject the so-called implicit predicate use as a matter of Greek grammar, though in some instances I see it as a necessary convention of English translation.

and much more.[27] In the rest of this chapter I examine the aforementioned passages in greater detail.

a. John the Baptist and the Messiah: John 1:20; 3:28

The first two occurrences of the "I am" saying in John's Gospel are instances of the predicate usage. These two occurrences are sometimes not included in discussion of the Johannine "I am" language because neither appears on the lips of Jesus.[28] Both are recorded as being uttered by John the Baptist. However, I consider it important to include both of these instances in an analysis of the Johannine use of the "I am" saying for the simple reason that they are virtually identical to statements used elsewhere, though in different places in the Gospel and not used by Jesus. However, in the light of the role of John the Baptist in announcing the coming of Jesus, it is not surprising to find such usage, and it demands examination.

The first occurrence is in the opening scene after the prologue (John 1:1-18). John 1:19 begins by saying, "This is the testimony of John, when the Jews sent to him from Jerusalem priests and Levites so that they might ask him, 'Who are you?'" The answer is then introduced using highly emphatic and repetitious word order (translated literalistically to make the point): "He both confessed and he did not deny and he confessed that 'I am not the

---

27. There are many works on Christology, including John's Christology. My attempt here is not to define John's Christology according to fixed categories but to see how the "I am" statements are used to create an unfolding Christology throughout the narrative, starting with John the Baptist's initial "I am" statement, enfolding the prologue, and pro-ceeding until the brink of Jesus' death. Some works that examine the ways these depictions of Jesus in John's Gospel are made and understood include B. F. Westcott, *The Revelation of the Father: Short Lectures on the Titles of the Lord in the Gospel of St. John* (London: Mac-millan, 1884); E. M. Sidebottom, *The Christ of the Fourth Gospel in the Light of First-Century Thought* (London: SPCK, 1961); V. Taylor, *The Names of Jesus* (London: Macmillan, 1962); R. N. Longenecker, *The Christology of Early Jewish Christianity* (SBT, 2nd ser., 17; London: SCM Press, 1970); L. W. Hurtado, *Lord Jesus Christ: Devotion to Jesus in Earliest Christianity* (Grand Rapids: Eerdmans, 2007), 349-407; R. Bauckham, "Jewish Messianism according to the Gospel of John," in his *The Testimony of the Beloved Disciple: Narrative, History, and Theology in the Gospel of John* (Grand Rapids: Baker, 2007), 207-38; and M. F. Bird, *Jesus Is the Christ: The Messianic Testimony of the Gospels* (Downers Grove, IL: InterVarsity Press, 2012), 97-140 and notes (whereas I agree with his overall argument, I disagree with several specifics, such as Bird's approach to John 20:30-31).

28. E.g., Williams, *I Am He*, who begins with the Samaritan woman in John 4.

Christ'" (1:20).[29] Apart from the use of the compound titular name Jesus Christ in 1:17, this is the first mention of the Christ (the Messiah) in John's Gospel. Furthermore, John's emphatic declaration comes not in response to a direct question but in response to the more general question of his own identity. He emphatically states that he is not the Christ. This structured question and response indicates several important features of this narrative opening. One feature is the implication that there was a general question in the air of who the Messiah was,[30] and John is made to indicate right from the outset that, lest there be any confusion, he is not the one. Another implication is that the Gospel itself wants to position itself as being concerned with determining who the Christ is. As already noted, the first use of Jesus' name in John's Gospel is in 1:17, where Jesus and Christ are linked together. This is the first introduction of Jesus, and it occurs in climactic fashion at the end of the prologue. The prologue begins with its *logos*-centered emphasis and moves to John and then to the incarnation, at which point the incarnate one is named: Jesus Christ. Thus, the topic of the Christ is already linked with Jesus — before John the Baptist, in the opening narrative scene in the Gospel following the more abstract prologue, clearly denies that he is the Christ.[31]

The second occurrence of an "I am" saying in John's Gospel occurs in John 3:28. Jesus has been baptized, he has been to the wedding at Cana, he has cleansed the temple, and he has conversed with Nicodemus. John the Baptist is now in prison, and his disciples are concerned with this man who is baptizing people and to whom the people are all flocking. It might strike us as odd that John's disciples are so confused at this point as to who Jesus is, except when we hear John's response. In John 3:28, he states: "You yourselves bear witness

29. See E. Freed, "*Ego Eimi* in John 1.20 and 4.25," *CBQ* 41 (1979): 288-91.

30. This is not the place to discuss all that was understood by the notion of the Messiah in the first century. It was a complex term that could encompass any of the roles chosen for God's anointed, including being in the line of David (and hence including shepherd imagery), king (linked to David also), high priest, prophet (including the final eschatological prophet), servant, son of man, Son of God (as 4Q521 makes clear, when it links the actions of the Messiah with the actions of God), among others. On this linkage, see S. E. Porter, "The Messiah in Luke and Acts: Forgiveness for the Captives," in *The Messiah in the Old and New Testaments* (ed. S. E. Porter; Grand Rapids: Eerdmans, 2007), 144-64, esp. 154-55, as well as other essays in this volume. My point is that the notion of Messiah was an expansive term, as we see displayed in John's Gospel.

31. See B. M. Stovell, *Mapping Metaphorical Discourse in the Fourth Gospel: John's Eternal King* (LBS 5; Leiden: Brill, 2012), 152-66, where she treats the Messiah and John the Baptist. Stovell also reminds us that there are other metaphors used in the Gospel regarding Jesus, such as king (the one she emphasizes).

to me that I said 'I am not the Christ.'" The clause structure is similar to 1:20, except that the negative particle, which was just before the verb in 1:20, has been shifted so that it stands at the beginning of the entire construction;[32] also the order of the verb and pronoun has been shifted from the usual ἐγώ εἰμι of 1:20 (with the negative particle between the two) to the less usual εἰμὶ ἐγώ of 3:28. The result in 3:28 is to emphasize, both through negation placement and word order, that John is *not* the Christ. This second instance of the "I am" construction serves a number of important purposes within John's Gospel. The first is that this use of the similar though negated structure makes an antithetical statement to the first usage in 1:20, in which John himself draws a stark distinction between Jesus being the Christ and himself not being that Christ. The second purpose is that this frame serves to highlight what has happened in the intervening space, namely, that we have seen recounted in the narrative a number of instances where Jesus is already seen to be the Christ by his own actions and by the actions or affirmations of others: he is recognized by John as the lamb of God who takes away the sin of the world (John 1:29); he has demonstrated his control over the natural world by transforming basic elements (2:1-11); he has cleared his Father's house of the corrupt money changers and given the first reference to his resurrection (2:13-22); and in his talking with Nicodemus he has revealed that he is the one in whom God is working (3:1-15/21). In other words, the disciples and, more important, John's readers have already seen clear evidence that Jesus is the Christ. John the Baptist is not him, and the narrative makes this point clear also.

b. Jesus Is the Christ: John 4:26; 6:20

The initial two instances of "I am" sayings spoken by Jesus are found in John 4:26 and 6:20. Both use the absolute construction.

The occurrence in John 4:26 is in the first major scene after John the Baptist's statement denying that he is the Christ. In Jesus' confrontation with the woman of Samaria,[33] after his initial discussion regarding living

---

32. The two different placements of the negative are sometimes referred to as word negation and clause negation, respectively. In the former, an individual element, here the verb, is negated, while in the latter, the entire clause is negated. See S. E. Porter, *Idioms of the Greek New Testament* (2nd ed.; BLG 2; Sheffield: Sheffield Academic Press, 1994), 281-83.

33. As Williams points out (*I Am He*, 257), this is the only time Jesus addresses one of his "I am" statements to a single individual, the rest of the instances being addressed to the disciples or his antagonists. See pp. 257-66 for her discussion of the entire passage.

water, he says that salvation comes from the Jews. This statement prompts her to say, "I know that Messiah is coming, the one called Christ" (v. 25). In the climax to the entire episode, Jesus responds (literally): "I am, the one who speaks to you [ἐγώ εἰμι, ὁ λαλῶν σοι]." This construction has been understood in a variety of ways.[34] Apart from simply attributing its meaning to its background, there are three possible explanations worth considering. The construction could be construed as an instance of the predicate structure, except that the sense would be redundant ("I am the one who is speaking to you," a truism that does not actually respond to the statement by the Samaritan woman). It is better to analyze it as an instance of the absolute use, followed by the articular participle used appositionally, defining who the "I" is.[35] In other words, Jesus is saying that "I am he, the Messiah, the one who is speaking to you." Jesus' first response is a direct affirmation of his messianic status, in which the woman's acknowledgment that the salvific figure from the Jews is the Messiah is met with the direct declaration that Jesus himself, the very one speaking to her, is that Messiah. Some scholars have taken the absolute construction as a form of elided construction, in which the implied predicate is that of Messiah, that is, Jesus is saying in abbreviated form that "I am the Messiah."[36] There is a sense in which this is the correct understanding of the construction, as this particular episode, as well as those above, indicates. However, there seems to be more going on than the author simply choosing to use the elided construction, since the construction of the individual units, the selection of the speakers, and their use in the structure of the narrative indicate that the "I am" construction has a particular importance not only to designate the Messiah but to do more and make a specific and direct affirmation. The use is in this sense revelatory, as we shall see further below.[37]

The second occurrence, in John 6:20, is also an absolute use. Between the affirmation in 4:26 and 6:20, Jesus performs a number of healings and

34. See Williams, *I Am He,* 259-62, for a survey of such opinions, although she relies too heavily upon establishing the background, probably for theological reasons. Her theology may be correct, but I believe that this needs to be found in the narrative, rather than brought from outside the text.

35. See Porter, *Idioms,* 84-85.

36. See Freed, *"Ego Eimi,"* 288-91.

37. G. R. O'Day, *Revelation in the Fourth Gospel: Narrative Mode and Theological Claim* (Philadelphia: Fortress Press, 1986), 49-92, esp. 73. This position does not, however, justify reading a fully formed theology of divinity into the first usage.

other miracles, which include his healing the official's son, healing the lame man at the pool of Bethesda, and feeding the five thousand. In this last episode we have the miracle of Jesus walking on the water. The disciples are rowing at sea when they see Jesus walking on the sea and approaching the boat. The account says that they were terrified. At that point Jesus says to them: "I am, do not fear." In this instance, one might legitimately argue for the implicit predicate, in which Jesus is affirming, "I am he" or "It is I." If this is the case, it is also not surprising that many scholars examining the "I am" sayings do not consider this passage, because it seems to be simply a matter of Jesus affirming that he is the one approaching. Besides the grammatical issues involved in construing the Greek in a particular way to make it more sensible in English, there is the problem that this implicit predicate answer does not seem any more contextually apt than the alternative absolute usage. The issue is not simply that Jesus is there, but who it is that has just walked out to meet them in the middle of the sea. He is the same man who has just performed a number of other startling miracles in their presence. There is no direct question asked whether it is Jesus or someone else — the disciples were not expecting anyone! There is also no direct question asked whether Jesus (or another) is or is not the Messiah, as there is in previous episodes, but the implication in context is the same, on the basis of the absolute usage (regardless of whether one translates with "I am he" or simply "I am"). The same Jesus who has been healing and feeding others is now, again, master of the elements, as demonstrated by his walking on the sea.

These two episodes provide explicit and graphic attestation to who Jesus is in the Johannine account. John the Baptist is not the Messiah, but Jesus is. Jesus is the Christ — and perhaps more. The revelation has begun, even if it is not complete.

c. Jesus Is Bread and Life: John 6:35, 41, 48, 51; 8:12, 18

This revelation and affirmation of Jesus' identity is supported by a series of alternating "I am" statements in John 6 and 8. These consist for the most part of a series of grouped predicate structures (the only possible exception being John 8:18) and locative structures (treated in the next section). The predicate statements are found in two blocks of material, each associated with a discourse of Jesus.

In John 6 and John 8 Jesus is recorded using two of his most famous "I am" sayings. John 6 has been subject to much discussion in scholarly circles, especially of its eucharistic overtones.[38] Whatever such overtones there may be, they are in some ways incidental to the messianic-christological thrust that they promote.[39] John 6:20-59 contains the bread-from-heaven discourse, which follows on immediately from the incident in which Jesus demonstrates his messianic status by walking on the sea (immediately preceded by his feeding of the five thousand). The link between the two episodes is explicitly made. In 6:22-24 those who had stayed on the other side of the lake, when they did not find Jesus, went searching for him and found him on the other side. They inquired about how he got there. Jesus links their coming, not with their seeking signs, but with their having been filled with bread, as was related in the episode of the feeding of the five thousand at the beginning of John 6. Jesus links the sign with the manna, but he makes clear that this came not from Moses but from God. Jesus then delivers his bread-from-heaven discourse, in which John uses "I am" sayings four times, in vv. 35, 41, 48, and 51, three of them on the lips of Jesus. John 6:35 marks the inauguration of the discourse, which begins boldly with "I am the bread of life." In v. 41 the Jews are depicted as angry that Jesus has said, "I am the bread that comes down from heaven," alluding to and paraphrasing v. 33, uttered by Jesus. Jesus repeats in v. 48 that he is the bread of life and then concludes in v. 51 by stating that he is the living bread that comes down from heaven. All of these are predicate structures. There are several strong and clear indicators that this series of statements and restatements is designed to reinforce the messianic emphasis of the Gospel regarding Jesus. First is the link between the "I am" statements and the feeding episode, which is one of the miracles that testifies to Jesus being the Messiah (see above). Jesus' initial "I am the bread of life" statement comes as a direct follow-up explanation and answer to those who sought him after the feeding of the five thousand. By stating it, he identifies the source of both the bread and, more important, the more valuable bread from heaven. The second indication follows on from the first and is the fact that the sign and bread are explicitly linked together by Jesus, who, he says of himself, is the one who fed the five thousand and

38. See, e.g., B. E. Gärtner, *Critical Readings of John 6* (CBNTS 17; Lund: Gleerup, 1959); Smalley, *John*, 204-6; D. M. Smith, *The Theology of the Gospel of John* (NTT; Cambridge: Cambridge University Press, 1995), 116, 136, 139; P. N. Anderson, *The Christology of the Fourth Gospel: Its Unity and Disunity in the Light of John 6* (Valley Forge, PA: Trinity Press International, 1997), ch. 6.

39. See J. H. Neyrey, *An Ideology of Revolt: John's Christology in Social-Science Perspective* (Minneapolis: Fortress Press, 1988), 130-36, who sees the christological significance of the predicate "I am" statements in their replacement theology.

who is the bread of God who comes down from heaven, whereas the source of the manna is said to be from heaven, not from a person. A third and final indicator is that the discourse itself begins with the explicit "I am" statement. In other words, the context for understanding this statement is more than simply the discourse that follows, but the discourse that proceeds. This discourse has already defined who Jesus is in relation to being the Messiah, and not John the Baptist. The bread-from-heaven discourse is thus seen as an elucidation of Jesus as the heaven-sent Messiah, who spiritually feeds and nourishes his people, as he did physically in the preceding feeding episode.

In John 8:12-20 we find the second discourse in this intermediate section, the discourse on Jesus as the light of the world. As in 6:35, Jesus again begins this discourse with an "I am" saying: "I am the light of the world" (8:12). The transition to this statement from John 7:52 is often clouded by the inclusion of the pericope concerning the woman caught in adultery (7:53–8:11), which is usually printed in Greek and English Bibles at this point (even if it is placed in brackets).[40] Between John 6 and this episode, there have been a number of episodes that depict adversity to Jesus, including the unbelief of Jesus' own brothers (7:1-9), but also that of the authorities, including the Pharisees and the chief priests. Jesus' exchange with the Pharisees in 8:12-20 grows out of these disputes and what constitutes grounds for establishing who Jesus is. Jesus states that he is the light of the world, but when he is questioned for making this statement (8:13), in v. 18 he states, "I am the one who testifies concerning myself [ἐγώ εἰμι ὁ μαρτυρῶν περὶ ἐμαυτοῦ]." This might be construed as an absolute construction, as in 4:26 (in which case the editors of the Greek text would probably indicate this interpretation with a comma after the "I am" construction), as Jesus is appositionally defining himself as the one bearing witness. However, it is more likely within the context that this is a predicate construction that does not create the same type of metaphorical linkage with natural phenomena (e.g., bread, light).[41] In this case, this is a statement by Jesus concerning who he is and who his relations are in relation to where he comes from. He states that he is not alone but that

---

40. This passage is a later addition and so probably not original to the Gospel, as is indicated by the best textual witnesses, as well as various linguistic criteria. For a useful discussion, see D. C. Parker, *The Living Text of the Gospels* (Cambridge: Cambridge University Press, 1997), 95-102. For a critique of Parker's overall approach to textual criticism, see S. E. Porter, *How We Got the New Testament: Text, Transmission, Translation* (Grand Rapids: Baker, 2013), 29-32.

41. In any case, it is not a periphrastic construction, as A. T. Lincoln thinks (*Truth on Trial: The Lawsuit Motif in the Fourth Gospel* [Peabody, MA: Hendrickson, 2000], 87).

he and the Father, who has sent him, are together. Even though the Father bears witness concerning him, Jesus says that he testifies concerning himself regarding who he is. In other words, Jesus bears witness to himself as the one who enlightens the world by being God's appointed one.

d. Where Jesus Is From: John 7:34, 36; 8:23 bis

The second type of supporting statement found in this section of John's Gospel consists of instances of locative constructions. These appear four times, in two groups of two — in John 7:34, 36, and twice in 8:23 — each following a discourse that uses the predicate structure.

In John 7:34 and 36 Jesus is embroiled in controversy with those who are sent to arrest him. Following on from the bread-from-heaven discourse, the leaders are angered and inquire about his identity. In the immediately preceding episode in 7:25-31, some are disputing the notion that Jesus could be the Messiah because, so they claim, no one will know where the Messiah is from. Jesus rejects this notion, pointing out that they do indeed know where he is from, and that he has not come on his own but from the one who sent him. His opponents clearly understand that Jesus' claim is messianic, which prompts their efforts to arrest him, but it also leads to further dialogue, in which he draws the clear distinction between where the authorities might search for him and where he is going. In John 7:33-34 we have, "Jesus therefore said: 'Still for a short time I am with you and I am going to the one who sent me. You will seek me and you will not find me, and where I am you are not able to come [ὅπου εἰμὶ ἐγὼ ὑμεῖς οὐ δύνασθε ἐλθεῖν].'" This statement is repeated in v. 36 by those pursuing him. This construction is not usually interpreted as an "I am" statement, even of the locative type. This is because the "I am" statement does not form its own independent clause but is adjunctive to the main clause. It is admittedly unusual to take this structure as an "I am" statement, but doing so would arguably make better sense of the flow of the narrative. The issue is not simply where Jesus is going (as the Jewish leaders interpret it in vv. 35-36), but who Jesus is and his relationship to the one who sent him. Hence, he states positively that this relationship is of an "I am" type, and their failure to accept this answer means that they are unable to enter this realm. He affirms that his realm is one that excludes them.

The final two locative occurrences are both found in John 8:23. After Jesus has affirmed that he is the light of the world and that he testifies for himself, he states again that he is going to a place where the Jewish leaders cannot find him. They are perplexed by this statement, which prompts their thinking that he is implying that he will kill himself. This is an error, however, as Jesus clarifies in 8:23, when he defines the two contrasting realms. He states: "You are from below; I am from above [ἐγὼ ἐκ τῶν ἄνω εἰμί]. You are from this world; I am not from this world [ἐγὼ οὐκ εἰμὶ ἐκ τοῦ κόσμου τούτου]." The contrast that Jesus draws is certainly between two locative realms, this world and the realm above. But it is more than this, as the two realms also represent realms of sinfulness and sinlessness linked directly to who Jesus is (see 8:24). As Jesus says, "I am [the sin-forgiving Messiah] from above; I am [the sin-forgiving Messiah] not from this world" — reminiscent of his conversation with the Samaritan woman about his identity as the Messiah. The two "I am" statements in John 7:34 and 36 were unusual by having the "I am" statement not forming its own free-standing clause. The instances in 8:23 more typically represent the locative "I am" construction, even though the first instance has the locative adjunct ("from above") placed between the pronominal subject ("I") and predicator ("am"). The second instance in 8:23 has more conventional syntax, with the "I am" construction at the front of the clause and only the negative intervening, but with the locative adjunct at the end ("from this world"). It is noteworthy, I believe, that the fourth instance here has the subject, "I," then the negative, and then the verb "am," with the locative phrase following. One could argue that the change from the first to the second instance is simply stylistic, but another explanation is that the phrasing changes to emphasize the "I am" structure, or in this case, its negative form. These particular instances are often overlooked by scholars because the passages do not apparently conform to the standard "I am" patterns. Nevertheless, in the light of the explanation above of how they are constructed and the contexts in which they are used, I think that these instances are used as part of a pattern of messianic affirmation in John's Gospel, including their use here in relation to forgiving sins.

e. Jesus and Abraham: John 8:24, 28, 58

The use of the word order in the second instance in John 8:23 to emphasize the "I am" structure is reinforced by the usage that follows. There are three instances of the absolute construction in 8:24, 28, and 58. These instances mark a significant point in the Johannine revelation of who Jesus is, especially the occurrence in 8:58, as has been widely recognized in previous Johannine scholarship.[42]

The discussion above has tried to capture the development of the argument from the opening of John's Gospel to ch. 8. John 8:24 and 28 shift the emphasis away from the negative, contrastive emphasis of the locative constructions to positive affirmations of who Jesus is. In 8:24 Jesus states that those who are talking with him will die in their sins because of their lack of belief. As he says, "If you do not believe that 'I am,' you will die in your sins." His opponents return again to the question of who he is, trying Jesus' patience. At this point, he introduces the concept of the son of man and states: "Whenever you will see the son of man, then you will know that 'I am' . . ." (8:28). This is the first time in John's Gospel where the son of man and Jesus are explicitly linked by an "I am" saying, even though on several occasions the two ideas are used in proximate contexts (e.g., 6:27, 53, 62).[43] The Johannine son of man, as in the Synoptics, is based on the apocalyptic imagery of the one like a son of man in Dan 7. This meaning is entirely consonant with this context, in which Jesus speaks of dual realms, coming and going, and being sent with a purpose. In this context, Jesus expands his messianic "I am" to become the son of man "I am" as well. Jesus links these notions to the idea that he does what the Father, who has sent him, has instructed him, apparently including the forgiveness of sins (a divine prerogative), and the response is that many believed in him.

The use of the "I am" saying in John 8:58 is undoubtedly the most well-known and potentially controversial of the "I am" constructions. The context itself is difficult because 8:31 states that Jesus' words are addressed to the Jews who believe (τοὺς πεπιστευκότας; perfect tense-form, stative aspect)

---

42. See, e.g., M. Davies, *Rhetoric and Reference in the Fourth Gospel* (JSNTSup 69; Sheffield: Sheffield Academic Press, 1992), 82-86; Bauckham, "Monotheism and Christology," 245; C. S. Keener, *The Gospel of John: A Commentary* (2 vols.; Peabody, MA: Hendrickson, 2003-6), 1:768-74, and references cited there.

43. Interpretation of the Johannine son of man has appreciated its christological significance at least since the time of F. J. Moloney, *The Johannine Son of Man* (2nd ed.; Biblioteca di Scienze Religiose 14; Rome: LAS, 1978). A larger question is whether the Johannine son of man is or is not apocalyptic. See R. Rhea, *The Johannine Son of Man* (AThANT; Zürich: Theologischer Verlag, 1990), who argues against; most recent interpreters, however, inspired by Dan 7, argue for an apocalyptic son of man: B. E. Reynolds, *The Apocalyptic Son of Man in the Gospel of John* (WUNT 2.249; Tübingen: Mohr Siebeck, 2008), and J. H. Ellens, *The Son of Man in the Gospel of John* (NTM 28; Sheffield: Sheffield Phoenix Press, 2010); cf. also J. Ashton, "The Johannine Son of Man: A New Proposal," *NTS* 57 (2011): 508-29, on the origins of the ascent and descent of the son of man.

in him. As the episode unfolds, however, it becomes clear early on that the audience is not sympathetic to Jesus and disputes with him over Abraham, to the point where their dispute leads to them taking up stones to stone him (v. 59). The disputative element is not unlikely if the episode takes place in the temple, as is stated in v. 59. Jesus even says in v. 40 that they are trying to kill him, and his opponents end up in v. 48 accusing him of having a demon. They attempt to substantiate this accusation by pointing to what they think is a claim to being greater than Abraham. When Jesus claims to have knowledge of Abraham, they are surprised. This reaction prompts Jesus' statement: "Truly, truly I say to you, before Abraham was, I am." At this point they pick up stones to hurl at him. On several counts, the absolute construction in 8:58 is a clear christological affirmation. The support for this is found in a number of explanations. One is the contrast between the reaction of the crowd earlier in the chapter and the reaction at the end. The reaction at the end is the most potentially violent reaction against Jesus thus far in John's Gospel, and it implies a suitable cause to warrant such a strong reaction. The kind of claim that Jesus is making in John 8 regarding Abraham would constitute such a cause — he appears to be making both a chronological claim and, by implication related to it, a status claim. Jesus indicates that he has previous existence, superior knowledge, and superior status to Abraham. A second explanation is found in the very enigmatic nature of the affirmation itself. The absolute construction, unlike the predicate or locative structures, in which there is some type of equation or situation specified, does not qualify what it is affirming or denying, but it uses the structure even where it may appear, at least to modern ears, to be unidiomatic. In English, "before Abraham was, I am," or as the NIV renders it, "before Abraham was born, I am!" sounds odd. It apparently sounded odd to the original hearers as well, according to John's narrative, as they then picked up stones. Third, although the emphatic phrase "truly, truly" used to introduce Jesus' "I am" statement is found throughout John's Gospel, this is the first place in John's Gospel where it is explicitly linked to an "I am" saying (the other being in 10:7; see subsection f below). In John's wording, Jesus makes this an emphatic "I am" statement. A final, and perhaps the most important, form of support is the resonance that this usage creates with the prologue to the Gospel. Abraham was seen as the Jewish forefather (cf. Rom 4), the one who stood at the head of the Jewish people, chronologically and positionally. The usage here states that Jesus posits himself as existing before Abraham. This statement harks back to the incarnational language of the prologue, in which the eternally existing *logos* becomes incarnate and lives among human beings. As Freed so aptly says, "The meaning here is something like 'Before Abraham was, I, the Christ, the Son of God, existed.'"[44]

Freed goes on to explicate the entire passage as follows:

> By using *ego eimi* three times ([John] 8:24, 25, 58) in a section of marked controversy with the Jews, the writer characteristically has developed his presentation of Jesus as the Messiah hidden to Jewish understanding. At the same time, the words, put on the lips of Jesus, are meant to reveal various aspects and functions of the Messiah to those who can comprehend their implications. Through the methodological devices of delaying tactics and misunderstanding, the points he wants to make come across with increasing effectiveness. At one point (8:31) some Jews even come to fleeting belief. But finally in a preconceived and well-prepared emotional climax, the Jews, as if suddenly realizing and rejecting the messianic implications of Jesus' words, take up stones to throw at him. They do not understand that Jesus as *ego eimi* is the Messiah who existed even before Abraham and whose person was represented by the name.[45]

The instances of the absolute construction in John 8 form a structural turning point in the Gospel, with regard to both its narrative action and the patterning of the use of the "I am" sayings. The use as found especially in John 8:58, but also in 8:24 and 28, forms a transition point in which the action of the first half of the book leads up to the clear and manifest statement of Jesus' divine, eternally existent messiahship, and then forms the basis for the second half of the book.

f. Jesus Is . . . : John 10:7, 9, 11, 14; 11:25; 14:6; 15:1, 5

The messiahship of Jesus is developed further in the second half of John's Gospel by additional instances of "I am" statements. Five sets of images are evoked, each using the predicate structure. This set of occurrences extends over much of the second half of John's Gospel, predicating of Jesus that he is the door of the sheep (John 10:7, 9), the good shepherd (10:11, 14), the

---

44. E. Freed, "Who or What Was before Abraham in John 8:58?" *JSNT* 17 (1983): 52-59, here 52. The usual equation made here is with Exod 3:14 (LXX), with Jesus making a claim to the divine nature (that is, being YHWH).

45. Freed, "Who or What?" 57. See Williams, *I Am He*, 275-83, who concludes similarly, though on the basis of usage in so-called Deutero-Isaiah.

resurrection and the life (11:25), the way, the truth, and the life (14:6), and the vine (15:1, 5). Once it has been clearly established in the Gospel that Jesus is the Messiah (defined in its full complexity) as highlighted in John 8 (see discussion above in section e), there is an increased concentration upon supportive imagery to further elaborate and establish his character.

John 10 includes two sets of closely related images used of Jesus. The first is the door of the sheep, and the second is the good shepherd.[46] There has been considerable discussion in the secondary literature about this shift and development of imagery, in which the one figure, Jesus, is first equated by means of predicate structure of a physical item and then of a person, in a composite image that seems to indicate contradiction. That is, how can Jesus be both the door of the sheep and the shepherd who leads his sheep through the door? Thankfully, some commentators can appreciate the use of figurative language, realizing that a single metaphor is limited in what it can express and that Jesus' messianic character is more complex than what a single image can convey. This complex imagery is seen in how the "I am" sayings are used in this passage. In the first set of predicate examples used in John's Gospel (John 6 and 8; see section c above), the "I am" statements introduce the imagery that is to be employed. In this set of "I am" statements in John 10, the imagery of the shepherd and the sheep is first laid out in John 10:1-6, and then in v. 7 Jesus introduces himself as the door of the sheep. In vv. 7-10 the text develops the messianic function of protection in opposition to the thief. Then in v. 11 we have introduced the second, related image: the good shepherd. Here the contrast is not with the thief, but between the good shepherd who is willing to lay down his life for his sheep and the hired hand who is unreliable and runs at the first sign of danger. The shepherd and king image are linked in John's thought, thus reinforcing the messianic force of the "I am" usage here. The final set of predicate-based "I am" sayings appears in John 15:1 and 5. Here we see the pattern noted earlier in the Gospel (John 6 and 8), in which the passage on the vineyard is introduced by the "I am" saying at the outset ("I am the true vine"; 15:1) and then essentially repeated in the course of the discourse ("I am the vine"; 15:5).

---

46. For thorough discussions, see J. van der Watt, *The Family of the King: Dynamics of Metaphor in the Gospel according to John* (BIS 47; Leiden: Brill, 2000), 54-86; and Stovell, *Mapping Metaphorical Discourse*, 221-55, who draws the metaphorical and historical linkage between king and shepherd particularly well. See also the various essays in J. Beutler and R. T. Fortna, eds., *The Shepherd Discourse of John 10 and Its Context: Studies by Members of the Johannine Writings Seminar* (SNTSMS 67; Cambridge: Cambridge University Press, 1991).

By contrast, the instance of predicate structure in John 11:25 does not occur in an extended metaphorical passage but in Jesus' conversation with Martha regarding the death of Lazarus, her brother. Jesus tells Martha that he is the resurrection and the life. Similarly, in John 14:6 Jesus says that he is the way and the truth and the life. These might at first appear to be odd occurrences of this predicate "I am" structure, since they do not appear as part of a set of extended discursive imagery, as do the other instances. This usage, however, seems consistent with the overall structuring effect of the use of the "I am" sayings in the Gospel. Whereas in the first half of the Gospel the "I am" predicate statements are used in only two blocks, both part of a concentrated set of images, in the second half of the book two major developments occur. One, as already noted above, is the increased frequency of "I am" statements, with a wider variety of images, five of them in all. The second is that they are interspersed throughout and do not occur only in sets of developed discursive images. This reflects the fact that, so far as the author of John's Gospel is concerned, once the clear affirmation of Jesus as Messiah has been made and reinforced, both at the beginning of Jesus' ministry and then especially in John 8, the messianic character of Jesus can be assumed; going forward, the Gospel further develops his character by the addition of pertinent and expressive images of his being and function.

g. Where Jesus Is From, Again: John 12:26; 14:3; 17:14, 16, 24

The locative "I am" construction is used five times in the second half of the Gospel of John. The formal usage in this half of the Gospel is similar to that in the first half, in which there are two major patterns of locative "I am" usage. John 12:26, 14:3, and 17:24 use the locative pattern as part of a "where" statement, as in 7:34 and 36, while 17:14 and 16 use a prepositional adjunct phrase.

The "where" locative structures may have the appearance of simply being incidental uses of the "I am" construction, expressing the location of the speaker. However, I think that the use of these phrases in their particular Johannine contexts indicates that the author, and perhaps even the speaker, is intending something more. In John 12:26 a number of Greeks come to see Jesus and make representations to him through the disciples Andrew and Philip. Their initiative results in Jesus stating that the hour has arrived for the son of man to be glorified. He concludes this set of pronouncements by making a call for obedient following. The language is framed in terms of master and servant, leader and follower, but also in locational terms (reminiscent of the two realms noted above). Jesus is depicted as equating his position of leader with that of being the surrogate of the Father. He states, "If someone might serve me, let him/her follow me, and where I am there also/indeed my servant shall be [καὶ ὅπου εἰμὶ ἐγὼ ἐκεῖ καὶ ὁ διάκονος ὁ ἐμὸς ἔσται]." As in the examples in John 7, the "I am" construction is not a freestanding clause. This one is made more complex by the double use of καί ("and/also/ indeed"). Nevertheless, I think that this statement is a locative use of the "I am" construction, with Jesus essentially stating, "Where I am [the Messiah sent by the Father], there my servant/follower is." This affirmation is consistent with the messianic designation of the "I am" saying. This notion is even clearer in John 14:3, where Jesus is speaking of his going to prepare a place for his followers, so that, when he returns, his followers can be with him (ὅπου εἰμὶ ἐγὼ καὶ ὑμεῖς ἦτε). In 17:24 Jesus addresses the Father directly, with the request regarding those who have been given to him that they may be with him (ὅπου εἰμὶ ἐγὼ κἀκεῖνοι ὦσιν μετ' ἐμοῦ). In both of these uses of the locative, Jesus is affirmed as the mediating Messiah between the Father and those who believe in him.

The second set of locative "I am" sayings is found in John 17:14 and 16. Used similarly to those in the first half of the Gospel (John 8), they distinguish between the world and where Jesus belongs, two separate realms of existence. Jesus does not belong in the world, and he prays that his followers will not be of this world also. As he says, "They are not of the world, as I am not of the world [ἐγὼ οὐκ εἰμὶ ἐκ τοῦ κόσμου, 17:14] . . . of the world they are not, as I am not of the world [ἐγὼ οὐκ εἰμὶ ἐκ τοῦ κόσμου, 17:16]."

There is a consistent thematic emphasis in the locative "I am" sayings, in which locational contrasts are drawn between Jesus, his Father, his followers, and the world. These contrasts line up with Jesus and the Father on one side, joined by his followers, as opposed to the others, who are of this world.

h. Jesus' Identity Confirmed: John 18:5, 6, 8

The final set of "I am" sayings uses the absolute construction. Three occurrences of this type of construction appear near the end of John's Gospel, all within ch. 18 and the episode in which Jesus is betrayed and arrested. As Williams says, "Considerably less attention" has been given to these passages, "because they are largely interpreted as examples of everyday usage possessing no particular christological significance."[47] Both Williams and I believe that this is not the case, and that these instances have great christological significance, even if we do not see this significance in exactly the same way.

The messianic function of these sayings is confirmed by the episode in which they are used. In John 18 Jesus is in the garden with his disciples when Judas approaches with a cohort of soldiers. In v. 4 Jesus is said to know all that was to happen to him, so he comes forward and asks those who are approaching whom they are looking for. They answer, "Jesus the Nazarene," at which point Jesus says to them, "I am." Many commentators interpret this as the implicit predicate use, as if Jesus were simply stating, "I am he" or "It's me." It seems to me, however, that there is more to the usage and the episode than this. The narrator at this point recapitulates for emphatic purposes and says that, when Jesus said "I am," those who were standing there stepped back and fell to the ground. Jesus then asks again whom they are seeking, and when they again say "Jesus the Nazarene," he repeats that he said to them, "I am."

There are several important observations to make about this account. One is the narrative buildup that takes place in this episode. A variety of literary techniques are used in John's Gospel, but this kind of incremental buildup and repetition is unusual.[48] Nevertheless, it occurs here right at the point where Jesus' identity is established before he is taken into custody, not only for those who are within his group of followers but for those outside as well. The second observation is to note the confirmatory response that is recorded. In this second use of "I am," the account says that, when Jesus said "I am," those who were intending to arrest him stepped back and fell to the ground. This repulsion comes as a response to the uttering of the absolute "I am" statement. This unusual response indicates that Jesus is depicted as more than simply using a self-designation. Instead, the saying is seen to carry the full impact of what it has come to mean throughout the entire Gospel. That is, the response to his "I am" statement clearly shows that Jesus meant to identify himself as the Messiah.[49] Jesus then repeats the request

---

47. Williams, *I Am He,* 287. Cf. 287-99, for her treatment of this passage. I do not agree with her, however, that these "I am" statements "serve as the centrepoint of a narrative in which key aspects of the Johannine understanding of this enigmatic construction are crystallized" (287). She seems to confuse literary structure with theological significance.

48. The classic work on John's literary character is Culpepper, *Anatomy of the Fourth Gospel.* So far as I can see, he does not cite this particular feature.

49. See R. E. Brown, *The Death of the Messiah: From Gethsemane to the Grave* (2 vols.; ABRL; New York: Doubleday, 1994), 1:260-62.

regarding whom they are seeking and confirms that "I am" a third time. A third observation is the fact that, even though those who are there to arrest him fall to the ground, Jesus allows himself to be arrested. He first requests that his followers be released. This request confirms words that Jesus had spoken earlier, in which he said that he would not lose a single one of those entrusted to him. This prophetic statement — one of the roles of Messiah — is found in 17:12, and partially echoed in 17:24, where a locative use of the "I am" construction is found (see above, section g).[50] Only at this point, once Jesus has ensured the safety of his followers (thus fulfilling this dimension of his messianic calling), does he allow himself to be arrested and taken into custody, the next step in drawing to a close his earthly, messianic ministry. The Messiah was to be God's appointed and anointed servant on earth. This role Jesus has fulfilled during the course of his ministry. There is a sense in which, in John's Gospel, Jesus' messianic status is a function primarily of his earthly ministry, hence the use of the "I am" sayings throughout most of the narrative, but its lack of use in the passion account. That is, once that ministry is completed, there is no need to establish Jesus' messianic identity through use of "I am" statements.

In the same way that the instances of absolute usage in John 8 firmly establish the messianic character of Jesus, these three instances mark the confirmation of that status as a fitting prelude to his death and resurrection, with his earthly task accomplished.

i. Other Examples: John 13:19; 9:9; 18:35

There are three other occurrences of "I am" sayings in John's Gospel that do not readily fit within the structure that I have outlined above. These instances occur in John 13:19, an instance of the absolute use on Jesus' lips; John 9:9, an instance of absolute use uttered by the blind man who has been healed; and John 18:35, a predicate use spoken by Pilate.

It may not be possible to satisfactorily explain each of these uses in a way that fits neatly within the schema that I have outlined above. The framework that I have outlined is an attempt to look at the range of evidence and weave an interpretive narrative around these instances in a way that gives coherence to the entire account. I think that the use of the "I am" sayings points to

50. On Jesus as prophet, see S. Cho, *Jesus as Prophet in the Fourth Gospel* (NTM 15; Sheffield: Sheffield Phoenix Press, 2006).

a creative and conscious effort by the Gospel writer to structure, frame, and develop his narrative. I would not pretend to think that he would articulate the same set of explanations as I have, nor would he necessarily be aware of what he has done in the same way as I have attempted to describe it. So in that sense it is probably not necessary to be able to explain every single episode, since this pushes beyond what might reasonably be expected of the author himself. Instead, an overall framework has been set forth that offers interpretive insights into the Johannine usage in most regards.

Having said this, however, I still think that some possible explanations of these apparently stray or recalcitrant uses can be given. The use of the absolute construction in John 13:19 is problematic only because it is an absolute use that does not fall into one of the three major groupings of absolute uses in which Jesus is the speaker (see above, sections b and e). But it is indeed an instance of the absolute "I am" saying being uttered by Jesus in a way that clearly indicates his messianic status. At the end of the episode in which Jesus washes the feet of his disciples (13:1-20), he tells them something about their relationship to him, but he indicates that he is not speaking to all of them, because he knows the character of those he has chosen. Jesus then says that what is happening is part of a pattern of fulfilling Scripture, concluding with a statement that he is saying this before it occurs so that they may believe that "I am." In other words, his indications that he is in control of his circumstances and that events are unfolding according to a larger plan are part of what must happen to him as the Messiah, or God's selected and chosen one.

The second example, John 9:9, is more problematic because it is an example of the absolute "I am" saying on the lips of someone other than Jesus.[51] Apart from the two initial instances that John the Baptist utters, this statement and 18:35 (to be discussed immediately below) are the only two "I am" constructions uttered by someone other than Jesus. One could plausibly argue that an "I am" statement on the lips of someone other than Jesus is not the same kind of statement as one uttered by Jesus, because the context in which the statement is used is the decisive factor in determining its meaning. I believe that this is probably the best way to understand this statement — as not directly relevant to the Christology of John's Gospel. Nevertheless, it is worth noting that this instance occurs in the second half of the Gospel, after

---

51. For discussion, see Williams, *I Am He,* 255 and n. 2. She is responding to M. C. Parsons, "A Neglected Εγω Ειμι Saying in the Fourth Gospel? Another Look at John 9:9," in *Perspectives on John: Method and Interpretation in the Fourth Gospel* (ed. R. B. Sloan and M. C. Parsons; Lewiston, NY: Mellen, 1993), 145-80.

Jesus' messianic status has been clearly identified, and that the use of this "I am" statement by the blind man — even if it is only to identify himself — is by someone who is further identified as a disciple of Jesus. In that sense, the use of the "I am" statement firmly places the user with Jesus the Messiah.

The final example, John 18:35, is an example of absolute use uttered by Pilate, the second example of such usage by someone other than Jesus or John the Baptist (see John 9:9 above). Again, it is possible that the context of usage makes this simply an instance of an "I am" saying without messianic implications. However, I think that it is also worth noting that, in contrast to the blind man who utters the statement in a positive way that identifies himself with Jesus, Pilate utters the "I am" statement as part of a denial of his being a Jew. Jesus has appeared before Pilate, and Pilate has heard the charges against Jesus, but the Jews are unhappy with his decision to let them take care of the matter. Then Pilate enters his headquarters again to question Jesus, asking him whether he is "King of the Jews." Rather than responding directly, Jesus answers with his own question: whether Pilate had asked this question on his own or at the bequest of others. Pilate replies, "I am not a Jew, am I? [μήτι ἐγὼ Ἰουδαῖός εἰμι;]." The negated question, expecting a negative answer, firmly places Pilate, and by implication those on whose side he stands, on the opposite side of Jesus, as those who reject his messianic status. It is as if to deny or negate the "I am" statement is tantamount to denying or negating Jesus' messianic status — or at least an attempt to do so by Pilate. John's Gospel makes clear that neither Pilate nor anyone else can do so.

5. Conclusion

John's Christology is obviously complex. However, I believe that the use of the "I am" statements serves as a structuring device for the presentation of Jesus as Messiah in John's Gospel. To be clear, this statement is not the same as claiming that anytime Jesus uses an "I am" statement in any of the other Gospels he is making a messianic claim. I am not saying that *all* instances of Jesus' use, nor anyone else's use for that matter, of "I am" must be interpreted in this manner. (This would be a clear example of what James Barr identified as theologizing.)[52] What I am saying, however, is that in John's Gospel these statements, in the light of my analysis above, seem to be used as a structuring

52. J. Barr, *The Semantics of Biblical Language* (Oxford: Oxford University Press, 1961), 212 and throughout.

device by the author, whether consciously or subconsciously, for invoking this christological framework and thought about Jesus. Furthermore, while most discussions of the "I am" statements have been centered on Jesus' self-identification as YHWH (cf. Exod 3:14 LXX), I have attempted to go beyond this standard discussion by suggesting another perspective on these statements in John's Gospel. John the Baptist denies that he is the Messiah (John 1:20), but Jesus affirms that he himself is the Christ (4:26). This sets the overt christological trajectory of the Gospel. Furthermore, Jesus in John 8 uses the absolute "I am" structure to affirm his messianic existence (vv. 23, 28) as ultimately before Abraham (v. 58). The statement clearly arouses the ire of the Jewish leaders. For the reader who knows the prologue of the Gospel, Jesus' statements in John 8 can be seen as making a claim to being the preexistent *logos*. Along the way, Jesus is also seen as Savior, Son of the Father, and forgiver of sins, among other things — all linked directly to his messianism and the use of the "I am" statements. However, messianic claims in the first-century world were bound to arouse opposition, and after this point in the Gospel (but beginning from John 6 on), Jesus is depicted as virtually always using pictorial or metaphorical descriptions of himself in the "I am" sayings, variously describing himself as the bread of life (John 6), the light of the world (John 8), the Sheep Gate and the good shepherd (John 10), the resurrection and the life (John 11), the way, the truth, and the life (14:6), and the true vine (John 15), or in relation to his location, where he is from and where he is going (John 7, 8, 12, 14, 17). There is a close correlation between several of the themes of the Gospel introduced in the prologue and several of these metaphorical equations, further reinforcing the messianic-christological depiction of Jesus. This usage also serves the function of helping Jesus to avoid further direct conflict with the religious leaders until he is at the point of being arrested by Judas. Then he reverts to emphatic use of the absolute structure and affirms "I am," at which time those arresting him fall to the ground before him (18:5, 6, 8). The "I am" sayings thus structure the christological development of John's Gospel and function on the lips of Jesus as important indicators of its expansive messianic Christology.[53]

53. For a similar conclusion, see K. B. Larsen, *Recognizing the Stranger: Recognition Scenes in the Gospel of John* (Leiden: Brill, 2008), 150: The "I am" statements "are Jesus' most explicit self-revelatory statement, but they do not pin him down to one, single title. They rather display various aspects of his identity, showing that he is not as easy to grasp as in simple, proper-name recognitions, and this diversity creates a sense of estrangement."

CHAPTER 6

Jesus, "the Jews," and John's Gospel

1. Introduction

John's Gospel has been accused by a number of scholars of having an anti-Jewish perspective. In fact, a major conference was held in Leuven, Belgium, in 2000 in order to address this very issue, with the results published in a massive volume on the subject.[1] The conclusions of this research indicate a wide range of disagreement. Some defend the perspective of John's Gospel and render οἱ Ἰουδαῖοι as "the Jews," others see John's Gospel as anti-Jewish and leave the rendering of οἱ Ἰουδαῖοι as "the Jews" to emphasize the anti-Jewish orientation of the Gospel, while still others lament and even excoriate John's clear anti-Jewish polemic as an embarrassment and, as a result,

---

1. R. Bieringer, D. Pollefeyt, and F. Vandecasteele-Vanneuville, eds., *Anti-Judaism and the Fourth Gospel: Papers of the Leuven Colloquium, 2000* (Jewish and Christian Heritage 1; Assen, Netherlands: Royal Van Gorcum, 2001) (used below). A selection of the papers has been published as *Anti-Judaism and the Fourth Gospel* (Louisville, KY: Westminster John Knox, 2001). Summaries of previous research are provided in U. C. von Wahlde, "The Johannine 'Jews': A Critical Survey," *NTS* 28 (1982): 33-60; and von Wahlde, "'The Jews' in the Gospel of John: Fifteen Years of Research (1983-1998)," *ETL* 76 (2000): 30-55. Works of importance since *Anti-Judaism and the Fourth Gospel* include R. Hakola, *Identity Matters: John, the Jews, and Jewishness* (NovTSup 118; Leiden: Brill, 2005); L. Kierspel, *The Jews and the World in the Fourth Gospel: Parallelism, Function, and Context* (WUNT 2.220; Tübingen: Mohr Siebeck, 2006); R. Bauckham and C. Mosser, eds., *The Gospel of John and Christian Theology* (Grand Rapids: Eerdmans, 2008), with chapters by S. Motyer, J. Lieu, T. Griffith, and S. K. Tonstad; C. Bennema, *Encountering Jesus: Character Studies in the Gospel of John* (Milton Keynes, UK: Paternoster, 2009), 38-46; Bennema, "The Identity and Composition of οἱ Ἰουδαῖοι in the Gospel of John," *TynBul* 60.2 (2009): 239-64; and R. Sheridan, "Issues in the Translation of οἱ Ἰουδαῖοι in the Fourth Gospel," *JBL* 132 (2013): 571-95. There are many others as well.

attempt to find ways to render οἱ Ἰουδαῖοι that are not offensive, such as "the Judeans." (This last alternative has been enshrined formally in lexicography by BDAG.) No doubt much of the recent sensitivity to the issue of how to render οἱ Ἰουδαῖοι grows out of legitimate post-Holocaust concerns. As children, we may have heard the old adage "Sticks and stones may break my bones, but words will never hurt me" — few, however, actually believe it. We all know from painful experience, no matter what our linguistic theory may say about the use of language, that some language does end up hurting and harming. If the problem were simply name-calling, we might think that it is unfortunate, unwise, and even cruel. When name-calling motivates people to take up sticks and stones — as they have on too many occasions — we must take a serious look at the language involved. Use of οἱ Ἰουδαῖοι in John's Gospel is a particularly important case in point.

After analyzing and assessing previous scholarship on the issue, this chapter will attempt to demonstrate that the fundamental issue at stake regarding "the Jews" in John's Gospel is not one of race or region but one of religion. As we have already seen in previous chapters in this volume, from the outset John's Gospel promotes a very high Christology, declaring that Jesus is the preexistent *logos*. Furthermore, the Gospel grounds this high Christology in Jesus' own self-understanding. Depicted as he is in John's Gospel with such a high christological position, it is not at all surprising that Jesus ends up running into conflict with established religious belief systems, including the Judaism of his day, of which he was a part. Although the critique of Judaism offered within John's Gospel is often trenchant, it accurately reflects the kinds of religious conflicts that inevitably result when exclusive religious claims are made, such as those made by the Jesus of John's Gospel.

I present my analysis in this chapter in two stages. First, I observe how οἱ Ἰουδαῖοι is used in John's Gospel, drawing in contemporary and recent discussion regarding the anti-Judaism of the Gospel. Then I briefly characterize the nature of the religious conflict between Jesus and "the Jews," before touching on the Gospel's date of composition and matters related to its historicity. Along the way, and as a result of my study, I will make some recommendations about how to understand reference to "the Jews" in John's Gospel.

2. John's Gospel, Anti-Judaism, and οἱ Ἰουδαῖοι

John's Gospel uses the term Ἰουδαῖοι approximately seventy times. Numerous proposals have been made for how to interpret this term, as already briefly noted above. Bieringer, Pollefeyt, and Vandecasteele-Vanneuville summarize five major interpretations of the references of this term that are prominent in recent literature on John's Gospel.[2] They find that οἱ Ἰουδαῖοι refers to (1) non-Johannine Jewish Christians (i.e., Jewish Christians not part of the specifically Johannine community),[3] (2) the Jewish leaders in Jerusalem,[4] (3) Torah-observing Jews in Jerusalem,[5] (4) residents of Judea, or Judeans,[6] and (5) the Jews as heirs of the particular Jews who openly opposed Jesus.[7] This list certainly represents a wide range of opinions, each of which has attracted a significant amount of discussion and debate.[8] In order

2. R. Bieringer, D. Pollefeyt, and F. Vandecasteele-Vanneuville, "Wrestling with Johannine Anti-Judaism: A Hermeneutical Framework for the Analysis of the Current Debate," in *Anti-Judaism and the Fourth Gospel*, 3-44. The authors cite the works I have referred to below as examples of the five major positions (apart from some of the later works and a few others that I cite but they did not).

3. E.g., H. J. de Jonge, "'The Jews' in the Gospel of John," in *Anti-Judaism and the Fourth Gospel*, 239-59. De Jonge relies upon the work of B. W. J. de Ruyter, *De gemeente van de evangelist Johannes: Haar polemiek en haar geschiedenis* (Delft: Eburon, 1998); J. M. C. Scott, "Jews or Christians? The Opponents of Jesus in the Fourth Gospel," in *Jesus and Paul: Global Perspectives in Honor of James D. G. Dunn for His Seventieth Birthday* (ed. B. J. Oropeza, C. K. Robertson, and D. C. Mohrmann; LNTS 414; London: T&T Clark, 2010), 83-101.

4. E.g., M. C. de Boer, "The Depiction of 'the Jews' in John's Gospel: Matters of Behavior and Identity," in *Anti-Judaism and the Fourth Gospel*, 260-80; U. C. von Wahlde, "'You Are of Your Father the Devil' in Its Context: Stereotyped Apocalyptic Polemic in John 8:38-47," in *Anti-Judaism and the Fourth Gospel*, 418-44; R. B. Edwards, *Discovering John* (London: SPCK, 2003), 112-22; D. M. Smith, *The Fourth Gospel in Four Dimensions: Judaism and Jesus, the Gospels, and Scripture* (Columbia: University of South Carolina Press, 2008), 18-19.

5. E.g., S. Motyer, "The Fourth Gospel and the Salvation of Israel," in *Anti-Judaism and the Fourth Gospel*, 92-110; Motyer, *Your Father the Devil? A New Approach to John and "the Jews"* (PBTM; Carlisle: Paternoster, 1997); Motyer, "Bridging the Gap: How Might the Fourth Gospel Help Us Cope with the Legacy of Christianity's Exclusive Claim over against Judaism?" in *Gospel of John and Christian Theology*, 143-67; Bennema, *Encountering Jesus*, 45; Bennema, "Identity," 260.

6. E.g., M. Lowe, "Who Were the Ἰουδαῖοι?" *NovT* 18 (1976): 101-30; von Wahlde, "The Johannine 'Jews'"; J. Ashton, "The Identity and Function of the Ἰουδαῖοι in the Fourth Gospel," *NovT* 27 (1985): 40-75.

7. E.g., R. Kysar, "Anti-Semitism and the Gospel of John," in *Anti-Semitism and Early Christianity: Issues of Polemic and Faith* (ed. C. A. Evans and D. A. Hagner; Philadelphia: Fortress Press, 1993), 113-27; R. A. Culpepper, "Anti-Judaism in the Fourth Gospel as a Theological Problem for Christian Interpreters," in *Anti-Judaism and the Fourth Gospel*, 68-91; A. Reinhartz, "'Jews' and Jews in the Fourth Gospel," in *Anti-Judaism and the Fourth Gospel*, 341-56; Hakola, *Identity Matters*, 231; Sheridan, "Issues."

8. The scope is even larger than these five interpretations. Kierspel, e.g., takes Ἰουδαῖοι and κόσμος as semantically overlapping, with the first a subgroup of the second (*The Jews,*

to analyze more successfully the various attempts to explain this usage, I examine the instances afresh before attempting to assess the various positions.

Obviously, one can categorize John's uses of Ἰουδαῖοι in a large variety of ways. In what follows, I suggest some categories that seem useful for interpretation.[9] One category consists of *instances where there is a clear relationship to Jewish religion or ethnicity:*

John 2:6	purification of the Jews
2:13; 6:4; 11:55	Passover of the Jews
4:22	salvation being from the Jews
5:1; 7:2	feast of the Jews
5:10, 16	Sabbath (cf. 5:1 with reference to a feast of the Jews; 19:31)
18:20	temple where the Jews gathered
19:21	chief priests of the Jews
19:31, 42	day of preparation of the Jews
19:40	burial custom for Jews

Another set of examples contains *instances where "the Jews" are defined by similarity or contrast in relation to some other group or person:*

John 1:19	Jews sending priests and Levites
3:1	Nicodemus described as a leader of the Jews and Pharisees
4:9	Jews vs. Samaritans
7:35; 8:22	Pharisees (see 7:32) and Greeks
8:31	the Jews who believed in Jesus
12:11; 19:20	many of the Jews
18:12	servants of the Jews
18:33, 39; 19:3, 19, 2 bis	king of the Jews

214-19); cf. Kysar, "Anti-Semitism," 118. Moloney takes them as "Israel" or "the nation," and the tension as one among those in the same group. See F. J. Moloney, "'The Jews' in the Fourth Gospel: Another Perspective," in *The Gospel of John: Text and Context* (BIS 72; Leiden: Brill, 2005), 20-44 (originally published in *Pacifica* 15 [2002]: 16-36).

9. Recent discussion tends to recognize the complexity of the topic and hence refers to such factors as social location, narrative context, and religious identity, among others. See, e.g., T. L. Donaldson, *Jews and Anti-Judaism in the New Testament: Decision Points and Divergent Interpretations* (London: SPCK; Waco, TX: Baylor University Press, 2010), 86-90; Kierspel, *The Jews*, 46-62; and Bennema, "Identity."

Another way of identifying "the Jews" is in relation to the response reflected in the context. There are a number of *instances where, from the context, one cannot identify or formulate an emotion-based (hence negative) opinion of the Jews* on the basis of their response. These references include:

John 7:15	The Jews marvel.
8:57	The Jews react to Jesus' reference to Abraham.
10:19	The Jews are divided in their opinion.
10:24	The Jews ask whether Jesus is the Christ.
11:19, 31, 33, 36, 45	Many Jews are with Mary and Martha.
12:9	A large crowd of the Jews came to see Lazarus.
13:33	Jesus says to the Jews, "Where I am going, you cannot come."
18:14	Caiaphas advises the Jews.
18:35	Pilate says, "I am not a Jew."

There are, however, a number of *instances with a definitely negative orientation* within the context:

John 2:18, 20	The Jews are indirectly identified with the ills of the temple.
5:16	The Jews pursue Jesus.
5:18; 7:1, 11	The Jews seek to kill Jesus.
6:41	The Jews grumble.
6:52	The Jews argue.
7:13; 9:22 bis	People fear the Jews.
8:48, 52	The Jews accuse Jesus of having a demon.
10:31, 33; 11:8	The Jews take up stones.
11:54	Jesus does not walk openly because of the Jews.
19:38; 20:19	Joseph fears the Jews; the disciples fear the Jews.

Also, a few contexts do not provide clear negative identifying features in the immediate environment but still appear to have overall negative connotations. Such instances are:

John 9:18	Jews do not believe.
18:31, 36, 38; 19:7, 12, 14	Jews are involved in Jesus' trial before Pilate.

So far, the results of my classification of instances point out two important considerations. The first is that no single proposal seems to include all of the examples. One gets the initial impression from reading much of the secondary literature, or at least discussion about the secondary literature, that the vast majority of Johannine usage of οἱ Ἰουδαῖοι reflects an anti-Jewish bias. This is simply not true. What is being disputed is in fact a much smaller number of instances, those that are problematic in what they say regarding who οἱ Ἰουδαῖοι are, and in what tone they say it, in John's Gospel. The second, related observation is that none of the major attempts at characterizing Johannine usage successfully accounts for all of the relevant passages. In other words, the diversity of contextual uses cannot be included in a single category. I consider each of the major positions in order.

a. Non-Johannine Jewish Christians

A number of examples in John of οἱ Ἰουδαῖοι do not refer to non-Johannine Jewish Christians. These examples include many instances that make reference to Jewish religion and ethnicity, since many of these uses do not seem to have in view a small group within the larger group of Jews, but rather the Jews in their entirety (i.e., not just Jewish Christians who are associated with Passover, but Jews as a whole who are associated with Passover). The same is true of instances where "the Jews" are defined in relation to other groups. Nicodemus is not a leader of the Jewish Christians but of the Jewish people. Instances where "the Jews" are identified as a group, such as those involved in the temple activities, are probably not best seen as referring to Jewish Christians. Perhaps the most problematic example for this position is the reference in John 4:22 to salvation being from the Jews. It is highly unlikely that the author would have said that salvation comes from the non-Johannine Jewish Christians, while himself writing as a Johannine Jewish Christian. It is further doubtful that Pilate or anyone else would have wanted to refer to Jesus as king of the non-Johannine Jewish Christians.

b. Jewish Leaders in Jerusalem

The same negative conclusion must be reached with respect to the proposal that Jewish leaders in Jerusalem are consistently in view. The instances that make reference to the Jewish religion or ethnicity are not confined to the Jewish leaders, to say nothing of their being in Jerusalem. Some of the instances where "the Jews" are defined in relation to other groups are patently absurd if they are understood as the Jewish leaders, such as Nicodemus being a leader of the Jewish leaders, or the Jewish leaders being seen as opposed to the priests and Levites (would they not have been overlapping groups in a way that makes this distinction untenable?), and Jesus as king (only?) of the Jewish leaders.

c. Torah-observing Jews in Jerusalem

In many instances, in the light of Jesus' conflict with "the Jews," the circumscription of them as Torah-observing Jews in Jerusalem makes some sense. However, in a number of instances this category also fails. There are many distinctions made in John's Gospel regarding Jewish religion or ethnicity where "the Jews" must be a larger group than the Torah-observing ones in Jerusalem, such as when they are contrasted with the Samaritans, or where salvation is said to be from the Jews (Jesus was, after all, a Galilean). The same is true when identification of the Jews with particular groups is made, such as those who are said to believe in Jesus.

d. Residents of Judea or Judeans

The notion that "the Jews" are residents of Judea, or Judeans, has gained recent currency because of BDAG's definitions. However, this proposal also fails. Features of Jewish religion or ethnicity extended beyond the boundaries of Judea, including the practice of Passover, Sabbath, and other customs. It becomes almost humorous to depict Jesus as king of the Judeans, when he was from Galilee and came with a message for "the world" (John 3:16). Furthermore, it is absurd to think that the author of John's Gospel was saying that salvation is from the Judeans, when Jesus and also most of his closest followers were Galileans.

e. The Jews as Heirs of the Particular Jews Who Betrayed Jesus

Some scholars attempt a bi-level analysis that contrasts the particular Jews who were involved in the betrayal of Jesus with Jews who are later mentioned or implied in the Gospel but who are seen in their disbelief as the heirs of those earlier Jews.[10] This approach may work for certain literary interpretations in some instances, but it clearly fails to account for all of the usage. Salvation is clearly not from this group, and Jesus was crucified as king of these Jews but also of a much wider group, as those of later Johannine communities recognized. Instances where "the Jews" is defined in relation to other groups cause further difficulties for this position, since it becomes difficult to tell which other group is being used to define "the Jews."

3. The Sense and Contexts of οἱ Ἰουδαῖοι

The above analysis, although it is brief, shows that previous attempts to define the uses of οἱ Ἰουδαῖοι within John's Gospel have not succeeded. Much of the difficulty, as Alan Culpepper seems to acknowledge,[11] is that most of these attempts are designed to account for the supposed problematic usage in John's Gospel, that is, the usage that some have interpreted as being anti-Jewish. Although previous scholarship has observed that some of the Johannine usage is neutral, Culpepper does not seem to fully accept such explanations. He notes instead Urban von Wahlde's conclusion from his study of ten surveys of Johannine usage that all ten scholars agreed that thirty-one instances were "hostile" uses of the term οἱ Ἰουδαῖοι.[12] In fact, von Wahlde adds seven more Johannine instances to this list of thirty-one

10. The bi-level analysis of John's Gospel is attributed to the 1968 work by J. L. Martyn, *History and Theology in the Fourth Gospel* (3rd ed.; Louisville, KY: Westminster John Knox, 2003 [1968]), developed by, among others, R. E. Brown, *The Community of the Beloved Disciple* (New York: Paulist Press, 1979), and followed by many since. This view has been widely criticized in Johannine studies of late (see below for further discussion and references).

11. Culpepper, "Theological Problem," 71-72.

12. The works examined by von Wahlde, "The Johannine 'Jews,'" are E. Grässer, "Die antijüdische Polemik im Johannesevangelium," *NTS* 11 (1964-65): 74-90; R. Schnackenburg, *The Gospel according to John* (trans. K. Smyth et al.; 3 vols.; London: Burns & Oates, 1968), 1:286-87; R. T. Fortna, "Theological Use of Locale in the Fourth Gospel," in *Gospel Studies in Honor of Sherman Elbridge Johnson* (ed. H. S. Massey and C. H. Edward; ATRSup 3; Evanston, IL: Anglican Theological Review, 1974), 58-95; R. G. Bratcher, "'The Jews' in the Gospel of John," *BT* 26 (1975): 401-9; R. Fuller, "The 'Jews' in the Fourth Gospel," *Dialog* 16 (1977): 31-37; G. J. Cuming, "The Jews in the Fourth Gospel," *ExpTim* 60 (1948-49): 290-92; G. Baum, *Is the New Testament Anti-Semitic? A Re-examination of the New Testament* (Glen Rock, NJ: Paulist Press, 1965); R. E. Brown, *The Gospel according to John* (2 vols.; AB 29, 29A; Garden City, NY: Doubleday, 1966), 1:lxx-lxxiii; M. C. White, "The Identity and Function of Jews and Related Terms in the Fourth Gospel" (Ph.D. diss., Emory University, 1972); and R. Leistner, *Antijudaismus im Johannesevangelium?* (TW 3; Bern: Herbert Lang, 1974).

(John 7:35; 8:31; 11:8; 18:12, 38; 19:12, 14), making a total of thirty-eight instances that are hostile toward οἱ Ἰουδαῖοι.[13] When this usage is examined more closely, however, one encounters further problems. The first, and major, difficulty is in confirming whether these instances are indeed all hostile uses. On what basis do these scholars determine that the following passages are hostile?

John 1:19	The Jews send priests and Levites to ask John who he is.
5:10, 15	The Jews point out that the healing took place on the Sabbath, whereas the hostility does not seem to begin until v. 16.
8:22	The Jews may be confused, but they are not overtly hostile.
10:24	The Jews demand to know whether Jesus is the Christ.
18:12	The officers of the Jews, not the Jewish people as a whole, arrest Jesus.
19:31	The Jews' breaking the legs before Passover is not depicted as an overtly hostile act but as one dictated by law or custom.[14]

One can be excused for thinking that interpretation of at least some of these passages as clearly hostile is based upon a prior conception of this hostility, and not upon examination in context. Similarly, I believe that one more instance should be included in the list of negative or hostile passages that are not included in von Wahlde's agreed list of thirty-one:

John 11:54	Jesus does not walk openly among the Jews, presumably because they are planning to kill him, as they are earlier in the immediate and larger context (v. 53).

This analysis indicates that there are a variety of factors at play in the analysis of the use of οἱ Ἰουδαῖοι, and that the linguistic situation is too complex simply to categorize usage on the basis of whether there is purported hostility or not indicated, especially when there is a thoughtful concern for

---

13. By way of contrast, my analysis concludes that twenty-six are probably negative in sense (see the two lists above).

14. See ch. 8 of this monograph for discussion of the nonbreaking of Jesus' legs as part of John's Passover theme.

the larger literary context. The determination of hostility is simply too neb-
ulous to provide a firm criterion for assessing what the phrase means.

Recently, Bieringer, Pollefeyt, and Vandecasteele-Vanneuville have endorsed the notion of differentiating sense and reference.[15] In their scheme,
reference involves an object in the real world to which one refers by using
a particular expression. Sense is the intralinguistic meaning or meanings
of such an expression, that is, its meaning(s) in relation to the other words
within a language.[16] They claim that attention must be paid to both but do
not make clear the nature of their relationship. Nevertheless, these authors
caution against views that neglect reference and that see the term "the Jews"
as "purely a literary category and of obscuring the fact that there remains
a connection with real people."[17] They are particularly concerned with examples in which the Jews are depicted in strongly adverse ways. However,
it appears that Bieringer, Pollefeyt, and Vandecasteele-Vanneuville, along
with those they represent, have confused sense and reference. One of their
mistakes is to fail to note that referentiality is a function of language users,
not simply of lexemes or of word groups. In this regard, there can never be
a separation of sense and reference, in that words with sense are used to
refer; sense mediates between the linguistic construction and the referent.[18]

15. Bieringer, Pollefeyt, and Vandecasteele-Vanneuville, "Wrestling with Johannine
Anti-Judaism," in *Anti-Judaism in the Fourth Gospel*, 18-22, esp. 21, citing J. Lyons, *Introduction to Theoretical Linguistics* (Cambridge: Cambridge University Press, 1968), 427 (see
425-28). For a basic discussion, see J. R. Hurford, B. Heasley, and M. B. Smith, *Semantics:
A Coursebook* (2nd ed.; Cambridge: Cambridge University Press, 2007), esp. 26-35 and
throughout. J. Ashton (*Understanding the Fourth Gospel* [Oxford: Clarendon Press, 1991],
132-33 [2nd ed., 2007, 66]) distinguishes between denotation and connotation, although it
is unclear how this helps solve the issue for him (pp. 131-37 [64-69] summarize his earlier
article, "Identity and Function").

16. J. Lyons, to whom Bieringer et al. refer, is actually more complex on this issue in his
later writings. Whereas he distinguished between sense and reference in his earlier work,
he came to differentiate between sense, reference, and denotation (J. Lyons, *Semantics* [2
vols.; Cambridge: Cambridge University Press, 1977], 1:174-229). If Culpepper's analysis
is accepted, that the use of οἱ Ἰουδαῖοι is on two levels of analysis, with at least one being
literary, then perhaps the category of denotation needs to be considered. However, I do not
believe that he is correct, and the notion of reference in this context will be sufficient for
the point that I am trying to make.

17. Bieringer, Pollefeyt, and Vandecasteele-Vanneuville, "Wrestling with Johannine
Anti-Judaism," 22.

18. S. Davis and B. S. Gillon, "Introduction," in *Semantics: A Reader* (ed. S. Davis and
B. S. Gillon; Oxford: Oxford University Press, 2004), 1-130, here 88. I admit that I too have
changed my perspective on this because of the cogent prompting of Christopher Land.

Reference is the procedure by which speakers or writers, by means of words (or word groups), identify and invoke entities in the real world. It is sense that relates the words to other words, and hence has the potential for negative meaning. Whereas Bieringer et al. seem to wish to invoke reference, what they are actually attempting to analyze is sense. Rather than attention to sense obscuring the reality of reference, I believe that paying close attention to sense relations — established by how words are used in relation to each other in context — helps us to establish the meaning of the word group οἱ Ἰουδαῖοι within John's Gospel. However, having said that, I believe that the author intends for us to understand the contextually specific senses that he establishes as referring to particular groups of people in the extratextual world. These particular groups vary in size, composition, and, to be sure, the emotive connotations sometimes associated with them — but these connotations come from the sense of the words used to identify these groups.

Confusion over reference has, nevertheless, been an apparent problem in previous discussion. The proposals that have been analyzed above all appear to endorse the notion that there is a single referent for the term οἱ Ἰουδαῖοι, with a large amount of negative connotative freight attached to it as well. These proposals, however, often have apparently got their categories reversed. They are confusing instances of reference for the sense of the term οἱ Ἰουδαῖοι. On the basis of the analysis presented above, I believe that, when the word group οἱ Ἰουδαῖοι is used in John's Gospel, it has as its monosemous sense a group of people (two or more) who are to be identified, by beliefs and practices, with the Jewish people as a religious-ethnic group.[19] In John's Gospel, the determination of this sense is perhaps made clearest by means of a significant number of instances where "the Jews" are mentioned in relation to various festivals, celebrations, or rituals, such as purification, Passover, and Sabbath, and to various positions of authority within such practices, among others. This usage identifies the sense of "the Jews" as a group of people distinguished by their particular sets of beliefs and practices and those who lead them in such practices. We know that the ancient Jews were in fact identified by their distinctive behavior and beliefs.

19. The foundation of this statement is in lexical monosemy. See S. E. Porter, "Greek Linguistics and Lexicography," in *Understanding the Times: New Testament Studies in the Twenty-First Century: Essays in Honor of D. A. Carson on the Occasion of His Sixty-Fifth Birthday* (ed. A. J. Köstenberger and R. W. Yarbrough; Wheaton, IL: Crossway, 2011), 19-61, esp. 31-37; G. P. Fewster, *Creation Language in Romans 8: A Study in Monosemy* (LBS 8; Leiden: Brill, 2013), 18-48; cf. C. Ruhl, *On Monosemy: A Study in Linguistic Semantics* (Albany, NY: SUNY Press, 1989).

John's usage seems to maintain this sense also when the Gospel sometimes simply contrasts "the Jews" with other groups or persons, or sometimes identifies them with certain other identifiable groups, as if to say that these people are "the Jews," as opposed to others who are not called "the Jews." Only if such a framework of contrast and identification is in place can we understand a number of other, less precisely defined uses. In many of these instances, nothing contextual indicates who "the Jews" are in relation to others in the context. One must know this religious-ethnic sense in advance, or these passages are difficult to interpret.

We begin with this sense of the term "the Jews." As noted above, many interpreters of the Johannine word group οἱ Ἰουδαῖοι conflate (or do not differentiate) sense and reference, so that the negative connotations conveyed in certain uses are attributed to the words themselves and then transferred to all their uses. Some then conclude that the author of John's Gospel had universally negative emotions toward "the Jews" in general.[20] There is no doubt that a number of instances, perhaps even close to half of the total instances, show negative connotations in the use of οἱ Ἰουδαῖοι. These negative connotations, however, come from the contexts in which the expression is used, including such acts as stoning, grumbling, arguing, and the like. One must also not forget, however, that, in well over half of the instances, the supposed anti-Jewish sentiments often associated with the use of the expression οἱ Ἰουδαῖοι are nowhere in view. Any successful explanation of the meaning of οἱ Ἰουδαῖοι in John's Gospel must account for this absence of negativity. These two broad categories of use — broadly, contextually differentiated meanings — can be accounted for as various contextual uses of the term οἱ Ἰουδαῖοι. In other words, the sense of οἱ Ἰουδαῖοι is modulated by context or realized in a given instance. That is, the sense of the phrase "the Jews" contextually varies in John's Gospel.

Before attempting to provide a more detailed examination of given instances, I wish to make several linguistic observations regarding the Greek article that are relevant to the investigation, as the use of the article οἱ with Ἰουδαῖοι has proved to be problematic in previous discussion. There is a tendency among scholars to take the articular use of οἱ Ἰουδαῖοι as indicating a specific and defined group (with the article indicating definiteness), as if the group were to be equated with all Jews, or "the Jews as a whole and entire people." Yet this is not how the article functions in Greek.

20. See, e.g., Reinhartz, "'Jews' and Jews in the Fourth Gospel," in *Anti-Judaism and the Fourth Gospel*, 213-14.

There has been widespread confusion and misunderstanding regarding the Greek article, much of it related to its supposed origins in the demonstrative pronoun.[21] A better approach is to see the article as a structural indicator that has various contextually based functional uses.[22] The article serves to define or disambiguate the sense relations of the words or phrases in construction with it. However, interpreters often confuse the structural uses of the article with the meanings of the substantive used with that article. The notion of so-called generic usage is a case in point. Many scholars seem to interpret the article in οἱ Ἰουδαῖοι as a generic use, so that the phrase designates Jews in general (i.e., a generic category of Jews), and so by implication (again) all Jewish people.[23] This interpretation allows for sweeping statements about the Gospel's characterization of the Jewish people, but this supposed use is impossible to sustain in so many instances that it must be dismissed out of hand — and with it perhaps many of the extreme claims made for the anti-Jewish bias of the Gospel. As just mentioned, the article can be used in various ways on the basis of its function in context. One of these functions is what might be termed a singularizing use (related perhaps to so-called demonstrative use, though without appealing to an original function of the article). In this case, οἱ Ἰουδαῖοι is identified as a structural (and, hence, meaning) unit as opposed to another group or other or wider groups (contrastive meaning units). A rendering might be "these Jews," or "the particular Jews here or involved in this situation," identifying them as the participants in a particular episode.

So when the author of the Gospel sometimes mentions that "the Jews" are involved in particular discussions, it is usually contextually clear that the reference to "the Jews" is specifying a particular group, as opposed to other possible groups (such as the Greeks) or some subgroup of Jewish people among other possible Jews (such as the Pharisees), whether it is possible to define them precisely or not. Some claim that the author is making this grammatically and conceptually identified group of people speak on behalf of all Jews, a claim that invariably forces the author of the Gospel into the

21. On the article, the best overall treatment now is R. D. Peters, *The Greek Article: A Functional Grammar of ὁ-items in the Greek New Testament, with Special Emphasis on the Greek Article* (LBS 9; Leiden: Brill, 2014).
22. I note that my developing view of the article as a structural indicator is consistent with an earlier discussion by R. W. Funk (*A Beginning-Intermediate Grammar of Hellenistic Greek* [3 vols.; Missoula, MT: SBL, 1973], 85-89), who calls the article a "structure indicator," though without precisely defining it beyond noting that it specifies a head term.
23. See, e.g., J. F. McHugh, *John 1-4* (ICC; London: T&T Clark, 2009), 207.

position of being anti-Jewish.[24] It is hard to accept this claim, however, given that the Johannine author clearly realizes that Jesus and virtually all of his followers are Jews. This usage instead supports the notion that the author is identifying "the Jews" as a contextually identified group within the larger sphere of Judaism, that is, those Jews who are opposed to Jesus. This understanding is related to what some might call a partitive usage of the article with οἱ Ἰουδαῖοι.[25] In this instance, a person or group of people is seen to be a part of the larger group called "the Jews." Quite clearly, therefore, the term "the Jews" is being used in the more comprehensive sense of the people who are religiously and ethnically identified as Jews, which comprises several subgroups recognized within this larger group. Sometimes these groups are explicitly identified, and sometimes they are not. Each of these features must be determined by the particular context in which the construction is found.

A fairly common use of the Greek article that makes its structural characteristics clear is its various discourse functions. One structural use of the Greek article, so-called anaphoric usage, creates discourse continuity. This explains instances when οἱ Ἰουδαῖοι is used to continue to invoke a group that has already been introduced (this is especially the case in the Lazarus episode in John 11 and the trial in John 19; see below). With this usage also, it is inappropriate to posit generalizations about the Jewish people in general on the basis of the meanings of these passages within context.

Taking all of the aforementioned into account, I believe that it is entirely appropriate to understand the sense of the word group οἱ Ἰουδαῖοι as meaning an ethnically/religiously identified group of people and to render it often as "the Jews." However, this sense is modulated or realized in varying contexts by a variety of co-textual constraints (i.e., various features, linguistic and other) that narrow that general sense in particular ways. Their basic sense relations, as well as their particular contextual modulations, are to be understood within their appropriate contexts and, depending upon the understanding of these constraints, may well be rendered in varying ways. The question of referentiality, therefore, is to a large extent out-

24. E.g., A. Reinhartz, *Befriending the Beloved Disciple: A Jewish Reading of the Gospel of John* (London: T&T Clark, 2001), 84-87, although she does not draw direct attention to the Greek article. This position, I believe, reveals the tendency to bias of some interpreters who wish to find the biblical author guilty, rather than realizing that the author of John's Gospel himself differentiates among various Jews.

25. On the nature of partitive usage, see J. M. Anderson, *The Grammar of Names* (Oxford: Oxford University Press, 2007), 41 and throughout.

side the parameters of this discussion — without minimizing the issue of connecting the world of the text with the extratextual world by means of sense relations. Simplistically, we could say that the referents of the term οἱ Ἰουδαῖοι in their various linguistic and co-textual configurations are the historically identified groups of people indicated by the word group in its various textual contexts.[26]

The following are the major contextually based meanings that are to be found in John's Gospel.

a. "The Jews" as the Jewish People

The major category of usage of οἱ Ἰουδαῖοι is one that indicates the Jews as a whole. We see this usage exemplified in two major ways. The first and primary means is semantico-syntactically. These instances typically include two constraints, one semantic and the other syntactic. The semantic constraint is that οἱ Ἰουδαῖοι is collocated with vocabulary that encompasses features of Jewish religion and ethnicity. The syntactic constraint is that οἱ Ἰουδαῖοι is used within a genitive word group modifying a head term indicating a feature of Jewish religion-ethnicity. The governed genitive word group indicating the Jewish people as a whole restricts the meaning of the head term, often identifying it by restricting the range of options.[27] The semantic linkage may involve customs, practices, or people associated with Judaism. An example would be Passover, where the construction τὸ πάσχα τῶν Ἰουδαίων (literally "the Passover of the Jews") can be rendered "the Jewish Passover," restricting the Passover to the Jewish one. Examples of this sense of "the Jews" include the following with customs and practices:

2:6	Jewish purification
2:13; 11:55	Jewish Passover
5:1; 6:4; 7:2	Jewish feast
18:20	Jewish temple
19:40	Jewish custom
19:42	Jewish preparation

26. I have not dealt with singular usage. This occurs in John 3:25, 4:9 and 19:35, each time where reference is made to a particular instance of one being a Jew identified by religion or ethnicity.

27. On the genitive, see S. E. Porter, *Idioms of the Greek New Testament* (2nd ed.; BLG 2; Sheffield: Sheffield Academic Press, 1994), 92.

Examples with individuals include:

3:1	Jewish leader (Nicodemus)
11:19; 12:9, 11; 19:20	many of the Jews
18:33, 39; 19:3, 19, 21 bis	Jewish king
19:21	Jewish chief priests

b. "The Jews" as Restricted Groups

The second major category of usage of οἱ Ἰουδαῖοι is that of definition by opposition. For example, in John 4:9 "the Jews" are defined in opposition to the Samaritans, a case of semantic antinomy.

A number of other instances require special attention to context to understand the sense more fully. I discuss here four extensive passages, and then consider several individual instances. Whereas in some instances the Jews as a whole are indicated by context and, often, by various syntactic indicators, in the vast majority of the instances here they are modulated (i.e., restricted) to designate a restricted subsection of the Jewish people pertinent to the particular context. In other words, the terminology of "the Jews" in many instances has the sense of a restricted subgroup within the Jews as a whole.

The first set of examples is in John 10, where Jesus delivers his good shepherd discourse. In 10:19 the author says that there was a division among the Jews (ἐν τοῖς Ἰουδαίοις) because of his words. The prepositional phrase is used to indicate the larger group within which the division occurs.[28] "The Jews" here must be those Jews who heard this discourse. To argue otherwise, I believe, is needlessly tendentious. The division arises on account of the words and thus is restricted to those who heard the words, as is indicated in the result: many of them (πολλοὶ ἐξ αὐτῶν) were saying that he had a demon, and others (ἄλλοι) that his words were not those of someone demon possessed. The composite of those with differing opinions represents "the Jews" in this context (i.e., the Jews who were divided, certainly not all Jews everywhere).

The scene changes in John 10:22 to the temple. Jesus is walking there, and "the Jews" surround him. Those surrounding Jesus are clearly not all Jews but a group of Jews who happen to be in the temple and who have

28. See Porter, *Idioms*, 156-57.

questions about who Jesus is. The context does not necessarily say more specifically who they are, but they may have been some from either of the groups specified above, or at least Jews who had similar questions about Jesus. It is likely that they should be closely identified with his skeptics, because before the episode is over, they take up stones to kill him (10:31, 33; cf. 11:8, where these Jews are again referred to as seeking to stone Jesus).

John 11, the healing of Lazarus, includes a number of instances to consider. John 11:19 says that many of the Jews (πολλοὶ . . . ἐκ τῶν Ἰουδαίων) came to Martha and Mary. The "many" are defined as part of a larger group of Jews. This usage resembles the first category above, which includes the Jews as a whole but is probably better seen as simply designating the identity of the group from which the many originated. When Jesus arrives, he speaks with Martha and then wishes to speak with Mary. The Jews who are with her (οἱ . . . Ἰουδαῖοι οἱ ὄντες μετ᾽ αὐτῆς, v. 31) go out when she does, thinking she is heading for the tomb. "The Jews" here are constrained (i.e., in this instance, restricted) by the articular modifying participle to those accompanying her. Jesus sees her and those Jews coming with her crying (τοὺς συνελθόντας αὐτῇ Ἰουδαίους κλαίοντας, v. 33). It is these Jews who comment on how much Jesus loved Lazarus (v. 36), even though certain ones (τινὲς . . . ἐξ αὐτῶν, v. 37), an even smaller group within those accompanying her, comment that he was not able to save Lazarus from death. After Lazarus is raised, many of these Jews (πολλοὶ . . . ἐκ τῶν Ἰουδαίων) who have come to Mary and seen what Jesus has done believe in him (v. 45). However, certain ones go to the Pharisees. The chief priests and the Pharisees gather the Sanhedrin, and they end up plotting to kill Jesus (vv. 46-53). Thus, the narrator of the Gospel says that Jesus no longer walked openly among the Jews (ἐν τοῖς Ἰουδαίοις, v. 54). Here "the Jews" includes any Jews who were hostile to him, including the leaders (Pharisees and chief priests and members of the Sanhedrin), but it is probably also meant to include a broader group of people who might potentially go to such leaders, like those Jews mentioned in v. 46 as plotting against him.[29] If a more general expression had been used, such as "some (Jewish) people" rather than simply "the Jews," the meaning here would have been referentially the same. The sense is larger than simply the leaders, but it is not all-inclusive, since it would not include Jews who were sympathetic to what Jesus was doing.

---

29. An important factor is Jesus no longer openly walking among the Jewish people, since it says that Jesus went into the country near the desert, where he stayed with his disciples.

John 18 contains many uses of οἱ Ἰουδαῖοι. The usage in this chapter begins with 18:12, where it says that the cohort and the chiliarch and the servants of the Jews (οἱ ὑπηρέται τῶν Ἰουδαίων) take Jesus to Annas the high priest, father-in-law of Caiaphas, the high priest that year. Caiaphas, however, had advised the Jews (τοῖς Ἰουδαίοις, v. 14) that it was necessary for one to die for the people. John 18:3 indicates that these servants are the servants of the chief priests and the Pharisees. This usage resembles the first category above, where the sense is modulated by the defining (restrictive) genitive word group. The use here is probably more restrictive, as servants are not an integral part of Judaism, but are those servants who serve Jewish leaders. These are servants of a particular group within Judaism, and so the construction could well be rendered "servants of the Jewish leaders." This is an instance where the article is used to structurally identify the Jews involved, that is, certain servants of the leaders. Likewise, Caiaphas had already advised a similar group, as noted in 11:47, when the chief priests and Pharisees convened the Sanhedrin as Caiaphas had advised them (vv. 49-50). When Jesus is interrogated by Annas regarding his disciples and teaching, Jesus says that he had spoken boldly to the world. This includes his teaching in the synagogue and in the temple, where all the Jews (πάντες οἱ Ἰουδαῖοι) gathered (18:20). This inclusive use does not, of course, include every Jew, but only those Jews who made it to the temple, including those who gathered at Pentecost, but nevertheless is indicative of potential representatives of all subgroups of the Jews. Later, after being sent to Caiaphas (v. 24), Jesus is taken to Pilate. The group that takes him presumably consists of the same group of servants of the chief priests and Pharisees, as well as their leaders. The leaders stay outside the praetorium so that they are not ritually defiled (v. 28), and Pilate returns to them (v. 38). When Pilate says that they should punish Jesus according to their own law, the Jews (οἱ Ἰουδαῖοι) who respond must be these same Jews, that is, the Jewish leaders (v. 31). These same Jews are the ones that Jesus refers to in v. 36, when he says that, if his kingdom were of this world, his servants would have fought so that he might not be handed over to the Jews, that is, the leaders who were responsible for his arrest (τοῖς Ἰουδαίοις). Within the trial scene, however, there are several uses that are more inclusive. In particular are the occurrences in John 18:33 and 39 identifying Jesus as the king of the Jews (ὁ βασιλεὺς τῶν Ἰουδαίων). Here "the Jews" would certainly include the Jewish leaders and their servants, but the phrase also seems to have a much wider sense, since the discussion is in the context of considering the kingdoms of this world. Nevertheless, along with these uses, throughout this section there is the more circumscribed sense of the "the Jews" as indicating the Jewish leaders and their servants.

The last section is John 19. Despite the depiction by some of this scene as involving large crowds,[30] there is contextual evidence that this scene involves a much smaller group of people. When Pilate presents Jesus as king of the Jews (19:3), it is the chief priests and their servants (vv. 6 and 15) who demand that Jesus be crucified: these Jews (v. 7) answer that their law demands that Jesus be crucified, challenge Pilate's loyalty to Caesar (v. 12), and are subsequently addressed by Pilate (v. 14). Later in the episode, in the dispute over the words on the *titulus* (see above on the expression ὁ βασιλεὺς τῶν Ἰουδαίων in 18:33, 39), John's Gospel says that many of the Jews (πολλοὶ . . . τῶν Ἰουδαίων) read it (19:20) because of its prominent location on the cross. The sense here is similar to that above, indicating many people from the larger group of the Jewish religious-ethnic group — though admittedly restricted to those who have access to Jerusalem. However, it is the Jewish chief priests (οἱ ἀρχιερεῖς τῶν Ἰουδαίων) who react negatively to the wording on the cross (v. 21). In this context, it is possible that the phrase in v. 20 has the sense of the Jewish leaders and their servants and followers. Certainly, this smaller group represents "the Jews" who are concerned about Jesus' body staying on the cross during Passover (cf. earlier 18:28) and who therefore ask Pilate to ensure that Jesus is dead (19:31). When Nicodemus comes to ask for the body of Jesus and is fearful of the Jews (διὰ τὸν φόβον τῶν Ἰουδαίων, v. 38), these leaders are the ones whom he fears, since he is one of them (see 3:1). Similarly, in an episode in John 7:13 during a celebration, the people there, who are no doubt Jews, since it is the Feast of Tabernacles, are said to be afraid of the Jews (διὰ τὸν φόβον τῶν Ἰουδαίων), using the same language as in 19:38. In this instance, one group of Jews is said to be fearful of another group. Also similar is 20:19 with the same phrasing, and 9:22 with slightly different wording. All of these instances have a sense in which the Jews involved are various configurations of the leaders, and hence the appropriateness of a rendering such as "the Jewish leaders."

Besides the examples treated above, there are several uses that have not already been discussed. They are as follows.

John 1:19 ("the Jews from Jerusalem sent priests and Levites"): These Jews are probably the Jewish leaders, including the chief priests

---

30. See, e.g., C. S. Keener, *The Gospel of John: A Commentary* (2 vols.; Peabody, MA: Hendrickson, 2003), 2:1118.

and other members of the Sanhedrin (see also John 18 and 19). The
phrase οἱ Ἰουδαῖοι specifies a group in a particular location who
have authority to send out other Jews of rank, that is, some level
of Jewish leaders.

John 2:18, 20 (the Jews question Jesus after his cleansing the temple): In
2:14 Jesus is said to have found those selling animals and changing
money, whom he throws out. "The Jews" in vv. 18 and 20 who then
speak to him would appear to be this same group or their super-
visors, since they directly ask about his actions in the temple (see
v. 20).

John 4:22 ("salvation is from the Jews"; ἡ σωτηρία ἐκ τῶν Ἰουδαίων
ἐστίν): This appears to be an inclusive use that refers to the Jews
religiously/ethnically. The modifying prepositional phrase limits
the type of salvation by indicating its origins, but the context does
not further restrict who these "Jews" are.

John 5:10, 15, 16, 18: This set of uses occurs after Jesus has healed the man
in the pool at Bethesda. The Jews point out that it was on the Sabbath (v. 10). Then, after Jesus finds the man in the temple and speaks
to him, the man goes away (ἀπῆλθεν) and announces to the Jews
that Jesus is the one who has healed him (v. 15). On account of this
action by Jesus, the Jews (v. 16) are seeking Jesus to kill him (v. 18).
It appears that these Jews, who are linked to either the temple or
other Jews nearby, occupy a position of leadership. The similarities
to the group that will finally decide to kill Jesus at a meeting of the
Sanhedrin (see John 18 above) are noteworthy.

John 6:41, 52 (the Jews objected to Jesus' words concerning the bread
of life): In these two instances, the Jewish leaders — or at any rate
a group of Jews capable of being distinguished from others — are
apparently being referred to, since they are defined as a portion of
the crowd that heard Jesus' words (6:22).

John 7:1, 11, 13, 15 (Jesus was in Galilee, not in Judea, because the Jews
were seeking to kill him): In this instance the interpretation of "the
Judeans" has its greatest support. However, whereas it may be true
that those seeking to kill Jesus are from Judea, it is not simply the
Judeans who are seeking to kill him. The distinction here is more
likely one about geographic jurisdiction. Judea was under the control of Pilate as Roman procurator, whereas the Galilee region was
under Herod Antipas. Thus the Jewish leaders in Jerusalem (Judea)
would have been outside of their authority in Galilee, and they are

the ones seeking to kill Jesus. This understanding is supported by subsequent usage, when the author says that Jesus went to Jerusalem for the Feast of Tabernacles; that is, he left Galilee and reentered the Judean territory (vv. 11, 15).

John 7:35 (after the chief priests and Pharisees send servants to arrest Jesus [v. 32], the Jews question each other regarding what Jesus is saying): Although it may be the servants who are asking these questions, the context here is probably better seen as indicating the chief priests and the Pharisees, or the Jewish leaders, doing the questioning.

John 8:22 (cf. 13:33), 31, 48, 52, 57 (the Jews inquire about Jesus): In 8:13 John says that the Pharisees speak to Jesus. Then, in v. 21, Jesus speaks again to them (πάλιν αὐτοῖς). These Jews (v. 22) are the Pharisees of v. 13, as are the Jews of vv. 48, 52, and 57. In v. 31 "the Jews" are syntactically defined as the Jews who believe in Jesus ("the Jews" is limited by the modifying participle to indicate those who believe), but the ensuing context identifies those who are trying to kill him (vv. 37, 40) and indicates that the Pharisees are in view. The intervening reference to those who believe in Jesus, using the modifying participle, may indicate a group different from that defined by οἱ Ἰουδαῖοι, while the simple reference to "the Jews" retains the anaphoric reference (using the article) to the Pharisees.

John 9:18, 22 (the healing of the man born blind): Verse 13 refers to the man being brought to the Pharisees. These same Pharisees are the ones who, in v. 18 designated as "the Jews," do not believe that the man was born blind, and whom the parents, themselves Jews, fear in v. 22.

John 13:33 ("even as I told the Jews"): The sense of "the Jews" here is the same as in 8:22, the Pharisees, since it is to these Pharisees that Jesus first makes the comment that they are not able to follow him where he is going.

One can see that a common pattern is for the word group "the Jews" to have various modulations, or limitations, of its sense on the basis of context (sometimes including structural indicators) so as to restrict its meaning to a variety of subgroups within Judaism, such as the Pharisees, chief priests, or other leaders. These groups are often invoked earlier in the discourse (in this sense the two constructions with different senses, "the Jews" and another group, have the same referent).

4. Jesus and the Jews in Religious Conflict

The above discussion has indicated quite clearly that the major religious conflict in John's Gospel is between two fundamentally differing religious orientations. The one orientation is that of Jesus and those who follow him, a group that later came to be known as Christians. The other is that of Judaism as a religious-ethnic group, especially as it is represented by the chief priests, Pharisees, and other Jewish leaders.

In his classic formulation of the two levels of the Johannine discourse, J. Louis Martyn has proposed that the book of John reflects circumstances in the late first century, by which time the Jews had expelled from the synagogue those who believed that Jesus was the Messiah (a situation supposedly reflected in John 9:22; cf. also 12:42; 16:2).[31] His scenario supposes that Jewish Christians were still worshipping in synagogues until the addition of the Birkat ha-Minim (the "blessing" [i.e., curse] on the heretics) made it untenable for Christians to remain. Accordingly, it was the Jews who came to believe that Christians were incompatible with Judaism, rather than Christians rejecting Judaism. Although a number of scholars still hold to this viewpoint, often as an attempt to provide an explanation for the supposed anti-Jewish passages in John's Gospel, the theory has fallen on hard times.[32]

The objections to Martyn's position are several.[33] Some scholars do not

---

31. Martyn, *History and Theology.*

32. Recent works supporting Martyn's thesis include Ashton, *Understanding the Fourth Gospel*, 107-9; S. G. Wilson, *Related Strangers: Jews and Christians, 70-170 CE* (Minneapolis: Fortress Press, 1995), 71-80; R. B. Hays, *The Moral Vision of the New Testament* (New York: HarperSanFrancisco, 1996), 407-43; A. Reinhartz, "On Travel, Translation, and Ethnography: Johannine Scholarship at the Turn of the Century," in *"What Is John?"* vol. 2: *Literary and Social Readings of the Fourth Gospel* (ed. F. F. Segovia; SympS 7; Atlanta: Scholars Press, 1998), 249-56; E. W. Stegemann and W. Stegemann, *The Jesus Movement: A Social History of Its First Century* (Minneapolis: Fortress Press, 1999), 226-31; J. H. Charlesworth, "The Gospel of John: Exclusivism Caused by a Social Setting Different from That of Jesus (John 11:54 and 14:6)," in *Anti-Judaism and the Fourth Gospel*, 479-513; de Boer, "Depiction of 'the Jews,'" 260-80; Smith, *Fourth Gospel*, 47-56; J. Marcus, "Birkat Ha-Minim Revisited," *NTS* 55 (2009): 523-51.

33. For a thorough discussion of the various criticisms of Martyn's hypothesis, see E. W. Klink, "Expulsion from the Synagogue? Rethinking a Johannine Anachronism," *TynBul* 59.1 (2008): 99-118; Klink, "The Overrealized Expulsion in the Gospel of John," in *John, Jesus, and History*, vol. 2: *Aspects of Historicity in the Fourth Gospel* (ed. P. N. Anderson, F. Just, and T. Thatcher; Atlanta: SBL, 2009), 175-84; and in particular on the question of "the Jews," by Hakola, *Identity Matters*, 41-86. See also W. V. Cirafesi, "The Johannine Community Hypothesis (1968–Present): Past and Present Approaches and a New Way Forward," *CBR* 12.2 (2014): 173-93.

think that the Johannine passages that mention departure from the synagogue do in fact refer to the split between Judaism and Christianity. These texts are seen by some to reflect some form of local conflict, rather than a widespread and complete separation. A further problem is the Birkat ha-Minim itself. Pertinent questions have been raised concerning the dating of inclusion of the supposed benediction against Christians, whether it was required that Christians and Jews say it, and whether in fact it even referred to Christians.[34] If it did not, then no matter how one construes the other issues, it could not have been used to exclude Christians from the synagogue.

A further set of considerations must enter into the equation. First, the allegedly anti-Jewish passages are not necessarily anti-Jewish. They can all be interpreted otherwise, either as neutral references to Judaism religiously or ethnically, as references to some contrastive group, or as references to some group within Judaism itself, often Jewish leaders such as the chief priests, Pharisees, or their servants (see above). Second, although the standard parting-of-the-ways scenario coheres nicely with the claim that we observe a late first-century anti-Judaism in John's Gospel, there is plenty of evidence that the separation between Judaism and what was to become identified as Christianity began during the ministry of Jesus; it was already well underway during the time of Paul's missionary endeavors and was nearly complete by the time of the fall of Jerusalem.[35] This timeline pushes Jewish-Christian tensions much earlier and makes it possible to argue that the tensions reflected in John's Gospel are reflections of tensions that already existed during Jesus' ministry and that resulted in his crucifixion. This tension arose because of competing religious models. As E. P. Sanders, J. D. G. Dunn, and others have clearly noted, the Jews during this time took great pride in religious bound-

---

34. On the benediction, see esp. Y. Y. Teppler, ed., *Birkat haMinim: Jews and Christians in Conflict in the Ancient World* (TSAJ 120; Tübingen: Mohr Siebeck, 2007); see also R. Kimelman, "Birkat ha-Minim and the Lack of Evidence for an Anti-Christian Jewish Prayer in Late Antiquity," in *Jewish and Christian Self-Definition*, vol. 2: *Aspects of Judaism in the Greco-Roman Period* (ed. E. P. Sanders, A. I. Baumgarten, and A. Mendelson; Philadelphia: Fortress Press, 1981), 226-44; W. Horbury, "The Benediction of the Minim and Early Jewish-Christian Controversy," *JTS* 33 (1982): 19-61; Reinhartz, *Befriending the Beloved Disciple*, 37-53; D. Boyarin, "The Ioudaioi in John and the Prehistory of 'Judaism,'" in *Pauline Conversations in Context: Essays in Honor of Calvin J. Roetzel* (ed. J. C. Anderson, P. Sellew, and C. Setzer; JSNTSup 221; London: Sheffield Academic Press, 2002), 216-39; and Edwards, *Discovering John*, 47-48.

35. On the issue of the separation of Jews and Christians, see S. E. Porter and B. W. R. Pearson, "Why the Split? Christians and Jews by the Fourth Century," *JGRChJ* 1 (2000): 82-119.

ary markers, such as the law, rituals and feasts, and of course the importance of the temple.[36] This tension is reflected in John's Gospel, where Jesus seems to be in conflict with the Jewish leaders over each one of them. For example, he confronts the law by healing on the Sabbath. He runs into conflict with the Jerusalem leaders when he is in Jerusalem for various feasts, and because of his teaching they begin to seek to kill him. Lastly, Jesus directly confronts the temple cult by cleansing the temple and making pronouncements about it (which the Jewish leaders interpret as referring to the actual physical temple). These factors do not necessarily point to an early date of composition for John's Gospel (although they might fit within such a scenario), but they do indicate that the events depicted in John's Gospel reflect tensions present during Jesus' ministry. They reach even to the point of the author not seeing "the Jews" as fellow religious-ethnic followers but as antagonists perhaps even during the life and ministry of Jesus, hence his identification of them, though he shares ethnicity with them, as "the Jews." In that sense, the language regarding "the Jews" reflects internecine debate, with the added dimension that such debate indicates even more fundamental disagreements that led early on to a parting of the ways of Judaism and Christianity.[37]

5. Conclusions

There has been much discussion of language regarding "the Jews" in John's Gospel. Much of the recent discussion has attempted to explain how it is that the author of John's Gospel can use what is often characterized as a blanket condemnation of the Jews. As a result, various proposals have been put forward to attempt to mitigate the problem and "save" the text from apparently justified condemnation. This climate of suspicion and accusation has warranted my detailed investigation of the use of such language in John's Gospel, especially as this language is used by and about and in relationship to Jesus and his depiction in the Gospel. My investigation indicates that the various major previous views regarding "the Jews" in John's Gospel all reveal themselves to be inadequate, for a variety of reasons. None of them presents an analysis that is comprehensive in scope. Few pay attention to

36. See, e.g., E. P. Sanders, *Paul and Palestinian Judaism: A Comparison of Patterns of Religion* (London: SCM Press, 1977); J. D. G. Dunn, *The New Perspective on Paul* (Grand Rapids: Eerdmans, 2007).

37. Thanks are due to Christopher Land for this idea.

fundamental linguistic distinctions, especially between sense and reference, and in particular the need to modulate the sense of "the Jews" on the basis of contextual and other factors. Many take a literalistic view and then read this throughout the entire Gospel and, as a result, condemn the biblical text. Undoubtedly, John's Gospel has been abused by certain individuals and groups wishing to exploit its depiction of severe tension between Jesus and the Jewish authorities. Yet those who wish to fault the biblical text for being anti-Jewish take an equally inflexible view and similarly abuse the text. If my analysis is plausible, then the author of John's Gospel, rather than having strong anti-Jewish tendencies, merely employed clear terms and used reasonable linguistic means to depict Jesus' opponents. In their opposition to Jesus, these opponents indicate a fundamental split between Judaism and what was to become Christianity, grounded in the language of the Gospel.[38]

38. I note that A. J. Köstenberger has adopted my explanation of "the Jews" in his commentary on John's Gospel, based upon an earlier draft of this chapter when it was delivered as a paper. See his *John* (BECNT; Grand Rapids: Baker, 2004), 59 n. 6. Note however that I have modified my methodology, though not my final conclusions, in the light of further thought.

CHAPTER 7

John's Gospel, Truth, and Jesus

1. Introduction

One of the distinguishing concepts in John's Gospel is "truth." In fact, words for truth (in this case, words derived from the root ἀληθ-) appear more often in John's Gospel than in any other book in the New Testament.[1] It would therefore seem prudent to consider how words for truth are used throughout John's Gospel. Various studies have addressed the subject, but far less than one might expect.[2] In this chapter, I consider the question afresh.

1. John leads all NT books with 55 occurrences, compared with Matthew (6x), Mark (6x), Luke (8x), Acts (5x), Romans (9x), 1 Corinthians (2x), 2 Corinthians (9x), Galatians (4x), Ephesians (7x), Philippians (2x), Colossians (2x), 1 Thessalonians (2x), 2 Thessalonians (2x), 1 Timothy (6x), 2 Timothy (6x), Titus (3x), Hebrews (4x), James (3x), 1 Peter (2x), 2 Peter (3x), 1 John (15x), 2 John (5x), 3 John (7x), and Revelation (10x). I am including all of the positive words in semantic domain 72A ("True, False") of the Louw-Nida lexicon, apart from ἀμήν. See J. P. Louw and E. A. Nida, *Greek-English Lexicon of the New Testament: Based on Semantic Domains* (2nd ed.; 2 vols.; New York: United Bible Societies, 1989).

2. Some of the more obvious studies that I have found include C. H. Dodd, *The Bible and the Greeks* (London: Hodder & Stoughton, 1935), 65-75; R. H. Strachan, *The Fourth Gospel: Its Significance and Environment* (London: SCM Press, 1941), esp. 141-45; W. F. Howard, *Christianity according to St. John* (London: Duckworth, 1943); E. K. Lee, *The Religious Thought of St. John* (London: SPCK, 1950), 38-42; C. H. Dodd, *The Interpretation of the Fourth Gospel* (Cambridge: Cambridge University Press, 1953), 170-78; R. E. Brown, *The Gospel according to John* (2 vols.; AB 29, 29A; Garden City, NY: Doubleday, 1966-70), 1:499-501; Y. Ibuki, *Die Wahrheit im Johannesevangelium* (Bonn: Peter Hanstein, 1972); J. Painter, *John: Witness and Theologian* (London: SPCK, 1977); I. de la Potterie, *La vérité dans Saint Jean* (2 vols.; Rome: Biblical Institute Press, 1977); S. S. Smalley, *John: Evangelist and Interpreter* (Exeter: Paternoster, 1978); A. C. Thiselton, "Truth," in *New International Dictionary of New*

For reasons that should be obvious, I do not wish to fall into the lexico-graphical trap of simply equating word and concept (e.g., κύριος = Lord, as indicating God).[3] Neither do I wish to suggest that one can determine conceptual importance on the basis of simple lexical counting. I do think, however — and I am hardly alone in this opinion — that the Johannine use of "truth" language points to something of significance in the Gospel. Pilate's provocative question to Jesus, "What is truth?" (John 18:38), is no doubt the most memorable instance of truth language in the Gospel. It has perplexed scholars and students of John's Gospel, however, that Pilate's question is not answered directly in its immediate context, nor is an explicit and exhaustive answer given in any single episode in John's Gospel. As the Gospel relates this discourse between Jesus and Pilate, there seems to be no response to this seemingly fundamental question by Jesus or the narrator, and the narrative continues as if the question was never even asked. Yet the entire Gospel of John, as I will show, is a graphic narrative and conceptual depiction of embodied and explicated truth. As a whole, the Gospel indicates that truth originates in the tripartite relationship of Father-Son-Spirit, and it is realized in truthful relations between the Son and human beings. This complex tripartite notion forms the basis of instances of "propositional" truth found within the Gospel itself. Thus, the Gospel writer asserts that God is truth (3:33; 7:28; 8:26; 17:3), that Jesus as the preexistent *logos* is truth and that what he does and says is truth (1:9, 14, 17; 8:14, 16; 14:6), and that the Paraclete, sent as the divine continuation of the work of God on earth, is truth (14:17; 15:26; 16:13).[4] On the

---

Testament Theology (ed. C. Brown; 3 vols.; Grand Rapids: Zondervan, 1975), 3:874-902, esp. 889-94; R. B. Edwards, *Discovering John* (London: SPCK, 2003).

3. See the very helpful discussion in J. Barr, *The Semantics of Biblical Language* (Oxford: Oxford University Press, 1961), 187-205. Unfortunately, there is some of this confusion in R. Bultmann, "Ἀλήθεια," *TDNT* 1 (1964): 238-51; E. Hoskyns and F. N. Davey, *The Riddle of the New Testament* (3rd ed.; London: Faber & Faber, 1947), 25-31; E. C. Blackman, "Truth," in *A Theological Word Book of the Bible* (ed. A. Richardson; London: SCM Press, 1950), 269-70; C. Senft, "Truth," in *Vocabulary of the Bible* (ed. J.-J. Von Allmen; London: Lutterworth, 1958), 430-33. A clear example of the word-concept fallacy can be found in E. W. Mburu, *Qumran and the Origins of Johannine Language and Symbolism* (Jewish and Christian Texts, ser. 8; London: T&T Clark, 2010). Mburu's entire study rests on the erroneous premises that (1) a word is equal to a concept and (2) Greek words have underlying Hebrew meanings. For her, John's use of ἀλήθεια can (and perhaps must) be understood, e.g., in the light of the use of the Hebrew word אמת in *Rule of the Community* (1QS; see pp. 141-52). Whether Mburu is aware of it or not, Barr specifically criticized this notion of bringing the thought structure of a Hebrew language user to bear on the analysis of Greek.

4. A. J. Köstenberger and S. R. Swain (*Father, Son, and Spirit: The Trinity and John's Gospel* [NSBT; Downers Grove, IL: InterVarsity Press, 2008]) cast their net wider than I do

basis of God's truth as thus defined, humans are expected to act in truth, particularly in relation to and response to God (3:21; 4:23-24; 5:31, 33; 8:31). This formulation, then, is the further basis of Johannine propositions about truth, by which I mean other statements about truth that are not contained within the tripartite or human relational depiction of truth (8:45-46; 16:7; 17:17; 18:37; 21:24). Truth is, therefore, both relational and propositional (8:32).

In this chapter I define each of these strands independently before bringing them together into a cohesive, even if complex, whole. Most treatments of this sort would probably start with the statement about the *logos* in the prologue to John's Gospel, but I start instead with statements about God. Mainly, I want to address the question of Pilate that seems to go unanswered: what is truth? I believe that, when readers pay attention to the broader usage of "truth" language in the entire Gospel, they discover that what truth is has already been presented to them. As a result, the answer is obvious and explicit enough in John's Gospel that Jesus, or the narrator, does not need to answer Pilate's question directly.

2. God Is True/Truth

Four passages in John's Gospel include the statement, either directly or indirectly, that God is true or truth: John 3:33; 7:28; 8:26; and 17:3.

a. Jesus, John the Baptist, and God as True: John 3:33

John 3:33, the first instance of the use of explicit truth language regarding God, comes at the end of two previous discussions. One is between Jesus and Nicodemus, who represents the Jewish leadership; and the other is between John the Baptist, who represents counterculture religion, and his followers. It is typical of John's Gospel that it is not always clear when a character in the narrative is speaking and when the narrator is speaking. This uncertainty is readily seen in the episode with Nicodemus, where it is not clear when the statements by Jesus in dialogue with Nicodemus end and when the narrator takes over (if he takes over at all; some have speculated that this occurs as late as at 3:16). There is a similar ambiguity at John 3:31. After John the Baptist has

---

and are much more overtly theological in their stated intentions and approach. Nevertheless, my more focused study has some of the same implications as their analysis of John's Gospel.

clarified that, in relation to the Messiah, he must decrease, there is language regarding the one who comes from above. The NASB, for example, puts vv. 31-36 in quotation marks, presumably as the continuing words of John the Baptist, while the Holman Christian Standard Bible does not, treating these verses presumably as the wording of the narrator. If the former is the case, then we have John the Baptist making statements regarding the one from above, but if the latter is the case, then we have these words spoken by the narrator. It is difficult to determine which interpretation to accept, but it seems that the narrator of John's Gospel rarely engages in overt or explicit theological discussion. The narrator most often relates narrative facts. Therefore, I think that it is better to take these words as those of John the Baptist. They are addressed primarily to his own followers.

Regardless of whether the words are from John or from the narrator of the Gospel, the fact that they are placed at the end of this unit involving two different yet significant discussions is important; these words occur within a passage of "consummate Johannine Christology."[5] The first, with Nicodemus, reflects the establishment, or status quo, religious orientation. This perspective is what prompts Jesus' comment to Nicodemus that he is surprised that Nicodemus, as a teacher of Israel, does not know what it means to be born again or be born of the Spirit (John 3:10). In his conversation with Nicodemus, Jesus emphasizes that the kingdom of God is an operative concept and that one must experience a new birth to enter it. Those on earth are testifying to what they know but do not see regarding the work of God, who is intent upon loving and saving the world. The second conversation, between John the Baptist and his followers regarding the baptisms that Jesus is performing, recognizes the temporary nature of John's ministry as appointed by God (i.e., from heaven, v. 27) and as preparatory for the work of the Messiah.

In John 3:31-36 John the Baptist contrasts the heavenly and the earthly.[6] The heavenly is from above and therefore is positionally above everything else. Jesus, as the one who has come from above, John the Baptist says, is therefore above all and testifying to what he has seen and heard when he was above, or in heaven, the realm of God. God is the one who sent him to speak God's words and in fact has entrusted him with all things. Therefore, John the

---

5. C. S. Keener, *The Gospel of John: A Commentary* (2 vols.; Peabody, MA: Hendrickson, 2003), 1:581; cf. W. R. G. Loader, "The Central Structure of Johannine Christology," *NTS* 30 (1984): 188-216.

6. On the descent and ascent theme, see G. C. Nicholson, *Death as Departure: The Johannine Descent-Ascent Scheme* (Chico, CA: Scholars Press, 1983), 21-74.

Baptist says, to accept what Jesus says is to tacitly affirm that God is true or truthful, and also that what God says is true or truthful. John the Baptist uses an interesting logic here. It is something of the sort that, if a = b and b = c, then a = c. That is, if one accepts Jesus and what he says, and if Jesus speaks on God's behalf, then to accept Jesus' words is to accept what God says. By accepting the validity of what Jesus says and noting that Jesus is the surrogate for God, then one affirms God; or in the words of John the Baptist, one affirms that God is true. In other words, one would be inconsistent with what John the Baptist is saying to affirm, for example, the moral teaching of Jesus, without also affirming that whatever Jesus taught was grounded in the truthfulness of God and, by implication, all else that God had taught and revealed as well.[7]

b. Jesus, the Jerusalemites, and the One Who Sent Him: John 7:28

A similar scenario is found in John 7 in Jesus' confrontation with certain ones from Jerusalem (vv. 25-31). These representatives sent by the Jerusalemites know that Jesus has already caused controversy, even to the point that some want to kill him (v. 25), yet the fact that no one approaches him while he is speaking makes them wonder whether he is the Messiah (even though they believe that he cannot be the Messiah because of his lowly origins). Jesus cries out to them that they in fact do know him and know where he is from, yet he points to God as the one who sent him. He states that the one who sent him, God, is true (v. 28), but they do not know God as he does, since he is the sent one.[8] Whereas John the Baptist in the earlier episode notes that acceptance of Jesus implies acceptance of the one who sent him, here we have a case in which Jesus bears witness to God, but despite their knowing Jesus — though clearly not accepting him as Messiah, since they do know

7. D. A. Carson (*The Gospel according to John* [PNTC; Grand Rapids: Eerdmans; Leicester: InterVarsity Press, 1991], 213) is right that the converse is also true, i.e., that "not to believe Jesus is to call God a liar." Perhaps this passage was what stood behind C. S. Lewis's well-known statement, sometimes called a trilemma, that one must accept Jesus either as what he claimed to be or as a madman or as a liar.

8. Note the use of the perfect tense-forms (stative aspect) throughout the verse, including three instances of οἶδα and ἐλήλυθα, in response to the use of the perfect by the Jerusalemites who claim to know where Jesus is really from (John 7:27). These marked forms and here frontgrounded processes are consonant with Jesus crying out in the temple; all are good examples of markedness assimilation. See S. E. Porter, *Verbal Aspect in the Greek of the New Testament, with Reference to Tense and Mood* (SBG 1; New York: Peter Lang, 1989), 286-87; cf. E. L. Battistella, *The Logic of Markedness* (New York: Oxford University Press, 1996), 61-65.

who he is and where he is from — they do not know God. As D. A. Carson points out, it is not that they doubt that God exists, but that they doubt that he truly is the one who sent Jesus.[9] This doubt indicates that their knowledge is not the kind of knowledge and reception that John the Baptist is speaking of, nor does it represent acceptance of Jesus as God's sent and anointed one.

c. Jesus, the Pharisees, and the One Who Sent Him: John 8:26

In confrontation with the Pharisees in John 8:21-30, Jesus tells them that he is going to depart and they will not be able to accompany him. They are understandably confused about what this means, so he explicates the notion already discussed above that he is from above (heaven), while they are from below and of this earthly, worldly sphere.[10] He equates one's allegiance with one's salvation, in that being of the world or aligned with it means being sinful. The basis for these statements, Jesus tells them, is that he is the sent one of God. God, who is true or truthful, has told him many things to tell to the world, and hence God's truthfulness validates or guarantees Jesus' message. As Craig Keener says, "Jesus ultimately defines his identity never in terms of his relationship to them, but rather only in terms of his relationship with the Father."[11] The Johannine narrator says that Jesus' hearers did not recognize that, in speaking of the one who sent him, Jesus was speaking of the Father.

d. Jesus and the Only True God: John 17:3

In Jesus' high priestly prayer in John 17,[12] in which he prays for himself, for his disciples, and then for all believers, Jesus begins by addressing God, his

9. Carson, *John*, 318.

10. See Nicholson, *Death as Departure*, 105-23.

11. Keener, *John*, 1:745.

12. The bibliography on Jesus' prayer is huge. Some of the more important works that I have found useful here are H. B. Swete, *The Last Discourse and Prayer of Our Lord: A Study of St. John XIV–XVII* (London: Macmillan, 1913); J. W. Pryor, "The Great Thanksgiving and the Fourth Gospel," *BZ* 35 (1991): 157-79; J. E. Staton, "A Vision of Unity — Christian Unity in the Fourth Gospel," *EvQ* 69 (1997): 291-305; C. L. Blomberg, *The Historical Reliability of John's Gospel: Issues and Commentary* (Downers Grove, IL: InterVarsity Press, 2001), 218-27; A. R. Kerr, *The Temple of Jesus' Body: The Temple Theme in the Gospel of John* (JSNTSup 220; London: Sheffield Academic Press, 2002), ch. 9; G. L. Parsenios, *Departure and Consolation: The Johannine Farewell Discourses in Light of Greco-Roman Literature* (NovTSup

Father. Jesus knows that his hour has come, and he prays for God to glorify him. He recognizes that God has given him power, and he now prays for the power to give eternal life. This relational continuum puts Jesus in the middle as the mediator between God and humanity.[13] He defines eternal life as knowing the only true God and the one whom God has sent, Jesus Christ.[14] We notice that the notion of truth here is not predicated of God as it has been in the previous instances, but instead it is an attribute of the only true God. The statement is not implying that there are other untrue gods, but that this is the only God, and to be God means to be true or truthful. This is the basis for belief that what this God reveals has veracity. The conceptual framework is similar to the above passages, in which God has sent Jesus, the sent one, and eternal life, or knowing God, is determined by how one responds to the sent one and hence, through him, to God.

In summary of the passages that directly address God as true or truthful, each one has a framework dependent upon the truthfulness of God, as opposed to his being untrue or a liar. God stands above the earthly sphere, but he has mediated himself to the world through sending his Son. There is thus a relational component to God's truth in that it is mediated through Jesus. The way in which one gains access to God is through the Son. True acceptance of the Son implies acceptance of the one who stands behind the Son, the only true God.

3. Jesus Is Truth

Besides God being described using language of truth, similar language is used of Jesus in John's Gospel. There are essentially four passages that describe Jesus and his relationship to truth. These passages are found in the prologue of the Gospel (John 1:9, 14, 17) and in chs. 5 (vv. 31-33), 8 (vv. 14, 16), and 14 (v. 6).

117; Leiden: Brill, 2005); and D. B. Stevick, *Jesus and His Own: A Commentary on John 13–17* (Grand Rapids: Eerdmans, 2011).

13. Some scholars take John 17:3 as a parenthetical insertion by the author between John 17:2 and 4, defining eternal life. See C. K. Barrett, *The Gospel according to St. John* (2nd ed.; Philadelphia: Westminster, 1978), 503; Blomberg, *The Historical Reliability of John's Gospel*, 219-20. However, the connection between vv. 2 and 4 is not as straightforward as posited, and v. 3 seems to follow from v. 2. See Carson, *John*, 555-56.

14. On the grammar of John 17:3, see M. J. Harris, *Jesus as God* (Grand Rapids: Baker, 1992), 258-59, in which the object of the verb "know" may well be "the only true God whom you sent, Jesus Christ." Keener (*John*, 2:1054) is quick to dismiss this option, as is Harris.

a. Jesus, Logos, and the True Light: John 1:9, 14, 17

In the prologue to John's Gospel,[15] there is a progression from the *logos* to the
witness to the *logos,* to the incarnation of the *logos.* Even though the enfleshment of the *logos,* or the incarnation itself, is not mentioned until 1:14, an earlier
reference in the prologue is worth noting. The prologue says that the *logos* was
life and this life was the light of humanity. In 1:9 the author says that John the
Baptist was not the light, but that he came to testify about the light. This light
is then called the "true light" that enlightens everyone. The sense here is that
this is the "genuine," or "real," light, as opposed to John the Baptist.[16] Although
the identity of this light, and certainly its incarnation, does not occur until
v. 14, the prologue goes on to talk of the presence of the *logos* in the world, its
creative powers, its rejection by its own people, and its acceptance by some.
When the *logos* is said to have become flesh and to have resided in the human
sphere, this fleshly *logos* is said to have glory as the one and only Son of the
Father, and to be "full of grace and truth" (v. 14). This phrase "full of grace and
truth" has certainly aroused widespread discussion, much of it focused upon
the (Old Testament) conceptual background of the use of "truth" language in
John's Gospel.[17] My impression is that too much time has been spent on trying
to determine this background, since the sense that seems to prevail is one that
encompasses many of the different suggestions. The sense is that Jesus was
full of "divine favor" and "divine reality."[18] Jesus was more than a witness to

15. The bibliography on the prologue to John's Gospel is immense, as was seen in ch. 4.
Just a few of the more useful works that I have found include C. K. Barrett, *The Prologue of
St John's Gospel* (Ethel M. Wood Lecture 1970; London: Athlone Press, 1971); C. H. Dodd,
"The Prologue to the Fourth Gospel and Christian Worship," in *Studies in the Fourth Gospel*
(ed. F. L. Cross; London: Mowbray, 1957), 9-22; E. J. Epp, "Wisdom, Torah, Word: The
Johannine Prologue and the Purpose of the Fourth Gospel," in *Current Issues in Biblical
and Patristic Interpretation: Studies in Honor of Merrill C. Tenney Presented by His Former
Students* (ed. G. F. Hawthorne; Grand Rapids: Eerdmans, 1975), 128-46; C. A. Evans, *Word
and Glory: On the Exegetical and Theological Background of John's Prologue* (JSNTSup 89;
Sheffield: JSOT Press, 1993); and P. M. Phillips, *The Prologue of the Fourth Gospel: A Sequential Reading* (LNTS 294; London: T&T Clark, 2006). See also chs. 2 and 4 in this volume
for a fuller discussion, but reflecting a different approach and concerns.
16. Thiselton, "Truth," 3:893; cf. Keener, *John,* 1:393.
17. E.g., see M. D. Hooker, "John's Prologue and the Messianic Secret," *NTS* 21 (1974):
40-58; A. T. Hanson, "John 1.14-18 and Exodus 34," *NTS* 23 (1976): 90-101; H. Mowvley,
"John 1:14-18 in the Light of Exodus 33:7–34:35," *ExpTim* 95 (1984): 135-37. For a survey of
alternatives, see Keener, *John,* 1:416-18.
18. R. Schnackenburg, *The Gospel according to St. John* (trans. K. Smyth et al.; 3 vols.;
London: Burns & Oates, 1968-82), 1:273.

God's reality; as Anthony Thiselton says, "The reality itself, to which everything else witnesses, is encountered in Christ."[19] Thus, the incarnation is connected with the Son's being full of grace and truth. In v. 17 this notion is repeated by contrasting the law as being given through Moses,[20] whereas grace and truth came through Jesus Christ. Thus, in the opening chapter of John's Gospel, Jesus Christ as the incarnate *logos* is seen to have been the true light and, in his earthly incarnation, full of divine grace and truth, in contrast to the law given through Moses.

b. Jesus and the Jews: John 5:31-33

In the context of charges against him that he was making himself equal with God (John 5:18), Jesus says that, if he is the only one who testifies about himself, then his testimony is not true, or valid.[21] As elsewhere in the Gospel (e.g., 15:26 below), Jesus notes that there is collaborative testimony regarding his identity. Here he provides, according to Jewish law, the two witnesses required to substantiate his claim.[22] The first one, God, provides true testimony regarding him, as Jesus himself knows. Furthermore, he says, even John the Baptist himself had testified to the truth. The idea here is that Jesus knows that he is a reliable witness to the truth, but that he does not make that assertion on his own. He has joint testimony to collaborate his claims. Not only does he have John the Baptist's testimony, but he has the valid testimony of God himself.

c. Jesus and the Pharisees: John 8:14, 16

Before predicting his departure back to the Father (see the example of John 8:26 above), Jesus has a confrontation with the Pharisees, who tell him that

---

19. Thiselton, "Truth," 3:890.

20. There is much discussion of the relation between Jesus and Moses, especially in John's Gospel. See J. W. Pryor, *John: Evangelist of the Covenant People* (London: Darton, Longman & Todd, 1992), 117-22; S. Harstine, *Moses as Character in the Fourth Gospel: A Study of Ancient Reading Techniques* (JSNTSup 229; London: Sheffield Academic Press, 2002); and J. Lierman, *The New Testament Moses* (WUNT 2.173; Tübingen: Mohr Siebeck, 2004).

21. Some translations, such as the Holman Christian Standard Bible, render the word ἀληθής with "valid" in John 5:31 and 32. See Thiselton, "Truth," 3:890, who makes the case for the notion here of validity based upon God himself.

22. Keener, *John*, 1:655-56.

his testimony is not true, or valid (8:13).[23] In response, Jesus maintains that his testimony is true (v. 14), because he knows who he is, where he has come from, and where he is going. They, he says, do not know who he is, because they judge by human or earthly standards, rather than knowing the one who sent him, God (again, God is seen as the validator of Jesus' true testimony). Jesus goes on to note that his judgment also is true (v. 16), because he is a judge along with God. Jesus' statement about his testimony being true is placed within the larger context of Jesus having a relationship with the Father who has sent him. As Keener states, "Jesus' judgment is true because his Father is with him in it."[24] Within the framework of the earthly and the heavenly, Jesus is the one who mediates between the two, representing the truth of God in his true testimony to those who either accept or reject it.

d. Jesus and the Way, the Truth, and the Life: John 14:6

In what is perhaps the best-known passage in John's Gospel regarding the notion of truth, except perhaps John 18:38, Jesus states that he is the way, the truth, and the life (14:6). This statement is uttered within the larger context of Jesus telling his disciples during the last time that they are to-gether as a group that they need to believe in God and also in him. He is going away to prepare a place for them, and he is going to return to take them to be with him. When Thomas expresses doubt regarding knowing how to get to where Jesus has indicated, Jesus responds by stating that he himself is the way, the truth and the life, and that no one is able to come to the Father except through him. There has been much discussion of this formulation with regard to its use of a predicate "I am" formulation,[25] its

---

23. Again, some translations, such as the Holman Christian Standard Bible, translate the word ἀληθής with "valid" in John 8:13, 14. The sense may be correct (and "valid" is a good translation to use in v. 17 regarding the witness of two people), but there is a loss in the use of "valid" because of the importance of the "truth" regarding Jesus as a theme in John's Gospel. See Thiselton, "Truth," 3:890.

24. Keener, *John*, 1:741.

25. On the "I am" passages, see ch. 5 in this volume for a more detailed study. See also Brown, *John*, 1:535-37; P. B. Harner, *The "I Am" of the Fourth Gospel* (Philadelphia: Fortress Press, 1970); J. Neyrey, *An Ideology of Revolt: John's Christology in Social-Science Perspective* (Philadelphia: Fortress Press, 1988), 130-33, who sees the figure as part of a replacement program; D. M. Ball, *"I Am" in John's Gospel: Literary Function, Background, and Theological Implications* (JSNTSup 124; Sheffield: Sheffield Academic Press, 1996); C. H. Williams, " 'I Am' or 'I Am He,' " in *Jesus in Johannine Tradition* (ed. R. T. Fortna and T. Thatcher;

conceptual background, whether there is emphasis placed on one or more of the three elements, and the relationship among the three.[26] There is no need to discuss all of these issues here. In fact, I think that there is perhaps a simpler explanation of what is being said. The use of the tripartite formulation is in keeping with the context, in which there is an indication of traveling occurring or about to occur, when Jesus speaks of his Father's house having many rooms and his going to prepare a place (14:2-3). Thomas is confused regarding how the disciples are going to know the proper way to this destination. Thus, Jesus notes that he himself is that way, as well as being the truth and the life. I do not think that it is stretching the ideas here to see an emphasis upon Jesus as the way to God, but with the truth of God's revelation in Jesus as the means, and eternal life as the goal.[27] Jesus says that the only way to the Father is accessed by believing in him both as the truth and as the one who provides the mediated path between God and humanity. Regarding the truth, this formulation and analysis mean that truth is a concrete notion that is embodied within Jesus, the divine revelation of God coming as the sent one.[28]

In summary, Jesus' view of God and truth is consistent with how he sees himself in relation to truth. God is from above and separate from the world of humanity. Jesus is the true mediator who is able to bridge the divide between the two and to mediate between the two realms, that of the things above and the things below, so that human beings can reach God — but only through Jesus as he provides the true way to God.

Louisville, KY: Westminster John Knox, 2001), 343-52; R. Bauckham, "Monotheism and Christology in the Gospel of John," in his *The Testimony of the Beloved Disciple: Narrative, History, and Theology in the Gospel of John* (Grand Rapids: Baker, 2007), 239-52. For a history of research, see R. Kysar, *The Fourth Evangelist and His Gospel: An Examination of Contemporary Scholarship* (Minneapolis: Augsburg, 1975), 119-22.

26. See, e.g., M. Scott, *Sophia and the Johannine Jesus* (JSNTSup 71; Sheffield: Sheffield Academic Press, 1992), 125-28.

27. Scholars who have said similar things include R. Bultmann, *The Gospel of John: A Commentary* (trans. G. R. Beasley-Murray et al.; Philadelphia: Westminster, 1971), 605-6; Carson, *John,* 491; A. Reinhartz, *The Word in the World: The Cosmological Tale in the Fourth Gospel* (Atlanta: Scholars Press, 1992), 35; Ball, *"I Am,"* 126-27. Cf. A. T. Robertson, *The Divinity of Christ in the Gospel of John* (New York: Revell, 1916; repr. Grand Rapids: Baker, 1979), 116 n. 1, who notes the use of the article with each substantive. The article's structural function indicates each of these as a distinct entity in the tripartite structure.

28. See Thiselton, "Truth," 3:892, who notes three implications regarding truth for his analysis. Cf. E. M. Sidebottom, *The Christ of the Fourth Gospel* (London: SPCK, 1961), 137-48, esp. 148, who sees the Trinity being foreshadowed in this formulation.

4. The Spirit of Truth

Having discussed the language of truth regarding God and Jesus in John's Gospel, I now turn to the Spirit. Three passages are related to the Paraclete, or Spirit, as truth — John 14:17; 15:26; 16:13 — and the language used to refer to this figure is identical in each, as is the function that the Spirit plays. It is noteworthy that the phrase "Spirit of truth" is used in three of the five Paraclete sayings in John's Gospel.[29] There has been much discussion regarding the Paraclete, often formulated in terms of its relationship to the Holy Spirit, its relationship to Old Testament mediatorial figures or other sources, its role as possible counselor, comforter, prosecutor or advocate (prosecutor or defender), and its function in relation to Jesus and his departure. These issues are all important ones, but to consider them fully would take us beyond the scope of this chapter. I think it is sufficient to say for the sake of my discussion that it appears that the Paraclete is to be seen in John's Gospel as an advocate on behalf of humans, serving the role that Jesus performs, after his departure.[30] Raymond Brown even goes so far as to say that the Spirit of

---

29. See Thiselton, "Truth," 3:892. But the spirit is referred to as Paraclete only in John 14–16. See M. M. Thompson, *The God of the Gospel of John* (Grand Rapids: Eerdmans, 2001), 179.

30. The advocacy role is propounded by Barrett, *John*, 76; Thiselton, "Truth," 3:982; Keener, *John*, 2:951-71, esp. 961; among others, including some of those below. There is an abundance of literature on the Paraclete, or Holy Spirit, in John's Gospel. See, e.g., G. B. Stevens, *The Johannine Theology* (London: Dickinson, 1894), 189-217; H. B. Swete, *The Holy Spirit in the New Testament: A Study of Primitive Christian Teaching* (London: Macmillan, 1910); P.-H. Menoud, *L'évangile de Jean d'après les recherches récentes* (Neuchâtel: Delachaux & Niestlé, 1947), 57-60; E. C. Colwell and E. L. Titus, *The Gospel of the Spirit: A Study in the Fourth Gospel* (New York: Harper, 1953); Brown, *John*, 1:533-58; J. T. Forestell, "Jesus and the Paraclete in the Gospel of John," in *Word and Spirit: Essays in Honor of David Michael Stanley, S.J., on His Sixtieth Birthday* (ed. J. Plevnik; Toronto: Regis College Press, 1975), 151-98; E. Franck, *Revelation Taught: The Paraclete in the Gospel of John* (CBNTS 14; Malmö: Gleerup, 1985); G. M. Burge, *The Anointed Community: The Holy Spirit in the Johannine Tradition* (Grand Rapids: Eerdmans, 1987); L. L. Morris, *Jesus Is the Christ: Studies in the Theology of John* (Grand Rapids: Eerdmans, 1989), 145-69; S. S. Smalley, " 'The Paraclete': Pneumatology in the Johannine Gospel and Apocalypse," in *Exploring the Gospel of John: In Honor of D. Moody Smith* (ed. R. A. Culpepper and C. C. Black; Louisville, KY: Westminster John Knox, 1996), 299-300; M. Turner, *The Holy Spirit and Spiritual Gifts: Then and Now* (Carlisle: Paternoster, 1996), 57-102; S. H. Ringe, *Wisdom's Friends: Community and Christology in the Fourth Gospel* (Louisville, KY: Westminster John Knox, 1999), 84-92; T. G. Brown, *Spirit in the Writings of John: Johannine Pneumatology in Social-Scientific Perspective* (JSNTSup 253; London: T&T Clark, 2003), esp. 170-234; and A. C. Thiselton, *The Holy Spirit — in Biblical Teaching, through the Centuries, and Today* (Grand Rapids: Eerdmans,

truth is a Paraclete because of his carrying on Jesus' earthly work of representation after Jesus' departure.[31]

a. The Paraclete and Spirit of Truth: John 14:17

In John 14:6 (see section 3d above), Jesus says that he is the way, the truth, and the life. He continues speaking to his disciples and instructs them regarding believing in him, but also awaiting another who will come to be their advocate, the Paraclete (14:16).[32] This is the Spirit of truth (14:17). Jesus says that the world will be unable to receive the Paraclete, because it does not see or know him. The disciples, however, will know him, because he will remain with them until Jesus returns to them. It is interesting to note that the Spirit, or Holy Spirit (using the language used elsewhere in the New Testament, such as in Paul, for the most part), is here called the Spirit of truth. Whereas the terminology of Holy Spirit utilizes a noun and modifying adjective (τὸ πνεῦμα τὸ ἅγιον, or grammatical variations), here the noun for Spirit is modified with a dependent genitival phrase, "the Spirit of truth" (τὸ πνεῦμα τῆς ἀληθείας). Even though the grammar is not parallel,[33] and the sense is clearly different, the referent is almost certainly meant to be the same. As we have already noted above, it is God who is true, and it is Jesus who is truth. Now the Johannine author wishes to include the Spirit within the scope of that attribution by saying that the Spirit is characterized by truth as well. The Spirit may be known elsewhere in the New Testament as being holy, but for John it is truth that characterizes God, Jesus, and the Spirit. The

---

2013), esp. 135-44. Cf. Kysar, *Fourth Evangelist*, 234-40; G. S. Sloyan, *What Are They Saying about John?* (New York: Paulist, 1991), 69-74.

31. Brown, *John*, 1:644.

32. See Ringe, *Wisdom's Friends*, 87.

33. The constructions are formulated differently but have both semantic and structural similarities. The adjectival attributive genitive came to be widely employed in Greek as a way of using genitive modification to perform functions often and usually associated with the attributive adjective. On the characteristics of the adjectival attributive genitive in ancient Greek and the New Testament, see S. E. Porter, "The Adjectival Attributive Genitive in the New Testament: A Grammatical Study," *TrinJ*, n.s., 4 (1983): 3-17; cf. Porter, *Idioms of the Greek New Testament* (2nd ed.; BLG 2; Sheffield: Sheffield Academic Press, 1994), 116-18. The construction in John 14:17 is not treated in my article, because it conforms to the most widely used pattern in the New Testament. The notion of the spirit of truth is known in other literature of the time. See Keener, *John*, 2:969-70 (although he is apparently flummoxed by the use of the Greek tense-forms; e.g., 2:972-73).

advocate sent by God to be with believers until Jesus again returns represents the same characteristics as the two figures for whom he now becomes the mediator. He is the mediator of the presence of Jesus while he is away, and, by virtue of this role, he is the mediator between humans and God, since the Paraclete stands in the role that Jesus had occupied while in the worldly realm — he is the other Paraclete given by God, Jesus being the first. The second Paraclete begins his mediatorial role once the first Paraclete, Jesus, departs and is glorified (see John 7:38-39).[34] In fact, one could say that it is the Spirit of truth that then is designated to lead people into the way, the truth, and the life.[35]

b. Paraclete Sent by the Father, the Spirit of Truth: John 15:26

The mediatorial function of the Paraclete is made even clearer in John 15:26. Jesus tells his disciples that the Paraclete will be sent to them from the Father by Jesus himself. He is sent by Jesus, but he proceeds from the Father, Jesus says, and testifies about Jesus. This mediatorial bearer of truth, as well as, by implication, probable prosecutor of those who have not received Jesus, is referred to again as the Spirit of truth. The same narrative pattern and conceptual framework is in place as we have seen above: the Paraclete is designated as being given (by the Father), and is called the Spirit of truth. In this framework, God is above and the world is below, and this humanly unbridgeable divide is mediated by Jesus. However, Jesus is now departing and leaves in his stead another truthful divine being as advocate, or Paraclete, the Spirit of truth, who proceeds from the Father though sent by the Son.

---

34. On "another paraclete," see A. T. Lincoln, *Truth on Trial: The Lawsuit Motif in the Fourth Gospel* (Peabody, MA: Hendrickson, 2000), 111, who interprets the Paraclete in forensic terms; and J. R. Michaels, *The Gospel of John* (NICNT; Grand Rapids: Eerdmans, 2010), 785.

35. Cf. Morris, *Jesus Is the Christ*, 156-57. T. G. Brown (*Spirit*, 190) lists the activities that the Paraclete and Jesus perform in common. These include (using her language): being given by the Father, accompanying the disciple, not being received by the world, not being known by the world, not being seen by the world, being sent by the Father, coming from the Father into the world, giving testimony, convicting the world, speaking what is heard, glorifying its sender, revealing, disclosing and proclaiming, leading into the fullness of truth, being the spirit of truth, and being a Paraclete.

c. Paraclete Leads into All Truth: John 16:13

In John 16:4-15 Jesus continues his comments about his imminent departure but then reassures his followers regarding his departure to the one who sent him, God (v. 5), by reiterating the dual advocacy role of the Paraclete. The Paraclete will be sent by Jesus with the function of convicting the world of sin, righteousness, and judgment (v. 8). This is the Spirit of truth, who will guide them into or toward all truth, with truth both the characterization of the Spirit and the goal toward which the Spirit leads (v. 13).[36] The reason the Spirit is able to do so is that he is not going to be speaking simply on his own, but he will be speaking what he hears from the departed Jesus.

In summary, the Paraclete (or advocate; less likely: comforter or counselor, as in various translations) is described as one who takes over the mediatorial function of Jesus once Jesus departs. The conceptual framework is one in which God is the one above who has sent Jesus. Now that Jesus is returning to the Father, Jesus is sending the Paraclete, who in fact originates with the Father, to assume Jesus' functions until the time when Jesus returns. The Spirit's role is not simply a passive one, however, since he has the several roles of testimony, guidance, and mediation, as well as performing the role of convicting humans regarding their behavior during this time.

5. Humans Are to Act in Truth

We have now discussed the role of truth in relation to God, Jesus, and the Spirit in John's Gospel. At this point, we turn to human beings. Three passages in John's Gospel address truth in relation to human beings: John 3:21, 4:23-24; and 8:32.

---

36. There are textual variants here: (1) "into all truth" / εἰς τὴν ἀλήθειαν πᾶσαν or εἰς πᾶσαν τὴν ἀλήθειαν (found in Codexes Alexandrinus and Vaticanus, a number of other majuscule manuscripts, a large number of minuscules, and the Byzantine and lectionary traditions), (2) "in all truth" / ἐν τῇ ἀληθείᾳ πάσῃ or ἐν πάσῃ τῇ ἀληθείᾳ (found in the first correcting hand of Codex Sinaiticus and a number of other majuscule manuscripts, among others), and (3) "in truth" ἐν τῇ ἀληθείᾳ (found in Codex Sinaiticus and some Coptic manuscripts). I think that "into all truth" (εἰς τὴν ἀλήθειαν πᾶσαν) is probably the best reading, because of its early and widespread attestation. If "in all truth" is correct (this is the reading found in the *UBSGNT* and Nestle-Aland editions), then it probably "suggests an exploration of truth already principally disclosed" (Carson, *John*, 539), taking the preposition ἐν as locative, rather than directional, as with εἰς.

a. Doing the Truth, Coming to the Light: John 3:21

Picking up on a theme that was first introduced in the prologue to John's Gospel,[37] Jesus, in his dialogue with Nicodemus (if the words from John 3:16-21 are those of Jesus rather than those of the narrator),[38] speaks of how the light has come into the world, a world that is equated with darkness and wickedness. The passage reaches its conclusion with a pronouncement regarding the light. The coming of the light exposes people for who they are and their actions for what they are. But, Jesus says, anyone who "does the truth" — probably language for doing what is ethically right[39] — moves toward the light. What the light exposes as one draws near is whether the works done have been performed by God. In other words, what it means to live by the truth is to do actions that are in fact accomplished by God, that is, through his strength rather than through one's own human efforts.[40] The same framework is in place as we have seen above regarding God, Jesus, and the Paraclete. There is a realm above the world, and one below the world, in which humans live and act. The light is equated with the realm above, since that is its source, the realm from which the light has come into the world. Those who are enlightened are able to do the truth, which means that they are doing actions not of their own but ones that are sanctioned and empowered by God.

b. Worship in Spirit and Truth: John 4:23-24

When Jesus confronts the Samaritan woman at the well and speaks to her (see John 4:1-42, esp. vv. 7-26), he says many profound things to her so as to impress upon her that he is a prophet (v. 19). In answer, she makes comments about spiritual things. The observations that she makes to Jesus regarding the proper place to worship are confined to the earthly or worldly realm (v. 20). In contrast, Jesus tells her that the time is coming when people will worship on neither mountain — hers or his — but that true worshippers will worship God in spirit and truth (vv. 23-24). The phrase "in spirit and truth" (ἐν πνεύματι καὶ ἀληθείᾳ) links the two substantives together by means of a single preposition,

37. I note that this is a pattern within John's Gospel, as we have seen elsewhere. See, e.g., ch. 2 of this volume, where this similar pattern is examined in other ways.

38. Many think that they are not, such as Carson, *John*, 203.

39. Keener, *John*, 1:574.

40. See Carson, *John*, 208.

rather than using a preposition with each substantive. The effect is to join the two concepts represented together; spirit and truth are both within the same realm, or sphere. Spirit-and-truth worship is the focus. True worshippers are not necessarily either Jews or Samaritans, but any who are worshippers devoted to God's revealed truth. They are the ones who will worship him in spirit and truth.[41] The necessity of worship in spirit is because God is spirit. But God is also truth (see section 2 above). Therefore, those who wish to worship him must approach him in both spirit and truth. The Samaritan woman does not understand what Jesus is saying (it is admittedly cryptic at first), but she appeals to the fact that the Messiah will make it clear. Jesus then tells her that he is the Messiah, the anointed one, who will explain everything. The framework in which this conversation takes place adds a new dimension to the worship of God. This passage contrasts the world of God, which is spirit (above), with the earthly or worldly realm of human worship. God must be worshipped with recognition that he is spirit and, hence, not containable or capturable in a particular place, such as on this mountain or that. True worship also recognizes the truth and truthfulness of God, as the one who stands as the source and origin of life from above, not below in the earthly realm. There is only one way to mediate the divide between these realms, and it is by means of Jesus. In a full theological exposition of the passage, Carson says of this worship, "It must be 'in spirit and truth', i.e. essentially God-centered, made possible by the gift of the Holy Spirit, and in personal knowledge of and conformity to God's Word-made-flesh, the one who is God's 'truth', the faithful exposition and fulfillment of God and his saving purposes."[42]

c. Truth Will Set You Free: John 8:32

Some Jews believe in Jesus and follow him (John 8:31).[43] To those Jews who believe, Jesus says that, if they continue to follow what he has said, they

---

41. For recent treatments of the Johannine concept of worship that is "in spirit and truth," see S. Um, *The Theme of Temple Christology in John's Gospel* (LNTS 312; London: T&T Clark, 2006); and B. Thettayil, *In Spirit and Truth: An Exegetical Study of John 4:19-26 and a Theological Investigation of the Replacement Theme in the Fourth Gospel* (CBET 46; Leuven: Peeters, 2007).

42. Carson, *John*, 225; contrast Keener, *John*, 1:615, who puts the emphasis upon "worship empowered by the Spirit." Cf. Brown, *Spirit*, 137-38, who does not distinguish spirit and truth.

43. On the meaning of "the Jews" in this context, see ch. 6 above.

prove that they truly are his disciples. This process of continuing to obey his word means that they can come to expect to know the truth, and the truth will set them free (8:32). The response of the Jewish believers is one of some perplexity, because, as they say in response to the idea that they might need to be freed, they have never been enslaved to anyone.[44] These interlocutors are thinking horizontally, that is, regarding the earthly realm of human slavery and freedom, while Jesus is thinking vertically, concerning God's freedom. Jesus' comments regarding truth are related to the God who is true and whose will is mediated to the worldly realm through the sent one Jesus, who embodies the truth. The Jews confine their question regarding their descent and slavery simply to the earthly realm, rather than recognizing that the liberation or freedom that Jesus is speaking of would free them from slavery to sin, so that they too could be in true and free relation with God.[45]

In summary, the repeated tension for the various people to whom Jesus speaks is their inability to recognize, and certainly to break free of, their bondage to the earthly or worldly realm of sin. The light comes from above to earth, and God resides in the realm of light above. In order for people to truly worship God or to be in relation with him, they must be able to span the gap between the earthly and the heavenly realms — realms physically represented but spiritually conceived. This mediation comes about through their being liberated by the truth and recognizing that Jesus is that mediator sent by God.

6. John's Gospel and Johannine Propositional Truth

A number of passages in John's Gospel that we have not yet considered further develop the notion of truth. In most of what has been said above, the notion of truth is not strictly propositional but relational, that is, it is explicated through relational patterns among the Father, Son, and Spirit and by human beings in relation to them, especially Jesus. However, as I have tried to adumbrate in my handling of the respective passages, there are also statements in

---

44. The difficulties with this assertion are addressed by Keener (*John*, 1:749-50), who notes that the Jews had been enslaved (e.g., in Egypt) and that possibly they were referring to their personal enslavement. They may also have simply wished to ignore this episode in their history or rewrite it as a moment of triumph.

45. However, they were mistaken even from this horizontal perspective, as it is clear that Israel as a nation had been in slavery to various other nations, including Persia, Assyria, Babylon, and, at the time, the Roman Empire.

John's Gospel to the effect that the truth is depicted as propositional. That is, these are statements concerned not so much with the relational dimension of God, Jesus, the Spirit, or humanity, but with raising questions or expressing something about truth outside of these relational paradigms. These propositional statements are often stated as incontrovertible assertions and often stand on their own as if unimpeachable. These passages are John 8:44-46; 16:7; 17:17; 18:37-38; and 21:24. As these passages indicate, however, the relationship between propositional and relational truth in John's Gospel is not a simple one.

a. The Devil and Truth: John 8:44-46

In talking with a group of Jews who had previously believed (John 8:31), Jesus apparently gets frustrated (see 8:39-47). He states that, if God were their Father, his hearers would not be responding as they are after his identification with God's actions. In that case, they would recognize that Jesus has come from God. In reality, he says, they are of their father the devil, who is a murderer, a liar, and the father of lies. The devil does not stand or position himself in the realm of truth, and there is no truth in him (v. 44). By way of contrast, Jesus tells them the truth, and for this reason they do not believe him (v. 45). They are not able to accuse or convict him of sin, but even though he tells the truth, they do not believe him (v. 46).

On the surface, this scene seems to be simply a dispute over various assertions of truthfulness, depicting Jesus' frustration that, even though he has told them the truth, his hearers do not believe him. One may also argue that this is a relational discussion of truth, as it involves Jesus, those opposing him, and their relation to the devil. As some scholars have thought, there may well be implicit reference in the dialogue about the devil to the temptation of Adam and Eve by the serpent, who lies as a matter of course.[46] The context makes clear, however, that there is more to the situation than simply a conversation with assertions of differing opinions. Even though there is a relational dimension, the heart of the dialogue is about the notion of truth itself, not the relationship of his hearers to Jesus. Jesus states categorically, or, we might say, propositionally, that the devil and the truth are not compatible because there is no truth in the devil. This reality simply is the truth, Jesus says, even if they do not believe him. This is the propositional element

46. See Thiselton, "Truth," 3:892; Carson, *John*, 353.

to the truth about the devil. Nevertheless, Jesus frames his response within the perspective shared with the rest of John's Gospel when he notes that the one who is from God listens to God's words (v. 47). Jesus is from God, and he consequently speaks the truth. Since Jesus' listeners have not accepted the truth of God and his sending of his Son, they cannot accept the truth. This instance shows that the notion of a propositional truth, as Jesus states it, is grounded in the larger conceptual notion of God as truth and as the one who is the source of truth in the world.

b. The Paraclete and Jesus' Departure: John 16:7

Regarding the sending of the Paraclete as advocate, Jesus says that he is telling the truth; that truth is that the Paraclete will not come until Jesus goes away (John 16:7). Again, the propositional truth — that the Paraclete will not come unless Jesus departs — is grounded in a much larger conceptual framework, one shared by the rest of John's Gospel. God is above and the world is below, and the mediation between the two occurs through Jesus (who must go away to be with God). Jesus is now departing, so he is sending another, the Paraclete, whose origins are in God, to act in his stead. This framework of God as true and the guarantor of the outworking of these events is the basis of the propositional assertion regarding the Paraclete.

c. God's Word Is Truth: John 17:17

While praying for himself, his disciples, and then for all believers (John 17), Jesus requests that God make his followers pure in or by the truth (v. 17). He then states that God's word is truth (v. 17). This statement certainly seems to be making a propositional assertion, formulated as if not susceptible to contradiction, for it is apparently grounded in the nature of God and his revelatory word. However, the larger context sets these remarks within the framework that we have seen elsewhere in John's Gospel. In the preceding context, Jesus says that he is praying not that his followers would be taken out of the world, but that they would be protected from the evil one (v. 15). He goes on to say that, just as God has sent him into the world, he has sent his followers into the world (v. 18). In other words, God has sent Jesus into the world, and Jesus has continued the mission that God sent him to do by sending his own followers out (with the power of the Paraclete to comfort and guide them in Jesus' absence, as other passages indicate; see section 4 above). God's word is truth because God himself is true, and because he has undertaken to communicate this truth from above to those in the world by means of Jesus, the sent one. This truth is the means by which Jesus' followers are made pure or sanctified. As Carson says, "No-one can be 'sanctified' or set apart for the Lord's use without learning to think God's thoughts after him, without learning to live in conformity with the 'word' he has graciously given."[47]

d. Testifying to the Truth: John 18:37-38

This passage may not best be placed in the category of stating a proposition; nevertheless, I think that it offers insight into the Johannine discussion of truth. Jesus stands before Pilate and tells him, "My kingdom is not of this world" (John 18:36). He has a kingdom, but it is not located here. A kingdom naturally suggests a king, so Pilate asks Jesus whether he is a king (v. 37). Jesus' elusive answer implies that he is a king but not the kind of king that Pilate has in mind. Instead, Jesus says, he was born for the purpose of coming into the world to testify to the truth. Everyone who also has their origins in the truth (i.e., is "of the truth") responds to him or hears his voice (v. 37). When Jesus says that his purpose for coming into the world is to testify to the truth, it may be that he is simply testifying to God, because we have seen that God and truth are associated in that God is the source of truth (cf. 5:37: "everyone who is from the truth hears my voice"). But God and the truth are not equated in John's Gospel. (God is true, to be sure, but is never said to be truth.) Nevertheless, when Jesus elsewhere speaks of testifying or of others testifying, it is usually concerning a person and often concerning himself (e.g., John 5:31-32, 36-37, 39; 8:14, 18; 10:25; 15:26). The only other place where someone testifies concerning the truth (5:33) records John testifying to the truth regarding Jesus. This instance in John 18:37 may, therefore, be a way of Jesus indirectly testifying to himself as the truth. This seems unlikely, however, since the reference would be doubly obscure. Instead, this passage seems to be one in which Jesus claims that his mission is to bear witness to and testify to the truth as a notion in and of itself — even though it has its origins and basis in the only

---

47. Carson, *John*, 566. Thiselton ("Truth," 3:892) raises the question of whether this passage implies the truthfulness of the Bible. He does not think so. However, if the Bible is the "word of God," then it would seem logical to imply that it would be true. At this point, perhaps Thiselton's desire to avoid a propositional content to the notion of truth has preempted his analysis.

true God.[48] Jesus as the sent one, and the returning one who has his kingdom elsewhere, is the one who is appointed to make clear that there is a notion of truth in this world. This is what prompts Pilate's question in response, "What is truth?" (v. 38). This question is often interpreted as a turning point in the Gospel, but instead it marks the pathetic close to the discussion between Jesus and Pilate. A situation of potential enlightenment ends with Pilate asking a question that exposes his ignorance. In a sense, as we have seen in the previous discussion, the entire Gospel is an answer to this question — at this point, in an act of dramatic irony, Pilate, as one who is not "of the truth," is the only one who does not know what, or rather who, it is.[49]

e. The Writer's Testimony Is True: John 21:24

At the very close of the Gospel,[50] the author says that he is the disciple who testifies to these things and who wrote them down, and that we know that his testimony is true (John 21:24). This statement stands as a proposition by the author about the reliability of his testimony. This language is reminiscent of several other passages (see discussions above of references in John 8 and 18) where testimony to the truth is important in John's Gospel. Here it serves as a concluding endorsement of what has been written by the author of the Gospel that what he has said is in fact true.

7. Conclusion

In the immediate context, there is not a simple or explicit answer to Pilate's almost pathetic question to Jesus, "What is truth?" (John 18:38). However, it

---

48. Contra Keener, *John,* 2:1113, who draws too firmly the lines between Hellenism and Judaism regarding truth. In the context, Jesus surely uses the idea with the sense of truth as a concept or proposition, "the truth."

49. See P. Duke, *Irony in the Fourth Gospel* (Atlanta: John Knox Press, 1985), 130, followed by Lincoln, *Truth on Trial,* 129; contra C. Bennema, "The Character of Pilate in the Gospel of John," in *Characters and Characterization in the Gospel of John* (ed. C. W. Skinner; LNTS 461; London: Bloomsbury, 2013), 240-53, esp. 243, who seems to miss the point entirely.

50. Many scholars do not include ch. 21 as part of the original text of John's Gospel (e.g., Bultmann, *John,* 700-701; cf. Carson, *John,* 665-68). I discuss this issue in ch. 9 of this volume.

does not follow that no answer is provided within John's Gospel. Throughout the Gospel, there is a consistent presentation of truth — even though there is relatively little overlap among sections of the Gospel in its presentation of the notion of truth (John 8 being the exception, as noted above with analysis under most of the major categories discussed). There are explicit references to truth using ἀληθ- words in the following chapters: John 1, 3 bis, 4, 5, 7, 8 (four times), 14 bis, 15, 16 bis, 17 bis, 18, and 21. In other words, over half of the chapters of the book have some specific discussion of the notion of truth focusing around words in this group. It is appropriate that some scholars have identified "truth" as one of the major concepts in the book. Out of this evidence, several patterns emerge.

In the first place, the question that Pilate asks is germane, and he is in a number of ways addressing it to the right person. Throughout the Gospel, Jesus stands at the center of discussion regarding truth and is the major instructor regarding truth.[51] He is the one who is described in the prologue as the light that brings truth, he is the one who describes God, the one who is above, as truth, and he is the one who describes the Paraclete as the one who is coming to represent him after he goes away and before he returns. In other words, the major discussion of what is meant by truth in John's Gospel revolves around Jesus explicating in various ways the notion of truth. He does so by speaking about himself, about God, and about the Paraclete. Thus, when Pilate asks Jesus the question of what is truth, it is a question asked of the very one who has been repeatedly explicating the notion through his actions and teachings throughout the Gospel. The question should come as no surprise to the reader, since the reader has been aware since John 1 that Jesus is the one who is truth and who, for John, reveals truth to others, including both friends and foes, and readers and hearers alike.

The second factor to consider is how the notion of truth forms a cohesive device in order to aid the coherence of the Gospel.[52] The notion of the truth is, as early as John's prologue, linked to the imagery of light and enlightenment, and then to the incarnate Jesus. This is one of the major early thrusts of the Gospel. The subsequent references to the notion of truth occur at a number of crucial junctures in the Gospel itself. For example, there is discussion of the notion of truth with regard to several of Jesus'

51. Cf. Lincoln, *Truth on Trial*, 419-31. See also Lincoln, *The Gospel according to Saint John* (BNTC; Peabody, MA: Hendrickson, 2005), throughout, who treats the "truth" notion with reference to the lawsuit motif.

52. I distinguish cohesion (formal elements that make a discourse a discourse) from coherence (the semantic patterns of a discourse that govern its consistent understanding).

major conversational partners (e.g., Nicodemus, the woman at the well, Jerusalemites), Jesus' confrontation with others regarding his departure and his relationship to the great patriarch Abraham (John 8), his words to the disciples during their last time together (John 14), his major prayer (John 17), and the near-final words of the Gospel as the author concludes (John 21:24). One cannot help but see that the notion of truth forms a crucial part of the substance of many of the major teaching episodes of the Gospel and binds the entire narrative within a conceptual framework that has something to do with presenting and explicating the truth.

The third consideration is what exactly the Gospel says about truth. There are two major distinctions to be made in the way that the notion of truth is handled in the Gospel. Truth is seen as both a relational and a propositional term, with the propositional content growing out of the relational substance. The discussion of truth is formulated around the notion that God is true. However, God is in the realm above, heaven, whereas humanity lives in the realm below, the world. Jesus, who as the *logos* was with God in the realm above, has been sent by God and mediates the relationship between the realm above and the realm below. Therefore, although the basis of truth is God, the only true God, the relational interface of truth with individual humans occurs in their response to Jesus as the incarnation of truth. The Gospel emphasizes that the way that people respond to Jesus is the way that they respond to God and his truth. If people are obedient and truly do the truth by following Jesus, then they are demonstrating acceptance of and obedience to God. A person cannot have one without the other. The Paraclete as advocate is given by Jesus as another heavenly being who originates with God as a substitute for Jesus when he departs from the earth and before he returns. Most of the formulations of truth in regard to God, Jesus, and the Paraclete are in terms of their "being" true or the truth. The propositional content of truth, clearly less important in John's Gospel than the relational representation, is formulated in terms of what someone might say is true and, even in its propositional form, depends upon the relational dimension, that is, whether it is grounded in Jesus as God's emissary sent from above, or even in God himself.

CHAPTER 8

Jesus, the Passover Theme, and John's Gospel

1. Introduction

In this chapter, I am concerned with what might be considered a literary-theological theme in John's Gospel, namely, John's use of the Passover theme — that Jesus is the Passover lamb, slain for the sins of his people — in its presentation of Jesus. As we will see, this theme in its fullest expression has, until recently, been generally neglected by exegetical treatments of John's Gospel, especially in its literary-critical dimensions.[1] In this chapter, we will see that, although reference is fairly frequently made to the Passover theme in John's Gospel, most studies manifest a general failure to appreciate the theme's significance as one that, in conjunction with the Old Testament fulfillment motif, elucidates the role and person of Jesus and serves to bind together the entire Gospel.[2] That is, the Passover theme serves both theological and literary functions in the Gospel. Throughout this chapter, I establish the importance of the fulfillment motif and the Passover theme in John's Gospel, noting especially how they converge in John 19.

There has been a recent and welcome upsurge in interest in the topic of

1. I have made a comprehensive survey of the literary study of John's Gospel in S. E. Porter, "Study of John's Gospel: New Directions or the Same Old Paths?" In *Linguistic Analysis of the Greek New Testament: Studies in Tools, Methods, and Practice* (Grand Rapids: Baker, 2015), 277-306.

2. In some ways, my treatment of the Passover theme as a unifying theme of John's Gospel is similar to A. T. Lincoln's *Truth on Trial: The Lawsuit Motif in the Fourth Gospel* (Peabody, MA: Hendrickson, 2000), for he uses the lawsuit motif as a unifying concept for the Gospel.

the use of the Old Testament in John's Gospel.[3] Nevertheless, despite this increased interest, there has been much less systematic attention given to a passage as important as John 19:36-37 in relationship to the larger context of the entire Gospel or to the sustained treatment throughout the Gospel of the Passover theme.[4] These two factors — the use of the Old Testament and development of the Passover theme — work together in John's Gospel to create a pattern that is worth exploring not only from a traditional exegetical standpoint but from a distinctive literary standpoint. Although commentators virtually always take note of the citation of the Old Testament in John 19:36 and 37, usually to dispute which Old Testament text is cited in v. 36, few go much further to explore the significance of the citations for the entire Gospel.[5] This significance will be explored here in terms of three categories:

3. Some more recent work in this area includes M. J. J. Menken, *Old Testament Quotations in the Fourth Gospel: Studies in Textual Form* (CBET 15; Kampen: Kok Pharos, 1996); C. A. Evans and J. A. Sanders, eds., *Early Christian Interpretation of the Scriptures of Israel: Investigations and Proposals* (JSNTSup 148; Sheffield: Sheffield Academic Press, 1997); J. Lieu, "Narrative Analysis and Scripture in John," in *The Old Testament in the New Testament: Essays in Honour of J. L. North* (ed. S. Moyise; JSNTSup 189; Sheffield: Sheffield Academic Press, 2000), 144-63; A. J. Köstenberger, "John," in *Commentary on the New Testament Use of the Old Testament* (ed. G. K. Beale and D. A. Carson; Grand Rapids: Baker, 2007), 415-512; and R. Sheridan, *Retelling Scripture: 'The Jews' and the Scriptural Citations in John 1:19–12:15* (BIS 110; Leiden: Brill, 2012).

4. Exceptions regarding the Passover theme are C. Schlund, *"Kein Knochen soll gebrochen werden": Studien zur Bedeutung und Funktion des Pesachfests in Texten des frühen Judentums und im Johannesevangelium* (WMANT 107; Neukirchen-Vluyn: Neukirchener, 2005), but without the Passover's atoning significance; J. T. Nielsen, "The Lamb of God: The Cognitive Structure of a Johannine Metaphor," in *Imagery in the Gospel of John: Terms, Forms, Themes, and Theology of Johannine Figurative Language* (ed. J. Frey, J. van der Watt, and R. Zimmermann; WUNT 200; Tübingen: Mohr Siebeck, 2006), 217-56; P. M. Hoskins, "Deliverance from Death by the True Passover Lamb: A Significant Aspect of the Fulfillment of the Passover in the Gospel of John," *JETS* 52.2 (2009): 285-300, although Hoskins does not seem to be aware of some of the most important literature on this topic; and D. Lee, "Paschal Imagery in the Gospel of John: A Narrative and Symbolic Reading," *Pacifica* 24 (2011): 13-28.

5. See, e.g., the commentary by A. J. Köstenberger, *John* (BECNT; Grand Rapids: Baker, 2004), 553-54, who notes the relation of vv. 36-37 to the Passover lamb but does not unravel the significance of this in much detail. In contrast, the following scholars have noted the significance of the passage: M. J. J. Menken, "The Old Testament Quotation in John 19:36: Sources, Redaction, Background," in *The Four Gospels* (ed. F. Van Segbroeck, C. M. Tuckett, G. Van Belle, and J. Verheyden; Leuven: Leuven University Press, 1992), 2101-18; Menken, *Old Testament Quotations,* esp. 167-85 (originally published as "The Textual Form and the Meaning of the Quotation from Zechariah 12:10 in John 19:37," *CBQ* 55 [1993]: 159-74); C. M. Tuckett, "Zechariah 12:10 and the New Testament," in *The Book of Zechariah and Its Influence* (ed. C. M. Tuckett; Burlington, VT: Ashgate, 2003), 111-21; W. R. Bynum, *The*

(1) how the quotations in John 19:36-37 — the final quotations from the Old Testament in John's Gospel — bring to an end a series of references introduced by fulfillment formulas; (2) how the quotations in 19:36-37 are the final quotations in a group of quotations surrounding the death of Jesus; and (3) how they are the final climactic quotations in establishing the Passover theme in John's Gospel, a theme that is often not given its due in regarding how it is developed throughout the Gospel. Thus, in the death of Jesus, as climactically defined by the Old Testament quotations, the Old Testament fulfillment motif and the Passover theme converge. The way that these two threads are created and woven together merits further discussion.

2. The Old Testament Fulfillment Motif

The use of allusions to or direct quotations of Old Testament passages in John's Gospel is probably more complex than most realize,[6] but there are a number of patterns with regard to quotation formulas in John's Gospel that bear mentioning.[7] Craig Evans has discussed these quotation formulas and has noted a significant division between quotations in John 1:23–12:16, which are "regularly introduced or alluded to with 'it is written', or the like, while in 12:38–19:37 [they are] regularly introduced with the formula 'in

---

Fourth Gospel and the Scriptures: Illuminating the Form and Meaning of Scriptural Citation in John 19:37 (Leiden: Brill, 2012); and A. Kubiś, *The Book of Zechariah in the Gospel of John* (Pendé, France: J. Gabalda, 2012), 115-218.

    6. See, e.g., S. E. Porter, "The Use of the Old Testament in the New Testament: A Brief Comment on Method and Terminology," in *Early Christian Interpretation of the Scriptures of Israel: Investigations and Proposals* (ed. C. A. Evans and J. A. Sanders; Studies in Scripture in Early Judaism and Christianity 5; JSNTSup 148; Sheffield: Sheffield Academic Press, 1997), 79-96; Porter, "Further Comments on the Use of the Old Testament in the New Testament," in *The Intertextuality of the Epistles: Explorations of Theory and Practice* (ed. T. L. Brodie, D. R. MacDonald, and S. E. Porter; NTM 16; Sheffield: Sheffield Phoenix Press, 2006), 98-110; and Porter, "Allusions and Echoes," in *As It Is Written: Studying Paul's Use of Scripture* (ed. S. E. Porter and C. D. Stanley; SympS 50; Atlanta: Scholars Press, 2008), 29-40.

    7. See C. A. Evans, "On the Quotation Formulas in the Fourth Gospel," *BZ* 26 (1982): 79-83; Evans, *Word and Glory: On the Exegetical and Theological Background of John's Prologue* (JSNTSup 89; Sheffield: JSOT Press, 1993), esp. 172-77. See also D. A. Carson, "John and the Johannine Epistles," in *It Is Written: Scripture Citing Scripture; Essays in Honour of Barnabas Lindars* (ed. D. A. Carson and H. G. M. Williamson; Cambridge: Cambridge University Press, 1988), 245-64, esp. 247; P. Miller, "'They Saw His Glory and Spoke of Him': The Gospel of John and the Old Testament," in *Hearing the Old Testament in the New Testament* (ed. S. E. Porter; Grand Rapids: Eerdmans, 2006), 127-51.

order that [the Scripture or what was spoken] be fulfilled.' "[8] This pattern is even more regular than most scholars recognize. Not only does it appear that all direct quotations of the Old Testament in John's Gospel are introduced by a formula, but, apart from 1:23 and 12:13, neither passage of which is spoken by Jesus, within the first section (1:23–12:16), coinciding with the book of signs (John 2–11),[9] every direct quotation of the Old Testament is introduced by use of the perfect participle of γράφω, that is, γεγραμμένον, "stands written" (2:17; 6:31, 45; 10:34; 12:14; the plural form of the participle is used similarly to refer back to a previously cited quotation in 12:16).[10] Other nonperfect forms of γράφω are used in a quotation formula when no specific citation is produced (1:45; 5:46; 7:42; 8:17). In the second section (12:38–19:37), virtually all of the quotations, as well as the allusions, are introduced by formulas using the aorist passive subjunctive of πληρόω, that is, πληρωθῇ, "be fulfilled" (12:38-40; 13:18; 15:25; 17:12; 18:9, 32; 19:24, 28, 36-37). John 12:39 and 19:37 do not use this verb, but these verses do not constitute exceptions, since, as Evans and others have pointed out, they "are to be understood as extensions of the respective formulae in 12:38 and 19:36 (as is also indicated by the presence of the linking word πάλιν [again])."[11] It is further to be noted that the initial and final quotations in this second section are double quotations, that is, they cite two Old Testament passages linked together. The only exception to the use of the subjunctive of πληρόω is in 19:28, where τελειωθῇ is used between two other cognate forms, one reporting Jesus' knowledge regarding his "end," and the other quoting his cry that the "end" is come (τετέλεσται, 19:30).[12] (John 19:28 is not a direct quotation; neither are 17:12; 18:9, 32.) Most of the quotations and allusions are from the author or narrator of John's Gospel, the exceptions being 13:18; 15:25; and 17:12. Evans has well summarized the use of the Old Testament in John's Gospel: "The function of the Old Testament in the Fourth Gospel, as seen in the formal quotations, is not ad hoc but is systematic and progressive, showing that Jesus' public ministry (1:29–12:36a) conformed to

8. Evans, *Word and Glory*, 175-76.

9. See C. H. Dodd, *The Interpretation of the Fourth Gospel* (Cambridge: Cambridge University Press, 1953), 289.

10. See S. E. Porter, *Verbal Aspect in the Greek of the New Testament, with Reference to Tense and Mood* (SBG 1; New York: Peter Lang, 1989), 245-90, esp. 277, regarding the use of the perfect tense-form (stative aspect) for authoritative citation.

11. Evans, *Word and Glory*, 176.

12. M. Hengel, "The Old Testament in the Fourth Gospel," *HBT* 12.1 (1990): 12-41, here 33; cf. Evans, *Word and Glory*, 176.

scriptural expectations and requirements, while his Passion (12:36b–19:37) fulfilled scriptural prophecies."[13] The result of this patterning, it can be argued, is that, although there may be a number of other allusions to the Old Testament in John's Gospel, the author typically sees Jesus' ministry as in some way specifically foreshadowed in the Old Testament, as borne out by the typical use of a standard formula (γεγραμμένον) for introducing direct quotations. In the death of Jesus, however, the Johannine author sees the Old Testament as fulfilled, as revealed by his consistent use of πληρωθῇ for all direct quotations.

The significance of the quotations in John 19:36-37 needs to be further explicated. Within John 19 alone three direct quotations of the Old Testament are said to be fulfilled in the death of Jesus, and the quotations in vv. 36 and 37 form a suitable climactic double quotation. In John 12 there are four direct quotations of the Old Testament (vv. 13, 15, 38, 40); however, the author does not treat them in the same way as the quotations in John 19. John 12 is a transition chapter between the conclusion to Jesus' ministry and the beginning of his passion; the citation in 12:13 is not introduced by an "it is written" formula, and the quotation in 12:15 is the final quotation of the first section of the Gospel, both introduced and concluded with a formula using the perfect participle (vv. 14, 16). Thus, the double quotation of 12:38, 40, linked by the connective πάλιν, is the first of the fulfillment quotations of the second section of the Gospel. The double quotation appropriately introduces the fulfillment motif that continues into John 19.[14] In John 19 this motif is continued through the three direct quotations, each seen by the author as fulfillment of the Old Testament. The author not only alludes to the Old Testament in 19:28 (introduced by the word τελειωθῇ, "be completed") but quotes the Old Testament three times directly, one a single quotation and one a double quotation. John 19:24 and 19:36 are each introduced by the fulfillment formula, with 19:37 attached to v. 36 by πάλιν.

Whereas it is uniformly believed that the author of John's Gospel cites Zech 12:10 at John 19:37, there has been much discussion regarding which text is being cited and from which version at John 19:36.[15] There have been two major proposals: a Pentateuchal text, in particular, Exod 12:46 (also

13. Evans, *Word and Glory,* 174.

14. See Hengel, "Old Testament in the Fourth Gospel," 32, 34.

15. See, e.g., T. L. Brodie, *The Gospel according to John: A Literary and Theological Commentary* (Oxford: Oxford University Press, 1993), 554-55; Menken, *Old Testament Quotations,* 147; and Bynum, *Fourth Gospel,* 121-23.

12:10 LXX) or Num 9:12; or Ps 34:20 (34:21 MT; 33:21 LXX). Some scholars argue that the Psalm quotation lies behind this passage,[16] others that the passage(s) from the Pentateuch are being cited,[17] and others that both sets are being drawn upon.[18] The evidence points to at least some reference to the Pentateuchal quotations, although there may be secondary reference or allusion to Ps 34:20. The support for the Pentateuchal solution is seen on two levels: linguistic and contextual.[19] The Psalm passage and John's quotation use the third person singular passive voice verb, with an impersonal subject provided in the context ("one" with reference to bones, or ὀστᾶ). In other respects, however, the Pentateuchal passages are more appropriate to the Johannine quotation: use of the singular for bone, ὀστοῦν, although it is the subject of the verb in John but the object in the Pentateuchal quotations; singular personal possessive reference, αὐτοῦ; and word order of subject (John) / object (Pentateuch) / negation / verb / prepositional phrase. There are still several divergences, including use of the second person plural in Exod 12:10 and 46, and the third person plural in Num 9:12, although the last is closer to John 19:36.[20]

The second criterion is context. Besides the Passover context (devel-

16. See, e.g., Dodd, *Interpretation,* 230-38; Dodd, *Historical Tradition in the Fourth Gospel* (Cambridge: Cambridge University Press, 1963), 42-44; R. Bultmann, *The Gospel of John: A Commentary* (trans. G. R. Beasley-Murray et al.; Philadelphia: Westminster, 1971), 677 n. 1; R. Schnackenburg, *The Gospel according to St. John* (trans. K. Smyth et al.; 3 vols.; London: Burns & Oates, 1968-82), 3:191-92. Usually mentioned in support of this proposal is the use of the passive voice of the verb and the use of Psalm quotations in John's Gospel.

17. See, e.g., G. Reim, *Studien zum alttestamentlichen Hintergrund des Johannesevangeliums* (SNTSMS 22; Cambridge: Cambridge University Press, 1974), 52; E. Freed, *Old Testament Quotations in the Gospel of John* (NovTSup 11; Leiden: Brill, 1965), 113.

18. See, e.g., C. K. Barrett, "The Old Testament in the Fourth Gospel," *JTS* 48 (1947): 157; B. Lindars, *New Testament Apologetic: The Doctrinal Significance of the Old Testament Quotations* (London: SCM Press, 1961), 96; A. T. Hanson, *The Prophetic Gospel: A Study of John and the Old Testament* (Edinburgh: T&T Clark, 1991), 218-22; B. G. Schuchard, *Scripture within Scripture: The Interrelationship of Form and Function in the Explicit Old Testament Citations in the Gospel of John* (SBLDS 133; Atlanta: Scholars Press, 1992), 138-40; cf. Bultmann, *John,* 677; C. K. Barrett, *The Gospel according to St. John* (2nd ed.; Philadelphia: Westminster, 1978), 558, who think that the Evangelist may have had the Pentateuchal quotations in mind but that his source was referring to Ps 34; cf. Barrett, "The Lamb of God," *NTS* 1 (1954-55): 210-18, esp. 211.

19. See D. J. Moo, *The Old Testament in the Gospel Passion Narratives* (Sheffield: Almond Press, 1983), 314-16, and bibliography cited there.

20. Note that Num 9:12 LXX[A] and Exod. 12:46 LXX[A] read συντρίψεται.

oped throughout the Gospel, as will be shown below),[21] and although psalms regarding the suffering of the righteous are used in the passion account, the Pentateuchal quotations are more germane, since Ps 34:20 refers to the presentation of the living rather than to what happens to the one who is to be the victim, whether alive or dead. It is probably pushing the evidence to argue further that the unbroken bones were a symbol created by the author of John's Gospel to foretell Jesus' resurrection and the failure of the grave to hold him.[22] More likely, we should see the passage as fulfillment of the Passover theme.[23] Regarding whether the MT or LXX is being quoted,[24] it is not necessary to establish this detail here, so long as it is agreed that the author is referring to the Old Testament, which is beyond doubt,[25] and probably to the Pentateuchal passages, each of which appears in a Passover context. The citation in Exod 12 from the Passover account is as likely as any, although this cannot be proven beyond doubt.

3. The Passover Theme

In one of the better literary commentaries on John's Gospel, Mark Stibbe mentions the Passover theme at several places. On John 1:29-34, he states, "There is evidence in John's story of a rich Passover symbolism. The whole of the Gospel could be described as a Passover plot in that it moves through the three Passover festivals in 2:13, 6:4 and 13:1."[26] On 19:16b-42, and speaking about the author's implicit commentary, he mentions several symbolic

21. See Reim, *Studien,* 52-53; J. H. Bernard, *A Critical and Exegetical Commentary on the Gospel according to St. John* (ed. A. H. McNeile; 2 vols.; ICC; Edinburgh: T&T Clark, 1928), 2:651.

22. So D. Daube, *The New Testament and Rabbinic Judaism* (London: Athlone Press, 1956), 309; Dodd, *Historical Tradition,* 44; Lindars, *Apologetic,* 96; and Schuchard, *Scripture within Scripture,* 139.

23. Moo (*Old Testament,* 316) creates an unnecessary disjunction between the factuality of the crucifragium (the breaking of a victim's bones) and Jesus' depiction as the Passover lamb.

24. On the MT, see Reim, *Studien,* 90; Moo, *Old Testament,* 315; on the LXX, see Schuchard, *Scripture within Scripture,* 133-40; B. Lindars, *The Gospel of John* (NCB; London: Marshall, Morgan & Scott, 1981), 590.

25. Although see Freed, *Quotations,* 109-14, who is undecided.

26. Stibbe, *John* (Readings: A New Bible Commentary; Sheffield: JSOT Press, 1993), 35. This is contrary to his earlier position in his *John as Storyteller: Narrative Criticism and the Fourth Gospel* (SNTSMS 73; Cambridge: Cambridge University Press, 1992).

details, including the hyssop (19:29) used to spread the blood of the Passover lamb on the door lintels and the three references to its being the day of preparation (19:14, 31, 42) as coordinating events with the slaughter of the lambs. This linkage "in turn creates an implicit commentary on the death of Jesus as the perfect paschal sacrifice, and shows how narrative chronology and narrative Christology are inseparable in John."[27] But how implicit is the commentary? Perhaps it is as veiled as it is to Stibbe because the evidence he examines is quite narrow. Thus, although he recognizes the potential importance of the Passover theme for developing his theological-historical interpretive agenda, he goes no further in examining Passover in the rest of John's Gospel.

The evidence of a Passover theme in John's Gospel is stronger than many recognize.[28] The essential thrust of this theme is that Jesus is seen by the author of the Gospel as the suitable and, in fact, ideal or perfect Passover victim. Since the animal sacrificed at Passover symbolized deliverance from the angel of death, as well as redemption from the oppression of Egypt, which leads to the exodus and, eventually, entrance into Canaan, several supporting themes in John's Gospel could be cited as giving further support for the Passover theme.[29] These include reference to Moses, the leader of the people during the course of these events (John 1:17, 45; 3:14; 5:45-46; 6:32; 7:19, 22-23; 8:5; 9:28-29),[30] and possibly even reference to the serpent raised

---

27. Stibbe, *John,* 196.

28. Contra S. McKnight, *Jesus and His Death: Historiography, the Historical Jesus, and Atonement Theory* (Waco, TX: Baylor University Press, 2005), 264 n. 17. Not taking every reference to "lamb" as being a Passover lamb, I do not think that I "cast my net" a bit wide. Nevertheless, I appreciate his recognition that I have shown the "potential significance" of the Passover theme in John's Gospel.

29. For a treatment of the Passover theme in the Old Testament, see T. Prosic, *The Development and Symbolism of Passover until 70 CE* (London: T&T Clark, 2004).

30. For those who see the significance of Moses in John's Gospel, see T. F. Glasson, *Moses in the Fourth Gospel* (SBT 40; London: SCM Press, 1963); W. A. Meeks, *The Prophet-King: Moses Traditions and the Johannine Christology* (NovTSup 14; Leiden: Brill, 1967), esp. 228-30; S. Pancaro, *The Law in the Fourth Gospel: The Torah and the Gospel, Moses and Jesus, Judaism and Christianity according to John* (Leiden: Brill, 1975); M.-E. Boismard, *Moses or Jesus: An Essay in Johannine Christology* (trans. B. T. Viviano; Minneapolis: Fortress Press; Leuven: Peeters, 1993); S. Harstine, *Moses as Character in the Fourth Gospel: A Study of Ancient Reading Techniques* (JSNTSup 229; London: Sheffield Academic Press, 2002), esp. 40-75; J. Lierman, "The Mosaic Pattern of John's Christology," in *Challenging Perspectives on the Gospel of John* (ed. J. Lierman; WUNT 2.219; Tübingen: Mohr Siebeck, 2006), 210-34; and A. D. Myers, " 'The One of Whom Moses Wrote': The Characterization of Jesus through Old Testament Moses Traditions in the Gospel of John," in *"What Does*

by Moses in the desert (3:14). As important as these themes are, they cannot be pressed here, except as they impinge on the exegesis below. More to the point, although not significant without further elucidation (see below), is reference to the Passover either directly or as a "feast" (πάσχα, "Passover," is used in 2:13, 23; 6:4; 11:55 bis; 12:1; 13:1; 18:28, 39; 19:14; and ἑορτή, "feast," is used with reference to the Passover in 2:23; 4:45; 5:1; 6:4; 11:56; 12:12, 20; 13:1, 29). John's Gospel directly refers to the Passover ten times, which is more than any other New Testament book (the closest being Luke with seven and Matthew and Mark with four each). Although Stibbe admits to what he calls a "passover plot," he confines his discussion to John 1 and 19 and mention of the temporal references in 2:13; 6:4; and 13:1.

The significant literary and critical evidence for the Passover theme in John's Gospel, however, is far more significant than Stibbe and most other commentators admit.[31] Seven major passages interspersed throughout the Gospel demonstsrate the significance of the theme.[32] It is not appropriate here to argue in detail regarding every dimension of each passage, but it is worth noting the significant features that do establish the theme.

_____

the Scripture Say?" Studies in the Function of Scripture in Early Judaism and Christianity, vol 2: The Letters and Liturgical Traditions (ed. C. A. Evans and H. D. Zacharias; London: T&T Clark, 2012), 1-20.

31. Even among those who agree that John's Gospel contains a Passover theme (which is by far most commentators at some point or another), few see it in chapters other than 1 and 19. Those who go beyond those passages in a significant way include L. Morris, The New Testament and the Jewish Lectionaries (London: Tyndale, 1964), 64-72; J. K. Howard, "Passover and Eucharist in the Fourth Gospel," SJT 20.1 (1967): 329-37; Hoskins, "Deliverance from Death"; and Lee "Paschal Imagery." There have been notable disputants, including Dodd, Interpretation, 230-40; and J. Seynaeve, "Les citations scriptuaires en Jn. 19,36-37: Une preuve en faveur de la typologie de l'Agneau Pascal?" Revue Africaine de Théologie 1 (1977): 67-76. Despite the fairly widespread mention of the Passover theme by commentators, there has not been thorough discussion of this idea at many of the places where I argue that it appears. Perhaps one reason many have not followed it as thoroughly as it appears to be present in the Gospel is because of the statement of Robert Kysar (The Fourth Evangelist and his Gospel: An Examination of Contemporary Scholarship [Minneapolis: Augsburg, 1975], 140) that, though evident, the Passover motif tends to be exaggerated. To the contrary, given its appearance throughout the Gospel, I do not think that it has been appreciated as fully as it warrants.

32. McKnight (Jesus and His Death, 271) writes that, "if John is driving a theological agenda on the Lamb of God, he simply avoids direct comment over and over when he has opportunities in the passion account itself. The evidence is not as lopsided as one might think. John's lamb theology is hardly prominent." On the contrary, I contend that John's references to the Passover lamb motif in his Gospel are evident in the entire Gospel, with the final referent included in the Passion narrative itself.

a. John 1:29-36 (esp. vv. 29, 36)

The first passage, John 1:29-36, contains two significant acclamations (vv. 29 and 36), in which John the Baptist refers to Jesus as "the lamb [ἀμνός] of God."[33] These are the only two uses of ἀμνός in John's Gospel (out of a total of four in the entire New Testament; see also Acts 8:32 and 1 Pet 1:19).[34] These two references appear in concentrated fashion at a crucial initiatory point in the narrative, marking the Gospel's, as well as John the Baptist's, introduction of Jesus and the commencement of Jesus' ministry (John 1:19–12:16). The question for most interpreters, however, is what John the Baptist's words mean.

A number of alternatives to understanding the "lamb" reference have been suggested.[35] These include the apocalyptic lamb of Revelation and other apocalyptic literature,[36] the sacrifice of Isaac in Gen 22,[37] the daily sacrifice or some other sacrifice of a lamb for an offering in the Old Testament,[38] the "Son of God" on the basis of the parallel with John 1:34,[39] the

33. See Bernard, *John*, 1:43-47. U. C. von Wahlde also notes, "In keeping with other passages in the third edition [of John's Gospel, as von Wahlde analyzes it; i.e., 1:29-34] that see Jesus in relation to the Passover lamb, here the title identifies Jesus as the means of liberation from sin" (*The Gospel and Letters of John* [ECC; Grand Rapids: Eerdmans, 2010], 2:55-56).

34. L. Morris, *The Gospel according to John* (rev. ed.; NICNT; Grand Rapids: Eerdmans, 1995 [1971]), 126.

35. For a summary of the positions, see G. L. Carey, "The Lamb of God and Atonement Theories," *TynBul* 32 (1981): 101-7; D. B. Sandy, "John the Baptist's 'Lamb of God' Affirmation in Its Canonical and Apocalyptic Milieu," *JETS* 34 (1991): 447-60; C. W. Skinner, "Another Look at 'The Lamb of God,'" *BibSac* 161 (2004): 89-104; cf. Bultmann, *John*, 95-97 and 677 and n. 1; Morris, *John*, 126-31; D. A. Carson, *The Gospel according to John* (PNTC; Grand Rapids: Eerdmans; Leicester: InterVarsity Press, 1991), 147-51; C. S. Keener, *The Gospel of John: A Commentary* (2 vols.; Peabody, MA: Hendrickson, 2003), 1:452-54; S. M. Schneiders, "The Lamb of God and the Forgiveness of Sin(s) in the Fourth Gospel," *CBQ* 73 (2011): 1-29.

36. E.g., Rev. 5:6, 8, 12, 13; ch. 6; 7:14, 17; 14:1, 4, 10; 15:3, although Revelation uses ἀρνίον; *T. Jos.* 19:18-19; *1 En.* 89-90. Dodd, *Interpretation*, 230-38; R. E. Brown, "Three Quotations from John the Baptist in the Gospel of John," *CBQ* 22 (1960): 295-97; G. R. Beasley-Murray, *John* (2nd ed.; WBC 36; Dallas: Word, 1999 [1981]), 24-25; cf. J. C. O'Neill, "The Lamb of God in the Testaments of the Twelve Patriarchs," *JSNT* 2 (1977): 2-30.

37. See, e.g., Gen 22:8; Glasson, *Moses*, 100.

38. E.g., Lev 7:1-7; 14:1-32; Num 6:1-21. See M. Davies, *Rhetoric and Reference in the Fourth Gospel* (JSNTSup 69; Sheffield: JSOT Press, 1992), 234.

39. N. R. Petersen, *The Gospel of John and the Sociology of Light: Language and Characterization in the Fourth Gospel* (Valley Forge, PA: Trinity Press International, 1993), 26; contra Carson, *John*, 149.

Suffering Servant of Isa 53,[40] or some combination of these.[41] For example, T. F. Glasson notes that the church fathers combined the serpent of John 3:14, noted above as possibly suggesting Passover imagery, the outstretched hands of Moses, and the offering of Isaac as prefiguring Jesus' crucifixion (e.g., Tertullian, *Answer to the Jews* 10). This kind of interpretive linkage, though a bit extreme, perhaps not only supports a sacrificial view of Christ's death from the standpoint of the early church, but possibly links the cross with Isaac's sacrifice (cf. Rom 8:32) and with the Passover.[42] It is not appropriate to offer a thorough critique of each of these theories here, however. It is more important to note that, in the eyes of most interpreters, the "lamb" includes at least some reference to the Passover,[43] often stated in terms of the writer of John's Gospel understanding the reference in Passover terms, even if John the Baptist's understanding was, for example, of some other form of imagery.[44] Although ἀμνός is not used in Exod 12 to refer to the Passover animal (πρόβατον is used), in other places in the LXX in the context of the Passover ἀμνός is used, such as Num 28:19.[45] This verbal correspondence, the association of the lamb with the sacrificial system, the significance of

40. Evans, *Word and Glory*, 182-83; M. Turner, "Atonement and the Death of Jesus in John: Some Questions to Bultmann and Forestell," *EvQ* 62.2 (1990): 119-22. As Evans (p. 182 n. 2) points out, this theory is not dependent upon the idea that Aramaic טליא, which can be rendered "servant" or "lamb," was mistranslated as ἀμνός, instead of παῖς. Those who have argued this include D. J. Ball, "Had the Fourth Gospel an Aramaic Archetype?" *ExpTim* 21 (1909-10): 91-93; C. F. Burney, *Aramaic Origins of the Fourth Gospel* (Oxford: Clarendon Press, 1922), 104-8; and J. Jeremias, "Ἀμνός," *TDNT* 1 (1964): 339-40.

41. Nielsen, "Lamb of God," esp. 252, sees metaphorical conceptual blending of the Passover lamb of Exodus and the Suffering Servant of Isaiah 53. Köstenberger states that John's pronouncement in 1:29 "likely involves multiple levels of meaning. Very possibly, the Baptist here speaks better than he knows" ("John," 428). In his commentary, Köstenberger argues that John the Baptist was referring to Isaiah 53 but that the Evangelist had the Passover lamb in mind (*John*, 66-67).

42. Glasson, *Moses*, 98-99; contra Carey, "Lamb of God," 103, who argues that explicit atonement theory regarding the sacrifice of Isaac does not occur until *Barn.* 7:3.

43. See V. Taylor, *Jesus and His Sacrifice: A Study of the Passion-Sayings in the Gospels* (London: Macmillan, 1937), 226-27; Barrett, *John*, 176-77; R. E. Brown, *The Gospel according to John* (2 vols.; AB 29, 29A; Garden City, NY: Doubleday, 1966), 1:295 n. 9; Lindars, *John*, 109; Carey, "Lamb of God," 111; Moo, *Old Testament*, 312-14; Carson, *John*, 150; Evans, *Word and Glory*, 181-82; Davies, *Rhetoric and Reference*, throughout; Brodie, *Gospel according to John*, 555; Keener, *John*, 1:454.

44. On this question, see E. W. Burrows, "Did John the Baptist Call Jesus 'The Lamb of God'?" *ExpTim* 85 (1973-74): 245-47.

45. See also Exod 29:38-41; Lev 9:3; 12:6; 14:10, with reference to other sacrifices; Davies, *Rhetoric and Reference*, 234.

the Passover in this sacrificial system, and the function of both in John's or the Gospel's and later Jewish thought (see below) — these all point toward Jesus as the Passover lamb. J. K. Howard is probably right in saying that this early episode serves as an introduction to the idea of Jesus as the Passover lamb that is continued throughout the book.[46]

Perhaps more important in establishing the Passover theme than the simple reference to the lamb, however, is the further comment attributed to John the Baptist that Jesus is the lamb "who takes away the sin of the world" (John 1:29). Some commentators have been surprised at this statement, because it seems to imply that the author of John's Gospel sees Jesus' death as in some way a substitutionary sacrifice.[47] This certainly appears to be the case, and for two reasons. The first is that the author appears to be invoking the Suffering Servant motif of Isa 53.[48] The author shows knowledge of Isaiah at several points in the Gospel — including quotation at John 1:23 of Isa 40:3, and at John 12:38 of Isa 53:1 — as Frances Young has pointed out,[49] but the reference in John 1:29 is apparently more specifically focused. In Isa 53:7 the "servant of the Lord"[50] is the ἀμνός who makes no noise and does not open its mouth before its shearers. Although in his commentary Stibbe sees "evidence in John's story of a rich Passover sym-

46. Howard, "Passover and Eucharist," 332. C. R. Koester makes a similar comment: "Introducing Jesus as the Lamb at the beginning of the Gospel anticipates his death at Passover at the end of the Gospel" (*The Word of Life: A Theology of John's Gospel* [Grand Rapids: Eerdmans, 2008], 112-13). See also Barrett, *John*, 176, although he notes that "the reference cannot have been drawn directly from Judaism, since in Judaism the Lamb sacrificed at passover does not take away sins. The probable source of John's thought and language is the Paschal interpretation of the last supper and the eucharist." In contrast, Menken (*Old Testament Quotations*, 158-59) writes, "How far the typology of Christ as the true paschal lamb has also determined the identification of Jesus as the 'lamb of God' in 1:29, 36, must remain uncertain, although the thought is tempting." While the discussion of typology is best left for another discussion, why this identification must remain uncertain is not clear. At least Menken recognizes this identification of Jesus early in John's Gospel.

47. Morris (*John*, 130-31) states that, although the verb αἴρω does not offer a specific means of atonement, "it does signify atonement, and that by substitution."

48. See Isa 53:4, 5, 6, 7, 8, 10, 12. See J. Morgenstern, "The Suffering Servant: A New Solution," *VT* 11 (1961): 406-31, esp. 425, who sees the Suffering Servant as a single individual rather than a corporate entity.

49. F. W. Young, "A Study of the Relation of Isaiah to the Fourth Gospel," *ZNW* 46 (1955): 215-33; cf. also Stibbe, *John*, 35.

50. Note that the phrase "servant of the Lord" is similar to the language "lamb of God," which is found elsewhere in John only in John 1:36. See Schnackenburg, *John*, 1:300, but not requiring mistranslation of Aramaic טליא.

bolism,"[51] he does not appreciate the full force of these references, in part because he divides up John 1:29-42 at vv. 34 and 35, rather than seeing vv. 29 and 36 as part of a single literary unit. Jesus is twice directly equated in this early episode of the Gospel with the lamb of God. This equation moves beyond the language of Isa 53:7, where the Suffering Servant is said to be like a lamb, to represent Jesus directly as the sacrificial victim.[52] In his first appearance, Jesus is depicted as one whose life is sacrificial in nature, and the sacrifice is characterized as one that takes away the sin of all people (cf. Acts 8:32). The Johannine language is an expansion of the Isaianic language (cf. Isa 53:11-12). In Isa 53:7 it is the ἀμνός that is shorn, but the author of John's Gospel apparently takes what is said of the Isaianic comparison with the sheep and applies it to the Suffering Servant, who bears (φέρει, v. 4) the sins of Israel. Jesus is said in John's Gospel to be the one who takes away (ὁ αἴρων) the sin of the world (cf. 1 John 3:5, although with plural "sins"; see also John 11:49-52).[53] The verbs φέρω and αἴρω overlap semantically in extrabiblical Greek, although apparently not in the LXX.[54] The language of John 1:29 and 36 thus intensifies and expands what is said of the lamb, moving its role beyond simply taking sin upon itself to removing sin as a concept (taking the singular form to represent sin in its collective sense),[55] and removing this sin for the entire world, not just for Israel.[56]

Second, the reader should not be unduly surprised by the language of substitutionary sacrifice in John 1 because Paul makes such an explicit equa-

---

51. Stibbe, *John*, 35.

52. Contra J. R. Michaels, who argues that "takes away the sins of the world" resists an understanding of Jesus as a victim (*The Gospel of John* [NICNT; Grand Rapids: Eerdmans, 2010], 108).

53. Carey, "Lamb of God," 199-200; Schnackenburg, *John*, 1:298; Brown, "Three Quotations," 296 n. 14 (cf. 1 John 3:5, 8); Evans, *Word and Glory*, 183; contra G. E. Ladd, *New Testament Theology* (Grand Rapids: Eerdmans, 1975), 43 n. 35. The point is not dependent on it, but there is some evidence that reference is being made by the author of John's Gospel to the LXX version of Isaiah 53, which refers to ἁμαρτίας ἡμῶν rather than "sickness" in v. 4, gives κύριος παρέδωκεν αὐτὸν ταῖς ἁμαρτίαις ἡμῶν for "the Lord caused to fall upon him the iniquity of us all" in v. 6, and employs vicarious language in v. 10. Contra S. K. Williams, *Jesus' Death as Saving Event: The Background and Origin of a Concept* (HDR 2; Missoula, MT: Scholars Press, 1975), 112-14.

54. See Exod 28:38; 34:7; Num 14:18; 1 Sam 15:25; Mic 7:18, where removal of guilt is spoken of, rendered by forms of αἴρω in the LXX. See B. F. Westcott, *The Gospel according to St John* (2 vols.; London: John Murray, 1908), 1:38-40.

55. Westcott (*John*, 1:40) emphasizes the idea of "taking away" as a conscious substitution and expansion on the LXX, with the singular "sin" treating sin as a unity.

56. Köstenberger, *John*, 67-68.

tion between Jesus and the Passover lamb when he equates the death of Jesus with the Passover sacrifice (see 1 Cor 5:7). Paul's usage suggests that a sacrificial understanding of Jesus' death had precedent in early Christianity, which the author of John's Gospel apparently takes up in similar terms. Although the original Passover sacrifice may not have been seen as substitutionary, it apparently became so early on.[57] Stibbe concludes rightly, "The suggestion is that Jesus is the true passover Lamb, the Lamb of God who takes away the sin of the world."[58] For most who mention the Passover theme, this passage and John 19:31-37 are the only ones discussed at length. However, the theme is more pervasive in the Gospel, as subsequent discussion shows.[59]

b. John 2:13-25

The second major passage to illustrate the point that the author of John's Gospel views Jesus as the Passover sacrifice is the incident of his cleansing the temple (John 2:13-25). Several indications in this passage point to this view. First, the author states at the outset that, "near the Passover of the Jews" (v. 13), Jesus entered Jerusalem and went to the temple. This significant event, apparently placed by the author at the outset of Jesus' ministry, is thus coordinated with the Passover. Stibbe in his commentary recognizes that this reference, the first of three to the Passover (cf. 6:4 and 13:1), is significant, with these references "important in the creation of a sense of plot (beginning, middle and end)."[60] But Stibbe does not go far enough

---

57. See Num 28:22; Ezek 45:21-25. See Howard, "Passover and Eucharist," 332, who cites these and other passages to show a link between sin offerings and Passover. Later Judaism apparently continued this idea (see *Exod. R.* 15:12 [on Exod 12:6], in which the blood of the Passover sacrifice is said to be atoning blood). See G. Dalman, *Jesus-Jeshua: Studies in the Gospels* (trans. P. Levertoff; London: SPCK, 1929), 167.

58. Stibbe, *John*, 35; contra Bultmann, *John*, 96; Barrett, *John*, 68; Brown, *John*, 1:60-61, who do not see the death as sacrificial. Cf. G. A. Barton, "'A Bone of Him Shall Not Be Broken': John 19:36," *JBL* 49 (1930): 13-19, who sees the death as sacrificial, but based on a cannibalistic background.

59. B. H. Grigsby ("The Cross as an Expiatory Sacrifice in the Fourth Gospel," *JSNT* 15 [1982]: 54 and nn. 37, 38) notes that equating the Passover lamb with the Suffering Servant is found elsewhere in the New Testament and early Christian literature: see 1 Pet 2:22-25, where ideas of Isa 53:1-12 are developed in a Passover setting; and Justin Martyr, *Dial.* 111: ἦν γὰρ τὸ πάσχα ὁ Χριστός, ὁ τυθεὶς ὕστερον, ὡς καὶ Ἡσαΐας ἔφη· Αὐτὸς ὡς πρόβατον ἐπὶ σφαγὴν ἤχθη.

60. Stibbe, *John*, 49. See also Köstenberger's helpful chart on the major Jewish festivals

in reference to the Passover. There is reference not only in John 2:13 but again in 2:23 at the close of the incident narrated here. This inclusio usefully surrounds the intervening events of Jesus' temple cleansing with explicit reference to the Passover, so that it is seen that Jesus' temple actions are to be understood as Passover activities.[61] Furthermore, Stibbe's statement suggests that his understanding of plot is simply related to the marking of events. Plot, however, is better understood as requiring recognition of the motivation for these events. In this sense, equation of Jesus with the Passover lamb is not simply a plot marker but potentially a major motivating factor for Jesus' actions throughout the entire Gospel, including his actions in the temple. In subsection a above it was seen that Jesus was depicted from the outset of his ministry as the "lamb of God" who serves as a sacrifice for the sin of the world, and once introduced in this way, his entire ministry needs to be seen in this light. The Passover theme itself thus begins at the outset of Jesus' ministry and does not end until his death (see below on John 19), with further events throughout the Gospel specifying this relationship, including not only John 2:13, 6:4, and 13:1 but other places as well, to be noted below.

Second, what Jesus does in this episode in the temple is depicted by the author as instituting a new Passover, one with Jesus as the focus rather than the old sacrificial institution. This change is indicated in several ways. In graphic fashion Jesus drives those selling the animals, including sheep (πρόβατα) and cattle (βόας), out of the temple.[62] Then, through a series of interchanges with the leaders who interrogate him, Jesus is depicted as transferring himself by reference to his own body into the equation as the substitute for the temple sacrificial system, that is, the temple system oriented toward the Passover sacrifice.[63] He tells them to destroy "this temple [τὸν

in John's Gospel, three of them being the Passover feast (*John*, 104; note the omission of 13:1 in the final reference to the Passover, which should be included with 11:55 and 12:1).

61. G. L. Borchert, "Passover and the Narrative Cycles in John," in *Perspectives on John: Method and Interpretation in the Fourth Gospel* (ed. R. B. Sloan and M. C. Parsons; Lewiston, NY: Mellen, 1993), 303-16, here 307-8. See also Borchert, *John 1–11* (NAC; Nashville: Broadman & Holman, 1996), 161.

62. Πρόβατον is the more usual term for sheep, the one used in the Exod 12 account of the institution of Passover; see Exod 12:3, 4, 5, 21, and 32, where cattle are mentioned also.

63. W. V. Cirafesi makes a similar observation and suggests that John's Christology has a significant priestly element, with Jesus seen as embodying the temple sanctuary, where sacrifice is offered (τοῦ ναοῦ), in addition to being the sacrifice itself (ὁ ἀμνὸς τοῦ θεοῦ). See W. V. Cirafesi, "The Priestly Portrait of Jesus in the Gospel of John in the Light of 1QS,

ναὸν τοῦτον]", and he will raise it in three days. The Johannine author tells us that Jesus was speaking of "the temple of his body [τοῦ ναοῦ τοῦ σώματος αὐτοῦ]," a clear reference to his death and resurrection.[64] W. D. Davies goes so far as to use this comment about temples as a means of accounting for placement of the episode: "John places the Cleansing of the Temple very early in his Gospel, in 2:13-25, to signify that a New Order had arrived. The 'Holy Place' is to be displaced by a new reality, a rebuilt 'temple (naos),' which John refers to as 'the temple of his body.'"[65] Regardless of how one relates the temple cleansing in John's Gospel to the similar or same event in the Synoptic Gospels,[66] the point I want to emphasize is that the author is thus telling his readers that Jesus' death is the new temple institution, one that renders the old no longer serviceable.

c. John 6:1-14, 22-71

The next episode that helps to establish the Passover theme appears in John 6. Not only does the author state that the events of the chapter, in particular Jesus' feeding of the five thousand, take place near the time of the Passover (John 6:4),[67] as many others have noted, but there are other substantial

---

1QSa, and 1QSb," *JGRChJ* 8 (2011-12): 83-105; Cirafesi, "The Temple Attitudes of John and Qumran in the Light of Hellenistic Judaism," in *Christian Origins and Hellenistic Judaism: Social and Literary Contexts for the New Testament* (ed. S. E. Porter and A. W. Pitts; TENT 10; Early Christianity in Its Hellenistic Context 2; Leiden: Brill, 2013), 315-40.

64. Cf. Stibbe, *John*, 52.

65. W. D. Davies, *The Gospel and the Land: Early Christianity and Jewish Territorial Doctrine* (Berkeley: University of California Press, 1974), 289-90; cf. R. H. Lightfoot, *St. John's Gospel: A Commentary* (ed. C. F. Evans; Oxford: Clarendon Press, 1956), 114. Davies sees the temple incidents of John 8 and 9 as continuing this theme. See also M. Davies, *Rhetoric and Reference*, 231-33. For a more recent work, see Alan R. Kerr, *The Temple of Jesus' Body: The Temple Theme in the Gospel of John* (JSNTSup 220; London: Sheffield Academic Press, 2002), esp. 67-101; P. M. Hoskins, *Jesus as the Fulfillment of the Temple in the Gospel of John* (PBMS; Milton Keynes, UK: Paternoster, 2006).

66. See also ch. 3 in this volume. For an analysis of this passage in relation to the Synoptics, see Porter, "Study of John's Gospel," 294-97.

67. See Lindars, *John*, 240. See also A. T. Lincoln, *The Gospel according to Saint John* (BNTC; Peabody, MA: Hendrickson, 2005), 211, who argues, "Passover is a particularly appropriate setting for the exposition of the exodus events that will follow in Jesus' discourse and for the eucharistic motifs that emerge as its end, since the eucharist was instituted at a meal which, if not itself a Passover meal, was associated from the earliest times with the Passover." The eucharistic overtones of the passage are widely noted. For recent discussion,

reasons as well. First, there is much critical agreement (perhaps even verging on consensus) that this chapter was a form of Christian Passover haggadah, possibly read as a lectionary at Passover celebrations.[68]

Second, there are several Moses-Exodus allusions[69] that help to create a Passover milieu by reference to images often associated with Passover. For example, there is reference to divine provision through the heavenly manna of the exodus. This is seen in particular in four places:

1. John 6:4-5,[70] when, after mentioning that it was Passover, in v. 5 Jesus lifts up his eyes (heavenward?), sees a large, hungry crowd, and makes provision for them to eat bread.

2. John 6:31-33, where, when asked for a sign, Jesus says that the Jewish people of a previous generation ate the manna from heaven in the desert, but that it is not Moses but God the Father who gives the true bread from heaven, which is the one who comes down from heaven, with Jesus alluding to himself.[71]

---

see E. Kobel, *Dining with John: Communal Meals and Identity Formation in the Fourth Gospel and Its Historical and Cultural Context* (BIS 109; Leiden: Brill, 2011), 173-92.

68. P. Borgen, *Bread from Heaven: An Exegetical Study of the Concept of Manna in the Gospel of John and the Writings of Philo* (NovTSup 10; Leiden: Brill, 1965), esp. 1-27. The haggadah theory is supported by supposed verbal parallels with the Old Testament, the Passover haggadah about manna, extrabiblical writers such as Philo, and the text of John 6. The lectionary theory is based on less substantial evidence and more on inference, sometimes drawn from later textual evidence. See also A. Guilding, *The Fourth Gospel and Jewish Worship: A Study of the Relation of St John's Gospel to the Ancient Jewish Lectionary System* (Oxford: Clarendon Press, 1960), 58-68; Brown, *John,* 1:245. It has been criticized by Morris, *Lectionary,* 64-72; U. Schnelle, *Antidocetic Christology in the Gospel of John: An Investigation of the Place of the Fourth Gospel in the Johannine School* (trans. L. M. Maloney; Minneapolis: Fortress Press, 1992), 194-208, esp. 196 n. 128. See Grigsby, "Cross as an Expiatory Sacrifice," 67 n. 25, for further discussion.

69. See M. A. Daise, *Feasts in John* (WUNT 2.229; Tübingen: Mohr Siebeck, 2007), 138-42. Daise understands John 6:4 to be referring to a second Passover, noting the difficulty in placing the event near the Passover (pp. 104-52).

70. Schnackenburg (*John,* 2:14) notes that this reference is "not chronological but theological": "John, however, is alone in explicitly mentioning the nearness of the Passover. . . . For him the importance of the bread discourse is that it introduces the theme of manna, which is important in the Jewish lessons for Passover time." Schnackenburg (*John,* 2:440 n. 2) notes further that, "since manna does not appear as a theme in early Christian Easter homilies we must go back to the Jewish Passover haggada." See Guilding, *Fourth Gospel,* 61-62; Dodd, *Interpretation,* 333; contra Morris, *John,* 342 n. 12.

71. Westcott (*John,* 102) notes that "bread from God" in 6:33 is similar in phrasing to "lamb of God" in 1:29, 36, namely in indicating that it comes directly from God.

3. John 6:34-38, where Jesus equates himself with the bread that comes down from heaven, after the people have apparently recognized his capability in this regard and asked him to give to them this bread.
4. John 6:48-51, when, reiterating more explicitly what he has said above, Jesus not only calls himself the living bread that comes down from heaven and guarantees life, but equates this bread with his flesh, which he says will be given for the life of the world (v. 51), an invocation of sacrificial imagery in terms of the Passover theme.

It has been pointed out above (and by numerous interpreters of this passage) that John's Gospel emphasizes the role of Moses, the leader of the exodus and the instigator of Passover, and so allusion to the manna of the exodus is in keeping with the Passover theme. But Jesus goes further and equates himself with this heavenly bread, and also sees this bread as sacrificial. Thus, third, Jesus himself is depicted as making his sacrificial death even more explicit in John 6:53-58, where he explicates the idea of eating the bread that comes down from heaven as eating his flesh and drinking his blood.[72] Not only does this language reflect exodus language (cf. 1 Cor 10:3-4), but it is sacrificial and makes direct appeal to Passover practices by means of Last Supper imagery. This imagery is probably maintained throughout the chapter but is especially focused on the feeding miracle.[73]

---

72. See Howard, "Passover and Eucharist," 334. Πίνειν τὸ αἷμα is unique to John 6 in the New Testament (6:54, 56), and τρώγειν τὴν σάρκα, also unique to John, is used apparently exclusively by him for the Last Supper (6:54, 56, 57, 58; 13:18). See also Bernard, *John*, 1:210; and Schnackenburg, *John*, 2:56-59, who debates the critical issues related to 6:52-59, especially regarding their relation to the previous discourse.

73. See Exod 12:7, 22; 1 Cor 10:6-22. As Carson states (*John*, 268-69) regarding the reference to the Passover in John 6:4 in the context of this chapter and its relation to the Passover, "The connections become complex: the sacrifice of the lamb anticipates Jesus' death, the Old Testament manna is superseded by the real bread of life, the exodus typologically sets forth the eternal life that delivers us from sin and destruction, the Passover feast is taken over by the eucharist (both of which point to Jesus and his redemptive cross-work). 'The movement from the miracle to the discourse, from Moses to Jesus (vv. 32-5, cf. i.17), and, above all, from *bread* to *flesh,* is almost unintelligible unless the reference in v. 4 to the Passover picks up i.29, 36, anticipates xix.36 (Exod. xii.46; Num. ix.12), and governs the whole narrative'" (quoting from E. Hoskyns and F. N. Davey, *The Fourth Gospel* [2 vols.; London: Faber & Faber, 1940], 1:281). This may also allude to the Suffering Servant ascent-descent motif. See G. C. Nicholson, *Death as Departure: The Johannine Descent-Ascent Scheme* (SBLDS 63; Chico, CA: Scholars Press, 1983).

d. John 8:31-47

In the fourth section, John 8:31-47, Jesus addresses hard words to a group of believing Jews, saying, "If you continue in my word, you are truly my disciples; and you will know the truth, and the truth will set you free" (vv. 31-32). This provocative comment triggers a discussion of what they would be set free from. Jesus talks first of bondage to sin (vv. 34-38) and then bondage to the devil (vv. 42-47). However, Jesus stresses the freedom from bondage that he provides: "So if the Son makes you free, you will be free indeed" (v. 36).

The connections of this episode to the Passover theme are not nearly as firmly established as are the other sections in this chapter. One of the main reasons is that this exchange does not happen around the time of Passover (as with the previous section) but rather around the Festival of Tabernacles (John 7:2). In fact, when I first wrote on the Passover theme in John's Gospel, I did not include this section in my analysis. However, Paul Hoskins has made a strong case that this section contributes to the Passover theme in John.[74] He first argues that the Feast of Tabernacles and Passover are closely related — both look back to the events of the exodus (Passover) and the wandering of the Israelites before entering the Promised Land (Tabernacles). Furthermore, as Hoskins points out, John's Gospel does connect the events celebrated in these two different feasts. The example he points to is John 6:51-58, where the setting is the Passover but the focus on the bread from heaven is closer to the Feast of Tabernacles.[75] Hoskins rightly argues that the theme of freedom from slavery fits the context of the original Passover and correlates with the Passover theme in John's Gospel. In fact, the freedom and slavery concept here in the Gospel may not be explicit but may more aptly be labeled an echo, according to its definition as an "invocation by means of thematically related language of some more general notion or concept."[76] The Passover theme, then, or at the very least an exodus theme, is invoked here by the reference to slavery and freedom. This echo alone does not establish a Passover theme in John's Gospel, but considering the other sections in this chapter where a Passover theme is more explicit, it may be appropriate to consider this to be at least an echo of that theme. In the same vein, Hoskins argues that this section "provides the redemptive picture that

---

74. P. M. Hoskins, "Freedom from Slavery to Sin and the Devil: John 8:31-47 and the Passover Theme of the Gospel of John," *TrinJ*, n.s., 31 (2010): 47-63; cf. also Hoskins, "Deliverance from Death," 289-92. See also Nielsen, "Lamb of God," 249-52.

75. Hoskins, "Freedom from Slavery," 48.

76. Porter, "Allusions and Echoes," 39.

helps to fill out John's Passover typology. It clarifies both the nature of the slavery and the redemption that John has in view."[77] Hoskins may see more in this section than is there, but he is certainly right that John 8:31-47 is another important element in the overall development of John's Passover theme.

e. John 11:47–12:8

John 11 records an incident in which the intentions of the leaders of the Jewish people, captured in the words of Caiaphas the high priest, are depicted as pointing specifically to Jesus as the sacrificial Passover victim. In the light of the controversy caused by Jesus, Caiaphas states that he thinks that it is better that "one man die for the people than that the whole nation be destroyed" (11:50). The scene is full of dramatic and verbal irony. On the one hand, the author refers to Jesus in his sacrificial role as creating the unified children of God (11:51-52), while the high priest speaks with specific reference to the death of Jesus saving the Jewish people, in particular its leaders, from destruction at the hands of the Romans. On the other hand, Caiaphas's words create an equation that captures (for the Johannine author) the function of the Passover sacrifice, in that the substitutionary death of the one victim (the "lamb of God") prevents the destruction of an entire people because of their sin.[78] Although the preposition ὑπέρ ("in behalf of," not necessarily "instead of") is used, the substitutionary idea is paramount.[79] This is seen in two ways. First, the preposition ὑπέρ, dependent on context, is used with a substitutionary sense during the Hellenistic period. When an amanuensis was employed to write for someone illiterate, a line was often appended by the scribe to indicate that he had written "for" (ὑπέρ) someone incapable of writing.[80] Second, the context is clearly substitutionary, in which Caiaphas sees the single individual as providing a substitute for the nation, so that destruction will come only to one. This sense of the one taking the place of the whole is taken up by the Johannine author in explaining the meaning of Caiaphas's statement.

77. Hoskins, "Freedom from Slavery," 62.
78. Cf. Stibbe, *John*, 130-31.
79. As Köstenberger points out, "In Jesus's case, however, this [Caiaphas's ruling] coincided perfectly with God's plan that Jesus would serve as 'God's lamb' (1:29, 36), a substitutionary sacrifice for the sins of humankind (cf. 3:14-16; 6:51; 10:14-18; 12:24, 32)" (*John*, 352).
80. S. E. Porter, *Idioms of the Greek New Testament* (2nd ed.; BLG 2; Sheffield: Sheffield Academic Press, 1994), 176-77; Lindars, *John*, 406.

There are two further references to the approaching Passover in John 11:55 and 12:1. The first is a general reference to the Passover, and the second places the following events six days before the Passover.[81] The effect of these two explicit time markers is to link Caiaphas's words to Jesus' being anointed at Bethany by Mary (John 12:1-8), and then to link both of these events to Jesus' impending death. The author makes sure that the reader understands Jesus' anointing as following on from Caiaphas's words and in anticipation of Jesus' death in Jerusalem, when he depicts Jesus as stating that the purpose of Mary's action was to prepare Jesus' body for burial (John 12:7). In this way, Jesus is further depicted as the Passover victim being prepared for sacrifice.[82]

f. John 13:1–17:26

Whereas the first part of the Gospel (John 1–12) covers a number of years in Jesus' life (two and a half by Culpepper's reckoning), John 13–19 depicts a time period of approximately twenty-four hours.[83] This latter series of prolonged events that terminates in Jesus' death begins with what is probably best seen as a Passover meal that Jesus eats with his disciples (John 13–17).[84] It has been debated in many quarters whether this is a Passover meal, largely because of the chronological difficulties between the Synoptic and Johannine accounts of the final days of Jesus' life. This is not the place to discuss these chronological issues. Nevertheless, it appears fairly clear that, in the light of the overwhelming similarities between the Synoptic and Johannine accounts, the meal depicted in John 13–17 is seen by the author of John's Gospel as a Passover meal, or at least as one that is infused with numerous

81. As Köstenberger observes, these time markers "may intend to remind the reader that Jesus is the paradigmatic sacrificial lamb" (*John*, 359); see also Carson, *John*, 427.

82. Schnackenburg (*John*, 2:366) misses entirely the significance of the temporal reference.

83. R. A. Culpepper, *Anatomy of the Fourth Gospel: A Study in Literary Design* (FFNT; Philadelphia: Fortress Press, 1983), 72. On the larger issue of time in the Gospel of John, see D. Estes, *The Temporal Mechanics of the Fourth Gospel: A Theory of Hermeneutical Relativity in the Gospel of John* (BIS 92; Leiden: Brill, 2008).

84. There has been much discussion of the unity of John 13–17. For a recent statement, see F. J. Moloney, "The Function of John 13–17 within the Johannine Narrative," in *"What Is John?"* vol. 2: *Literary and Social Readings of the Fourth Gospel* (ed. F. F. Segovia; SympS 7; Atlanta: Scholars Press, 1998), 43-66, but who is not entirely convincing in his explanations.

Passover elements.[85] What is often less well established are the clear indications of Jesus' being depicted as the Passover lamb in several episodes within these chapters.

The indications that should be taken into account are the following. First, 13:1 sets the scene by saying that, just before the time of the Passover, Jesus realized what would happen to him.[86] This verse probably serves as a heading for all of John 13–17. The author continues by stating that, in the light of Jesus' knowledge and compassion, during the dinner (13:4) he did and said a number of things. Second, among the words that Jesus is said to have uttered were words regarding his identity as the true vine (15:1-10). The vine image probably alludes to the wine consumed at the Passover celebration, having apparently just been consumed in the events of the narrative above.[87] Furthermore, the language used in John 15–17 is reminiscent of

---

85. The strongest case for equating the meals in the Synoptic Gospels and John's Gospel is probably made by J. Jeremias (*The Eucharistic Words of Jesus* [NTL; London: SCM Press, 1966], 56-82, esp. 81). See also R. E. Brown, "The Problem of History in John," *CBQ* 24 (1962): 5, who argues for a meal with Passover features. For a position against such an equation, see A. J. B. Higgins, *The Lord's Supper in the New Testament* (SBT 6; London: SCM Press, 1952), 74-88, who argues that the Passover victim had to be killed before the meal. On chronology, the strongest advocates for two calendars being in use in Palestine are A. Jaubert (*La date de la cène: Calendrier biblique et liturgie chrétienne* [EBib; Paris: Gabalda, 1957]; "Jésus et le calendrier de Qumrân," *NTS* 7 [1960-61]: 1-30; "The Calendar of Qumran and the Passion Narrative in John," in *John and the Dead Sea Scrolls* [ed. J. H. Charlesworth; New York: Crossroad, 1990], 62-75) and E. Ruckstuhl (*Chronology of the Last Days of Jesus: A Critical Study* [trans. V. J. Drapela; New York: Desclee, 1965]); see also N. Walker, "Pauses in the Passion Story and Their Significance for Chronology," *NovT* 6 (1963): 16-19; K. A. Strand, "John as Quartodeciman: A Reappraisal," *JBL* 84 (1965): 251-58. They have been opposed by G. Ogg, "Review of Mlle Jaubert, La date de la cène," *NovT* 3 (1959): 149-60, besides numerous commentators. Cf. von Wahlde, *Gospel and Letters of John*, 2:576; Lincoln, *John*, 365. They both, however, argue that it was not a Passover meal. I note here that the current footnote is mine and is based on my previously published essay. I note this because a nearly identical footnote (apart from the two later references) appears in S. H. Khani, *Revelation and Concealment of Christ: A Theological Inquiry into the Elusive Language of the Fourth Gospel* (WUNT 2.120; Tübingen: Mohr Siebeck, 2000), 275 n. 184.

86. J. Rendel Harris ("The Early Christian Interpretation of the Passover," *ExpTim* 38 [1926-27]: 88-90) cites the use of μεταβῇ in John 13:1 as an allusion to the Passover, since Philo describes the exodus using similar language, but this is pretty thin evidence. See Glasson, *Moses*, 97-98.

87. See John 13:2, 4, 26, 30; Howard, "Passover and Eucharist," 335; Bernard, *John*, 2:478. Cf. Isa 5:1-7; 27:2-11. Note also that this usage probably extends and applies to Jesus' language regarding Israel as the true vine (e.g., Jer 2:21; 12:10-13; Ezek 15:1-8; 19:10-14; Hos 10:1; Ps 80:8-16). See Hoskyns and Davey, *Fourth Gospel*, 2:559-60.

the "bearing" and "taking away" language of 1:29 (see subsection a above) and of the glory language that refers to Jesus' death on the cross.[88] In John 17 the entire scene is brought to a close by Jesus' prayer for himself and his followers. The concept of glorification (see 17:5) seems to have been inspired by the Suffering Servant passages of Isaiah, especially Isa 53 (see 12:38, 41), which are used at the outset of Jesus' ministry to establish him as not only the one who suffers but as the one who dies as a sacrificial lamb (1:29; cf. v. 36; see subsection a above). In Jesus' prayer, as the meal draws to a close, it is perhaps not too much to see Jesus offering a new prayer of blessing and consecration for the Passover feast — one that he himself is about to reenact as its victim.[89]

g. John 19:13-42, especially vv. 14, 29, 31, 36-37, 42

In the light of what has been argued above, it should not come as a surprise that the Johannine author draws out the Passover theme in the actual depiction of Jesus' death in John 19. Many commentators are willing to concede that there are Passover elements in this scene, but they have failed to realize the force such a depiction would have because they have failed to see how the theme has been developed throughout John's Gospel. This passage is therefore not a simple equation of Jesus with the Passover victim on the basis of only the points of correlation mentioned in this particular passage, but it is a climactic scene that brings to a decisive conclusion a major thematic element developed throughout the Gospel. As J. Duncan Derrett states for the Johannine author, "Whatever Passover means, the [passion narrative] means."[90] There are a number of factors in this passage to consider in establishing the importance of the Passover theme, all of which point to the double quotation in John 19:36-37 as the climactic statement regarding this theme.

The first factor is the temporal references to the day on which Jesus died. John 18:28 and 39 say that it is the evening of the day before Passover; 19:14 says that it is the preparation for Passover (παρασκευὴ τοῦ πάσχα); and 19:31 and 42 say that it is the day of preparation — either for Passover

88. The glory language includes John 12:16, 23, 28; 13:31-32. See Evans, *Word and Glory*, 180.

89. See Howard, "Passover and Eucharist," 336.

90. J. D. M. Derrett, *The Victim: The Johannine Passion Narrative Reexamined* (Shipton-on-Stour: Drinkwater, 1993), 142.

or for Sabbath, since the two seem to have fallen on the same day, so far as the author's account is concerned.[91] Throughout John's Gospel, there is correlation of events in Jesus' ministry with events surrounding Passover (see above), and the same is true in the passion account, where there is direct correlation of specific events concerning Jesus' death with the events surrounding the Passover celebration. Not only is the mention of the specific timing important, but the repetition unites the account. John 18:28 and 39 prepare the reader for the specific chronology of events in John 19, and the crucial events surrounding Jesus' death are linked on three occasions to the day of preparation, once at the beginning, once in the middle, and once at the end (19:14, 31, 42). The significance of this linkage lies in the fact that the day of preparation was the day on which the Passover sacrifices were killed.[92] Thus Jesus' death not only is seen to occur on the day on which the Passover sacrifice was made but is equated with that sacrifice itself by virtue of its contemporaneity.

Second, Jesus is sentenced to death by Pilate at noon, or the eighth hour; according to the Jewish chronography,[93] this is the hour at which the slaughter of the Passover lambs was to begin (John 19:14; cf. Exod 12:6).[94] The presentation by Pilate of Jesus for death is accompanied both by the indication of the day, which is repeated twice more in the account, as noted above, and by the indication of the specific hour. The timing of the presentation of Jesus could be a coincidence, but it is an uncanny one that coordinates well with what is known of Passover practice and points to Jesus' impending death as being interpreted in the light of the Passover. Jesus' death has the same symbolic significance as the cleansing of the temple.[95]

---

91. See Barrett, *John*, 555, who claims that there is a significant difference between John 19:14 and vv. 31 and 42, on the basis of which day is being referred to. Cf. Schnackenburg, *John*, 3:264; Carson, *John*, 604. Stibbe (*John*, 191) takes them all as referring to Passover.

92. G. B. Gray, *Sacrifice in the Old Testament: Its Theory and Practice* (Oxford: Clarendon Press, 1925), 388.

93. There is some textual dispute regarding the time of Jesus' death, but readings for the sixth hour are almost certainly designed to bring the Fourth Gospel into harmony with the Synoptic accounts.

94. Gray, *Sacrifice*, 388-89; Brown, *John*, 2:833; Barrett, *John*, 545.

95. See Beasley-Murray, *John*, 341, who states: "The place, the day, and the hour are all mentioned, for the Evangelist is conscious of the momentous nature of the event now taking place. . . . It is the sixth hour (noon) of the Preparation Day; at this hour three things take place: Jews cease their work, leaven is gathered out of the houses and burned, and the slaughtering of the Passover lambs commences. The Passover festival, for all practical purposes, now begins. . . . The Evangelist's thought is plain: Passover is the great celebration

As Bultmann states, "The end of the Jewish cultus, or the uselessness of its further observance, is thereby affirmed."[96]

Third, specific events associated with Jesus' actual death are perhaps best interpreted in terms of the Passover.[97] For example, in Exod 12:22 and in John 19:29 (but not in the Synoptic Gospels), the hyssop branch is mentioned. There has been much debate regarding what the hyssop branch was and, if it was a small, weak plant (as it seems to have been), how it could be used to lift the sponge to Jesus' lips. If anything, these difficulties, as well as the apparently conscious departure from the Synoptic use of κάλαμος ("reed"),[98] point to the author's intentionally including this item to correlate it with the use of the hyssop branch at Passover.[99] They are described in the Passover and John 19 accounts as serving similar functions; that is, the hyssop branch is used to form a connection between the sacrificial victim and those for whom it or he is the sacrifice.[100] In John 19:34 the blood and water of Jesus that flow out when he is stabbed by the soldier may be reminiscent of the flow of blood and fluid out of the sacrificial animal (Exod 12:7, 22). Several later rabbinic passages describe the proper sacrifice in terms of the flow of blood and water or fluid. The idea appears to be that the blood was supposed to flow like water to prevent congealing.[101] Furthermore, Jesus'

---

of Israel's deliverance from slavery by God's almighty power; then it was that he showed himself as King, and they became his people. In this celebration the Jews gathered before Pilate are about to play a decisive part in the fulfillment of the Passover, a second Exodus, wherein God would achieve an emancipation for all nations, not for Israel alone, giving them life in the promised land of his eternal kingdom. The crucial hour of destiny for Jew and Gentile has arrived."

96. Bultmann, *John*, 677.

97. On issues of chronology and Passover practice, see Grigsby, "Cross as an Expiatory Sacrifice," 54-56 and notes. He shows that the Passover theme is essentially unaltered by the various chronologies proposed.

98. See Mark 15:36; Matt 27:48. Barrett, *John*, 553; Grigsby, "Cross as an Expiatory Sacrifice," 57; contra Schnackenburg, *John*, 3:284; Bultmann, *John*, 673 n. 5; Dodd, *Historical Tradition*, 123-24 n. 2.

99. Cf. Heb 8:19, where blood, water, and hyssop are related. Stibbe (*John*, 196) notes the hyssop branch as a reference to the Passover, where the Israelites used it to daub the blood on the doorposts during the first Passover. See also Nielsen, "Lamb of God," esp. 253.

100. See Lev 14:6-7; Num 19:6; Ps 50:9, where hyssop is related to cultic sprinkling. Barrett (*John*, 553) says that "the fact that hyssop could hardly be used in the manner described is not one that would greatly concern the evangelist."

101. The καί may be epexegetic: "blood, even water (fluid)." J. M. Ford ("'Mingled Blood' from the Side of Christ [John XIX.34]," *NTS* 15 [1968-69]: 337-38) also finds reference to the meaning "spurting" rather than dripping blood in ἐξῆλθον εὐθὺς αἷμα, but this

body is not allowed to stay on the cross until the next morning (John 19:31, 38), just as the remains of the Passover meal were not to be left until the next day but were to be burned (Exod. 12:19) — thus, another parallel between Jesus' crucifixion and the Passover is evident.[102]

Fourth, the scene is brought to a close by the two formulaic quotations (or a double quotation) from the Old Testament in John 19:36-37. The first is probably a quotation of Exod 12:46 (also 12:10 LXX) or Num 9:12,[103] both from Passover accounts. The second quotation is from Zech 12:10.[104] The first is introduced by John's fulfillment formula, which, as noted above, he uses frequently throughout the second half of the Gospel (the exception is John 19:28). Although the second quotation begins with πάλιν ἑτέρα γραφὴ λέγει, rather than πληρωθῇ, the two are apparently meant to be taken together, with the second quotation a further passage taken in support of the sacrificial imagery, here referring to the piercing of Jesus. This is the second compound quotation in John's Gospel, the first having begun the passion section of the Gospel and the "fulfillment" quotations (John 12:38–19:37). Although Margaret Davies contends that the author of John's Gospel is never explicit about referring to Jesus' death as related to the Passover except at this particular point,[105] perhaps in the light of the evidence marshaled above, it is better to see these quotations as simply making explicit in a summative way a major theme that has been developed throughout the Gospel.[106] The issue is not so much whether an explicit quotation is used to prove that the sacrificial Passover imagery comes from the Old Testament, as whether there has been sustained and consistent use of recognizable Passover language throughout. It is my contention that this has been the case at several significant junctures in the unfolding Gospel account.

---

understanding is less clear. See also Beasley-Murray, *John,* 353-58, for medical explanations; contra Stibbe, *John as Storyteller,* 115-16.

102. Davies, *Rhetoric and Reference,* 234, 305, 355.

103. Although, less likely, Ps 34:20 (34:21 MT; 33:21 LXX) has also been suggested.

104. Köstenberger, *John,* 553.

105. Davies, *Rhetoric and Reference,* 305-6.

106. See M. Stibbe, "Magnificent But Flawed: The Breaking of Form in the Fourth Gospel," in *Anatomies of Narrative Criticism: The Past, Present, and Futures of the Fourth Gospel as Literature* (ed. T. Thatcher and S. D. Moore; SBLRBS 55; Atlanta: SBL, 2008), 149-65, esp. 158. He observes the connection between John 1:29, 36 and 19:36, 37, with Jesus being the "perfect Passover lamb."

4. Conclusion

At the outset of Jesus' ministry, he is proclaimed the sacrificial lamb of God, introducing a theme that is maintained and developed throughout John's Gospel. At several significant junctures in the ministry of Jesus the author reaffirms Jesus' role as Passover victim. Then at the climactic events leading up to and including his death, he brings the passion story to a close by citing in double, emphatic fashion Old Testament quotations that make the sacrificial Passover death not only specific but virtually undeniable. This particular double quotation not only brings the Passover theme to its fitting conclusion, but it also brings to an end the series of Old Testament quotations by the author of John's Gospel, both of them occurring at the death of Jesus. The quotations in John 19:36-37 are to be seen, therefore, as final fulfillment statements that bring the entire course of plot development to a close. A primary motivation for the action of the story is Jesus' death as a substitute and replacement for the Passover sacrifice, seen in his fulfilling various features of that sacrifice.[107]

---

107. This position has essentially been adopted by A. J. Köstenberger, *A Theology of John's Gospel and Letters* (Grand Rapids: Zondervan, 2009), 414-20.

CHAPTER 9

Jesus and the Ending of John's Gospel

1. Introduction

The question of whether John 21 was originally part of John's Gospel has been debated in discussion of this Gospel for the last approximately one hundred years.[1] The issue has not gone away, despite there being no external textual evidence to indicate that John 21 belongs anywhere else but right after John 20, and that it belonged there from the start. In other words, no ancient Greek (or other) manuscript indicates that anything other than the Gospel as a whole (John 1–21) circulated, which should serve as a satisfactory answer to the question regarding the integrity of John 21.[2] Nevertheless, controversy over John 21 goes back to at least the time of Tertullian (*Prax.* 25).[3] A number of more recent scholars have argued that this chapter was not

---

1. For bibliography, see G. R. Beasley-Murray, *John* (2nd ed.; WBC 36; Dallas: Word, 1999), 392; and C. Claussen, "The Role of John 21: Discipleship in Retrospect and Redefinition," in *New Currents through John: A Global Perspective* (ed. F. Loazada Jr. and T. Thatcher; SBLRBS 54; Atlanta: SBL, 2006), 55-68, who illustrates more recent concern with reading the final chapter as a literary unity, even if it was written by someone else or later.

2. See P. S. Minear, "The Original Functions of John 21," *JBL* 102 (1983): 85-98, esp. 86. Nevertheless, some interpreters choose simply not to include John 21 in their study. See, e.g., G. R. O'Day, *Revelation in the Fourth Gospel: Narrative Mode and Theological Claim* (Philadelphia: Fortress Press, 1986), 136 n. 1; A. Reinhartz, *The Word in the World: The Cosmological Tale in the Fourth Gospel* (SBLMS 45; Atlanta: Scholars Press, 1992), 13 n. 57.

3. According to J. B. Lightfoot, *Biblical Essays* (London: Macmillan, 1893), 194. On other earlier interpreters, see J. Moffatt, *An Introduction to the Literature of the New Testament* (3rd rev. ed.; Edinburgh: T&T Clark, 1918), 571-72.

a part of the original Gospel but was written by the author of the Gospel and appended later, possibly quite soon after.[4] Some wish to argue that John 21 was written by another author and so should be separated from the rest of the Gospel.[5] Others believe that the chapter was added to retain "important material" for later readers.[6] Still others depict John 21 as an "epilogue" that was added "shortly after the gospel was completed," and that it "resolves some of the minor conflicts" found in the text by serving a literary purpose.[7] One scholar has recently proposed that the addition of John 21 reflects an added chapter for a second edition of the Gospel.[8] Finally, at least one author believes that the miraculous catch of fish (21:1-14) is a retelling for Johannine

---

4. Lightfoot, *Biblical Essays,* 194; B. F. Westcott, *The Gospel according to St. John* (2 vols.; London: John Murray, 1908), 2:359-60; W. Bauer, *Das Johannesevangelium* (HNT 6; Tübingen: Mohr Siebeck, 1933), 235; R. Schnackenburg, *The Gospel according to St. John* (trans. K. Smyth et al.; 3 vols.; London: Burns & Oates, 1968-82), 3:335; L. Morris, *The Gospel according to John* (rev. ed.; NICNT; Grand Rapids: Eerdmans, 1995 [1971]), 859; G. L. Borchert, *John 12–21* (NAC; Nashville: Broadman & Holman, 2002), 320.

5. F. Godet, *Commentary on the Gospel of St. John* (trans. M. D. Cusins; 3 vols.; Edinburgh: T&T Clark, 1899), 3:343; M. Boismard, "Le chapître xxi de saint Jean: Essai de critique littéraire," *RB* 54 (1947): 473-501; R. Bultmann, *The Gospel of John: A Commentary* (trans. G. R. Beasley-Murray et al.; Oxford: Blackwell, 1971), 700-706; B. Lindars, *The Gospel of John* (NCB; Grand Rapids: Eerdmans, 1972), 618; C. K. Barrett, *The Gospel according to St. John* (2nd ed.; Philadelphia: Westminster, 1978), 576.

6. R. Brown, *The Gospel according to John* (2 vols.; AB 29, 29A; Garden City, NY: Doubleday, 1966-70), 2:1077-82. Cf. T. Zahn, *Introduction to the New Testament* (trans. M. W. Jacobus; Edinburgh: T&T Clark, 1909), 234; J. H. Bernard, *A Critical and Exegetical Commentary on the Gospel according to St. John* (ed. A. H. McNeile; 2 vols.; ICC; Edinburgh: T&T Clark, 1928), 2:687-92; R. H. Lightfoot, *St. John's Gospel: A Commentary* (ed. C. F. Evans; Oxford: Clarendon Press, 1956), 339-42.

7. R. A. Culpepper, *Anatomy of the Fourth Gospel: A Study in Literary Design* (Philadelphia: Fortress Press, 1983), 96. Since this earlier publication, Culpepper has wanted to emphasize the literary unity of John 21. See his "Designs for the Church in the Imagery of John 21:1-14," in *Imagery in the Gospel of John* (ed. J. Frey, J. van der Watt, and R. Zimmermann; WUNT 200; Tübingen: Mohr Siebeck, 2006), 369-402; and Claussen, "Role of John 21," 69.

8. H. C. Waetjen, *The Gospel of the Beloved Disciple: A Work in Two Editions* (New York: T&T Clark, 2005), 3, who gives the above recent theories on p. 8 n. 23, as well as others. W. G. Kümmel (*Introduction to the New Testament* [trans. H. C. Kee; Nashville: Abingdon, 1973], 207) asserts that it is "uncontestable" that John 21 is a later addition; cf. G. Reim, *Jochanan: Erweiterte Studien zum alttestamentlichen Hintergrund des Johannesevangeliums* (Erlangen: Verlag der Ev.-Luth. Mission, 1995), 389-96. This conclusion may be uncontestable among a certain group of German scholars, but it is far from obvious that all scholars hold to this position, especially a number of recent ones (and many of them outside of Germany).

rhetorical purposes of a similar event in Luke 5:1-11.[9] Of course, there are also a number of scholars who, while recognizing various differences and even difficulties with John 21, believe that it was indeed the final chapter of the original Gospel.[10] In the light of these differing conclusions, an examination of the evidence for distinguishing between John 21 and the rest of the Gospel is in order.

A number of arguments that merit discussion have been marshaled on each side of this question. One must be careful in examining the alternatives, however. As noted above, some believe that John 21 was not written by the same author who wrote John 1–20, while others believe that John 21 was written by the same author but was not part of the original Gospel. In this section, I examine arguments regarding differences between John 21 and the rest of the Gospel as a means of examining the question of whether the chapter was written by a different author from the one who wrote the rest of the book. I first examine the language evidence, then turn to the evidence for and against internal and external unity of John 21. I conclude by examining the question of how John 21 fits with the rest of the Gospel in the light of the purported ending of John 20:30-31.

2. The Language of John 21

Questions of the language of John 21 can be usefully divided into two groups: those concerned with grammar and those concerned with vocabulary.

---

9. M. Labahn, "Fishing for Meaning: The Miraculous Catch of Fish in John 21," in *Wonders Never Cease: The Purpose of Narrating Miracle Stories in the New Testament and Its Religious Environment* (ed. M. Labahn and B. J. L. Peerbolte; LNTS 288; London: T&T Clark, 2006), 125-45.

10. E.g., E. C. Hoskyns, *The Fourth Gospel* (ed. F. N. Davey; 2nd ed.; London: Faber & Faber, 1947), 561-62; M. C. Tenney, *John: The Gospel of Belief* (Grand Rapids: Eerdmans, 1948), 258; S. S. Smalley, *John: Evangelist and Interpreter* (Exeter: Paternoster, 1978), 95-96; F. F. Bruce, *The Gospel of John* (Basingstoke, UK: Pickering & Inglis, 1983), 398; D. A. Carson, *The Gospel according to John* (PNTC; Grand Rapids: Eerdmans; Leicester: InterVarsity Press, 1991), 665-68; T. L. Brodie, *The Gospel according to John: A Literary and Theological Commentary* (New York: Oxford University Press, 1993), 576, 581-82; A. J. Köstenberger, *John* (BECNT; Grand Rapids: Baker, 2004), 583-86; R. Bauckham, "The 153 Fish and the Unity of the Fourth Gospel," in his *The Testimony of the Beloved Disciple: Narrative, History, and Theology in the Gospel of John* (Grand Rapids: Baker, 2007), 271-84 (reprinted from *Neot* 36 [2002]: 77-88).

a. Grammar

Rudolf Bultmann presents what at first glance appears to be one of the most significant sets of lists of items to consider regarding the authenticity and integrity of John 21.[11] He presents several lists dealing with language and style, sentence connections, and Semitisms. However, his lists are of limited worth for investigation of the question of authenticity. The reason for their limited value is that he presents a laundry list of items in John 21, but he does not present these in comparison with the rest of the Gospel. For example, Bultmann notes that there are two genitive absolutes in John 21 (vv. 4, 11). But are these proportionately more or less than is found throughout the rest of the Gospel, and is this significant? It is not surprising that Bultmann concludes that language and style "admittedly afford no sure proof" either way on the question of authenticity.[12] A better list is presented by J. B. Lightfoot (with some supplementary references):[13]

- historic οὖν characteristic of John's narrative: John 21:5, 6, 7 bis, 9, 11, 15, 21, 23[14]
- absence of narrative δέ[15]
- placement of the verb first: John 21:1, 2, 3, 4, 5, 7, 10, 11, 12, 13, 23, 25
- placement of the verb λέγει first: John 21:3, 5, 7, 12, 15 bis, 16, 17, 22
- avoidance of connecting particles: John 21:3, 12, 13, 16, 17[16]
- use of ἐκεῖνος: John 21:3, 7, 23
- indications of definiteness: "the right-hand side" (John 21:6), "200 cubits" (v. 8), "153" (v. 11), "this third time" (v. 14)

11. Bultmann, *John*, 700; cf. Barrett, *John*, 576-77. See also W. F. Howard, *The Fourth Gospel in Recent Criticism and Interpretation* (rev. C. K. Barrett; London: Epworth, 1955), 279-80.

12. Bultmann, *John*, 700.

13. Lightfoot, *Biblical Essays*, 194-95.

14. According to E. Ruckstuhl (*Die literarische Einheit des Johannesevangeliums* [NTOA 5; Freiburg: Universitätsverlag; Göttingen: Vandenhoeck & Ruprecht, 1987], 293), narrative-historical οὖν occurs in the following places in John 1–20: 2:22; 3:25; 4:1, 45, 46; 6:5, 11, 19, 24; 7:45; 8:12, 21, 28; 9:18, 20, 24; 10:7, 24; 11:20, 21, 32, 33, 56; 12:1, 9, 21; 13:12, 31; 18:4, 6, 7, 10, 17, 19, 24, 25, 27, 28, 33; 19:6, 8, 20, 23, 30, 31; 20:6, 8, 10, 19, 20, 21, 30.

15. Lightfoot (*Biblical Essays*, 194) disputes that δέ in John 21:12 is authentic, claiming it was "wrongly inserted" by scribes.

16. Ruckstuhl (*Literarische Einheit*, 94) offers the following examples of asyndeton in John 1–20: 1:40, 41, 42, 45, 47; 2:17; 4.6c, 7, 30, 50b; 5:12, 15; 6:23; 7:32, 41; 8:27; 9:9, 13, 16c, 35, 40; 10:21, 22b; 11:35, 44; 12:22a, 22b, 29b; 13:22, 23; 16:19; 19:29; 20:18, 26b. In John 21 he also lists vv. 2, 3c, 13, 17b.

- parenthetical explanations: John 21:7, 8
- familiar phrasing: ὑπάγω ἁλιεύειν . . . ἐρχόμεθα καὶ ἡμεῖς σὺν σοί (John 21:3), δεῦτε ἀριστήσατε . . . σὺ τίς εἶ; (v. 12), ἀκολούθει μοι (v. 19; cf. v. 22, with different wording),[17] κύριε, οὗτος δὲ τί; (v. 21), τί πρὸς σέ; σύ μοι ἀκολούθει (v. 22), etc.
- favorite Johannine expressions: καὶ τὸ ὀψάριον ὁμοίως (John 21:13; cf. 6:11), ἀμὴν ἀμήν (21:18),[18] τοῦτο δὲ εἶπεν σημαίνων ποίῳ θανάτῳ (21:19; cf. 12:33; 18:32)
- style of designation of people and places: "the sea of Tiberias" (John 21:1; cf. 6:1), "Nathanael from Cana of Galilee" (21:2; cf. 1:45; 12:21; 19:38), "Thomas called Didymus" (21:6; cf. 11:16; 20:24), "the disciple whom Jesus loved" (21:7, 20; cf. 13:23; 19:26; 20:2), "Simon, son of John" (21:15, 16; cf. 1:42)

Lightfoot believes that all these elements of language indicate that John 21 was written by the same author who wrote John 1–20.[19] A case for John 21 being demonstrably different from the rest of the Gospel on the basis of grammar clearly remains unmade.

b. Vocabulary

There are two kinds of vocabulary items to note in the discussion of the authenticity of John 21. First is a list of vocabulary items that are unique to John 21, as compared to the rest of the Gospel. These include the following, according to Bultmann's and Barrett's lists:[20]

---

17. This is an example of what Leon Morris calls twofold variation, which he finds throughout the Gospel. This twofold variation occurs when "a word or expression is used and then repeated once only," but with some variation. See L. Morris, *Studies in the Fourth Gospel* (Grand Rapids: Eerdmans; Exeter: Paternoster, 1969), 293-304, esp. 304 (quotation 293).

18. Ruckstuhl (*Literarische Einheit*, 300) lists the following uses in John 1–20: 1:51; 3:3, 5, 11; 5:19, 24, 25; 6:26, 32, 47, 53; 8:34, 51, 58; 10:1, 7; 12:24; 13:16, 20, 21, 38; 14:12; 16:20, 23.

19. The grammatical issues are discussed in detail verse by verse in A. Schlatter, *Der Evangelist Johannes: Wie er spricht, denkt und glaubt; Ein Kommentar zum vierten Evangelium* (4th ed.; Stuttgart: Calwer, 1975), 364-77. On problems with using such criteria, see M. Hengel, *The Johannine Question* (trans. J. Bowden; London: SCM Press; Philadelphia: Trinity Press International, 1989), 83-87.

20. Bultmann, *John*, 700-701 and n. 3; Barrett, *John*, 576.

αἰγιαλός ("beach"; John 21:4)
ἁλιεύειν ("fish"; v. 3)
ἀποβαίνειν ("get out"; v. 9)
ἀριστᾶν ("eat"; v. 12)
ἀρνίον ("lamb"; v. 15)
βόσκειν ("feed"; v. 15)
γηράσκειν ("age"; v. 18)
γυμνός ("naked"; v. 7)
δίκτυον ("fishing net"; vv. 6, 8)
ἐκτείνειν ("stretch out"; v. 18)
ἐξετάζειν ("ask"; v. 12)
ἐπενδύτης ("outer garment"; v. 7)
ἐπιστρέφειν ("turn around"; v. 20)
ζωννύναι ("fasten"; v. 18)

ἰσχύειν ("be able"; v. 6)
ἰχθύς ("fish"; vv. 6, 8, 11)
μακράν ("far"; v. 8)
νεώτερος ("younger"; v. 18)
οἴεσθαι ("think"; v. 25)
πῆχυς ("cubit"; v. 8)
ποιμαίνειν ("tend sheep"; v. 16)
προβάτιον ("sheep"; v. 16)
προσφάγιον ("fish"; v. 5)
πρωΐα ("early"; v. 4)
σύρειν ("drag"; v. 8)
τολμᾶν ("dare"; v. 12)
τρίτον ("third"; vv. 1, 14, 17)

This is a sizable and substantial list.

This list requires further scrutiny, however. Some of these examples are quickly dismissed, such as ἐπιστρέφειν, where the lexeme is simply the prefixed form of a verb that appears elsewhere in the Gospel (John 1:38; 12:40; 20:14, 16), or τολμᾶν, which is used no more frequently in John than it is in any of the other Gospels (Matthew = 1x, Mark = 2x, Luke = 1x).[21] It is worth noting that, of the twenty-eight words that Bultmann and Barrett list (the twenty-seven above, plus Ζεβεδαῖος, "Zebedee"), seventeen of them occur in the episode of Jesus' appearance to the disciples while they are fishing (John 21:1-14), with many of the words being related to fishing (e.g., "beach," "fish" [both noun and verbs], "get out," "naked," "fishing net," "outer garment," "drag," and possibly "eat" and "cubit"). As this is the only fishing episode in John's Gospel, these results are perhaps not too surprising, and the data not too telling.[22] Another seven words occur in the next episode in the exchange between Jesus and Peter (21:15-19) that reflect a high concentration of vocabulary particular to their discussion of sheep (e.g., "lamb," "feed," "tend sheep," "sheep"). As Bultmann himself even realizes, much of this word usage is "accidental and conditioned by the material."[23]

21. See Ruckstuhl, *Literarische Einheit*, 144.
22. See Brown, *John*, 1079. Labahn ("Fishing for Meaning") uses other criteria to argue for the integrity of this episode as a separate miracle story.
23. Bultmann, *John*, 700.

The second list comprises the words that are used in unusual ways. Bultmann notes the following examples: ἀδελφοί is used only in John 21:23 as a designation for Christians, the disciples are addressed by Jesus as παιδία (v. 5), the preposition ἀπό is used causatively in v. 6 and partitively in v. 10 (rather than ἐκ),[24] the preposition ἐπί is used differently in v. 1 than elsewhere in John's Gospel, the verb φανεροῦν is used differently in v. 1 than elsewhere, and πλέον (v. 15) is used instead of μᾶλλον (3:19; 12:43).[25]

This type of evidence is somewhat more difficult to evaluate, as there are a greater number of factors to consider, including style, content, and even significance of a variant as opposed to the regular pattern. As a result, there have been detailed scholarly responses to some of these suggestions (and responses to the first list as well). Ruckstuhl, for example, agrees with Bultmann regarding the use of ἀδελφοί for "Christians" in John 21:23 but claims that the concept of "Christian" as member of the community had not appeared in John's Gospel previously.[26] He further contends that the use of ἐξετάζειν (purportedly for ἐρωτᾶν, 21:12) is in the sense not of "ask" but of "test" or "interrogate," an example in which the use defines the sense of the word.[27] Ruckstuhl finds a parallel to the use of παιδία (21:5) in the use of τεκνία, which appears only in 13:33. Furthermore, Ruckstuhl disputes Bultmann's judgments regarding causal and partitive ἀπό. He does not think that there was a likely alternative for the former (21:6), and he defends the sense in 21:10 of the partitive use ("some of the fish").[28] Concerning the supposedly unusual use of ἐπί in 21:1, Ruckstuhl contends that the sense here is not that of "upon the sea," as in 6:19, but of "on the edge of the sea." In that sense it is closer to the use in 6:21: ἐπὶ τῆς γῆς ("on the ground"). Ruckstuhl notes that, throughout John's

---

24. Ruckstuhl (*Literarische Einheit,* 302) lists the following instances of partitive ἐκ in John 1–20: 1:16, 24, 35; 3:1; 6:11, 39, 50b, 51b, 60, 66b; 7:19, 31, 40; 9:40; 10:20, 26; 11:19, 45; 12:3, 9a, 42; 16:5, 14, 15; 17:12; 18:3 bis, 9, 17, 25. He also notes an instance of partitive ἐκ in John 21:2.

25. Not all of Bultmann's examples are of the same value. His comments on the use of ἕως (John 21:22) instead of ἕως ὅτου (9:18) or ἕως οὗ (13:38), οὐ μακράν (John 21:8) rather than ἐγγύς (e.g., 11:18), and ὑπάγειν + infinitive (John 21:3) as compared to John 4:16; 9:7; 15:16 are essentially inconsequential. Ruckstuhl (*Literarische Einheit,* 144-45) points out that the first is of no consequence, the second is not an accurate opposition (ἐγγύς and πλησίον are opposed to each other, not the words that Bultmann cites), and the last is the only way to express what the author wanted to say. It is surprising that Barrett simply takes over Bultmann's entire list (*John,* 576).

26. Ruckstuhl, *Literarische Einheit,* 143.

27. Ruckstuhl, *Literarische Einheit,* 143.

28. Ruckstuhl, *Literarische Einheit,* 144.

Gospel, Jesus wanders near the seashore.[29] Ruckstuhl also disputes that the use of φανερόω in 21:1 is different, as the reflexive use is found also in 7:4.[30]

A survey of the vocabulary evidence must conclude similarly to that of the grammar — that the case for a distinction between John 21 and the rest of the Gospel clearly remains unmade. So far, the text-critical evidence is nonexistent, and the language evidence is at best inconclusive regarding the authenticity and integrity of John 21. Thus, no clear case for disputing the authenticity has been made.

3. The Thematic Unity of John 21

Bultmann's major contention, however, was that John 21 was not a consistent unity. By that he meant that it was not internally unified. However, his comments also indicate that he believed it was not externally united either. In this he has been followed by a number of scholars.[31] Bultmann contended that there were two sections, vv. 1-14 and 15-23, and that they did not originally belong together.[32] John 21:1-14 is, according to Bultmann, an "independent Easter story," in which Jesus appears to a group of his disciples. Nevertheless, there have been a number of editorial additions to this story. These include the addition of the disciples not recognizing Jesus in 21:4, as a means of preparing the reader for the role played by the Beloved Disciple in v. 7; the announcement that it is the Lord, also in v. 7; and the confusion over where the fish Jesus was roasting came from (v. 9) in the light of the disciples fishing and being commanded by Jesus to bring their catch, which then Jesus distributes (v. 13). There are other incidental details that Bultmann also identifies as indicating redaction of the original Easter appearance story (e.g., reference in v. 8 to "other disciples"; reference in v. 11a to the disciples and not Peter). Bultmann distinguishes further those editorial changes that introduced the motif of Peter and were designed to introduce the subsequent episode (vv. 15-23) and those that transformed an ordinary meal into a "miraculous cultic meal."[33] The story of the catch

29. Ruckstuhl, *Literarische Einheit*, 144.
30. Ruckstuhl, *Literarische Einheit*, 144. Morris (*Studies in the Fourth Gospel*, 308-13) labels the use of φανερόω in 21:1, 14 an instance of triple variation, with all instances different.
31. E.g., Brown, *John*, 2:1082-85.
32. Bultmann, *John*, 702-6, followed in essence by R. Brown, *An Introduction to the New Testament* (New York: Doubleday, 1997), 360-61.
33. Bultmann, *John*, 704.

of fish has long been thought to be related to Luke 5:1-11 (see below). Bultmann believes that the John 21:1-14 account is the original and reflects the
original context of being an Easter story.[34] To this story has been added two
further conversations between Jesus and Peter in John 21:15-23. In the first
(vv. 15-17), perhaps part of the tradition, Peter is given the position of leader
of the Christian community, and in the second (vv. 18-22), a creation of the
redactor, Peter's relationship to the Beloved Disciple is explained. Bultmann
notes that there is no connection between vv. 1-14 and these two episodes,
and no connection between the two episodes themselves. The purpose of
the account, according to Bultmann, is to transfer authority from Peter to
the Beloved Disciple, who takes over his position.[35]

Bultmann has made what appears to be a compelling case for textual
disunity by bringing into question a number of apparent inconsistencies in
the text, and by showing its relation to other texts. These inconsistencies
include the confusion in the fishing episode over the origin of the fish and
the motivation and sequencing of the action. There have been many other
discussions of this passage since then, but most have seen the same elements
at play. The factors that Bultmann lays out as evidence for disunity, while
convincing for some, have not proved as compelling for other scholars.

At least three issues raise questions about Bultmann's conclusions. The first
concerns his use of sources. One of the criticisms of John 21 by Bultmann and
others is that it appears that the chapter utilizes a number of sources — such
as a Galilee Easter appearance of Jesus, the story of the disciples fishing (both
in vv. 1-14), Jesus' dialogue with Peter (vv. 15-19), events around Jesus, Peter,
and the Beloved Disciple (vv. 20-24), and possibly v. 25, the final verse of the
Gospel. One of the most widely discussed theories of sources is the purported
relationship between the fishing episode in John 21 and the fishing episode in
Luke 5:1-11.[36] The fact that there may be sources used by the author of John 21
is not in itself compelling to dispute the authorship or integrity of the chapter,

34. Brown (*John*, 2:1092) believes that the episode is the combination of a Galilean
Easter appearance story involving a meal and a fishing story involving Peter.

35. Interestingly, Bauckham suggests a similar idea while, nevertheless, maintaining
that John 21 is part of the original Gospel (R. Bauckham, "John for Readers of Mark," in *The
Gospels for All Christians: Rethinking the Gospel Audiences* [ed. R. Bauckham; Grand Rapids:
Eerdmans, 1998], 147-71).

36. The latest of these is Labahn, "Fishing for Meaning," although he does not refer to
Bultmann's commentary on this correlation. He instead simply repeats what he apparently
sees as compelling evidence that John's Gospel ended at 20:31 and that John 21 consists of
additional material.

however. That sources may have been used is consistent with the widely held belief by Johannine scholars that the author (or authors, especially if a community was involved) of John's Gospel made use of a number of sources. Here is not the place to discuss these sources (see ch. 3 of this volume), but the Gospel itself seems to give some indications that there were such sources as the prologue (John 1:1-18),[37] a signs source,[38] a passion account, possibly a discourse source, and even perhaps the Synoptic Gospels as sources.[39]

There has been much discussion of John 21 and Luke 5. Grant Osborne notes that there are a number of parallels between the accounts, while also noting a number of differences.[40] The evidence is sufficiently complex that there is a major question of whether John 21:1-14 uses Luke 5:1-11 or the reverse, or whether they possibly stem from two independent traditions.[41] Nev-

37. There has been much discussion of the prologue as a separate source. For a discussion of the evidence, see R. N. Longenecker, *New Wine into Fresh Wineskins: Contextualizing the Early Christian Confessions* (Peabody, MA: Hendrickson, 1999), esp. 111-14.

38. See R. Fortna, *The Fourth Gospel and Its Predecessor: From Narrative Source to Present Gospel* (Minneapolis: Fortress Press, 1988).

39. See U. Schnelle, *The History and Theology of the New Testament Writings* (trans. M. E. Boring; Minneapolis: Fortress Press, 1998), 492-504.

40. G. R. Osborne, "John 21: Test Case for History and Redaction in the Resurrection Narratives," in *Studies of History and Tradition in the Four Gospels* (vol. 2 of *Gospel Perspectives;* ed. R. T. France and D. Wenham; Sheffield: JSOT Press, 1981), 293-328, esp. 296-97, notes the following similarities: "(1) Fishing all night but catching nothing; (2) Command to cast the nets together with a promise that they would catch fish; (3) The presence of other disciples; (4) Obedience to the command and fulfillment of the promise; (5) Peter's impulsive act and the peripheral place of the others in the story; (6) Jesus as Lord; (7) The missionary motif." Osborne also notes the following differences: "(1) Seven disciples in John vs. three in Luke; (2) The nets breaking and others called to assist in Luke vs. dragging the nets to shore in John; (3) The confession of Peter in Luke vs. the B[eloved] D[isciple] in John; (4) The non-recognition motif in John (v. 19); (5) The BD in John is the central figure; (6) Peter's swimming to shore in John; (7) The different conclusions ('fishers of men' in Luke and the meal fellowship in John)." Labahn ("Fishing for Meaning," 128 n. 23) too readily dismisses Osborne's argument without first actually considering it.

41. All of these possibilities have been suggested. F. Neirynck ("John 21," *NTS* 36 [1990]: 321-36; repr. in his *Evangelica II, 1982-1991: Collected Essays* [ed. F. Van Segbroeck; BETL 99; Leuven: Peeters/Leuven University Press, 1991], 601-16) proposes that Luke was the source of John; Brown (*John*, 2:1090) that John has priority; and Osborne ("John 21," 297) that they are two independent traditions — that is, that the event took place twice, a position favored by J. A. Bailey (*The Traditions Common to the Gospels of Luke and John* [NovTSup 7; Leiden: Brill, 1963], 9-11) and C. L. Blomberg (*The Historical Reliability of John's Gospel: Issues and Commentary* [Downers Grove, IL: InterVarsity Press, 2001], 274). W. S. Vorster (*Speaking of Jesus: Essays on Biblical Language, Gospel Narrative, and the Historical Jesus* [ed. J. E. Botha; NovTSup 92; Leiden: Brill, 1999], 199-215) disputes Neirynck at most points, taking the

ertheless, there is enough recognition of the use of sources in John's Gospel that the use of sources in John 21 is not a sufficient reason to doubt its status. In fact, one might well argue that this constitutes an argument in favor of its status as, at least from a source-critical standpoint, integral to the Gospel.

The second issue in response to Bultmann relates to finding unity within the chapter itself. Whereas Bultmann and others have found a lack of unity, on the basis of what they contend are narrative discrepancies, clear use of sources, and the introduction of material that is new or foreign to John's Gospel, not all have concluded similarly. For example, Patrick Spencer finds a literarily well-structured narrative design in five scenes, with an introduction (John 21:1) and a conclusion (vv. 24-25). The five scenes are as follows:

Scene One: "Unsuccessful Fishing Expedition" (John 21:2-3)
Scene Two: "Miraculous Catch" (vv. 4-8)
Scene Three: "Breakfast on the Beach" (vv. 9-14)
Scene Four: "Confrontation of Love" (vv. 15-19)
Scene Five: "The Other Guy?" (vv. 20-23)[42]

Wolfgang Schenk, on the basis of a text-linguistic analysis, has found a number of internally unifying features in John 21. Drawing upon both internal evidence of structure (e.g., the opening of John 21:1 and the "thus" of v. 14) and vocabulary (e.g., words for "witness"), besides comparisons with epilogical material in other ancient writers (such as Euripides), Schenk posits that John 21 offers "an orderly temporal sequence,"[43] from the opening dialogue between Peter and the other disciples through his dialogue with Jesus, the focal point of the chapter, to the end. As a result, he sees John 21 functioning as a conclusion to the book that is in balance with the prologue

---

position that the story in John 21 is independent of Luke 5 (his chapter, "The Growth and Making of John 21," is reprinted from *The Four Gospels: Festschrift Frans Neirynck* [3 vols.; ed. F. Van Segbroeck, C. M. Tuckett, G. Van Belle, and J. Verheyden; Leuven: Peeters, 1992], 3:2207-21). Labahn ("Fishing for Meaning," 130 n. 27) again simply dismisses Vorster's argument, rather than responding to it.

42. P. E. Spencer, "Narrative Echoes in John 21: Intertextual Interpretation and Intratextual Connection," *JSNT* 75 (1999): 49-68, esp. 56. Cf. B. R. Gaventa, "The Archive of Excess: John 21 and the Problem of Narrative Closure," in *Exploring the Gospel of John: In Honor of D. Moody Smith* (ed. R. A. Culpepper and C. C. Black; Louisville, KY: Westminster John Knox, 1996), 240-52.

43. W. Schenk, "Interne Strukturierungen im Schluss-Segment Johannes 21: Συγγραφή + Σατυρικόν/'Επίλογος," *NTS* 38 (1992): 507-30, esp. 521, citing Neirynck, "John 21," 326.

of John 1:1-18.[44] Lars Hartman, also using a text-linguistic method, notes the literary context and organization, as well as common themes (e.g., fish and shepherding), characters (e.g., Peter), and information flow.[45] Other examples could be cited. One of the possible conclusions that this discussion brings to the fore is that whether one finds or disputes unity (sometimes called cohesion or even coherence) is often a matter of where one begins the discussion.[46] This is not to say that such unifying or disjunctive factors do not exist, but how much weight one gives to them is often the result of larger interpretive decisions. Bultmann clearly wishes to minimize unity, while others wish to maximize it. The fact that so many scholars have been able to offer coherent readings of the chapter in the light of the overall Gospel cannot, however, be easily dismissed.

The third issue with regard to Bultmann's argument concerns the themes that are found in John 21, and how they relate to the rest of the Gospel. There have been a number of attempts to illustrate these lines of thematic and ideational connection. For example, John Marsh, even though he recognizes a certain independence to John 21, admits that it is "an indispensable part of the gospel" on theological, if not historical, grounds.[47] He marshals a number of themes, including dominical authority, fulfillment of expectations regarding Jesus' postresurrection appearances, the nature of discipleship, among other possibilities.[48] Spencer, who argues for a conscious narrative design to John 21, also sees "narrative echoes" of other parts of the Gospel. These include echoes between John 21:1-14 and 6:1-71 regarding the feeding by the Tiberian sea, and between John 21:15-19 and a number of episodes involving Peter, including 10:1-18, 13:3-5, 36-38, and 18:15-18, 25-27. The episode in John

44. Schenk, "Interne Strukturierungen," 508. See also Carson, *John*, 665-68; M. W. G. Stibbe, *John* (Readings: A New Bible Commentary; Sheffield: JSOT Press, 1993), 207; Köstenberger, *John*, 586. Cf. C. Keener, *The Gospel of John: A Commentary* (2 vols.; Peabody, MA: Hendrickson, 2003), 2:1221-22, who talks about epilogues that ruin a book's cohesion; and A. J. Köstenberger, "'I Suppose' (Οἶμαι): The Conclusion of John's Gospel in Its Literary and Historical Context," in *The New Testament in Its First-Century Setting: Essays on Context and Background in Honour of B. W. Winter on His Sixty-Fifth Birthday* (ed. P. J. Williams, A. D. Clarke, P. M. Head, and D. Instone-Brewer; Grand Rapids: Eerdmans, 2004), 72-88.

45. L. Hartman, "An Attempt at a Text-Centered Exegesis of John 21," in his *Text-Centered New Testament Studies: Text-Theoretical Essays on Early Jewish and Early Christian Literature* (ed. Hellholm; WUNT 102; Tübingen: Mohr Siebeck, 1997), 69-87 (orig. *Studia Theologica* 38 [1984]: 29-45).

46. Cf. Ruckstuhl, *Literarische Einheit*, 134-42, in his criticism of Bultmann.

47. J. Marsh, *Saint John* (Harmondsworth: Penguin, 1968), 654.

48. Marsh, *Saint John*, 654-60.

18:15-18, 25-27 revolves around Peter's threefold denial and the need for his rehabilitation; 13:3-5, 36-38 revolves around Peter's desire for being rehabilitated and restored to the community, and 10:1-18 revolves around Peter's obligations to provide pastoral care.[49] It might be argued that these lines of connection were formulations by the Johannine author, who either created and/or appended John 21 to the rest of the Gospel. However, the argument for disjunction between the two is predicated upon a lack of unity to the chapter, something that can be readily disputed.

A fourth and final issue is whether a coherent explanation of John 21 can be offered that in some way plausibly fulfills or even supplements the rest of the Gospel. Here Bultmann himself seems to have provided the answer to his own dilemma. A number of scholars have had little difficulty identifying, along with Bultmann and others, the major focus of John 21 — besides Jesus, who superintends all of the action in his interactions with the various characters — as Peter, with secondary interest in the Beloved Disciple. Whether this focus reflects a source or sources regarding these figures, or whether it reflects important additional material that the Johannine author believed should be included in the Gospel, there is an apparent consensus among scholars, including those who dispute the origins and integrity of John 21, that the focus is upon Peter. Years ago, Lightfoot said that "the delineation of the character of St Peter, and of his relation to St John, has all the refinement of our Evangelist. This is the case in the two scenes in which they appear in contact. The spiritual insight of St John (John 21:7) is matched by the impetuosity (vv. 3, 7, 11) and the curiosity (v. 21) of St Peter."[50] More recently, Timothy Wiarda encapsulates John 21 as focusing upon five key events that involve Peter. These include his going fishing and his various responses and reactions to Jesus, as well as being rebuked.[51] As Helen Orchard states, "The final appearance of the resurrected Jesus is focused around the character of Peter. There is unfinished business between Peter and Jesus [see Spencer's analysis above,] and this pericope seeks to remedy the situation, resulting in a healing for Peter."[52] It appears that Bultmann himself, in drawing attention to the role of Peter in John 21, has provided his own best explanation.

---

49. Spencer, "Narrative Echoes," 59-64.

50. Lightfoot, *Biblical Essays*, 195.

51. T. Wiarda, "John 21.1-23: Narrative Unity and Its Implications," *JSNT* 14 (1992): 53-71, esp. 56.

52. H. C. Orchard, *Courting Betrayal: Jesus as Victim in the Gospel of John* (JSNTSup 161; Sheffield: Sheffield Academic Press, 1998), 257, who provides an analysis of the structure of the chapter. See also Stibbe, *John*, 207.

4. John 20:30-31 and Two Closings

Robert Kysar has said that John's Gospel has two endings, one at the end of
John 20 and the other at the end of John 21.[53] Many if not most commentators have observed that there is a sense of finality and closing to John 1–20
in 20:30-31.[54] This is so much the case that M.-J. Lagrange, even though he
thought that John 21 was authentic, believed that the ending had been displaced and that the material in John 21 should be placed before 20:30-31.[55]
The only truly significant attempt to mitigate the finality of John 20:30-31
that I can find is the work of Paul Minear.[56] He argues that John 20:30-31 is
the close only of the final chapter, not of the entire Gospel.[57] Most scholars
have not followed him in this view.[58] The notion of two endings, however,
has been picked up by Herman Waetjen in developing his recent theory regarding the two editions of John's Gospel. As with earlier theories regarding
Romans,[59] he proposes that one method of accounting for what has been
identified as a difficult textual problem is, in essence, to accept both theories. He contends that there was a first edition of the Gospel that consisted
of John 1–20, and a second edition of the Gospel with John 1–21 addressed
to a different audience. This approach allows him to recognize the tensions
between John 1–20 and ch. 21, on the basis that the redactor who added the

53. R. Kysar, *John's Story of Jesus* (Philadelphia: Fortress Press, 1984), 91.

54. E.g., J. N. Sanders, *The Gospel according to St. John* (ed. B. A. Mastin; BNTC; London: A&C Black, 1968), 440.

55. M.-J. Lagrange, *L'Évangile selon Saint Jean* (EBib; Paris: Gabalda, 1948), 520-21.

56. Minear, "Original Functions," esp. 89-90. See also Hoskyns (*John,* 550), who contends that a Gospel needs to end with a commissioning, and hence John with ch. 21. There
are two problems with his position. The one is that he includes the longer Markan ending in
his analysis. If the Gospel of Mark ends at 16:8, there is no sense of commissioning in it, thus
vitiating his theory (see Carson, *John,* 666). The second objection is that John's Gospel does
have a commissioning in 20:21, thus alleviating any further need for a final commissioning
(see Brown, *John,* 2:1078).

57. See also H. Thyen, "Noch einmal: Johannes 21 und 'der Jünger, den Jesus liebte,'" in
*Texts and Contexts: Biblical Texts in Their Textual and Situational Contexts; Essays in Honor
of Lars Hartman* (ed. T. Fornberg and D. Hellholm; Oslo: Scandinavian University Press,
1995), 147-89, esp. 154-55, who takes John 20:30-31 as serving the function of a bridge from
the body of the Gospel to its epilogue.

58. See Keener, *John,* 2:1219 n. 6.

59. T. W. Manson proposed that Romans was sent in two editions, one without Romans
16 and the other to Ephesus with Romans 16. See his "St. Paul's Letter to the Romans — and
Others," in his *Studies in the Gospels and Epistles* (ed. M. Black; Manchester: Manchester
University Press, 1962), 225-41.

final chapter was not able to create complete continuity in the text, while accepting that there was also from (nearly as) early times an edition that had all twenty-one chapters as well. This second edition had a more apologetic purpose, and so was not able to fully incorporate all of the elements of the earlier edition, which was evangelistic. One of the major planks in Waetjen's theory is that the similar textual variants in John 6:29, 19:35, and 20:31 regarding whether one should read πιστεύητε (present subjunctive) or πιστεύσητε (aorist subjunctive) illustrates the tension.

Waetjen believes that the present subjunctive "implies that the original addressees of the Gospel were Christians," while the aorist subjunctive "requires a non-Christian audience."[60] He goes on to note that, according to text-critical principles, the more difficult reading is more likely to be original, and hence the aorist subjunctive reading is the harder and therefore more likely as original. He thus concludes, "It is more probable that initially the Fourth Gospel was addressed to non-Christians" and was evangelistic in purpose.[61] Therefore the aorist subjunctive, which he renders as "you may begin to believe," was the original verb form in John 6:29, 19:35, and 20:31. When the Gospel was revised, so Waetjen believes, it was revised for Christian readers, and at that time the aorist was changed to the present subjunctive form "in order to reinforce their continuation in the Christian faith."[62] The present subjunctive is rendered by Waetjen as "you may continue to believe." Furthermore, at the time the verbs were changed from the aorist to the present subjunctive, the Gospel was also changed in other ways to adapt to its use in a Christian context, including adding material that would have helped the Gospel to be understandable in its new context.

As ostensibly plausible as Waetjen's proposal may seem in the light of the controversies over John 21, there are two major problems with his analysis — one text-critical and the other grammatical — that leave his explanation completely unsatisfactory.[63]

60. Waetjen, *Gospel of the Beloved Disciple*, 6.
61. Waetjen, *Gospel of the Beloved Disciple*, 7.
62. Waetjen, *Gospel of the Beloved Disciple*, 7.
63. This discussion parallels in many ways one that has recently been carried on between D. A. Carson and G. D. Fee. See D. A. Carson, "The Purpose of the Fourth Gospel: John 20:31 Reconsidered," *JBL* 106 (1987): 639-51; G. D. Fee, "On the Text and Meaning of John 20:30-31," repr. in *To What End Exegesis? Essays Textual, Exegetical, and Theological* (Grand Rapids: Eerdmans, 2001 [1992]), 29-42; and D. A. Carson, "Syntactical and Text-Critical Observations on John 20:30-31: One More Round on the Purpose of the Fourth Gospel," *JBL* 124 (2005): 693-714.

The text-critical problem itself consists of several more specific problems. One difficulty is that the text-critical evidence is not consistently found at each of the three places in John's Gospel where Waetjen believes that it should be found. Waetjen's theory really demands comparable text-critical evidence for each of the passages that he cites. This is simply not the case.[64] The evidence for the passages is as follows:

John 6:29
    Present subjunctive: $\mathfrak{P}^{75}$ ℵ A B L T 1 33 40 71 106 (Origen)[65]
    Aorist subjunctive: D K W Γ Δ 0145 f^{13} 700 892 1241 1424 Majority
John 19:35
    Present subjunctive: $\mathfrak{P}^{66vid}$ ℵ* B Ψ (Origen)[66]
    Aorist subjunctive: ℵ² A D^s L W Θ $f^{1,13}$ 33 Majority
John 20:31
    Present subjunctive: $\mathfrak{P}^{66}$ ℵ* B Θ 0250 892^s l2211
    Aorist subjunctive: ℵ² A C D L W Ψ $f^{1,13}$ 33 Majority

On the basis of the manuscript evidence, the present subjunctive should almost assuredly be accepted in each case, especially John 20:31.[67] For John 6:29 the second/third-century papyrus $\mathfrak{P}^{75}$ and the two fourth-century codexes Sinaiticus and Vaticanus have the present subjunctive. The aorist subjunctive is not found until the fifth-century codex Bezae, and then in the

---

64. I use the Nestle-Aland apparatus, with supplementation from C. Tischendorf, *Novum Testamentum Graece* (8th ed.; 2 vols.; Leipzig: Giesecke & Devrient, 1872-96); W. J. Elliott and D. C. Parker, *The New Testament in Greek*; vol. 4: *The Gospel according to St. John*; vol. 1: *The Papyri* (NTTS 20; Leiden: Brill, 1995); and P. W. Comfort and D. P. Barrett, *The Text of the Earliest New Testament Manuscripts* (2nd ed.; Wheaton, IL: Tyndale, 2001). The Nestle-Aland text itself is of little help at this point, as at both John 19:35 and 20:31 they leave the readings ambiguous and include the sigma of the aorist subjunctive in square brackets.

65. Waetjen (*Gospel of the Beloved Disciple*, 6) includes no evidence for the present subjunctive at John 6:29, apparently because the Nestle-Aland text does not. The reason for the lack of listing of evidence is not clear.

66. B. M. Metzger's commentary is misleading at this point (*A Textual Commentary on the Greek New Testament* [London: United Bible Societies, 1971]). It gives the impression (p. 256 n. 1) — but without including the reading of $\mathfrak{P}^{66}$ — that the evidence for the present subjunctive is slight compared to the evidence from "all other witnesses" for the aorist subjunctive. The same comments are found in the second edition (Stuttgart: German Bible Society, 1994), 219-20.

67. So Carson, "Syntactical and Text-Critical Observations," 703; contra M. F. Bird, *Jesus Is the Christ* (Downers Grove, IL: InterVarsity Press, 2012), 136 (the grounds he uses are very unclear).

Byzantine textual tradition. For John 19:35 the second/third-century $\mathfrak{p}^{66}$ (although the papyrus is lacunose at this point), the original hand of Sinaiticus, and Vaticanus appear to have the present subjunctive. The aorist subjunctive is not found until the fifth-century codex Alexandrinus, a later correcting hand of Sinaiticus, the fifth-century codex Bezae, and the Byzantine tradition. For John 20:31 the second/third-century papyrus $\mathfrak{p}^{66}$,[68] the original hand of Sinaiticus, and Vaticanus have the present subjunctive. The aorist subjunctive is again not found until the fifth-century codexes Alexandrinus and Bezae, a later corrector of Sinaiticus, and the Byzantine tradition. The pattern is clear. The Alexandrian tradition clearly has the present subjunctive much earlier than the appearance of the aorist subjunctive in the Western and then Byzantine traditions. In each case, the evidence for the present subjunctive is to be preferred, thus nullifying Waetjen's claim. Another text-critical problem is that the evidence itself indicates a late date — the fifth century — for any change from the present to the aorist subjunctive, the opposite of what Waetjen is proposing for the original reading. According to the textual evidence, there is no aorist subjunctive attested until the fifth century, far too late for his supposition of an early second edition of John's Gospel, whereas the present subjunctive reading is in place by the second or third century — or by at least as early as the evidence that exists.

The grammatical problem with Waetjen's proposal also contains several problems. The first difficulty is that he assumes a particular correlation between the aorist and present tense-forms and kinds of action. He seems to assume that the present subjunctive indicates continuous action and the aorist subjunctive punctiliar action, and especially ingressive punctiliar action.[69] To some extent this is understandable, as he appears to have accepted the kind of explanation found in Bruce Metzger's *Textual Commentary on the Greek New Testament*.[70] Metzger contends that, "strictly interpreted,"

---

68. Nestle-Aland lists $\mathfrak{p}^{66}$ as "videtur," but an examination of the photographs makes it seem unlikely that the η was preceded by a ς. The previous letter, though mostly broken away, appears more likely to be part of a right-hand portion of the arm of a υ. Hence the present subjunctive seems to be the reading of the papyrus. See V. Martin and J. W. B. Barns, *Papyrus Bodmer II Supplément: Evangile de Jean chap. 14–21* (rev. ed.; Cologny-Geneva: Bibliotheca Bodmeriana, 1962), 48, plate 145.

69. In a footnote Waetjen (*Gospel of the Beloved Disciple*, 6) expresses the opinion that two aorists in John 4:48 and 11:15 are to be understood as ingressive aorists.

70. Metzger, *Textual Commentary* (1st ed.), 256. It has been pointed out by Carson ("Syntactical and Text-Critical Observations," 697) that Metzger's comments are less about textual criticism than they are about Metzger's view of their (questionable) meanings.

the aorist tense-form would suggest "that the fourth Gospel was addressed to non-Christians" and the present subjunctive to "strengthen the faith of those who already believe."[71] The best we could say is that Metzger and now Waetjen are out of touch with the mainstream of recent research in Greek language study. Nineteenth-century *Aktionsart* theory may have tried to correlate tense-forms with kind of action, but current aspectual theory sees the aorist as perfective (action as complete) and the present/imperfect as imperfective (action as in process).[72] Categories such as ingressive, constative, iterative, and the like, as enshrined as they may be, are not indicated simply by choice of the tense-form.[73] There is therefore no necessary correlation between the aorist and punctiliar events (and hence being addressed to nonbelievers so that they might come to believe) or the present and continuous action (and hence being addressed to believers so that they might continue to believe). D. A. Carson has shown that this point is well illustrated by John's Gospel itself. He comments as follows on the use of the present subjunctive form πιστεύητε in John 6:29: "Jesus is making his demands of unbelievers, of opponents, of those who cannot in any sense be thought of as believers."[74] What, then, does the choice of tense-form convey? Though discussing a different proposal, Carson's comment here is relevant:

> Aspect theory would respond by saying that . . . the present tense πιστεύητε in John 20:31 reflects the evangelist's choice of presenting this believing as process. He might have chosen to present this belief as something else, but he chose to present it in this way. . . . Had the author

71. Metzger, *Textual Commentary* (1st ed.), 256. This is not the place to discuss the purpose of John's Gospel, which is closely linked in many interpreters' minds to the use of the Greek tense-forms (see Carson, "Purpose," 640-41).

72. See S. E. Porter, *Verbal Aspect in the Greek of the New Testament, with Reference to Tense and Mood* (SBG 1; New York: Peter Lang, 1989), ch. 4. One does not need to have aspect theory to recognize that this proposal of kinds of action may be pressing the meaning of the tense-forms. See Sanders, *John*, 440 n. 2. This issue was raised for New Testament scholars at least as far back as Frank Stagg in his "The Abused Aorist," *JBL* 91 (1972): 222-31. That it continues to be found in New Testament scholarship is quite astounding.

73. See Carson, "Syntactical and Text-Critical Observations," 704; contra, among recent statements, E. W. Klink, *The Sheep of the Fold: The Audience and Origin of the Gospel of John* (SNTSMS 141; Cambridge: Cambridge University Press, 2007), 214-15; and Bird, *Jesus Is the Christ*, 136, who persists in the old paradigm, not aided by the sources he cites. One suspects that they do not fully understand the linguistic issues and/or are bent on making a particular theological point regarding John's Gospel and its audience.

74. Carson, "Syntactical and Text-Critical Observations," 705.

chosen the aorist tense, that too would have been "meaningful,"[75] but the meaning would have been different. . . . This is not because no legitimate distinction can be made between the semantics of the aorist and the semantics of the present, but because the present tense forms . . . can clearly be applied to believers and unbelievers alike.[76]

Thus, Waetjen's contention is unproven regarding the two editions of John's Gospel on the basis of the textual variants.

As a result, we can see that there is no text-critical or language-based argument that prevents John 21 from being composed by the Johannine author and being integral to the Gospel itself. Even if one does not accept Minear's proposal that John 20:30-31 constitutes the ending only of John 20, there is a sense in which these two verses provide a suitable transition to John 21. The author states that Jesus did many other miraculous signs in front of his disciples, for the purpose of belief that the Christ, the Son of God, is Jesus ('Ιησοῦς ἐστιν ὁ Χριστὸς ὁ υἱὸς τοῦ θεοῦ).[77] This same Jesus then appears on the Sea of Tiberias, where Peter and the other disciples are fishing. Jesus calls out to them, instructs them, and then cooks breakfast for them. After eating, Jesus then addresses Peter, asking him three times whether he loves Jesus. Despite much current argument that the two different terms for love are synonyms, I believe that they are not synonyms semantically or contextually.[78] Two times Jesus asks Peter (using ἀγαπάω) whether he holds Jesus in the highest regard and esteem, and both times Peter answers affirmatively but

75. Carson is here responding to Fee's statement ("Text and Meaning," 35-42) that choice of the present-tense form is "meaningful." Carson rightly contends that the present and the aorist are both meaningful, but in different (aspectual) ways ("Syntactical and Text-Critical Observations," 704).

76. Carson, "Syntactical and Text-Critical Observations," 704, 707.

77. See Carson, "Syntactical and Text-Critical Observations," 709-14, with reference to his previous writings as well, for support of this rendering. I have not seen any convincing arguments against Carson's conclusion regarding the copulative construction here (based upon E. V. N. Goetchius, review of L. C. McGaughy, *Toward a Descriptive Analysis of Εἰναι as a Linking Verb in New Testament Greek* [SBLDS 6; Missoula, MT: Society of Biblical Literature, 1972], *JBL* 95 [1976]: 147-49); cf. S. E. Porter, *Idioms of the Greek New Testament* (2nd ed.; BLG 2; Sheffield: Sheffield Academic Press, 1994), 109-10. There are a number of unfortunate too-confident rejections of Carson's analysis that lack substantive counterargumentation or are based simply on assertion. I suspect that there is probably special pleading involved in support of particular theological positions.

78. See ch. 2 above in this volume, section 3i, and S. E. Porter, "Study of John's Gospel: New Directions or the Same Old Paths?" In *Linguistic Analysis of the Greek New Testament: Studies in Tools, Methods, and Practice* (Grand Rapids: Baker, 2015) 298-301.

uses a verb (φιλέω) indicating a less lofty kind of love. In Jesus' concluding
question about Peter's love, he uses Peter's verb, perhaps a subtle acknowledgment of the limitations of Peter's love. Peter replies a third time using
φιλέω. In the final episode of the chapter, Jesus then turns to the Beloved
Disciple, who is said to be the one who testifies to the things that have happened and whose testimony is true. The concluding verse affirms that Jesus
did many other things, the full descriptions of which, the author believes,
the entire world could not contain. Thus, even though John's Gospel might
appear to end at the end of ch. 20, the final chapter, John 21, continues to
portray the words and actions of the Messiah, the Son of God, Jesus.

5. Conclusion

After my investigation of the issues, I am more firmly convinced of the authenticity and integrity of John 21 than I was before undertaking the investigation. One of the major insuperable difficulties of arguments for ch. 20
as the ending proper of the Gospel is that there is no text-critical evidence
that the Gospel ever existed in a form other than John 1–21.[79] This lack of
evidence represents a significant difference from other passages erroneously
invoked as parallels, such as the various endings of Mark (16:9ff.) and the
pericope of the woman caught in adultery (John 7:53–8:11), where there
is clear manuscript evidence of some texts including the disputed unit and
other (earlier) texts not having it.

After consideration of the text-critical evidence, I believe that the language evidence is the most important. An examination of both grammatical
and vocabulary evidence — along with the admissions of such scholars as
Bultmann and Barrett, proponents of a disjunctive John 21 — indicates that
no clear case can be made for distinguishing the author of John 21 from that
of the rest of the Gospel. All of these arguments of course do not necessarily
mean that the chapter was integral to the first draft of the Gospel. I am not
sure when John 21 was included in John's Gospel, but I believe that there is
no substantive evidence for doubting that it was written by the same author
who wrote the rest of the Gospel, and that it was attached to the Gospel very
early — so early as to leave no substantive (only suppositional and specula-

79. This factor has been recognized by virtually all scholars. Those who take it into
special consideration in their estimations of the issue include Minear, "Original Functions,"
85-86, 98, and Vorster, *Speaking of Jesus,* 200.

tive) evidence of its being attached later. The recent attempt by Waetjen to defend two editions of the Gospel fails on both text-critical and linguistic grounds.

The final argument revolves around literary unity. As we have seen in previous essays in this volume, Jesus is the major figure of John's Gospel, and his activities and words dominate the development of the Gospel and give it the literary shape that it has. John's prologue introduces Jesus as the enfleshed *logos*. The depiction of Jesus continues throughout the various sections of the Gospel. This pattern of representation of Jesus is also continued in John 21, as a number of authors have shown.

Despite this evidence for inclusion of John 21, the least substantive and most potentially subjective evidence in a discussion such as this is the interpretation of questions of unity and thematic relations between John 1–20 and ch. 21. However, once these other, more substantive obstructions to seeing the authenticity and integrity of the chapter are eliminated, there is no reason not to view the positive proposals with sympathy, as plausible explanations from a conceptual level of what exists at a textual level. As a result, I can see no convincing reason to dispute the authenticity and even early integrity of John 1–21 and its attestation to the words and actions of Jesus the Christ.[80]

---

80. W. Sanday (*The Criticism of the Fourth Gospel* [Oxford: Clarendon Press, 1905], 81) makes a point that bears repeating and further contemplation. He notes that in John 21:24 another author writes, "This is the disciple who bears witness of these things, and wrote these things; and we know that his witness is true." Sanday continues: "The critics who assert that the Gospel is not the work of an eye-witness, and even those who say that the last chapter was not written by the author of the whole, wantonly accuse these last words of untruth. That is another of the methods of modern criticism that seem to me sorely in need of reforming. I hope that a time may come when it will be considered as wrong to libel the dead as it is to libel the living."

Conclusion

John, His Gospel, and Jesus: In Pursuit of the Johannine Voice is the title that
I have given to this monograph. Now that we have reached the conclusion
of the volume, I wish once more to reflect upon this title — not to justify
my selection of it, but to see how the individual chapters have fulfilled their
assigned purpose within the overall scheme. As I stated at the outset, this
volume is a series of essays that have been written around the foci of John's
Gospel and Jesus. From the beginning of this project, I sought to explore
John's Gospel in its various and multifaceted dimensions in order to discover
its distinctive voice. The Gospel has proved more than worthy of such exploration — and certainly merits much more than I have been able to do in
one relatively short volume. In every chapter I have uncovered more than
I could possibly explore in depth in a given essay. But I have had to limit
what I could say so that I could move on to other topics that have been
equally provocative, challenging, and rewarding. The other focus of these
essays, even if more subtly presented, is always Jesus. In some chapters and
in conjunction with certain topics, Jesus looms large in my exploration, but
in others he is perhaps not as paramount as is John's Gospel itself. Nevertheless, in each of these essays, I have wanted to remember and draw to my
own and my readers' attention that, whatever else John's Gospel is about, it
is a Gospel about Jesus. The reason for its writing, for its organization, and
for the various themes and ideas that are developed is to present who Jesus is
to the reader, often in uniquely Johannine ways. I hope that the essays have
accomplished that purpose.

This purpose has governed how I have organized this volume. The first
essay argues that John's Gospel, rather than being pulled again into the second century and isolated from the Synoptic Gospels (as has been the trend

246

in some recent research), should be grounded securely in the first century — temporally, if not in other ways, closer to the other Gospels. John's Gospel is not one of many products of second-century ecclesial literary production, as are some apocryphal gospels, but it is a fundamental Gospel written in the aftermath of the originating events of Jesus' life and ministry. The papyrological and related evidence supports this conclusion.

Once we have moved beyond establishing its rightful position as a Gospel about Jesus, I think that it is important to explore what John's Gospel says about Jesus in multiple ways. I have tackled this issue from a variety of often distinctive Johannine angles. One of my significant findings is that there are a number of different means by which the Johannine author organizes and shapes his Gospel, often related to concepts or patterns used throughout the Gospel. One of these means is the author's positioning his Gospel as a public proclamation of the ministry and teachings of Jesus, not as an isolated or private document that hides Jesus' words and actions. This positioning begins at the very outset of the Gospel in the prologue itself and encompasses many of the major episodes and people that Jesus meets, including his encounters with Galileans, Samaritans, the infirm, nobility, the Jews, and others.

A second organizing principle is created by means of the prologue. In fact, as has become evident, in this volume I treat the prologue in a number of different places, for a variety of reasons, because its contribution to understanding John's Gospel and its presentation of Jesus is immense. Nevertheless, some scholars continue to say that John's prologue stands apart from the rest of the Gospel. I do not believe that this is the case. There are definitely a number of unique and intriguing features of the prologue, but many of the major ideas of the Gospel, especially regarding Jesus, are found and first broached in the prologue. In the major chapter devoted to the prologue, I explore four different ways that have been used to interpretively examine the prologue, including form criticism, source criticism, musical-liturgical criticism, and functional criticism. Each of them has something to offer that the others do not. The last two are probably less familiar to most readers than the first two, but they perhaps have the most to offer those interested in going deeper in exploring the meaning and function of this important introduction to John's Gospel. What the last, functional criticism, illustrates especially well is that the incarnate *logos* becomes an organizing and functioning character throughout the rest of the entire Gospel as the incarnate, or enfleshed, Christ.

A third christological organizational principle revolves around the "I am" sayings in John's Gospel. These "I am" statements have been explored many times before, but my analysis, which defines the categories of description slightly differently, finds within the use of the "I am" sayings a means of defining the Johannine Christology, in particular, John's emphasis on Jesus being the promised Messiah. In other words, by means of his use of the "I am" sayings — first on the lips of John the Baptist and then by Jesus — John as the author of his Gospel establishes major teachings about Jesus. The major finding is that John uses the "I am" statements to develop the notion of what it means that Jesus is the Messiah, as the concept of Messiah is expanded and elucidated throughout the Gospel.

A fourth means of examining the organizational pattern of John's Gospel is focused on the question of truth. In a number of places throughout the Gospel, the question of truth is raised and discussed, in relation to God the Father, Jesus, and the Spirit/Paraclete. Many such discussions focus upon Pilate's question to Jesus, "What is truth?" found in John 18:38. Pilate asks this question at the end of the Gospel's exploration of the truth. By this time in the story, the Gospel has clearly established that Jesus is the truth; Pilate is the only one who appears not to know this.

The fifth and final means by which the Gospel is organized that I explore in this volume is the Passover theme. Many scholars have identified the Passover as significant in John 1 and 19. I argue that the Passover theme — that Jesus is the lamb of God sacrificed for his people — is found at a number of other places in the Gospel as well. The pattern begins in John 1 but also includes John 2, 6, 8, 11–12, 13–17, as well as 19. The culmination of the display is found in the words and depictions of Jesus' death as the sacrificial lamb offered up at Passover.

These five means by which John organized his Gospel are all ways of presenting Jesus — the one publicly proclaimed, the divine *logos,* the Messiah, the truthful mediator between God and humanity, and the Passover lamb. Some may raise questions whether all of these patterns can legitimately be found within one Gospel. I believe that they can, as I have attempted to illustrate, and to do so without either mitigating the significance of any of them or ending up in contradiction. John's Gospel is a complex work that presents Jesus in a variety of profound and provocative ways, with its own distinctive voice. Furthermore, Jesus himself as represented in John's Gospel is an equally complex character, one who cannot be fully articulated simply by means of a selection of titles or a reductionistic set of rubrics. As I have attempted to show, the Jesus of John's Gospel is a multifaceted character whose theological understanding is revealed through a variety of authorial means. The essays in this volume represent some of these means that I believe are worth exploring.

Besides overall plans for organization and development of the Gospel, however, I have also addressed a number of other issues of importance in John's Gospel and how they have relevance for Jesus. Because I have suggested that John's Gospel should be seen in relation to the other Gospels, I have also explored what these possible relations might look like. To this end, I examined twenty-three individual Gospel episodes. I believe that we can discover a number of different relations among the Synoptics and John's Gospel, finding in particular a number of passages that seem to attest to independent sources being used to describe the same event. This conclusion has important implications for historical Jesus research that I hope can be taken up in other venues.

The topic of Jesus and "the Jews" is another major issue that has been of much current interest. This topic has provoked many opinions, some quite strident. Drawing upon an important distinction between sense and reference, I attempt to differentiate the uses of the language regarding "the Jews," seeing that the Gospel cannot be stereotyped or easily categorized as promoting one particular view. In fact, its view of "the Jews" is highly contextually dependent, often identifying only a specific group in opposition to Jesus. I hope that my findings here may go some way toward alleviating what I consider to be undue and unnuanced castigation of John's Gospel for its view of "the Jews."

The final chapter of this volume treats the ending of John's Gospel. I end this book with the end of the Gospel, for a number of reasons. John 21 has aroused much controversy regarding whether it belongs with the original Gospel or whether it was a later addition. After examining the relevant arguments, I conclude that the chapter is integral to the entire Gospel both linguistically and structurally. Furthermore, I conclude that it brings the Gospel to a fitting end just as it has done throughout the work — in presenting Jesus as the Messiah.

I WOULD BE THE FIRST to admit that this volume of essays is in many ways only a preliminary exploration of topics of importance. I have endeavored to examine particular topics that, over the years, I have found intriguing and provocative. I believe that I have taken some unusual positions, argued in some new and different ways, rejected some of the standard or more usual answers, and discovered new solutions even to traditional problems — and as a result have arrived at some interesting and even provocative conclusions regarding John's Gospel and, with it, the Jesus that John presents. I hope that I have identified at least some of the Johannine voice. If nothing else, I have discovered an unfathomable depth of profundity in the Gospel that has rewarded all of the effort involved, and I trust that these essays will help others in that task of exploration as well.

Bibliography

Adam, J. *The Religious Teachers of Greece*. Edinburgh: T&T Clark, 1909.

Akala, A. J. *The Son-Father Relationship and Christological Symbolism in the Gospel of John*. LNTS 505. London: Bloomsbury, 2014.

Aland, K., ed. *Synopsis of the Four Gospels*. 6th ed. Stuttgart: United Bible Societies, 1983.

Aland, K., and B. Aland. *The Text of the New Testament: An Introduction to the Critical Editions and to the Theory and Practice of Modern Textual Criticism*. Translated by E. F. Rhodes. 2nd ed. Grand Rapids: Eerdmans, 1989. (German original, 1981.)

Anderson, J. M. *The Grammar of Names*. Oxford: Oxford University Press, 2007.

Anderson, P. N. *The Christology of the Fourth Gospel: Its Unity and Disunity in the Light of John 6*. Valley Forge, PA: Trinity Press International, 1997.

———. "The Origin and Development of the Johannine *Ego Eimi* Sayings in Cognitive-Critical Perspective." *JSHJ* 9 (2011): 139-206.

Anonymous. *The New Gospel Fragments*. London: Trustees of the British Museum, 1935. (Rev. ed., 1951, 1955.)

Ashton, J. "The Identity and Function of Ἰουδαῖοι in the Fourth Gospel." *NovT* 27 (1985): 40-75.

———. "The Transformation of Wisdom: A Study of the Prologue of John's Gospel." Pages 5-35 in his *Studying John: Approaches to the Fourth Gospel*. Oxford: Clarendon Press, 1994 (1986).

———. *Understanding the Fourth Gospel*. Oxford: Clarendon Press, 1991. 2nd ed., 2007.

———. "The Johannine Son of Man: A New Proposal." *NTS* 57 (2011): 508-29.

Athanassakis, A. N. *The Orphic Hymns: Text, Translation, and Notes*. SBLTT 12. GRRS 4. Atlanta: Scholars Press, 1977.

Bacon, B. W. *The Fourth Gospel in Research and Debate*. London: Fisher Unwin, 1910.

Bailey, J. A. *The Traditions Common to the Gospels of Luke and John*. NovTSup 7. Leiden: Brill, 1963.

Baird, W. *History of New Testament Research*. Vol. 2: *From Jonathan Edwards to Rudolf Bultmann*. Minneapolis: Fortress Press, 2003.

Ball, D. J. "Had the Fourth Gospel an Aramaic Archetype?" *ExpTim* 21 (1909-10): 91-93.

Ball, D. M. *"I Am" in John's Gospel: Literary Function, Background, and Theological Implications.* JSNTSup 124. Sheffield: Sheffield Academic Press, 1996.

Barnes, J. *The Presocratic Philosophers.* London: Routledge & Kegan Paul, 1979.

Barr, J. *The Semantics of Biblical Language.* Oxford: Oxford University Press, 1961.

—————. *Biblical Words for Time.* London: SCM Press, 1962.

Barrett, C. K. "The Old Testament in the Fourth Gospel." *JTS* 48 (1947): 155-69.

—————. "The Lamb of God." *NTS* 1 (1954-55): 210-18.

—————. *The Prologue of St John's Gospel.* Ethel M. Wood Lecture 1970. London: Athlone Press, 1971.

—————. "The Prologue of St John's Gospel." Pages 27-48 in his *New Testament Essays.* London: SPCK, 1972.

—————. *The Gospel of John and Judaism.* London: SPCK, 1975.

—————. *The Gospel according to St. John.* 2nd ed. Philadelphia: Westminster, 1978.

Barton, G. A. "'A Bone of Him Shall Not Be Broken': John 19:36." *JBL* 49 (1930): 13-19.

Barton, S. "Early Christianity and the Sociology of the Sect." Pages 140-62 in *The Open Text: New Directions for Biblical Studies?* Edited by F. Watson. London: SCM Press, 1993.

Battistella, E. L. *The Logic of Markedness.* New York: Oxford University Press, 1996.

Bauckham, R. "John for Readers of Mark." Pages 147-71 in *The Gospels for All Christians: Rethinking the Gospel Audiences.* Edited by R. Bauckham. Grand Rapids: Eerdmans, 1998.

—————. *Jesus and the Eyewitnesses: The Gospels as Eyewitness Testimony.* Grand Rapids: Eerdmans, 2006.

—————. *The Testimony of the Beloved Disciple: Narrative, History, and Theology in the Gospel of John.* Grand Rapids: Baker, 2007.

—————. "The Fourth Gospel as the Testimony of the Beloved Disciple." Pages 120-39 in *The Gospel of John and Christian Theology.* Edited by R. Bauckham and C. Mosser. Grand Rapids: Eerdmans, 2008.

Bauckham, R., ed. *The Gospels for All Christians: Rethinking the Gospel Audiences.* Grand Rapids: Eerdmans, 1998.

Bauckham, R., and C. Mosser, eds. *The Gospel of John and Christian Theology.* Grand Rapids: Eerdmans, 2008.

Bauer, W. *Das Johannesevangelium.* HNT 6. Tübingen: Mohr Siebeck, 1933.

Baum, G. *Is the New Testament Anti-Semitic? A Re-examination of the New Testament.* Glen Rock, NJ: Paulist Press, 1965.

Baur, F. C. *The Church History of the First Three Centuries.* Translated by Allan Menzies. 3rd ed. 2 vols. London: Williams & Norgate, 1878, 1879.

Beasley-Murray, G. R. *John.* 2nd ed. WBC 36. Dallas: Word, 1999 (1981).

Beilner, W., and M. Ernst. *Unter dem Wort Gottes.* Thaur, Austria: Kulturverlag, 1993.

Bell, H. I., and T. C. Skeat. *Fragments of an Unknown Gospel and Other Early Christian Papyri.* London: Trustees of the British Museum, 1935.

Bennema, C. *Encountering Jesus: Character Studies in the Gospel of John.* Milton Keynes, UK: Paternoster, 2009.

———. "The Identity and Composition of οἱ Ἰουδαῖοι in the Gospel of John." *TynBul* 60.2 (2009): 239-64.

———. "The Character of Pilate in the Gospel of John." Pages 240-53 in *Characters and Characterization in the Gospel of John.* Edited by C. W. Skinner. LNTS 461. London: Bloomsbury, 2013.

Bernard, J. H. *A Critical and Exegetical Commentary on the Gospel according to St. John.* Edited by A. H. McNeile. 2 vols. ICC. Edinburgh: T&T Clark, 1928.

Bieringer, R., D. Pollefeyt, and F. Vandecasteele-Vanneuville, eds. *Anti-Judaism and the Fourth Gospel: Papers of the Leuven Colloquium, 2000.* Jewish and Christian Heritage 1. Assen, Netherlands: Royal Van Gorcum, 2001.

———. *Anti-Judaism and the Fourth Gospel.* Louisville, KY: Westminster John Knox, 2001.

Bird, M. F. *Jesus is the Christ: The Messianic Testimony of the Gospels.* Downers Grove, IL: InterVarsity Press, 2012.

Bittner, W. J. *Jesu Zeichen im Johannesevangelium.* WUNT 2.26. Tübingen: Mohr Siebeck, 1987.

Black, M. *An Aramaic Approach to the Gospels and Acts.* 3rd ed. Oxford: Clarendon Press, 1967.

Blackman, E. C. "Truth." Pages 269-70 in *A Theological Word Book of the Bible.* Edited by A. Richardson. London: SCM Press, 1950.

Blomberg, C. L. "The Historical Reliability of John: Rushing in Where Angels Fear to Tread?" Pages 71-82 in *Jesus in Johannine Tradition.* Edited by R. T. Fortna and T. Thatcher. Louisville, KY: Westminster John Knox, 2001.

———. *The Historical Reliability of John's Gospel: Issues and Commentary.* Downers Grove, IL: InterVarsity Press, 2001.

Bock, D. L. *Jesus according to Scripture: Restoring the Portrait from the Gospels.* Grand Rapids: Baker, 2002.

Boismard, M. "Le chapître xxi de saint Jean: Essai de critique littéraire." *RB* 54 (1947): 473-501.

———. *Moses or Jesus: An Essay in Johannine Christology.* Translated by B. T. Viviano. Minneapolis: Fortress Press; Leuven: Peeters, 1993.

Borchert, G. L. "Passover and the Narrative Cycles in John." Pages 303-16 in *Perspectives on John: Method and Interpretation in the Fourth Gospel.* Edited by R. B. Sloan and M. C. Parsons. Lewiston, NY: Mellen, 1993.

———. *John 1–11.* NAC. Nashville: Broadman & Holman, 1996.

———. *John 12–21.* NAC. Nashville: Broadman & Holman, 2002.

———. *Worship in the New Testament: Divine Mystery and Human Response.* St. Louis: Chalice, 2008.

Borgen, P. *Bread from Heaven: An Exegetical Study of the Concept of Manna in the Gospel of John and the Writings of Philo.* NovTSup 10. Leiden: Brill, 1965.

Boring, M. E. *An Introduction to the New Testament: History, Literature, Theology.* Louisville: Westminster John Knox, 2012.

Bousset, W. *Kyrios Christos: A History of the Belief in Christ from the Beginnings of Chris-*

tianity to Irenaeus. Translated by J. E. Steely. Nashville: Abingdon, 1969 (German original, 1913).

Boyarin, D. "The Ioudaioi in John and the Prehistory of 'Judaism'." Pages 216-39 in *Pauline Conversations in Context: Essays in Honor of Calvin J. Roetzel*. Edited by J. C. Anderson, P. Sellew, and C. Setzer. London: Sheffield Academic Press, 2002.

Bradshaw, P. F. *The Search for the Origins of Christian Worship: Sources and Methods for the Study of Early Liturgy*. Oxford: Oxford University Press, 1992.

Bradshaw, P. ed. *The New Westminster Dictionary of Liturgy and Worship*. Louisville, KY: Westminster John Knox, 2002.

Bradshaw, P. F., and L. A. Hoffman, eds. *The Making of Jewish and Christian Worship*. Notre Dame: University of Notre Dame Press, 1991.

Bratcher, R. G. "'The Jews' in the Gospel of John." *BT* 26 (1975): 401-409.

Braumann G., and H.-G. Link. "I am." Pages 2:278-83 in *New International Dictionary of New Testament Theology*. Edited by C. Brown. 3 vols. Grand Rapids: Zondervan, 1975.

Broadhead, E. K. "The Fourth Gospel and the Synoptic Sayings Source: The Relationship Reconsidered." Pages 291-301 in *Jesus in Johannine Tradition*. Edited by R. T. Fortna and T. Thatcher. Louisville: Westminster John Knox, 2001.

Brodie, T. L. *The Gospel according to John: A Literary and Theological Commentary*. New York: Oxford University Press, 1993.

———. *The Quest for the Origin of John's Gospel: A Source-Oriented Approach*. New York: Oxford University Press, 1993.

Brown, R. E. "Three Quotations from John the Baptist in the Gospel of John." *CBQ* 22 (1960): 292-98.

———. "The Problem of Historicity in John." *CBQ* 24 (1962): 1-14.

———. *The Gospel according to John*. 2 vols. AB 29, 29A. Garden City, NY: Doubleday, 1966-70.

———. *The Community of the Beloved Disciple*. New York: Paulist Press, 1979.

———. *The Death of the Messiah: From Gethsemane to the Grave*. ABRL. New York: Doubleday, 1994.

———. *An Introduction to the New Testament*. New York: Doubleday, 1997.

———. *An Introduction to the Gospel of John*. Edited by F. J. Moloney. New York: Doubleday, 2003.

Brown, T. G. *Spirit in the Writings of John: Johannine Pneumatology in Social-Scientific Perspective*. JSNTSup 253. London: T&T Clark, 2003.

Bruce, F. F. *The Gospel of John*. Basingstoke: Pickering & Inglis, 1983.

Büchsel, F. "Ειμί, ὁ ὤν." Pages 2:398-400 in *Theological Dictionary of the New Testament*. Edited by G. Kittel and G. Friedrich. Translated by G. W. Bromiley. 10 vols. Grand Rapids: Eerdmans, 1964-76.

Bultmann, R. "Die Bedeutung der neuerschlossenen mandäischen und manichäischen Quellen für das Verständnis des Johannesevangeliums." *ZNW* 24 (1925): 100-46.

———. *Das Evangelium des Johannes*. KEK 2. Göttingen: Vandenhoeck & Ruprecht, 1941; repr., Berlin: Evangelische Verlagsanstalt, 1963.

————. *The Gospel of John: A Commentary.* Translated by G. R. Beasley-Murray et al. Oxford: Blackwell, 1971.

————. "The History of Religions Background of the Prologue to the Gospel of John." Pages 27-46 in *The Interpretation of John.* Edited by J. Ashton. 2nd ed. Edinburgh: T&T Clark, 1997.

Burge, G. M. *The Anointed Community: The Holy Spirit in the Johannine Tradition.* Grand Rapids: Eerdmans, 1987.

————. *Interpreting the Gospel of John.* Grand Rapids: Baker, 1992.

————. " 'I Am' Sayings." Pages 354-56 in *Dictionary of Jesus and the Gospels.* Edited by J. B. Green, S. McKnight, and I. H. Marshall. Downers Grove, IL: InterVarsity Press, 1992.

————. "Gospel of John." Pages 37-163 in *The Bible Knowledge Background Commentary: John's Gospel, Hebrews-Revelation.* Edited by C. A. Evans. Colorado Springs: Cook, 2005.

Burney, C. F. *The Aramaic Origin of the Fourth Gospel.* Oxford: Clarendon Press, 1922.

Burrows, E. W. "Did John the Baptist Call Jesus 'The Lamb of God'?" *ExpTim* 85 (1973-74): 245-47.

Bury, R. G. *The Fourth Gospel and the Logos-Doctrine.* Cambridge: Heffer, 1940.

Buss, M. J. *Biblical Form Criticism in Its Context.* JSOTSup 274. Sheffield: Sheffield Academic Press, 1999.

————. *The Concept of Form in the Twentieth Century.* Sheffield: Sheffield Phoenix Press, 2008.

————. *The Changing Shape of Form Criticism: A Relational Approach.* Edited by N. M. Stipe. Hebrew Bible Monographs 18. Sheffield: Sheffield Phoenix Press, 2010.

Buttrick, G. A., ed. *Interpreter's Dictionary of the Bible.* 4 vols. Nashville: Abingdon, 1962.

Bynum, W. R. *The Fourth Gospel and the Scriptures: Illuminating the Form and Meaning of Scriptural Citation in John 19:37.* Leiden: Brill, 2012.

Carey, G. L. "The Lamb of God and Atonement Theories." *TynBul* 32 (1981): 101-107.

Carson, D. A. "The Purpose of the Fourth Gospel: John 20:31 Reconsidered." *JBL* 106 (1987): 639-51.

————. "John and the Johannine Epistles." Pages 245-64 in *It is Written: Scripture Citing Scripture: Essays in Honour of Barnabas Lindars.* Edited by D. A. Carson and H. G. M. Williamson. Cambridge: Cambridge University Press, 1988.

————. *The Gospel according to John.* Leicester: InterVarsity Press, 1991.

————. "Syntactical and Text-Critical Observations on John 20:30-31: One More Round on the Purpose of the Fourth Gospel." *JBL* 124 (2005): 693-714.

Carson, D. A., D. J. Moo, and L. Morris. *An Introduction to the New Testament.* Grand Rapids: Zondervan, 1992. 2nd ed., 2005.

Carter, W. "The Prologue and John's Gospel: Function, Symbol and the Definitive Word." *JSNT* 39 (1990): 35-58.

————. *John: Storyteller, Interpreter, Evangelist.* Peabody, MA: Hendrickson, 2006.

Charlesworth, J. H. *The Beloved Disciple: Whose Witness Validates the Gospel of John?* Valley Forge, PA: Trinity Press International, 1995.

―――. "The Gospel of John: Exclusivism Caused by a Social Setting Different from That of Jesus (John 11:54 and 14:6)." Pages 479-513 in *Anti-Judaism and the Fourth Gospel: Papers of the Leuven Colloquium, 2000.* Edited by R. Bieringer, D. Pollefeyt, and F. Vandecasteele-Vanneuville. Assen, Netherlands: Royal Van Gorcum, 2001.

Childs, B. S. *Biblical Theology in Crisis.* Philadelphia: Westminster, 1970.

Cho, S. *Jesus as Prophet in the Fourth Gospel.* NTM 15. Sheffield: Sheffield Phoenix Press, 2006.

Cirafesi, W. V. "The Priestly Portrait of Jesus in the Gospel of John in the Light of 1QS, 1QSa and 1QSb." *JGRChJ* (2011-12): 83-105.

―――. "The Temple Attitudes of John and Qumran in the Light of Hellenistic Judaism." Pages 315-40 in *Christian Origins and Hellenistic Judaism: Social and Literary Contexts for the New Testament.* Edited by S. E. Porter and A. W. Pitts. TENT 10. Early Christianity in Its Hellenistic Context 2. Leiden: Brill, 2013.

―――. "The Johannine Community Hypothesis (1968-Present): Past and Present Approaches and a New Way Forward." *CBR* 12.2 (2014): 173-93.

Claussen, C. "The Role of John 21: Discipleship in Retrospect and Redefinition." Pages 55-68 in *New Currents through John: A Global Perspective.* Edited by F. Loazada Jr. and T. Thatcher. SBLRBS 54. Atlanta: SBL, 2006.

Colwell, E. C., and E. L. Titus. *The Gospel of the Spirit: A Study in the Fourth Gospel.* New York: Harper, 1953.

Comfort, P. W. *Early Manuscripts and Modern Translations.* Grand Rapids: Baker, 1990.

Comfort, P. W., and D. P. Barrett. *The Text of the Earliest New Testament Manuscripts.* 2nd ed. Wheaton, IL: Tyndale, 2001.

Copenhaver, B. P. *Hermetica.* Cambridge: Cambridge University Press, 1992.

Cosgrove, C. *An Ancient Christian Hymn with Musical Notation: Papyrus Oxyrhynchus 1786. Text and Commentary.* STAC 65. Tübingen: Mohr Siebeck, 2011.

Cotterell, F. P. "The Nicodemus Conversation: A Fresh Appraisal." *ExpTim* 96 (1984-85): 237-42.

Cribbs, F. L. "A Reassessment of the Date of Origin and the Destination of the Gospel of John." *JBL* 89 (1970): 38-55.

Cullmann, O. *Les Premières Confessions de foi Chrétiennes.* Paris: Presses Universitaires, 1943.

―――. *Early Christian Worship.* SBT 10. London: SCM Press, 1953.

―――. *The Christology of the New Testament.* Translated by S. C. Guthrie and C. A. M. Hall. 2nd ed. London: SCM Press, 1963.

―――. *The Johannine Circle.* Translated by J. Bowden. London: SCM Press, 1976.

Culpepper, R. A. "The Pivot of John's Prologue." *NTS* 27 (1980-81): 1-31.

―――. *Anatomy of the Fourth Gospel: A Study in Literary Design.* FFNT. Philadelphia: Fortress Press, 1983.

―――. "Anti-Judaism in the Fourth Gospel as a Theological Problem for Christian Interpreters." Pages 68-91 in *Anti-Judaism and the Fourth Gospel: Papers of the Leuven Colloquium, 2000.* Edited by R. Bieringer, D. Pollefeyt, and F. Vandecasteele-Vanneuville. Assen, Netherlands: Royal Van Gorcum, 2001.

―――. "Designs for the Church in the Imagery of John 21:1-14." Pages 369-402 in *Imagery in the Gospel of John*. Edited by J. Frey, J. van der Watt, and R. Zimmerman. WUNT 200. Tübingen: Mohr Siebeck, 2006.

Cuming, G. J. "The Jews in the Fourth Gospel." *ExpTim* 60 (1948-49): 290-92.

Cumming, C. G. *The Assyrian and Hebrew Hymns of Praise*. New York: Columbia University Press, 1934; repr. 1966.

Daise, M. A. *Feasts in John*. WUNT 2.229. Tübingen: Mohr Siebeck, 2007.

Dalman, G. *Jesus-Jeshua: Studies in the Gospels*. Translated by P. Levertoff. London: SPCK, 1929.

Danove, P. L. *The End of Mark's Story: A Methodological Study*. Leiden: Brill, 1993.

Daube, D. *The New Testament and Rabbinic Judaism*. London: Athlone Press, 1956.

Davies, M. *Rhetoric and Reference in the Fourth Gospel*. JSNTSup 69. Sheffield: JSOT Press, 1992.

Davies, W. D. *The Gospel and the Land: Early Christianity and Jewish Territorial Doctrine*. Berkeley: University of California Press, 1974.

Davis, S., and B. S. Gillon. "Introduction." Pages 1-130 in *Semantics: A Reader*. Edited by S. Davis and B. S. Gillon. Oxford: Oxford University Press, 2004.

de Boer, M. C. "The Depiction of 'the Jews' in John's Gospel: Matters of Behavior and Identity." Pages 260-80 in *Anti-Judaism and the Fourth Gospel: Papers of the Leuven Colloquium, 2000*. Edited by R. Bieringer, D. Pollefeyt, and F. Vandecasteele-Vanneuville. Assen, Netherlands: Royal Van Gorcum, 2001.

Deeks, D. "The Structure of the Fourth Gospel." Pages 77-101 in *The Gospel of John as Literature: An Anthology of Twentieth-Century Perspectives*. Edited by M. W. G. Stibbe. NTTS 17. Leiden: Brill, 1993.

Deichgräber, R. *Gotteshymnus und Christushymnus in der frühen Christenheit*. Göttingen: Vandenhoeck & Ruprecht, 1967.

Deissmann, A. *Light from the Ancient East*. Translated by L. R. M. Strachan. 4th ed. London: Hodder & Stoughton, 1927.

―――. "Ein Evangelienblatt aus den Tagen Hadrians." *Deutsche allgemeine Zeitung* 564 (3 December 1935). ET *British Weekly* (12 December 1935): 219.

de Jonge, H. J. " 'The Jews' in the Gospel of John." Pages 239-59 in *Anti-Judaism and the Fourth Gospel: Papers of the Leuven Colloquium, 2000*. Edited by R. Bieringer, D. Pollefeyt, and F. Vandecasteele-Vanneuville. Assen, Netherlands: Royal Van Gorcum, 2001.

de la Potterie, I. *La vérité dans Saint Jean*. 2 vols. Rome: Biblical Institute Press, 1977.

Derrett, J. D. M. *The Victim: The Johannine Passion Narrative Reexamined*. Shipton-on-Stour: Drinkwater, 1993.

de Ruyter, B. W. J. *De gemeente van de evangelist Johannes: Haar polemiek en haar geschiedenis*. Delft: Eburon, 1998.

Dibelius, M. *Die Formgeschichte des Evangeliums*. 2nd ed. Tübingen: Mohr Siebeck, 1933; repr. ed. G. Iber, 1971. ET *From Tradition to Gospel*. Translated by B. L. Woolf. London: Ivor Nicholson & Watson, 1934.

Diels, H. *Die Fragmente der Vorsokratiker*. 3 vols. Berlin: Weidmannsche Buchhandlung, 1912.

Dix, D. G. *The Shape of the Liturgy*. Westminster: Dacre Press, 1954.

Dodd, C. H. *The Bible and the Greeks*. London: Hodder & Stoughton, 1934.

———. *The Interpretation of the Fourth Gospel*. Cambridge: Cambridge University Press, 1953.

———. "A New Gospel." Pages 12-52 in his *New Testament Studies*. Manchester: Manchester University Press, 1953 (1936).

———. "The Prologue to the Fourth Gospel and Christian Worship." Pages 9-22 in *Studies in the Fourth Gospel*. Edited by F. L. Cross. London: Mowbray, 1957.

———. *Historical Tradition in the Fourth Gospel*. Cambridge: Cambridge University Press, 1963.

Donaldson, T. L. *Jews and Anti-Judaism in the New Testament: Decision Points and Divergent Interpretations*. London: SPCK; Waco, TX: Baylor University Press, 2010.

Duke, P. D. *Irony in the Fourth Gospel*. Atlanta: John Knox Press, 1985.

Dunn, J. D. G. *Christology in the Making*. Philadelphia: Westminster, 1980.

———. *Jesus Remembered*. Christianity in the Making 1. Grand Rapids: Eerdmans, 2003.

———. *The New Perspective on Paul*. Grand Rapids: Eerdmans, 2007.

Edwards, R. *Discovering John*. London: SPCK, 2003.

Ehrenberg, V., and A. H. M. Jones. *Documents Illustrating the Reigns of Augustus and Tiberius*. 2nd ed. Oxford: Clarendon Press, 1955.

Elliott, W. J., and D. C. Parker. *The Gospel according to St. John*. Vol. 1: *The Papyri*. Vol. 4 of *The New Testament in Greek*. NTTS 20. Leiden: Brill, 1995.

Ellis, E. E. *The Making of the New Testament Documents*. BIS 39. Leiden: Brill, 1999.

Epp, E. J. "Wisdom, Torah, Word: The Johannine Prologue and the Purpose of the Fourth Gospel." Pages 128-46 in *Current Issues in Biblical and Patristic Interpretation: Studies in Honor of Merrill C. Tenney Presented by His Former Students*. Edited by G. F. Hawthorne. Grand Rapids: Eerdmans, 1975.

Estes, D. *The Temporal Mechanics of the Fourth Gospel: A Theory of Hermeneutical Relativity in the Gospel of John*. BIS 92. Leiden: Brill, 2008.

———. *The Questions of Jesus in John: Logic, Rhetoric and Persuasive Discourse*. BIS 115. Leiden: Brill, 2013.

Evans, C. A. "On the Quotation Formulas in the Fourth Gospel." *BZ* 26 (1982): 79-83.

———. *Word and Glory: On the Exegetical and Theological Background of John's Prologue*. JSNTSup 89. Sheffield: JSOT Press, 1993.

Evans, C. A., and J. A. Sanders, eds. *Early Christian Interpretation of the Scriptures of Israel: Investigations and Proposals*. JSNTSup 148. Sheffield: Sheffield Academic Press 1997.

Evelyn-White, H. G. *Hesiod, the Homeric Hymns and Homerica*. LCL. London: Heinemann; Cambridge, MA: Harvard University Press, 1950.

Falcetta, A., ed. *James Rendel Harris: New Testament Autographs and Other Essays*. NTM 7. Sheffield: Sheffield Phoenix Press, 2006.

Faure, A. "Die alttestamentlichen Zitate im 4. Evangelium und die Quellenscheidungshypothese." *ZNW* 21 (1922): 99-121.

Fee, G. D. "On the Text and Meaning of John 20:30-31." Reprinted as pages 29-42 in

To What End Exegesis? Essays Textual, Exegetical, and Theological. Grand Rapids: Eerdmans, 2001 (1992).

Fewster, G. P. *Creation Language in Romans 8: A Study in Monosemy.* LBS 8. Leiden: Brill, 2013.

Finegan, J. *Encountering New Testament Manuscripts.* London: SPCK, 1975.

Fletcher-Louis, C. *Luke-Acts: Angels, Christology and Soteriology.* WUNT 2.94. Tübingen: Mohr Siebeck, 1997.

Ford, J. M. "'Mingled Blood' from the Side of Christ (John XIX.34)." *NTS* 15 (1968-69): 337-38.

Forestell, J. T. "Jesus and the Paraclete in the Gospel of John." Pages 151-98 in *Word and Spirit: Essays in Honor of David Michael Stanley, S.J., on his 60th Birthday.* Edited by J. Plevnik. Toronto: Regis College Press, 1975.

Fortna, R. T. *The Gospel of Signs: A Reconstruction of the Narrative Source Underlying the Fourth Gospel.* SNTSMS 11. Cambridge: Cambridge University Press, 1970.

———. "Theological Use of Locale in the Fourth Gospel." Pages 58-95 in *Gospel Studies in Honor of Sherman Elbridge Johnson.* Edited by H. S. Massey and C. H. Edward. ATRSup 3. Evanston, IL: Anglican Theological Review, 1974.

———. *The Fourth Gospel and Its Predecessor: From Narrative Source to Present Gospel.* Philadelphia: Fortress Press, 1988.

Foster, P. "Memory, Orality, and the Fourth Gospel: Three Dead-Ends in Historical Jesus Research." *JSHJ* 10 (2012): 191-227.

Fowl, S. *The Story of Christ in the Ethics of Paul: An Analysis of the Function of the Hymnic Material in the Pauline Corpus.* JSNTSup 36. Sheffield: JSOT Press, 1990.

Franck, E. *Revelation Taught: The Paraclete in the Gospel of John.* CBNTS 14. Malmo: Gleerup, 1985.

Freed, E. *Old Testament Quotations in the Gospel of John.* NovTSup 11. Leiden: Brill, 1965.

———. "Ego Eimi in John 1.20 and 4.25." *CBQ* 41 (1979): 288-91.

———. "Who or What was before Abraham in John 8:58?" *JSNT* 17 (1983): 52-59.

Frye, N. *Anatomy of Criticism.* Princeton: Princeton University Press, 1957.

Fuller, R. "The 'Jews' in the Fourth Gospel." *Dialog* 16 (1977): 31-37.

Funk, R. W. *A Beginning-Intermediate Grammar of Hellenistic Greek.* 3 vols. Missoula, MT: SBL, 1973.

Gardner-Smith, P. *Saint John and the Synoptic Gospels.* Cambridge: Cambridge University Press, 1938.

Gärtner, B. E. *Critical Readings of John 6.* CBNTS 17. Lund: Gleerup, 1959.

Gaventa, B. R. "The Archive of Excess: John 21 and the Problem of Narrative Closure." Pages 240-52 in *Exploring the Gospel of John: In Honor of D. Moody Smith.* Edited by R. A. Culpepper and C. C. Black. Louisville: Westminster John Knox, 1996.

Giblin, C. H. "Two Complementary Literary Structures in John 1:1-18." *JBL* 104 (1985): 87-103.

Glasson, T. F. *Moses in the Fourth Gospel.* SBT 40. London: SCM Press, 1963.

Glover, T. R. *The Conflict of Religions in the Early Roman Empire.* London: Methuen, 1909.

Godet, F. *Commentary on the Gospel of St. John.* Translated by M. D. Cusin. 3 vols. Edinburgh: T&T Clark, 1899.

Goetchius, E. V. N. Review of L. C. McGaughy, *Toward a Descriptive Analysis of Εἶναι as a Linking Verb in New Testament Greek. JBL* 95 (1976): 147-49.

Grässer, E. "Die antijüdische Polemik im Johannesevangelium." *NTS* 11 (1964-65): 74-90.

Gray, G. B. *Sacrifice in the Old Testament: Its Theory and Practice.* Oxford: Clarendon Press, 1925.

Grigsby, B. H. "The Cross as an Expiatory Sacrifice in the Fourth Gospel." *JSNT* 15 (1982): 51-80.

Gronewald, M. "Unbekanntes Evangelium oder Evangelienharmonie (Fragment aus dem 'Evangelium Egerton')." Pages 136-45 in *Kölner Papyri,* vol. 6. Edited by M. Gronewald et al. Papyrologica Coloniensia 7. Cologne: Westdeutscher Verlag, 1987.

Guilding, A. *The Fourth Gospel and Jewish Worship: A Study of the Relation of St John's Gospel to the Ancient Jewish Lectionary System.* Oxford: Clarendon Press, 1960.

Gundry, R. H. *Jesus the Word according to John the Sectarian.* Grand Rapids: Eerdmans, 2002.

Guthrie, D. *New Testament Introduction.* 3rd ed. Downers Grove, IL: InterVarsity Press, 1970; 4th ed. Leicester: Apollos, 1990.

Guthrie, W. K. C. "Hymns." Page 534 in *The Oxford Classical Dictionary.* Edited by N. G. L. Hammond and H. H. Scullard. Oxford: Clarendon Press, 1970.

Hagner, D. A. *The New Testament: A Historical and Theological Introduction.* Grand Rapids: Baker, 2012.

Hakola, R. *Identity Matters: John, the Jews, and Jewishness.* NovTSup 118. Leiden: Brill, 2005.

Hannick, C. "Christian Church, Music of the Early." Pages 4:363-71 in *New Grove Dictionary of Music and Musicians.* Edited by S. Sadie. 20 vols. London: Macmillan, 1980.

Hanson, A. T. "John 1.14-18 and Exodus 34." *NTS* 23 (1976): 90-101.

——. *The Prophetic Gospel: A Study of John and the Old Testament.* Edinburgh: T&T Clark, 1991.

Harner, P. B. *The "I Am" of the Fourth Gospel.* Philadelphia: Fortress Press, 1970.

Harrington, W. J. *Record of the Fulfillment: The New Testament.* Chicago: Priory, 1965.

Harris, E. *Prologue and Gospel: The Theology of the Fourth Evangelist.* JSNTSup 107. Sheffield: Sheffield Academic Press, 1994.

Harris, J. R. *The Origin of the Prologue to St John's Gospel.* Cambridge: Cambridge University Press, 1917.

——. "The Early Christian Interpretation of the Passover." *ExpTim* 38 (1926-27): 88-90.

Harris, M. J. *Jesus as God.* Grand Rapids: Baker, 1992.

Harrison, E. F. *Introduction to the New Testament.* Grand Rapids: Eerdmans, 1964.

Harstine, S. *Moses as Character in the Fourth Gospel: A Study of Ancient Reading Techniques.* JSNTSup 229. London: Sheffield Academic Press, 2002.

Hartman, L. "An Attempt at a Text-Centered Exegesis of John 21." *Studia Theologica* 38 (1984): 29-84. Reprinted on pages 69-87 in his *Text-Centered New Testament Studies: Text-Theoretical Essays on Early Jewish and Early Christian Literature.* Edited by D. Hellholm. WUNT 102. Tübingen: Mohr Siebeck, 1997.

Hays, R. B. *The Moral Vision of the New Testament.* New York: HarperSanFrancisco, 1996.

Headlam, A. C. *The Fourth Gospel as History.* Oxford: Blackwell, 1948.

Hengel, M. *Hellenism and Judaism.* Translated by J. Bowden. 2 vols. Philadelphia: Fortress Press, 1974.

———. *The Johannine Question.* Translated by J. Bowden. London: SCM Press; Philadelphia: Trinity Press International, 1989.

———. "The Old Testament in the Fourth Gospel." *HBT* 12.1 (1990): 12-41.

———. "The Song about Christ in Earliest Worship." Pages 227-91 in his *Studies in Early Christology.* Edinburgh: T&T Clark, 1995.

Higgins, A. J. B. *The Lord's Supper in the New Testament.* SBT 6. London: SCM Press, 1952.

Hill, C. E. "Did the Scribe of P52 Use the *Nomina Sacra?* Another Look." *NTS* 48.4 (2002): 587-92.

———. *The Johannine Corpus in the Early Church.* Oxford: Oxford University Press, 2004.

Hooker, M. D. "John's Prologue and the Messianic Secret." *NTS* 21 (1974): 40-58.

Horbury, W. "The Benediction of the Minim and Early Jewish-Christian Controversy." *JTS* 33 (1982): 19-61.

Hoskins, P. M. *Jesus as the Fulfillment of the Temple in the Gospel of John.* PBMS. Milton Keynes: Paternoster, 2006.

———. "Deliverance from Death by the True Passover Lamb: A Significant Aspect of the Fulfillment of the Passover in the Gospel of John." *JETS* 52.2 (2009): 285-300.

———. "Freedom from Slavery to Sin and the Devil: John 8:31-47 and the Passover Theme of the Gospel of John." *TrinJ*, n.s., 31 (2010): 47-63.

Hoskyns, E. C. *The Fourth Gospel.* Edited by F. N. Davey. 2nd ed. London: Faber & Faber, 1947.

Hoskyns, E., and F. N. Davey. *The Fourth Gospel.* 2 vols. London: Faber & Faber, 1940.

———. *The Riddle of the New Testament.* 3rd ed. London: Faber & Faber, 1947.

Howard, J. K. "Passover and Eucharist in the Fourth Gospel." *SJT* 20.1 (1967): 329-37.

Howard, W. F. *Christianity according to St. John.* London: Duckworth, 1943.

———. *The Fourth Gospel in Recent Criticism and Interpretation.* Revised by C. K. Barrett. 4th ed. London: Epworth, 1955 (1931).

Hunt, S. A. *Rewriting the Feeding of Five Thousand: John 6.1-15 as a Test Case for Johannine Dependence on the Synoptic Gospels.* StBL 125. New York: Peter Lang, 2011.

Hurford, J. B., B. Heasley, and M. B. Smith, *Semantics: A Coursebook.* 2nd ed. Cambridge: Cambridge University Press, 2007.

Hurtado, L. W. "The Origin of the *Nomina Sacra:* A Proposal." *JBL* 117.4 (1998): 655-73.

———. *At the Origins of Christian Worship.* Carlisle: Paternoster, 1999.

———. "The Earliest Evidence of an Emerging Christian Material and Visual Culture:

The Codex, the Nomina Sacra, and the Staurogram." Pages 271-88 in *Text and Artifact in the Religions of Mediterranean Antiquity*. Edited by S. G. Wilson and M. Desjardins. Waterloo: Wilfrid Laurier University Press, 2000.

———. "P52 (P.Rylands Gk. 457) and the Nomina Sacra: Method and Probability." *TynBul* 54.1 (2003): 1-14.

———. *The Earliest Christian Artifacts: Manuscripts and Christian Origins*. Grand Rapids: Eerdmans, 2006.

———. *Lord Jesus Christ: Devotion to Jesus in Earliest Christianity*. Grand Rapids: Eerdmans, 2007.

Ibuki, Y. *Die Wahrheit im Johannesevangelium*. Bonn: Peter Hanstein, 1972.

Idelsohn, A. Z. *Jewish Music in Its Historical Development*. New York: Tudor, 1948 (1929).

Inge, W. R. *Christian Mysticism*. London: Methuen, 1899.

Jasper, A. *The Shining Garment of the Text: Gendered Readings of John's Prologue*. JSNTSup 165. GCT 6. Sheffield: Sheffield Academic Press, 1998.

Jaubert, A. *La date de la cène: Calendrier biblique et liturgie chrétienne*. EBib. Paris: Gabalda, 1957.

———. "Jésus et le calendrier de Qumrân." *NTS* 7 (1960-61): 1-30.

———. "The Calendar of Qumran and the Passion Narrative in John." Pages 62-75 in *John and the Dead Sea Scrolls*. Edited by J. H. Charlesworth. New York: Crossroad, 1990.

Jeremias, J. "An Unknown Gospel with Johannine Elements (Pap. Egerton 2)." Pages 1:94-97 in *New Testament Apocrypha*. Edited by E. Hennecke and W. Schneemelcher. 2 vols. London: Lutterworth, 1963.

———. *The Central Message of the New Testament*. London: SCM Press, 1965.

———. *The Eucharistic Words of Jesus*. NTL. London: SCM Press, 1966.

Jones, C., G. Wainwright, and E. Yarnold, eds. *The Study of Liturgy*. Rev. ed. New York: Oxford University Press, 1992 (1978).

Käsemann, E. "A Primitive Christian Baptismal Liturgy." Pages 149-68 in his *Essays on New Testament Themes*. Translated by W. J. Montague. London: SCM Press, 1964.

———. "The Structure and Purpose of the Prologue to John's Gospel." Pages 138-67 in his *New Testament Questions of Today*. Philadelphia: Fortress Press, 1969.

Keener, C. S. *The Gospel of John: A Commentary*. 2 vols. Peabody, MA: Hendrickson, 2003.

———. *The Historical Jesus of the Gospels*. Grand Rapids: Eerdmans, 2009.

Kennel, G. *Frühchristliche Hymnen? Gattungskritische Studien zur Frage nach den Leidern der frühen Christenheit*. WMANT 71. Neukirchen-Vluyn: Neukirchener Verlag, 1995.

Kent, C. F. *The Songs, Hymns, and Prayers of the Old Testament*. London: Hodder & Stoughton, 1914.

Kermode, F. "St John as Poet." *JSNT* 28 (1986): 3-16.

Kerr, A. R. *The Temple of Jesus' Body: The Temple Theme in the Gospel of John*. JSNTSup 220. London: Sheffield Academic Press, 2002.

Kierkegaard, S. *The Concept of Irony with Constant Reference to Socrates.* Translated by L. M. Capel. Bloomington: Indiana University Press, 1965.

Kierspel, L. *The Jews and the World in the Fourth Gospel: Parallelism, Function, and Context.* WUNT 2.220. Tübingen: Mohr Siebeck, 2006.

Kimelman, R. "Birkat ha-Minim and the Lack of Evidence for an Anti-Christian Jewish Prayer in Late Antiquity." Pages 226-44 in *Jewish and Christian Self-Definition.* Vol. 2 of *Aspects of Judaism in the Greco-Roman Period.* Edited by E. P. Sanders. London: SCM Press, 1981.

Kirk, G. S., J. E. Raven, and M. Schofield. *The Presocratic Philosophers.* 2nd ed. Cambridge: Cambridge University Press, 1983.

Kittel, G., and G. Friedrich, eds. *Theological Dictionary of the New Testament.* Translated by G. W. Bromiley. 10 vols. Grand Rapids: Eerdmans, 1964-76.

Khani, S. H. *Revelation and Concealment of Christ: A Theological Inquiry into the Elusive Language of the Fourth Gospel.* WUNT 2.120. Tübingen: Mohr Siebeck, 2000.

Klink, E. W. *The Sheep of the Fold: The Audience and Origin of the Gospel of John.* SNTSMS 141. Cambridge: Cambridge University Press, 2007.

———. "Expulsion from the Synagogue? Rethinking a Johannine Anachronism." *TynBul* 59.1 (2008): 99-118.

———. "The Overrealized Expulsion in the Gospel of John." Pages 175-84 in *John, Jesus, and History.* Vol. 2: *Aspects of Historicity in the Fourth Gospel.* Edited by P. N. Anderson, F. Just, and T. Thatcher. Atlanta: SBL, 2009.

Klink, E. W., III, ed. *The Audience of the Gospels: Further Conversation about the Origin and Function of the Gospels in Early Christianity.* LNTS 353. New York: T&T Clark, 2010.

Knopf, R. *Einführung in das Neue Testament.* New York: Ökumenischen Rates der Kirchen, 1929.

Knox, W. L. *St Paul and the Church of the Gentiles.* Cambridge: Cambridge University Press, 1939.

———. *Some Hellenistic Elements in Primitive Christianity.* Schweich Lectures. London: British Academy, 1944.

Kobel, E. *Dining with John: Communal Meals and Identity Formation in the Fourth Gospel and Its Historical and Cultural Context.* BIS 109. Leiden: Brill, 2011.

Koester, C. R. *The Word of Life: A Theology of John's Gospel.* Grand Rapids: Eerdmans, 2008.

Koester, H. *Ancient Christian Gospels: Their History and Development.* Philadelphia: Trinity Press International, 1990.

Köstenberger, A. J. "The Seventh Johannine Sign: A Study in John's Christology." *BBR* 5 (1995): 87-103.

———. "'I Suppose' (Οἶμαι): The Conclusion of John's Gospel in Its Literary and Historical Context." Pages 72-88 in *The New Testament in Its First Century Setting: Essays on Context and Background in Honour of B. W. Winter on His 65th Birthday.* Edited by P. J. Williams, A. D. Clarke, P. M. Head, and D. Instone-Brewer. Grand Rapids: Eerdmans, 2004.

———. *John.* BECNT. Grand Rapids: Baker, 2004.

————. "The Destruction of the Second Temple and the Composition of the Fourth Gospel." Pages 69-108 in *Challenging Perspectives on the Gospel of John*. Edited by J. Lierman. WUNT 2.219. Tübingen: Mohr Siebeck, 2006.

————. "John." Pages 415-512 in *Commentary on the New Testament Use of the Old Testament*. Edited by G. K. Beale and D. A. Carson. Grand Rapids: Baker, 2007.

————. *A Theology of John's Gospel and Letters*. Grand Rapids: Zondervan, 2009.

Köstenberger, A. J., and S. R. Swain. *Father, Son, and Spirit: The Trinity and John's Gospel*. NSBT. Downers Grove, IL: InterVarsity Press, 2008.

Kraus, T., M. Kruger, and T. Nicklas. *Gospel Fragments*. Oxford: Oxford University Press, 2009.

Krebs, E. *Der Logos als Heiland im ersten Jahrhundert: Ein religions- und dogmengeschichtlicher Beitrag zur Erlösungslehre*. Freiburg: Herder, 1920.

Kreitzer, L. J. *Striking New Images: Roman Imperial Coinage and the New Testament World*. JSNTSup 134. Sheffield: Sheffield Academic Press, 1996.

Kroll, J. *Die christliche Hymnodik bis zu Klemens von Alexandria*. Königsberg: Harlung, 1921.

Kubiś, A. *The Book of Zechariah in the Gospel of John*. Pendé, France: J. Gabalda, 2012.

Kümmel, W. G. *Introduction to the New Testament*. Translated by H. C. Kee. Nashville: Abingdon, 1973.

Kysar, R. *The Fourth Evangelist and his Gospel: An Examination of Contemporary Scholarship*. Minneapolis: Augsburg, 1975.

————. *John: The Maverick Gospel*. Rev. ed. Louisville: Westminster John Knox, 1993 (1976).

————. *John's Story of Jesus*. Philadelphia: Fortress Press, 1984.

————. "Anti-Semitism and the Gospel of John." Pages 113-27 in *Anti-Semitism and Early Christianity: Issues of Polemic and Faith*. Edited by C. A. Evans and D. A. Hagner. Philadelphia: Fortress Press, 1993.

Labahn, M. "Fishing for Meaning: The Miraculous Catch of Fish in John 21." Pages 125-45 in *Wonders Never Cease: The Purpose of Narrating Miracle Stories in the New Testament and Its Religious Environment*. Edited by M. Labahn and B. J. L. Peerbolte. LNTS 288. London: T&T Clark, 2006.

Ladd, G. E. *New Testament Theology*. Grand Rapids: Eerdmans, 1975.

Lagrange, M.-J. *L'Évangile selon Saint Jean*. EBib. Paris: Gabalda, 1948.

Lamarche, P. "The Prologue of John." Pages 47-65 in *The Interpretation of John*. Edited by J. Ashton. 2nd ed. Edinburgh: T&T Clark, 1997.

Lang, M. *Johannes und die Synoptiker*. Göttingen: Vandenhoeck & Ruprecht, 1999.

Larsen, K. B. *Recognizing the Stranger: Recognition Scenes in the Gospel of John*. Leiden: Brill, 2008.

Lattke, M. *Hymnus: Materialien zu einer Geschichte der antiken Hymnologie*. NTOA 19. Göttingen: Vandenhoeck & Ruprecht, 1991.

Layton, B. *The Gnostic Scriptures*. London: SCM Press, 1987.

Lee, D. A. *The Symbolic Narratives of the Fourth Gospel: The Interplay of Form and Meaning*. JSNTSup 95. Sheffield: Sheffield Academic Press, 1994.

―――. "Paschal Imagery in the Gospel of John: A Narrative and Symbolic Reading." *Pacifica* 24 (2011): 13-28.

Lee, E. K. *The Religious Thought of St John*. London: SPCK, 1950.

Leistner, R. *Antijudaismus im Johannesevangelium?* TW 3. Bern: Herbert Lang, 1974.

Lierman, J. *The New Testament Moses*. WUNT 2.173. Tübingen: Mohr Siebeck, 2004.

―――. "The Mosaic Pattern of John's Christology." Pages 210-34 in *Challenging Perspectives on the Gospel of John*. Edited by J. Lierman. WUNT 2.219. Tübingen: Mohr Siebeck, 2006.

Lietzmann, H. *The Beginnings of Christianity*. Translated by B. L. Woolf. London: Lutterworth, 1949 (1937).

Lieu, J. "Narrative Analysis and Scripture in John." Pages 144-63 in *The Old Testament in the New Testament: Essays in Honour of J. L. North*. Edited by S. Moyise. JSNTSup 189. Sheffield: Sheffield Academic Press, 2000.

Lightfoot, J. B. *Biblical Essays*. London: Macmillan, 1893.

Lightfoot, R. H. *History and Interpretation in the Gospels*. London: Hodder & Stoughton, 1935.

―――. *St John's Gospel: A Commentary*. Edited by C. F. Evans. Oxford: Clarendon Press, 1956.

Lincoln, A. T. *Truth on Trial: The Lawsuit Motif in the Fourth Gospel*. Peabody, MA: Hendrickson, 2000.

―――. *The Gospel according to Saint John*. BNTC. Peabody, MA: Hendrickson, 2005.

Lindars, B. *New Testament Apologetic: The Doctrinal Significance of the Old Testament Quotations*. London: SCM Press, 1961.

―――. *The Gospel of John*. NCB. London: Oliphants, 1972.

―――. *John*. NTG. Sheffield: JSOT Press, 1990.

Lindars, B., R. B. Edwards, and J. M. Court. *The Johannine Literature*, with an Introduction by R. A. Culpepper. Sheffield: Sheffield Academic Press, 2000.

Loader, W. R. G. "The Central Structure of Johannine Christology." *NTS* 30 (1984): 188-216.

Loisy, A. *The Birth of the Christian Religion*. Translated by L. P. Jacks. London: Allen & Unwin, 1948.

Long, A. A. *Hellenistic Philosophy: Stoics, Epicureans, Sceptics*. 2nd ed. London: Duckworth, 1986.

Longenecker, R. N. *The Christology of Early Jewish Christianity*. SBT 2nd Series 17. London: SCM Press, 1970.

―――. *New Wine into Fresh Wineskins: Contextualizing the Early Christian Confessions*. Peabody, MA: Hendrickson, 1999.

Louw, J. P., and E. A. Nida. *Greek-English Lexicon of the New Testament: Based on Semantic Domains*. 2 vols. 2nd ed. New York: United Bible Societies, 1989.

Lowe, M. "Who Were the Ἰουδαῖοι?" *NovT* 18 (1976): 101-30.

Lowth, R. *De Sacra Poesie Hebraeorum Praelectiones Academicae*. Oxford: Clarendon Press, 1821. ET *Lectures on the Sacred Poetry of the Hebrews*. Translated by G. Gregory. London: Chadwick, 1847.

Lyons, J. *Introduction to Theoretical Linguistics.* Cambridge: Cambridge University Press, 1968.

———. *Semantics.* 2 vols. Cambridge: Cambridge University Press, 1977.

Maas, P., and C. Trypanis. *Sancti Romani Melodi Cantica: Cantica Genuina.* Oxford: Clarendon Press, 1963.

Maccini, R. G. *Her Testimony Is True: Women as Witnesses according to John.* JSNTSup 125. Sheffield: JSOT Press, 1996.

Mandilaras, B. *The Verb in the Greek Non-Literary Papyri.* Athens: Hellenic Ministry of Culture and Sciences, 1973.

Manson, T. W. "St. Paul's Letter to the Romans — and Others." Pages 225-41 in his *Studies in the Gospels and Epistles.* Edited by M. Black. Manchester: Manchester University Press, 1962.

———. "The Johannine Logos Doctrine." Pages 136-59 in his *On Paul and John: Some Selected Theological Themes.* Edited by M. Black. SBT 38. London: SCM Press, 1963.

Manson, W. *Jesus and the Christian.* London: James Clark, 1967.

Marcus, J. "*Birkat ha-Minim* Revisited." *NTS* 55 (2009): 523-51.

Marsh, J. *Saint John.* Harmondsworth: Penguin, 1968.

Martin, D. B. *New Testament History and Literature.* New Haven: Yale University Press, 2012.

Martin, R. P. "Aspects of Worship in the New Testament Church." *Vox Evangelica* 2 (1963): 6-32.

———. *The Four Gospels.* Vol. 1 of *New Testament Foundations.* Grand Rapids: Eerdmans, 1975.

———. *Worship in the Early Church.* 2nd ed. London: Marshall, Morgan, & Scott, 1978.

Martin, V., and J. W. B. Barns. *Papyrus Bodmer II Supplément: Evangile de Jean chap. 14–21.* Rev. ed. Cologny-Geneva: Bibliotheca Bodmeriana, 1962.

Martyn, J. L. *History and Theology in the Fourth Gospel.* 3rd ed. Louisville: Westminster John Knox, 2003 (1968).

Matson, M. A. "The Temple Incident: An Integral Element in the Fourth Gospel's Narrative." Pages 145-53 in *Jesus in Johannine Tradition.* Edited by R. T. Fortna and T. Thatcher. Louisville: Westminster John Knox, 2001.

Mayeda, G. *Das Leben-Jesu-Fragment Papyrus Egerton 2 und seine Stellung in der urchristlichen Literaturgeschichte.* Bern: Paul Haupt, 1946.

Mburu, E. W. *Qumran and the Origins of Johannine Language and Symbolism.* Jewish and Christian Texts Series 8. London: T&T Clark, 2010.

McDonald, L. M., and S. E. Porter. *Early Christianity and Its Sacred Literature.* Peabody, MA: Hendrickson, 2000.

McGaughy, L. C. *Toward a Descriptive Analysis of Εἶναι as a Linking Verb in New Testament Greek.* SBLDS 6. Missoula, MT: Society of Biblical Literature, 1972.

McHugh, J. F. *John 1–4.* ICC. London: T&T Clark, 2009.

McKay, K. L. "Style and Significance in the Language of John 21:15-17." *NovT* 27 (1985): 319-33.

———. "'I Am' in John's Gospel." *ExpTim* 107 (1996): 302-303.

McKinnon, J., ed. *Music in Early Christian Literature.* CRLM. Cambridge: Cambridge University Press, 1987.

McKnight, S. *Jesus and His Death: Historiography, the Historical Jesus, and Atonement Theory.* Waco, TX: Baylor University Press, 2005.

McNeile, A. H. *An Introduction to the Study of the New Testament.* Oxford: Clarendon Press, 1927. 2nd ed., 1953.

Meeks, W. A. *The Prophet-King: Moses Traditions and the Johannine Christology.* NovTSup 14. Leiden: Brill, 1967.

———. "The Man from Heaven in Johannine Sectarianism." *JBL* 91 (1972): 44-72.

Menken, M. J. J. "The Old Testament Quotation in John 19:36: Sources, Redaction, Background." Pages 2101-118 in *The Four Gospels.* Edited by F. Van Segbroeck, C. M. Tuckett, G. Van Belle, and J. Verheyden. Leuven: Leuven University Press, 1992.

———. "The Textual Form and the Meaning of the Quotation from Zechariah 12:10 in John 19:37." *CBQ* 55 (1993): 159-74.

———. *Old Testament Quotations in the Fourth Gospel: Studies in Textual Form.* CBET 15. Kampen: Kok Pharos, 1996.

Menoud, P.-H. *L'évangile de Jean d'après les recherches récentes.* Neuchâtel: Delachaux & Niestlé, 1947.

Metzger, B. M. *A Textual Commentary on the Greek New Testament.* London: United Bible Societies, 1971. 2nd ed., Stuttgart: German Bible Society, 1994.

———. *Manuscripts of the Greek Bible.* Oxford: Oxford University Press, 1981.

Meyer, E. *Ursprung und Anfänge des Christentums.* 3 vols. Stuttgart: Cotta'sche Buch-handlung, 1921-23.

Michaels, J. R. *The Gospel of John.* NICNT. Grand Rapids: Eerdmans, 2010.

Micklem, N., ed. *Christian Worship: Studies in its History and Meaning.* Oxford: Clarendon Press, 1936.

Miller, P. "'They Saw His Glory and Spoke of Him': The Gospel of John and the Old Testament." Pages 127-51 in *Hearing the Old Testament in the New Testament.* Edited by S. E. Porter. Grand Rapids: Eerdmans, 2006.

Minear, P. S. "The Original Functions of John 21." *JBL* 102 (1983): 85-98.

Moffatt, J. *An Introduction to the Literature of the New Testament.* 3rd rev. ed. Edinburgh: T&T Clark, 1918.

Moloney, F. J. "The Function of John 13–17 within the Johannine Narrative." Pages 43-66 in *"What Is John?"* Vol. 2: *Literary and Social Readings of the Fourth Gospel.* Edited by F. F. Segovia. SympS 7. Atlanta: Scholars Press, 1998.

———. "'The Jews' in the Fourth Gospel: Another Perspective." Pages 20-44 in his *The Gospel of John: Text and Context.* BIS 72. Leiden: Brill, 2005.

———. "The Fourth Gospel and the Jesus of History." Pages 45-65 in his *The Gospel of John: Text and Context.* BIS 72. London: Brill, 2005.

Moo, D. J. *The Old Testament in the Gospel Passion Narratives.* Sheffield: Almond Press, 1983.

Morgenstern, J. "The Suffering Servant: A New Solution." *VT* 11 (1961): 406-31.

Morris, L. *The New Testament and the Jewish Lectionaries.* London: Tyndale, 1964.

———. *Studies in the Fourth Gospel*. Grand Rapids: Eerdmans; Exeter: Paternoster, 1969.

———. *The Gospel according to John*. NICNT. Grand Rapids: Eerdmans, 1971. Rev. ed. 1995.

———. *Jesus is the Christ: Studies in the Theology of John*. Grand Rapids: Eerdmans, 1989.

Motyer, S. *Your Father the Devil? A New Approach to John and "the Jews."* PBTM. Carlisle: Paternoster, 1997.

———. "The Fourth Gospel and the Salvation of Israel." Pages 92-110 in *Anti-Judaism and the Fourth Gospel: Papers of the Leuven Colloquium, 2000*. Edited by R. Bieringer, D. Pollefeyt, and F. Vandecasteele-Vanneuville. Assen, Netherlands: Royal Van Gorcum, 2001.

———. "Bridging the Gap: How Might the Fourth Gospel Help Us Cope with the Legacy of Christianity's Exclusive Claim over Against Judaism?" Pages 143-67 in *The Gospel of John and Christian Theology*. Edited by R. Bauckham and C. Mosser. Grand Rapids: Eerdmans, 2008.

Mowvley, H. "John 1:14-18 in the Light of Exodus 33:7–34:35." *ExpTim* 95 (1984): 135-37.

Mussner, F. *The Historical Jesus in the Gospel of St John*. Translated by W. J. O'Hara. Freiburg: Herder; London: Burns & Oates, 1965.

Myers, D. "'The One of Whom Moses Wrote': The Characterization of Jesus through Old Testament Moses Traditions in the Gospel of John." Pages 1-20 in *"What Does the Scripture Say?" Studies in the Function of Scripture in Early Judaism and Christianity*. Vol. 2: *The Letters and Liturgical Traditions*. Edited by C. A. Evans and H. D. Zacharias. London: T&T Clark, 2012.

Neirynck, F. "John 4,46-54: Signs Source and/or Synoptic Gospels." *ETL* 60 (1984): 367-75. Reprinted as pages 679-88 in his *Evangelica II, 1982-1991: Collected Essays*. Edited by F. Van Segbroeck. BETL 99. Leuven: Peeters/Leuven University Press, 1991.

———. "John and the Synoptics: The Empty Tomb Stories." *NTS* 30 (1984): 161-87. Reprinted as pages 571-600 in his *Evangelica II, 1982-1991: Collected Essays*. Edited by F. Van Segbroeck. BETL 99. Leuven: Peeters/Leuven University Press, 1991.

———. "Papyrus Egerton 2 and the Healing of the Leper." *ETL* 61 (1985): 153-60. Reprinted as pages 773-83 in his *Evangelica II, 1982-1991: Collected Essays*. Edited by F. Van Segbroeck. BETL 99. Leuven: Peeters/Leuven University Press, 1991.

———. "John 21." *NTS* 36 (1990): 321-36. Reprinted as pages 601-16 in his *Evangelica II: 1982-1991: Collected Essays*. Edited by F. Van Segbroeck. BETL 99. Leuven: Peeters, 1991.

———. "The Signs Source in the Fourth Gospel: A Critique of the Hypothesis." Pages 651-78 in his *Evangelica II, 1982-1991 Collected Essays*. Edited by F. Van Segbroeck. BETL 99. Leuven: Peeters/Leuven University Press, 1991.

———. "John and the Synoptics: 1975-1990." Pages 3-62 in *John and the Synoptics*. Edited by A. Denaux. Leuven: Leuven University Press, 1992.

Neyrey, J. *An Ideology of Revolt: John's Christology in Social-Science Perspective*. Philadelphia: Fortress Press, 1988.

Nicholson, G. C. *Death as Departure: The Johannine Descent-Ascent Scheme.* SBLDS 63. Chico, CA: Scholars Press, 1983.

Nielsen, J. T. "The Lamb of God: The Cognitive Structure of a Johannine Metaphor." Pages 217-56 in *Imagery in the Gospel of John: Terms, Forms, Themes, and Theology of Johannine Figurative Language.* Edited by J. Frey, J. van der Walt, and R. Zimmerman. WUNT 200. Tübingen: Mohr Siebeck, 2006.

Nongbri, B. "The Use and Abuse of P52: Papyrological Pitfalls in the Dating of the Fourth Gospel." *HTR* 98.1 (2005): 23-48.

Norden, E. *Agnostos Theos: Untersuchungen zur formengeschichte religiöser Rede.* Leipzig: Teubner, 1913. Repr., Darmstadt: Wissenschaftliche Buchgesellschaft, 1956.

———. *Die Antike Kunstprosa vom VI. Jahrhundert V. Chr. bis in die Zeit der Renaissance.* Reprint ed. Stuttgart: Teubner, 1995 (1898).

O'Day, G. R. *Revelation in the Fourth Gospel: Narrative Mode and Theological Claim.* Philadelphia: Fortress Press, 1986.

Ogg, G. "Review of Mlle Jaubert, La Date de la Cène." *NovT* 34 (1959): 149-60.

O'Neill, J. C. "The Lamb of God in the Testaments of the Twelve Patriarchs." *JSNT* 2 (1977): 2-30.

Orchard, H. C. *Courting Betrayal: Jesus as Victim in the Gospel of John.* JSNTSup 161. Sheffield: Sheffield Academic Press, 1998.

Osborne, G. R. "John 21: Test Case for History and Redaction in the Resurrection Narratives." Pages 293-328 in *Studies of History and Tradition in the Four Gospels.* Vol. 2 of *Gospel Perspectives.* Edited by R. T. France and D. Wenham. Sheffield: JSOT Press, 1981.

Painter, J. *John: Witness and Theologian.* London: SPCK, 1977.

———. *The Quest for the Messiah: The History, Literature, and Theology of the Johannine Community.* Edinburgh: T&T Clark, 1991.

Pancaro, S. *The Law in the Fourth Gospel: The Torah and the Gospel, Moses and Jesus, Judaism and Christianity according to John.* Leiden: Brill, 1975.

Parker, D. C. *The Living Text of the Gospels.* Cambridge: Cambridge University Press, 1997.

Parsenios, G. L. *Departure and Consolation: The Johannine Farewell Discourses in Light of Greco-Roman Literature.* NovTSup 117. Leiden: Brill, 2005.

Parsons, M. C. "A Neglected Εγω Ειμι Saying in the Fourth Gospel? Another Look at John 9:9." Pages 145-80 in *Perspectives on John: Method and Interpretation in the Fourth Gospel.* Edited by R. B. Sloan and M. C. Parsons. Lewiston, NY: Mellen, 1993.

Peters, R. D. *The Greek Article: A Functional Grammar of ὁ-items in the Greek New Testament with Special Emphasis on the Greek Article.* LBS 9. Leiden: Brill, 2014.

Petersen, N. R. *The Gospel of John and the Sociology of Light: Language and Characterization in the Fourth Gospel.* Valley Forge, PA: Trinity Press International, 1993.

Peterson, D. *Engaging with God: A Biblical Theology of Worship.* Grand Rapids: Eerdmans, 1992.

Phillips, P. M. *The Prologue of the Fourth Gospel: A Sequential Reading.* LNTS 294. London: T&T Clark, 2006.

Pöhlmann, E. *Denkmähler altgriechischer Musik: Sammlung Übertragung und Erläuterung aller Fragmente und Fälshungen.* Nürenberg: Verlag Hans Carl, 1970.

Porter, S. E. "The Adjectival Attributive Genitive in the New Testament: A Grammatical Study." *TrinJ* 4 NS (1983): 3-17.

―――. *Verbal Aspect in the Greek of the New Testament, with Reference to Tense and Mood.* New York: Lang, 1989.

―――. "Can Traditional Exegesis Enlighten Literary Analysis of the Fourth Gospel? An Examination of the Old Testament Fulfilment Motif and the Passover Theme." Pages 396-428 in *Gospels and the Scriptures of Israel.* Edited by C. A. Evans and W. R. Stegner. Studies in Scripture in Early Judaism and Christianity 3. JSNTSup 104. Sheffield: Sheffield Academic Press, 1994. (Reprinted in edited form in this volume as ch. 8.)

―――. *Idioms of the Greek New Testament.* 2nd ed. BLG 2. Sheffield: JSOT Press, 1994.

―――. "Literary Approaches to the New Testament: From Formalism to Deconstruction and Back." Pages 77-128 in *Approaches to New Testament Study.* Edited by S. E. Porter and D. Tombs. JSNTSup 120. Sheffield: JSOT Press, 1995.

―――. "The Use of the Old Testament in the New Testament: A Brief Comment on Method and Terminology." Pages 79-96 in *Early Christian Interpretation of the Scriptures of Israel: Investigations and Proposals.* Edited by C. A. Evans and J. A. Sanders. Studies in Scripture in Early Judaism and Christianity 5. JSNTSup 148. Sheffield: Sheffield Academic Press, 1997.

―――. *The Criteria for Authenticity in Historical-Jesus Research: Previous Discussion and New Proposals.* JSNTSup 191. Sheffield: Sheffield Academic Press, 2000.

―――. "Further Comments on the Use of the Old Testament in the New Testament." Pages 98-110 in *The Intertextuality of the Epistles: Explorations of Theory and Practice.* Edited by T. L. Brodie, D. R. MacDonald, and S. E. Porter. NTM 16. Sheffield: Sheffield Phoenix Press, 2006.

―――. "The Messiah in Luke and Acts: Forgiveness for the Captives." Pages 144-64 in *The Messiah in the Old and New Testaments.* Edited by S. E. Porter. Grand Rapids: Eerdmans, 2007.

―――. "Allusions and Echoes." Pages 29-40 in *As It Is Written: Studying Paul's Use of Scripture.* Edited by S. E. Porter and C. D. Stanley. SympS 50. Atlanta: Scholars Press, 2008.

―――. "Canon: New Testament." Pages 1:109-20 in *The Oxford Encyclopedia of the Books of the Bible.* Edited by M. D. Coogan. 2 vols. Oxford: Oxford University Press, 2011.

―――. "Paul Confronts Caesar with the Good News." Pages 164-96 in *Empire in the New Testament.* Edited by S. E. Porter and C. L. Westfall. MNTS. Eugene, OR: Pickwick, 2011.

―――. "Der Papyrus Egerton 2 (P.Egerton 2/P.Lond.Christ 1)." Pages 360-65 in *Antike christliche Apokryphen in deutscher Übersetzung,* vol. 1, part 1. Edited by C. Markschies and J. Schröter. Tübingen: Mohr Siebeck, 2012.

————. "Der Papyrus Köln VI 255 (P.Köln VI 255)." Pages 366-67 in *Antike christliche Apokryphen in deutscher Übersetzung,* vol. 1, part 1. Edited by C. Markschies and J. Schröter. Tübingen: Mohr Siebeck, 2012.

————. *How We Got the New Testament: Text, Transmission, and Translation.* Grand Rapids: Baker, 2013.

————. "Recent Efforts to Reconstruct Early Christianity on the Basis of Its Papyrological Evidence." Pages 71-84 in *Christian Origins and Greco-Roman Culture: Social and Literary Contexts for the New Testament.* Edited by S. E. Porter and A. W. Pitts. TENT 9. Early Christianity in Its Hellenistic Context 1. Leiden: Brill, 2013.

————. "What Do We Know and How Do We Know It? Reconstructing Early Christianity from Its Manuscripts." Pages 41-70 in *Christian Origins and Greco-Roman Culture: Social and Literary Contexts for the New Testament.* Edited by S. E. Porter and A. W. Pitts. TENT 9. Early Christianity in Its Hellenistic Context 1. Leiden: Brill, 2013.

————. "How Do We Know What We Think We Know? Methodological Reflections on Jesus Research." Pages 82-99 in *Jesus Research: New Methodologies and Perceptions. The Second Princeton-Prague Symposium on Jesus Research.* Edited by J. H. Charlesworth with B. Rhea and P. Pokorný. Grand Rapids: Eerdmans, 2014.

————. "Study of John's Gospel: New Directions or the Same Old Paths?" Pages 277-306 in *Linguistic Analysis of the Greek New Testament: Studies in Tools, Methods, and Practice.* Grand Rapids: Baker, 2015.

Porter, S. E., ed. *Handbook to Exegesis of the New Testament.* NTTS 25. Leiden: Brill, 1997.

————, ed. *Dictionary of Biblical Criticism and Interpretation.* London: Routledge, 2007.

Porter, S. E., and K. D. Clarke. "What Is Exegesis? An Analysis of Various Definitions." Pages 3-21 in *Handbook to Exegesis of the New Testament.* Edited by S. E. Porter. NTTS 25. Leiden: Brill, 1997.

Porter, S. E., and A. K. Gabriel. *Johannine Writings and Apocalyptic: An Annotated Bibliography.* JOST 1. Leiden: Brill, 2013.

Porter, S. E., and G. L. Heath. *The Lost Gospel of Judas: Separating Fact from Fiction.* Grand Rapids: Eerdmans, 2007.

Porter, S. E., and H. T. Ong. "Memory, Orality, and the Fourth Gospel: A Response to Paul Foster with Further Comments for Future Discussion." *JSHJ* 12 (2014): 143-64.

Porter, S. E., and B. W. R. Pearson. "Why the Split? Christians and Jews by the Fourth Century." *JGRChJ* 1 (2000): 82-119.

Porter, S. E., and W. J. Porter. "P.Vindob. G 26225: A New Romanos Melodus Papyrus in the Vienna Collection." *Jahrbuch der österreichischen Byzantinistik* 52 (2002): 135-48 with plate.

————. *New Testament Greek Papyri and Parchments: New Editions.* 2 vols. Mitteilungen aus der Papyrussammlung der Nationalbibliothek in Wien (Papyrus Erzherzog Rainer) New Series 29, 30. Berlin: Walter de Gruyter, 2008.

Porter, S. E., and J. T. Reed. "Philippians as a Macro-Chiasm and its Exegetical Significance." *NTS* 44 (1998): 213-31.

Porter, S. E., and J. C. Robinson. *Hermeneutics: An Introduction to Interpretive Theory.* Grand Rapids: Eerdmans, 2011.

Porter, S. E., and B. M. Stovell, eds. *Biblical Hermeneutics: Five Views.* Downers Grove, IL: InterVarsity Press, 2012.

Porter, W. J. "Music." Pages 711-19 in *Dictionary of New Testament Background.* Edited by C. A. Evans and S. E. Porter. Downers Grove, IL: InterVarsity Press, 2000.

————. "The Use of Ekphonetic Notation in Vienna New Testament Manuscripts." Pages 581-86 in *Akten des 23. Internationalen Papyrologenkongresses Wien, 22.-28. Juli 2001.* Edited by B. Palme. Vienna: Österreichischen Akademie der Wissenschaften, 2007.

Prosic, T. *The Development and Symbolism of Passover until 70 CE.* London: T&T Clark, 2004.

Pryor, J. W. "The Great Thanksgiving and the Fourth Gospel." *BZ* 35 (1991): 157-79.

————. *John: Evangelist of the Covenant People.* London: Darton, Longman & Todd, 1992.

Quasten, J. *Music and Worship in Pagan and Christian Antiquity.* Translated by B. Ramsey. Washington, DC: National Association of Pastoral Musicians, 1980 (1930).

Queck, T.-M. "A Text-Critical Study of John 1:34." *NTS* 55 (2009): 22-34.

Reim, G. *Studien zum alttestamentlichen Hintergrund des Johannesevangeliums.* SNTSMS 22. Cambridge: Cambridge University Press, 1974.

————. *Jochanan: Erweiterte Studien zum alttestamentlichen Hintergrund des Johannesevangeliums.* Erlangen: Verlag der Ev.-Luth. Mission, 1995.

Reinhartz, A. *The Word in the World: The Cosmological Tale in the Fourth Gospel.* SBLMS 45. Atlanta: Scholars Press, 1992.

————. "On Travel, Translation, and Ethnography: Johannine Scholarship at the Turn of the Century." Pages 249-56 in *"What Is John?"* Vol. 2: *Literary and Social Readings of the Fourth Gospel.* Edited by F. F. Segovia. SympS 7. Atlanta: Scholars Press, 1998.

————. *Befriending the Beloved Disciple: A Jewish Reading of the Gospel of John.* London: T&T Clark, 2001.

————. " 'Jews' and Jews in the Fourth Gospel." Pages 341-56 in *Anti-Judaism and the Fourth Gospel: Papers of the Leuven Colloquium, 2000.* Edited by R. Bieringer, D. Pollefeyt, and F. Vandecasteele-Vanneuville. Assen, Netherlands: Royal Van Gorcum, 2001.

Reitzenstein, R. *Die hellenistischen Mysterienreligionen: Nach ihren Grundgedanke und Wirkungen.* Reprint ed. Darmstadt: Wissenschaftliche Buchgesellschaft, 1966 (1910).

————. *Poimandres: Studien zu griechisch-ägyptischen und frühchristlichen Literatur.* Reprint ed. Darmstadt: Wissenschaftliche Buchgesellschaft 1966.

Reitzenstein, R., and H. H. Schaeder. *Studien zum antiken Synkretismus aus Iran und Griechenland.* Reprint ed. Darmstadt: Wissenschaftliche Buchgesellschaft, 1965.

Renan, E. *The Life of Jesus.* London: Watts, 1935 (1863).

Rhoads, D., J. Dewey, and D. Michie. *Mark as Story: An Introduction to the Narrative of a Gospel.* 2nd ed. Minneapolis: Fortress Press, 1999.

Ringe, S. H. *Wisdom's Friends: Community and Christology in the Fourth Gospel.* Louisville: Westminster John Knox, 1999.

Roberts, C. H. *An Unpublished Fragment of the Fourth Gospel in the John Rylands Library.* Manchester: Manchester University Press, 1935. Reprinted with corrections in *BJRL* 20 (1936): 45-56.

————. *Catalogue of the Greek and Latin Papyri in the John Rylands Library Manchester.* Vol. 3. Manchester: Manchester University Press, 1938.

————. *Manuscript, Society, and Belief in Early Christian Egypt.* London: British Academy, 1979.

Robertson, A. T. *The Divinity of Christ in the Gospel of John.* New York: Revell, 1916. Repr., Grand Rapids: Baker, 1979.

Robinson, J. A. T. "The Relation of the Prologue to the Gospel of St John." *NTS* 9 (1963): 120-29. Reprinted as pages 65-76 in his *Twelve More New Testament Studies.* London: SCM Press, 1984.

————. *Redating the New Testament.* Philadelphia: Westminster, 1975.

————. *The Priority of John.* Edited by J. F. Coakley. London: SCM Press, 1985.

Robinson, J. M. "The Johannine Trajectory." Pages 232-68 in *Trajectories through Early Christianity,* by J. M. Robinson and H. Koester. Philadelphia: Fortress Press, 1971.

Robinson, J. M., ed. *The Nag Hammadi Library in English.* New York: Harper & Row, 1988.

Ronning, J. *The Jewish Targums and John's Logos Theology.* Peabody, MA: Hendrickson, 2010.

Ruckstuhl, E. *Chronology of the Last Days of Jesus: A Critical Study.* Translated by V. J. Drapela. New York: Desclee, 1965.

————. *Die literarische Einheit des Johannesevangeliums.* NTOA 5. Freiburg: Universitätsverlag; Göttingen: Vandenhoeck & Ruprecht, 1987 (1951).

Ruhl, C. *On Monosemy: A Study in Linguistic Semantics.* Albany, NY: SUNY Press, 1989.

Sanday, W. *The Criticism of the Fourth Gospel.* Oxford: Clarendon Press, 1905.

Sandbach, F. H. *The Stoics.* London: Chatto & Windus, 1975.

Sanders, E. P. *The Tendencies of the Synoptic Tradition.* SNTSMS 9. Cambridge: Cambridge University Press, 1969.

————. *Paul and Palestinian Judaism: A Comparison of Patterns of Religion.* London: SCM Press, 1977.

Sanders, J. N. *The Gospel according to St John.* Edited by B. A. Mastin. BNTC. London: A. & C. Black, 1968.

Sanders, J. T. *The New Testament Christological Hymns: Their Historical Religious Background.* SNTSMS 15. Cambridge: Cambridge University Press, 1971.

Sandy, D. B. "John the Baptist's 'Lamb of God' Affirmation in Its Canonical and Apocalyptic Milieu." *JETS* 34 (1991): 447-60.

Schenk, W. "Interne Strukturierungen im Schluss-Segment Johannes 21: Συγγραφή + Σατυρικόν/'Επίλογος." *NTS* 38 (1992): 507-30.

Schille, G. *Frühchristliche Hymnen.* Berlin: Evangelische Verlagsanstalt, 1962.

Schlatter, A. *Der Evangelist Johannes: Wie er spricht, denkt und glaubt; Ein Kommentar zum vierten Evangelium.* 4th ed. Stuttgart: Calwer, 1975.

Schlund, C. *"Kein Knochen soll gebrochen werden": Studien zur Bedeutung und Funktion des Pesachfests in Texten des frühen Judentums und im Johannesevangelium.* WMANT 107. Neukirchen-Vluyn: Neukirchener, 2005.

Schmidt, A. "Zwei Anmerkungen zu Ryl. III 457." *APF* 35 (1989): 11-12.

Schnackenburg, R. *The Gospel according to St. John.* Translated by K. Smyth et al. 3 vols. London: Burns & Oates, 1968-82.

Schneiders, S. M. "The Lamb of God and the Forgiveness of Sin(s) in the Fourth Gospel." *CBQ* 73 (2011): 1-29.

Schnelle, U. *Antidocetic Christology in the Gospel of John: An Investigation of the Place of the Fourth Gospel in the Johannine School.* Translated by L. M. Maloney. Minneapolis: Fortress Press, 1992.

——. *The History and Theology of the New Testament Writings.* Translated by M. E. Boring. Minneapolis: Fortress Press, 1998.

Schubart, W. *Griechische Palaeographie.* Berlin: Beck, 1925.

Schuchard, B. G. *Scripture within Scripture: The Interrelationship of Form and Function in the Explicit Old Testament Citations in the Gospel of John.* SBLDS 133. Atlanta: Scholars Press, 1992.

Schweizer, E. *Ego Eimi: Die religionsgeschichtliche Herkunft und theologische Bedeutung der johanneischen Bildreden, zugleich ein Beitrag zur Quellenfrage des vierten Evangeliums.* FRLANT 56. Göttingen: Vandenhoeck & Ruprecht, 1939.

Scott, E. F. *The Fourth Gospel: Its Purpose and Theology.* 2nd ed. Edinburgh: T&T Clark, 1908.

Scott, J. M. C. "Jews or Christians? The Opponents of Jesus in the Fourth Gospel." Pages 83-101 in *Jesus and Paul: Global Perspectives in Honor of James D. G. Dunn for his 70th Birthday.* Edited by B. J. Oropeza, C. K. Robertson, and D. C. Mohrmann. LNTS 414. London: T&T Clark, 2010.

Scott, M. *Sophia and the Johannine Jesus.* JSNTSup 71. Sheffield: JSOT Press, 1992.

Sedgewick, G. G. *Of Irony: Especially in Drama.* 2nd ed. Toronto: University of Toronto Press, 1948.

Senft, C. "Truth." Pages 430-33 in *Vocabulary of the Bible.* Edited by J.-J. Von Allmen. London: Lutterworth, 1958.

Seynaeve, J. "Les Citations Scriptuaires en Jn. 19,36-37: Une Preuve en Faveur de la Typologie de l'Agneau Pascal?" *Revue Africaine de Théologie* 1 (1977): 67-76.

Shepherd, D. " 'Do You Love Me?' A Narrative-Critical Raeappraisal of Ἀγαπάω and Φιλέω in John 21:15-17." *JBL* 129 (2010): 777-92.

Sheppard, W. S. *Musical Aspects of the New Testament.* Amsterdam: Ten Have, 1962.

Sheridan, R. "Issues in the Translation of οἱ Ἰουδαῖοι in the Fourth Gospel." *JBL* 132 (2013): 671-95.

——. *Retelling Scripture: 'The Jews' and the Scriptural Citations in John 1:19–12:15.* BIS 110. Leiden: Brill, 2012.

Sidebottom, E. M. *The Christ of the Fourth Gospel in the Light of First-Century Thought.* London: SPCK, 1961.

Siegert, F. *Das Evangelium des Johannes in seiner ursprünglichen Gestalt: Widerherstellung und Kommentar.* Göttingen: Vandenhoeck & Ruprecht, 2008.

Skinner, C. W. "Another Look at 'The Lamb of God.'" *BibSac* 161 (2004): 89-104.

Sloyan, G. S. *What Are They Saying about John?* New York: Paulist, 1991.

Smalley, S. S. *John: Evangelist and Interpreter.* Exeter: Paternoster, 1978.

———. "'The Paraclete': Pneumatology in the Johannine Gospel and Apocalypse." Pages 289-300 in *Exploring the Gospel of John: In Honor of D. Moody Smith.* Edited by R. A. Culpepper and C. C. Black. Louisville: Westminster John Knox, 1996.

Smith, D. M. *Johannine Christianity: Essays on Its Setting, Sources, and Theology.* Edinburgh: T&T Clark, 1984.

———. *The Theology of the Gospel of John.* Cambridge: Cambridge University Press, 1995.

———. *John among the Gospels.* 2nd ed. Columbia: University of South Carolina Press, 2001 (1992).

———. *The Fourth Gospel in Four Dimensions: Judaism and Jesus, the Gospels, and Scripture.* Columbia: University of South Carolina Press, 2008.

Sparks, K. "Form Criticism." Pages 111-14 in *Dictionary of Biblical Criticism and Interpretation.* Edited by S. E. Porter. New York: Routledge, 2007.

Spencer, P. E. "Narrative Echoes in John 21: Intertextual Interpretation and Intratextual Connection." *JSNT* 75 (1999): 49-68.

Stagg, F. "The Abused Aorist." *JBL* 91 (1972): 222-31.

Staley, J. "The Structure of John's Prologue." *CBQ* 48 (1986): 241-64.

Stanton, V. H. *The Gospels as Historical Documents.* Vol. 3: *The Fourth Gospel.* Cambridge: Cambridge University Press, 1920.

Staton, J. E. "A Vision of Unity — Christian Unity in the Fourth Gospel." *EvQ* 69 (1997): 291-305.

Stauffer, E. *Die Theologie des Neuen Testaments.* Genf: Oikumene Verlag, 1941. ET *New Testament Theology.* Translated by J. Marsh. London: SCM Press, 1955.

Stegemann, E. W., and W. Stegemann. *The Jesus Movement: A Social History of Its First Century.* Minneapolis: Fortress Press, 1999.

Stettler, C. *Der Kolosserhymnus.* WUNT 2.131. Tübingen: Mohr Siebeck, 2000.

Stevens, G. B. *The Johannine Theology.* London: Dickinson, 1894.

Stevens, W. A., and E. D. Burton. *A Harmony of the Gospels for Historical Study.* New York: Scribners, 1904.

Stevick, D. B. *Jesus and His Own: A Commentary on John 13–17.* Grand Rapids: Eerdmans, 2011.

Stibbe, M. W. G. *John as Storyteller: Narrative Criticism and the Fourth Gospel.* SNTSMS 73. Cambridge: Cambridge University Press, 1992.

———. *John.* Readings: A New Biblical Commentary. Sheffield: JSOT Press, 1993.

———. "Magnificent But Flawed: The Breaking of Form in the Fourth Gospel." Pages 149-65 in *Anatomies of Narrative Criticism: The Past, Present, and Futures of the Fourth Gospel as Literature.* Edited by T. Thatcher and S. D. Moore. SBLRBS 55. Atlanta: SBL, 2008.

Stovell, B. M. *Mapping Metaphorical Discourse in the Fourth Gospel: John's Eternal King.* LBS 5. Leiden: Brill, 2012.

Strachan, R. H. *The Fourth Gospel: Its Significance and Environment.* London: SCM Press, 1917. 3rd ed., 1941.

Strand, K. A. "John as Quartodeciman: A Reappraisal." *JBL* 84 (1965): 251-58.

Strauss, D. F. *The Life of Jesus Critically Examined.* Translated by Georg Eliot from 4th German ed. London: George Allen, 1848 (1835).

————. *A New Life of Jesus.* 2 vols. London: Williams & Norgate, 1879 (1865).

Strecker, G. *The Johannine Letters: A Commentary on 1, 2, and 3 John.* Translated by L. M. Maloney. Minneapolis: Fortress Press, 1996.

Streeter, B. H. *The Four Gospels: A Study of Origins.* London: Macmillan, 1930.

Stringer, M. D. *A Sociological History of Christian Worship.* Cambridge: Cambridge University Press, 2005.

Swete, H. B. *The Holy Spirit in the New Testament: A Study of Primitive Christian Teaching.* London: Macmillan, 1910.

————. *The Last Discourse and Prayer of Our Lord: A Study of St. John XIV–XVII.* London: Macmillan, 1913.

Taylor, V. *Jesus and His Sacrifice: A Study of the Passion-Sayings in the Gospels.* London: Macmillan, 1937.

————. *The Names of Jesus.* London: Macmillan, 1962.

Tenney, M. C. *John: The Gospel of Belief.* Grand Rapids: Eerdmans, 1948.

Teppler, Y. Y., ed. *Birkat haMinim: Jews and Christians in Conflict in the Ancient World.* TSAJ 120. Tübingen: Mohr Siebeck, 2007.

Thatcher, T. "Introduction." Pages 1-9 in *Jesus in Johannine Tradition.* Edited by R. T. Fortna and T. Thatcher. Louisville: Westminster John Knox, 2001.

————. *Greater than Caesar: Christology and Empire in the Fourth Gospel.* Minneapolis: Fortress Press, 2009.

Thettayil, B. *In Spirit and Truth: An Exegetical Study of John 4:19-26 and a Theological Investigation of the Replacement Theme in the Fourth Gospel.* CBET 46. Leuven: Peeters, 2007.

Thiselton, A. C. "Truth." Pages 3:874-902 in *New International Dictionary of New Testament Theology.* Edited by C. Brown. 3 vols. Grand Rapids: Zondervan, 1975.

————. *The Holy Spirit — In Biblical Teaching, through the Centuries, and Today.* Grand Rapids: Eerdmans, 2013.

Thompson, M. M. *The Humanity of Jesus in the Fourth Gospel.* Philadelphia: Fortress Press, 1988.

————. *The God of the Gospel of John.* Grand Rapids: Eerdmans, 2001.

Thyen, H. "Aus der Literatur zum Johannesevangelium." *TR* 39 (1975): 53-69, 222-52.

————. "Noch einmal: Johannes 21 und 'der Jünger, den Jesus liebte.'" Pages 147-89 in *Texts and Contexts: Biblical Texts in Their Textual and Situational Contexts. Essays in Honor of Lars Hartman.* Edited by T. Fornberg and D. Hellholm. Oslo: Scandinavian University Press, 1995.

Tischendorf, C. *Novum Testamentum Graece.* 2 vols. 8th ed. Leipzig: Giesecke & Devrient, 1872.

Tovey, D. *Narrative Art and Act in the Fourth Gospel.* JSNTSup 151. Sheffield: Sheffield Academic Press, 1997.

Tuckett, C. M. "The Fourth Gospel and Q." Pages 281-90 in *Jesus in Johannine Tradition.* Edited by R. T. Fortna and T. Thatcher. Louisville: Westminster John Knox, 2001.

———. "P52 and *Nomina Sacra.*" *NTS* 47.4 (2001): 544-48.

———. "Zechariah 12:10 and the New Testament." Pages 111-21 in *The Book of Zechariah and Its Influence.* Edited by C. M. Tuckett. Burlington, VT: Ashgate, 2003.

Turner, E. G. *Greek Manuscripts of the Ancient World.* Edited by P. J. Parsons. 2nd ed. London: Institute of Classical Studies, 1987.

Turner, M. "Atonement and the Death of Jesus in John: Some Questions to Bultmann and Forestell." *EvQ* 62:2 (1990): 119-22.

———. *The Holy Spirit and Spiritual Gifts: Then and Now.* Carlisle: Paternoster, 1996.

Um, S. *The Theme of Temple Christology in John's Gospel.* LNTS 312. London: T&T Clark, 2006.

van Arnim, S. *Stoicorum Veterum Fragmenta.* 4 vols. Stuttgart: Teubner, 1964.

Vanderburgh, F. A. *Sumerian Hymns from Cuneiform Texts in the British Museum.* New York: Columbia University Press, 1908. Repr. ed., 1966.

van der Horst, P. "'The Elements Will Be Dissolved with Fire': The Idea of Cosmic Conflagration in Hellenism, Ancient Judaism, and Early Christianity." Pages 271-92 in his *Hellenism-Judaism-Christianity: Essays on their Interaction.* Leuven: Peeters, 1998.

van der Watt, J. *The Family of the King: Dynamics of Metaphor in the Gospel according to John.* BIS 47. Leiden: Brill, 2000.

van Haelst, J. *Catalogue des papyrus littéraires Juifs et Chrétiens.* Paris: Publications de la Sorbonne, 1976.

von Wahlde, U. C. "The Johannine 'Jews': A Critical Survey." *NTS* 28 (1982): 33-60.

———. *The Earliest Version of John's Gospel: Recovering the Gospel of Signs.* Wilmington, DE: Michael Glazier, 1989.

———. "'The Jews' in the Gospel of John: Fifteen Years of Research (1983-1998)." *ETL* 76 (2000): 30-55.

———. "'You Are of Your Father the Devil' in Its Context: Stereotyped Apocalyptic Polemic in John 8:38-47." Pages 418-44 in *Anti-Semitism and the Fourth Gospel: Papers of the Leuven Colloquium, 2000.* Edited by R. Bieringer, D. Pollefeyt, and F. Vandecasteele-Vanneuville. Assen, Netherlands: Royal Van Gorcum, 2001.

———. *The Gospel and Letters of John.* ECC. 3 vols. Grand Rapids: Eerdmans, 2010.

Vorster, W. S. "The Growth and Making of John 21." Pages 3:2207-21 in *The Four Gospels: Festschrift Frans Neirynck.* 3 vols. Edited by F. Van Segbroeck, C. M. Tuckett, G. Van Belle, and J. Verheyden. Leuven: Peeters, 1992. Reprinted as pages 199-215 in his *Speaking of Jesus: Essays on Biblical Language, Gospel Narrative & the Historical Jesus.* Edited by J. E. Botha. NovTSup 92. Leiden: Brill, 1999.

———. *Speaking of Jesus: Essays on Biblical Language, Gospel Narrative, and the Historical Jesus.* Edited by J. E. Botha. NovTSup 92. Leiden: Brill, 1999.

Waetjen, H. C. *The Gospel of the Beloved Disciple: A Work in Two Editions.* New York: T&T Clark, 2005.

Wainwright, G., and K. B. Westerfield Tucker, eds. *The Oxford History of Christian Worship*. Oxford: Oxford University Press, 2006.

Walker, N. "Pauses in the Passion Story and Their Significance for Chronology." *NovT* 6 (1963): 16-19.

Wallace, D. B. "John 5,2 and the Date of the Fourth Gospel." *Bib* 71 (1990): 177-205.

Warrack, J., and E. West. "Overture." Pages 531-32 in *The Oxford Dictionary of Opera*. Oxford: Oxford University Press, 1992.

Watson, F. *Gospel Writing: A Canonical Perspective*. Grand Rapids: Eerdmans, 2013.

Weiss, J. *Earliest Christianity: A History of the Period A.D. 30-150*. Edited by R. Knopf. Translated by F. C. Grant. 2 vols. Repr., Gloucester, MA: Peter Smith, 1970.

Wellesz, E. "Early Christian Music." Pages 1-13 in *Early Mediaeval Music up to 1300*. Edited by D. A. Hughes. Rev. ed. NOHM 2. London: Oxford University Press, 1955.

———. *A History of Byzantine Music and Hymnography*. 2nd ed. Oxford: Clarendon Press, 1961.

Wellesz, E., ed. *Ancient and Oriental Music*. NOHM 1. London: Oxford University Press, 1957.

Wendland, P. *Die hellenistisch-römische Kultur in ihren Beziehungen zu Judentum und Christentum: Die urchristlichen Literaturformen*. Tübingen: Mohr Siebeck, 1912.

Wengst, K. *Christologische Formeln und Lieder des Urchristentums*. Gütersloh: Mohn, 1972.

Werner, E. *The Sacred Bridge: The Interdependence of Liturgy and Music in Synagogue and Church during the First Millennium*. 2 vols. Vol. 1 London: Dobson; New York: Columbia University Press, 1959. Vol. 2 New York: Ktav, 1984.

West, M. L. *Greek Meter*. Oxford: Clarendon Press, 1982.

———. "Analecta Musica." *ZPE* 92 (1992): 1-54.

———. *Ancient Greek Music*. Oxford: Clarendon Press, 1992.

Westcott, B. F. *The Revelation of the Father: Short Lectures on the Titles of the Lord in the Gospel of St. John*. London: Macmillan, 1884.

———. *The Gospel according to St John*. 2 vols. London: John Murray, 1908.

Wheelwright, P. *Heraclitus*. Oxford: Clarendon Press, 1959.

White, J. F. *Introduction to Christian Worship*. 3rd ed. Nashville: Abingdon, 2000 (1980).

White, M. C. "The Identity and Function of Jews and Related Terms in the Fourth Gospel." Unpublished Ph.D. diss., Emory University, 1972.

Wiarda, T. "John 21.1-23: Narrative Unity and Its Implications." *JSNT* 46 (1992): 53-71.

Wikenhauser, A. *New Testament Introduction*. New York: Herder & Herder, 1958.

Wilken, U. "Die Bremer Papyrus Sammlung." *Forschungen und Fortschritte* 12 (1936): 89-90.

Williams, C. H. *I Am He: The Meaning and Interpretation of Anî Hû in Jewish and Early Christian Literature*. WUNT 2.113. Tübingen: Mohr Siebeck, 2000.

———. "'I Am' or 'I Am He'? Self-Declaratory Pronouncements in the Fourth Gospel and Rabbinic Tradition." Pages 343-52 in *Jesus in Johannine Tradition*. Edited by R. T. Fortna and T. Thatcher. Louisville, KY: Westminster John Knox, 2001.

———. "'I Am' Sayings." Pages 396-99 in *Dictionary of Jesus and the Gospels*. 2nd ed.

Edited by J. B. Green, J. K. Brown, and N. Perrin. Downers Grove, IL: InterVarsity Press, 2013.

Williams, P. J. "Not the Prologue of John." *JSNT* 33.4 (2011): 375-86.

Williams, S. K. *Jesus' Death as Saving Event: The Background and Origin of a Concept.* HDR 2. Missoula, MT: Scholars Press, 1975.

Wilson, S. *Related Strangers: Jews and Christians 70-170 CE.* Minneapolis: Fortress Press, 1995.

Yamauchi, E. M. "Jewish Gnosticism? The Prologue of John, Mandaean Parallels, and the Trimorphic Protennoia." Pages 467-97 in *Studies in Gnosticism and Hellenistic Religions: Presented to Gilles Quispel on the Occasion of His 65th Birthday.* Edited by R. van den Broek and M. J. Vermaseren. EPRO 91. Leiden: Brill, 1981.

Young, F. W. "A Study of the Relation of Isaiah to the Fourth Gospel." *ZNW* 46 (1955): 215-33.

Zahn, T. *Introduction to the New Testament.* Translated by M. W. Jacobus. Edinburgh: T&T Clark, 1909.

Zimmermann, H. "Das absolute 'ego eimi' als die neutestamentliche Offenbarungs-formel." *BZ* 4 (1960): 54-69, 266-76.

Zimmermann, R. "Imagery in John: Opening up Paths into the Tangled Thicket of John's Figurative World." Pages 1-43 in *Imagery in the Gospel of John: Terms, Forms, Themes, and Theology of Johannine Figurative Language.* Edited by J. Frey, J. van der Watt, and R. Zimmermann. WUNT 200. Tübingen: Mohr Siebeck, 2006.

Index of Modern Authors

Index of Ancient Sources